HEALER'S HANDBOOK

FOR PRACTITIONERS

Messages from the Body~
Condensed *Version*

Michael J. Lincoln, Ph.D.
Revised 2006

HEALER'S
HANDBOOK

FOR PRACTITIONERS

Copyright © 2006 Michael J. Lincoln, Ph.D.,
5th Print 2009 Talking Hearts
All Rights Reserved

Published by Talking Hearts
Printed in the USA

ISBN: 0-9772069-7-1

For all U.S. and International book orders and consultations with
Michael J. Lincoln, Ph.D. visit our website at www.talkinghearts.net or
write to P.O. Box 194, Cool, CA 95614

Also by the Author:

Allergies and Aversions: Their Psychological Meaning (1991, Rev. 2006)
Addictions and Cravings: Their Psychological Meaning (1991, Rev. 2006)
Animals: Their Psycho-Symbolic Meaning (1991, Rev. 2007)
Clothes Consciousness (1985 Rev. 2008)
Honey, I Blew Up The Kids! Comprehensive Approach to Parenting (1992, Rev. 2007)
Household Hot Spots: Their Psycho-Symbolic and Psycho-Utilitarian Meanings (1991, Rev. 2008)
How to Live Life (1972, Rev.2008)
It's All in the Family: Exploration of the Life Scripts (1992, Rev. 2007)
Messages from the Body: Their Psychological Meaning (1991, Rev. 2006)
My Car, Myself (1991, Rev. 2008)
Nonverbal Messages "Body Language" (1995, Rev. 2008)
Our Personal Challenges A discussion on Relationships (1968, Rev. 2008)
Problematic Patterns: Behavioral, Psychological and Psychiatric Problems - Their Emotional Meaning (1991, Rev. 2007)
What's in a FACE? The Dictionary for Heart Centered Face Reading (1990, Rev. 2007)
What's Happening to ME!!?? (1981, Rev. 2007)
What was THAT All About? (1995, Rev. 2008)
Where the Hell Art Thou Romeo (1992, Rev. 2008)
Top 50 Messages from the Body (1991, 2008)

For more information visit our website at www.talkinghearts.net
or write to P.O. Box 194, Cool, CA 95614

CONTENTS

Words from the Author

INTRODUCTION

In an effort to help Healer's and Practitioner's bring new awareness to their clients Dr. Lincoln has taken the diseases from *"Messages from the Body"* to create this shorter version called *Healer's Handbook*.

Bodily functioning is a continuous adaptation process to our external and internal environments that is operated by the brain, which in turn reflects the contents of the mind, the emotions, and the soul.

The key factor in the maintenance of bodily health is the immune system, which is controlled by the brain via neural connections, chemical reactions, neurotransmitters, lymphocytes, neurohormones, endorphins, and the like.

Through these linkages, what is going on in our consciousness is continuously affecting our body -- and vice versa. In many ways, the body and the mind imitate and imprint each other.

Ultimately, of course, consciousness underlies and is the final determinant of everything, and the body reflects this vividly. It should be noted in this regard that "consciousness" will be used here to refer to both aware and unaware processes and phenomena, as well as what is happening in our brains and in our souls.

What is in our consciousness is determined by our life experiences and by the nature and history of our soul. We design our destiny, and then we encounter the interaction between ourselves and the world around us. And we react to what happens.

For instance, one way in which illnesses and such can happen is when the individual's life goals are not being met. The individual then feels so frustrated that bodily functioning goes awry. Their consciousness then becomes permeated with this process.

The resultant in such a situation is that the particular interpretations and interventions that the individual exhibits about this issue are reflective of the agitated state of their consciousness.

And that, in turn, shows up in the form of the disorder that develops. The illness, ailment or damaged condition then reflects the goal-thwarting impacts from our environment, and/or it reflects the effects of our efforts to try to get by without dealing with our goal(s).

The key factor in all this is the "thought form" or pattern of consciousness in the mind and soul, which affects the body via the processes described above. And when something is awry in our consciousness, the body is the place where our consciousness problem; that is precipitating the disorder, is played out.

Illnesses, ailments, disorders and damages in our bodies therefore represent the ***final warning system*** regarding the things in which we are caught up that are causing us significant, serious, and perhaps even lethal outcomes. These "Messages From The Body" point to what needs to be tracked and modified in our emotional/cognitive/behavioral/evaluational/spiritual system.

Symptoms and syndromes (clusters of symptoms) express what we are unconscious of, as well as what we are "shoving into our shadow." The "shadow" is that part of us where things that were (or are) not acceptable to us and/or to those around us are relegated.

This is especially true during the intensely impressionable childhood period, where at the beginning in particular, we tend to put God's face on the parents and other significant caretakers and relationships.

What the symptoms and syndromes of illness and disorders often represent, then, is a de-evolution of a "shadow-shoving" process, in which we are refusing to integrate our qualities or needs into our consciousness and lives, due to severely repressive, suppressive, exploitative and/or abusive reactions to these aspects of our nature when we were children.

There is an old saying to the effect that "As a person thinketh, so they shall be." In other words, what is in our consciousness determines the way our life goes. And that gets started in childhood. This means that how one handles one's core themes determines who and how one will become.

Some example core themes here are things like self-support, belonging, being safe, getting love, needing validation, being responsible, knowing and understanding, mutual support, honesty, perfection, being able to love, being able to have, cultural and community commitment, being without doing, attention input, abandonment, cosmic connection, etc.

A major source of bodily malaise is the impact of one's negative experiences on the neurotransmitter conditions that result from formative processes. Chronic and/or repeated traumatic experience patterns have specific impacts on the individual's neurotransmitters that tend to last the lifetime.

Specifically, what has been found is that:

1) Dopamine is lowered by joy-deprivation.

2) Norepinepherine is elevated by fear- and/or rage-induction.

3) Endorphine is lowered by love-deprivation.

4) Serotonin is lowered by status-deprivation and powerlessness-induction.

Illnesses and disorders are linked to beliefs and changes of beliefs about oneself, about the nature of one's relationships with others, about one's position in the social world, and about where one stands in relation to the Universe. And these, in turn, are determined by one's life experiences, by one's interventions in the world, and by one's soul history.

Things like the love or lack of love, joy and meaningful sexual contact that one has experienced, via such things as having undergone oppression, emotional conflict and trauma, the role of expectations and their play-outs, social acceptance or rejection experiences, having the feeling that one is able or unable to impact on the environment and the nature of one's quality of life, etc., are key factors here.

Such processes as not feeling a part of a social unit, not feeling valuable and valued, being caught up in loneliness, undergoing deep longing and frustration, traumatic patterns and being under the spell of unresolved detrimental residuals from infancy and childhood have the effect of causing disturbances in one's consciousness.

Living through uncontrollable stress, social instability, lack of resources, or failed ambitions, encountering conflicting signals from important others around crucial matters, having to deal with unexpected threats, finding oneself ensnared in compulsive and addictive behavior, and experiencing social rejection, isolation, devaluation and alienation also cause consciousness problems.

All of these, along with issues like learned helplessness, feelings of weakness, victimization, incompetence and lack of control and/or power, and the experience of rejection by or alienation from the Cosmos are the things that generate negative thoughts and emotions such as grief, fear, despair, guilt, resentment, nihilism, cynicism, hostility, greed, hate, unforgivingness, pride, cruelty, narcissism and ignorance.

These kinds of difficulties suppress the immune system by generating and maintaining negative self-reactions and beliefs about one's position/situation in the world. The mental thoughts and emotional patterns that most often precipitate disease and disorder in the body are criticism, anger, resentment, guilt, shame, grief and fear.

Criticism arises from a feeling of wanting to hands-on control everything, due to a childhood in which such control was critical for cosmic acceptance, physical and/or emotional survival, family protection, sense of worth, quality of life, etc. When this "control-mania" occurs, it results in disorders in which the environmental impact systems are affected, such as arthritis.

Anger comes from experiencing obstacles that can't be overcome, and the resulting impasse ends up in our turning from seeking to remove the obstacle to attacking other people, the environment, and the Universe. This tends to lead to conditions that emphasize infections, boils, burning, fevers and inflammations.

Resentment is based on a feeling of victimization and powerlessness, and it turns into smoldering fires that eat and fester away at the body, until diseases like cancer and tumors develop.

Guilt is anger turned against the self, with a resulting self-attacking. It leads to self-punishment and pain. Self-hobbling illnesses like emphysema and herpes are the result.

Shame is generalized guilt, and the attack that results from shame is on the general self-sustenance systems. As a result, it ends up in disorders of the life support system, such as the blood, the liver, and the immune system.

Grief is the reaction to loss and deprivation, and its expression involves the entire respiratory system, along with the fluid treatment systems such as the kidneys and the bladder. Suppressed grief therefore produces such things as lung problems, ear infections, and sinus difficulties, as well as heart problems.

Fear activates the adrenal system for all-out emergency action. It suppresses the vegetative systems such as digestion, regarding them as being of less importance during the emergency. Chronic fear thus tends to result in things like stomach and intestinal disorders, along with diseases of the kidneys and the bladder.

Physical symptoms arise from the condition of the individual's body, as generated by the negative thoughts the individual characteristically has, that shape their life and experiences through constant repetition.

They also represent the body trying to do things that the individual won't/can't/isn't manifesting and/or patterns that the family of origin forced upon them. Environmental influences like diet, bacteria/viruses, pollens, pollutants, etc. operate as the precipitant or "trigger" for the already loaded and aimed "gun." So are the events that produce traumas and assaults, such as falls, accidents, violence, losses, etc.

Current intensely emotionally loaded situations tend to precipitate disorders that heal quickly in response to interventions, though they will go on to generate physical ailments/complications if the condition-of-consciousness warnings are not heeded.

Meanwhile, chronic stress-producing and on-going emotional meaning pattern problems grind away at the body till it breaks down. These illness and disorders tend to take longer to heal, and to require more intensive interventions.

It should also be noted that this whole disorder-precipitating process pretty much centers around what we think of as "unconscious" phenomena that are out of awareness, that are beyond our conscious control, and/or that are continuously indirectly influencing what happens in our lives.

They reflect aspects of ourselves and of our lives that are so threatening to us or that were so threatening to those around us in our formative period that we had to repress them from our awareness.

Another situation that arises is where we have the operation of forces emanating from the soul or essence of the individual that influence the manifestation of unconscious motivations, interpretations and interventions in interaction with environmental phenomena.

Such things as accidental death, violence perpetrated on us, abortions, etc. reflect the intentions of the soul, showing up as either unconscious motivations and/or as externals that precipitate these outcomes.

All experiences are stored in the soul, and the soul also receives the karma for any cosmic contributions or cosmic transgressions. Consequently, some disorders and intense events are karmic resolutions. Congenital disorders are often of this nature.

One example of this type of thing is where marks or sores on the body often indicate soul memories that are "scarring" the soul. They require replacement with more positive programming via experiences in this life, and the marks or sores serve as a "catalyst message" to this effect. One's life goals as selected by the soul frequently reflect the need for "cosmic resolutions" of this sort.

Situations where external events and forces are operative in a manner that is not under our control or that are not directly in our consciousness, but which precipitate physical problems (such as work environment disorders) come from our unconscious in this way. They are the resultants of our soul needs and our inner motivations and interpretations interacting with the environmental phenomena around us.

Still another aspect of the processes involved in the production of illnesses and disorders by seemingly impersonal and independent causations are things like intense cold and other passing external stimuli that seem to us to be the full and total explanation of responses like sneezes.

However, it is true that these, too, are reflective of the underlying state of being of the individual, in the sense that we often experience such stimuli without reacting to them with sneezes, colds or whatever when there is not such an underlying disturbance operative.

It should be noted that there are three general correspondences with broad causative processes in life that are located in the body tissues. These tissues are composed of the bones, the soft tissues, and the fluids.

The bones are our fundamental support system and the foundation of our existence. It should not be too surprising, therefore, to learn that the bones reflect our deepest issues, and they are the representatives of our cosmic self, our spiritual foundation, and our relationship with the Universe.

The soft tissues such as the muscles and/organs, on the other hand, represent our thinking processes, parameters and phenomena, as well as *what* we are thinking. "As a person thinketh," so their soft tissues go.

Finally, the fluids of the body, especially the blood, are manifestations of our emotional processes and operations, along with our feelings about things. That includes the interpretation and meaning-achieving and -attributing system.

Breakdowns in these three tissue types will be very clearly manifesting the situation in these three arenas and areas of our being. The linkages involved are the resultant of one or more of four different processes. Some are the outcome of the direct physiological effects of the mental/emotional/soul determinants and precipitants of the disorder, such as the "fight or flight" reaction.

Others come from the indirect physical resultants of the mental/emotional/soul outcomes of the individual's interpretations and interventions in their lives, as in the "Oh my God!" or "So that means . . ." reactions that precipitate physical effects in the body.

Still others consist of mediated impacts via the mental/emotional/soul processes that flow along the meridian system of the body that oriental medicine is so familiar with. Here the effect is to alter our auric field in a manner that affects our physical body.

And finally, others are the outcome of direct "thought form"-generated symbolic representations of the person's pictures of their situation and the meanings they give the circumstances that show up as bodily metaphors of their interpretation for the person.

The more systems that are involved in a disorder that, when they are decoded, are saying the same thing, the more important it is that the message be heeded and that actions are taken to change the situation and the consciousness associated with it.

Every condition in our lives exists because there is a need for it in one way or another, either on the time-space level or on the soul level or both. The symptoms, reactions or conditions are the outward effect of the inner condition of the individual.

A specific sickness is the natural physical outcome of particular thought patterns and/or emotional disharmonies. They are coded messages from the body to the effect of what is happening and what needs to happen. In effect, then, illnesses and ailments teach us, expand us, and move us on -- if we can understand them and heed them.

There is a kind of "escalation chain" effect involved in this matter of consciousness distortions showing up in the body's malfunctioning. It starts out as psychological phenomena such as disturbing thoughts, wishes, fantasies, intentions, interpretations or repressions.

If these are ignored, avoided or resisted, it then moves to mild disruptions of our functioning such as fatigue, irritation reactions, or sleep pattern disruptions. If the situation continues to not be heeded, it then moves to acute physical disturbances like inflammations, wounds and minor accidents.

If we still don't get the message and we persist in the pattern of consciousness/functioning that is causing the problem, we move on to chronic conditions, where we receive a lasting reminder of our situation.

If we still stubbornly refuse to acknowledge our problem and to adjust our consciousness, the soul and/or the Cosmos will precipitate traumatic events such as accidents, assaults, lightening strikes, and the like.

If all this fails, the situation deteriorates into irreversible physical changes or incurable processes. The individual then proceeds to descend into such outcomes as cancer or degenerative disorders like "Lou Gehrig's disease" or AIDS.

If the individual continues in their patterns even then, this development leads to death, the ultimate acknowledgment that we are not a separate "I" in a strictly physical world. We are conscious beings in a sea of consciousness, where the requirement is to be "at one with the One."

It should be noted that all illnesses and disorders are based on the same source: a deep sense of separation from God. The situation of being in a physical body in time-space lays the ground work for this experience, and it then is exaggerated/exacerbated by non-optimal life experiences.

In effect, we feel at the deep unconscious level that "it's all our fault" and that we are "getting our just desserts," with the result that we respond with mental/emotional reactions that result ultimately in bodily breakdowns. The disorder then brings our attention to the particular ways in which we feel separated and isolated from the Cosmos, and to the interpretations and interventions that arise from this.

Incidentally, an excellent resource for understanding how this all works and how to work with the information that comes from the meanings of the diseases and disruptions is *"Feelings Buried Alive Never Die . . . ."* by Karol K. Truman.

In effect, when we are afflicted with a physical disorder, what we are being told in no uncertain terms is that this dysfunctional way of being must go. The meaning of bodily break-downs, then, can in effect be succinctly summarized in three words:

CHANGE THAT PATTERN!

The "prudent person's" reaction to all this is to accept and understand what the disturbance is telling us, as well as heeding its implications for changes in our consciousness. If we resist, avoid, deny or continue to pursue the "settle-for- substitutes" for resolutions and solutions to the consciousness problem, our symptoms will persist or worsen.

The basic reality here is that *awareness heals*. Tuning into and taking seriously the implications for changes in our consciousness manifestation are the "way to fly" when dealing with illnesses and disorders.

This doesn't mean, of course, that one doesn't do corrective interventions directly on the bodily effects of the conflict. It just means that in addition to the corrective efforts, you also go after the underlying source of the problem in your consciousness.

The process is like working from one side of a mountain on symptom treatment, while simultaneously working from the other side on the underlying emotional/mental/Cosmic issues. The two then meet in the middle, resulting in a permanent termination of the disorder after a greatly accelerated healing.

HELPFUL HINTS FOR WORKING WITH THE "Dictionaries"

This is a brief note regarding how to utilize the information contained in the "Dictionaries" written by Michael J. Lincoln, Ph.D. These books were composed from scientific literature, clinical experience, life learning, inner knowing and other-dimensional sources. As a result, they make rather audacious and at times seemingly off-the-wall statements regarding what is happening when an individual is experiencing one of the indicators of what is going on for them when they encounter a "disruption" in their life. This makes the "Dictionaries" rather difficult to work with at times.

What follows are some recommendations regarding how to proceed with the information contained in the "Dictionaries," particularly in reference to situations where the information doesn't seem to fit the circumstances or the person, or where it is hard to know what the information indicates.

First of all, it needs to be said that the task here is to PUT IT IN CONTEXT. These items are general purpose, and they must be related to the particulars of the situation in which they come up for the person.

They are basic generic statements of the pattern and dynamics of the disruption in the person's life. It is imperative that they therefore be interpreted in terms of the individual's situation, so as to be understandable and utilizable there.

Then there is the problem of the generic experiential histories presented. They frequently do not seem to fit the overall situation or the actual facts of the life history of any given individual.
The way to deal with this is to remember that the "histories" are given as a way of coming to comprehend that the problematic pattern described regarding the disruption is a natural resultant of understandable processes, not some flaw in their soul, some accident of nature or some in-born "bad seed" pathology.
The items are designed to generate compassionate comprehension -- whether for you or for the one who is experiencing the dynamics and circumstances involved in the problem.

The reality is that we don't need to know the exact history of circumstances, events and environmental influences that led to the individual's having the dynamics involved. We *do* need to know that it all makes sense of some sort, and that making sense of it is healing of the problem and healing for the person.

What happens when this material is read is that the person's "inner child," who had to take whatever happened to them in their formative process as "God's Gospel Truth" from the "Horse's Mouth, the Source Itself", comes to understand how it all started.

What was actually taking place is that normally or abnormally flawed human beings were trying to cope with the huge impact of this new person on a 24/7/365 basis, with inevitable failures and harms. We in effect reached for God, and we got God"(zilla)" in one form or another.
So we end up thinking God is some 24-story tall Tyrannosaurus Rex going around eating New York and looking for YOU.

We think that God is infallible so we therefore deserved the events we underwent. This book is designed to switch on the light so that you see the emperor's new clothes, and that was God(zilla) and not God. The postulated histories are designed to turn that light on.

A second major difficulty is when the description of the dynamics and processes involved do not seem to fit the overt nature of the person's personality, functioning patterns or history.

One source of this difficulty is that the descriptions are "set to medium level" in their intensity and implications. You may have to "tone down" the description or "amp up" the description to get a better fit to the situation. The important thing here is to understand the dynamics, not necessarily to have the description fit exactly in the person's life on the overt level.

The other source of this difficulty is that often the dynamics being referred to or described are taking place on some other level in the person's functioning. One such situation is where the dynamics and issues are reflecting the state and intensity of the pattern setting circumstances at the point of the formative process of the dynamics, rather than what they are currently or have historically manifested overtly.

Such a situation means that the person is in effect "back to the beginning" so as to finally heal it, and they are therefore re-experiencing the original situation internally so as to clear it out of their dynamics for once and for all.

The way this works is a "peeling the onion" process in which the individual works their way back from the most recently acquired wounds till they arrive at the point where the issue/experience/interpretation in question comes up full force. This involves a primordial part of the person which went into action when they first encountered the experience that "God is angry with me" somewhere along the way from conception to about age three.

It arises because we are hard-wired to believe that everything that comes to us in that foundational developmental period is the truth, the whole truth and nothing but the truth about whom and what we are.

We then think we have to get the "God Housekeeping Seal of Approval" so as to "save our soul," and the "inner child" commences to seek to achieve that outcome by doing what "God" (actually "God(zilla)" -- the parent(s) being caught up in their own unfinished business and/or trying circumstances at the time) the parent(s) seems to demand.

The purpose is for the person's "inner child" (who did not have mental equipment operating at the time of the wound) to be activated, so as to "educate Rita" about what it was REALLY all about with the now available full mental and experiential equipment to be able to do so.

Items will therefore sometimes reflect an on going representation of the original internal experience in the current context in order to free the person from the beliefs and agonies that were generated in the absence of any real understanding of what was going on back then. By far the most common inference/conclusion drawn is that it was all their fault and God said so.

This "illusional conclusion" produces the "three steps forward, two and a half steps back" phenomenon that is experienced as, "I have met the enemy and it is me!" Sometimes, therefore, the dynamics for the disruption pattern are referring to what is happening for their "inner child" at this particular point in the person's life.

If that is the case, it means that the issues and areas involved are now pushing for healing, and that the "inner child" needs compassionate comprehension and assistance in healing the wounds of their early formative process.

And the dynamics described in the item give the necessary information as to what is happening and what needs healing around their relationship with themselves and around their relationship with the "Home Office" from way back when.

This process can result in the item characterizing the person in a manner that flies in the face of their subsequently developed functioning, understanding and experience. The way to handle this is to go back to what was happening at the time the "illusional conclusions" were instilled and to sort it out, along with releasing the dammed up emotions and anxieties/angers/despairs generated at the time.

In such a situation, the item clarifies the person's reaction to what was happening to them at the time, as a function of the limitations of the mental equipment of the "inner child." It explains what's been bugging them all along, so they can liberate themselves from the ancient pattern and get on with their life with fully operative equipment unhampered by "ghosts of Christmases past."

Another situation that happens often is where the dynamics being described are those involved in their "shadow." This is where some aspects of the person's soul and/or biologic beingness were not allowed to manifest as a child, and these aspects were therefore "shoved into their shadow." The aspects then become distorted by being shunned and shunted like this. The item then serves as an indicator of this "shadow-clearing" process going on.

When you are encountering the effects of a "shadow aspect" of this nature, the implication is to find what the "shadow aspect" is a distortion of, to find what was not allowed and which is now pushing for acknowledgement, validation, acceptance and manifestation.

The trick here is not to try to "treat the symptom" -- either the disruption reflecting the situation or the "shadow aspect" manifestation. You work on releasing the underlying "shadow-shoved" self-beingness into full manifestation in their life.

You do repair the car, handle the medical problem, or whatever, as a practical matter. But that is not where the action is, and if you don't take care of the underlying cause, it will result in further disruptions until it is worked with.

For instance, suppose the disruption is pointing to an underlying rage that the individual is working with. Yet the person is a kind, gentle, wise and loving individual who is anything but rageful to all appearances.

What is going on here is that they were forced to shove their personal power and potency into their "shadow," where it turned into an incessant rage about being so suppressed and distorted that is always pushing to be released.

So you don't start accusing the person of being a rageful phony, and you don't start working on rage-reduction, unless the individual is showing the need to find positive anger-release methods per se.

What you DO, do is work with them to release their personal power and potency so that they can impact effectively in the world, and so that they can then manifest their full nature, contribution and destiny.

Still another way in which there may be a mismatch between the individual's overt or consciously knowable functioning and experience, on the one hand, and the dynamics description of the disruption in the item on the other, is when what is being dealt with is early formative experiences that never got handled or dealt with before.

When this occurs, it is like a "lawn rake," where you have a nice line of cut grass clippings you've already raked up, and you notice a big clump way back at the beginning that you forgot.

So you have to go back and bring that clump up in line with the rest of your life. And the dynamics description points you in the right direction, as well as indicating the time period of your development that needs work now.

One more way in which a seeming "mismatch" between the item contents and the person's situation can occur is where what is being referred to is the process of healing itself, in terms of its effects on the individual's emotional dynamics and functioning at present.

That is, the dynamics of the disruption being described are in reference to the processes and impacts of the healing process on the individual's experience and manifestation. In other words, the emotions and dynamics activated by the person's undergoing the healing of the original damage can have disruptive effects of their own.

You then see the implications regarding what the individual is experiencing on the unconscious emotional level, and you work to alleviate that and the resultants of the original damage that are creating this disruptive outcome simultaneously.

And of course, on some occasions for whatever reason, the description of the dynamics involved for the disruption are just plain wrong. After all, psychological and spiritual dynamics are not the only factors involved in the disruptions that occur in life. As Freud said in his last interview, "Sometimes gentlemen a cigar, is nothing but a cigar."

One common situation where this occurs is when the individual is either a very seasoned old soul and/or they have pretty much handled most of their damage repair. In such situations, the normal context of the human condition is not happening, and the events in their life activate unusual reactions from their body or whatever.

The other major difficulty that will on occasion arise when reading the items is the "So -- so what?" reaction. This is the problem of translating the abstractions into actions. This is sometimes raised as a request for there to be added to the "Dictionary" additional information for each item regarding intervention or correction.

In addition to the already out-of-hand problem of size of the "Dictionary" in most cases, this suggestion runs into another issue, which is that the actual process of handling the dynamics underlying the description is totally unique to each person's situation.

Consequently, to try and cover all possible ways of dealing with the dynamics involved would lead to a book of encyclopedic proportions for each "Dictionary," and it STILL wouldn't handle the need because of the multi-dimensional uniqueness factor. The reality is that "awareness heals" in idiosyncratically manifesting ways all by itself, largely on the subconscious and holographic level.

Since the disruptions are reflections of underlying dynamics and fundamental "premises" that the individual is working with and needing to work on, specific symptom intervention techniques are not the place where the action is. It is in the emotional and mental bodies of the individual, as well as in their soul and destiny dynamics. As such, the problem needs to be addressed on that level in the "awareness heals" manner.

If there were a kind of universal principle on how to utilize the information in the "Dictionaries," it would be to discern what the foundational "premise" and early emotional wound in their relationship with "God(zilla)" are that have shaped their formative and subsequent experiential history.

These are things like "God is angry with me," "I caused World War II," "I don't deserve to exist," "People are no damned good," "I am unfit for human consumption," "I am unlovable," "I am worthless," "Nothing makes any sense," etc.

Once you have a handle on the premise(s), you know roughly what is up for healing and what is causing the disruption. Then you work on reversing the premise(s) by whatever ways are appropriate for the person and their situation/process/point in their development/destiny via the "awareness heals" processes. And this almost never involves admonitions, accusations and acrimonious attacks or simple formulas like, "Just do it!," "Tell yourself not to do it" or "Just say no!" It just doesn't work that way.

What usually is helpful is to alert yourself or the person involved to the underlying premise(s), and then to search out the Truth that is based on a lot of personal experience the individual has had, and which is trying to "get out of prison" now in such a way as to cause the disruption.

For instance, if they have an "IT'S NOT ALLOWED!" premise, the Truth is that "It is required by God, by common sense, by human decency and your needs!" The past was, period!

It served its purpose, and it is now time to collect the gifts in the garbage and to start sharing what you have learned from it.

One way to approach this whole issue is the direct route. That is, you turn the alternative to the foundational premise into an affirmation which the individual repeatedly reminds themselves of, meditates on, and puts in their environment, like on the bathroom mirror, the refrigerator, the car, etc.

It is important to be careful how you word the affirmation, though. It should be generic and Universally serving, rather than some specific and selfish or unilateral goal statement. Remember, you will get just exactly what you put out there, so be conscious as you formulate it.

It is also helpful to examine situations, events, routines, relationships, processes, motivations, etc, in terms of how they relate to and are affected by the foundational premise and by the alternative affirmation. By making the whole thing a major focus, it helps to heal the issue.

Another way to heal the problem is to start studying when the fundamental premise and its behavioral/functional effects show up in your personal life, and then to start using "awareness training" to facilitate its retirement as no longer being needed.

"Awareness training" is where you as soon as possible notice that the premise dynamic functioning has showed up again. And then you give yourself a meaningful reward of self-congratulation and whatever else feels and is good for you for noticing it!

You do NOT beat yourself up for doing it again! You pay yourself off for noticing and being aware of it. This will give you both experiential validation that you are on the right track and the resulting awareness of functioning precipitation patterns. You will see what sets you off, what the situations that set you off have in common, and how they relate to the foundational premise and to the alternative affirmation.

If you keep doing this, you will find that the time between doing it and noticing that you did it gets shorter and shorter in a hurry. You get to the point where you notice it in midstream.

Sometimes you can stop working on it at that point and sometimes not. If you do terminate here, give yourself an extra reward for your accomplishment as well as for noticing again.

Eventually, you will notice it at the onset of the process, and then you will get to the place where you notice it at the intention point. When you have arrived there, you will have reached the goal of self-regulation on the pattern.

And if you are also inserting the alternative affirmation to the foundational premise while you are doing this, you will be amazed at how fast the pattern disappears and the disruption goes away.

The reason for this is that the disruption pattern came to your attention in the first place because it was time for healing the dynamic. This fact, in conjunction with the effectiveness of "awareness training" and "alternative affirmations," makes for a highly impactful change process.

Still another way to work with the information is to study how the premise dynamic and functioning pattern works in your life. If the relationship is symbolic and indicative of the "truth" of the foundational premise so that each instance is further "proof" of the premise, this can be worked on with the alternative affirmation.

And if the dynamic and functioning pattern are serving some purpose for you in its present process, see what you can do to meet the need(s) that the dynamic and its resultants serve, and look for better, more effective and non-destructive ways that those needs can be met.

Finally, one interesting way in which the "Dictionaries" have been applied is to read the dynamics for the disruptive pattern you are experiencing to see if it fits with you. If it does, work on it in the ways described above.

But if it doesn't and the dynamic and history are way off base, that might indicate that you are not going to have to experience the full impacts and implications of the disruptive pattern.

If that is the case, it then tells you that you don't have to work on that dynamic because in all likelihood it isn't there, and you can focus your energy on finding what else might be happening here.

For instance, if you don't have the dynamics for cancer but you got it anyway, it might be indicative of a psychic attack or of a genetic/familial vulnerability or of a self-endangering process that has led to a natural consequence outcome, or whatever.

Incidentally, one interesting application of the item content in the case of a psychic attack is to be aware that the attacker will invariably do their dirty work on the basis of their own dynamics and issues. In other words, they will seek to generate in others what they themselves are struggling with. That, in turn, can be helpful in identifying who is doing the attacking.

This is admittedly not a whole lot of information on how to deal with the data of the "Dictionaries." The reality is that it is in effect something of an art form that relies heavily upon a lot of information about a lot of things and on the skillful use of intuition, insight and inputs from other dimensions. But like any art form, it can be learned, improved upon, and even passed on to others.

A final hint. The "Dictionaries" were written by "talking" through the typewriter. As a result, it is almost imperative that when you read the description or information on the item(s), you should do so out LOUD -- even if you are by yourself. It does not follow the information patterns of written English, and it speaks more directly to your soul, so to speak. If you read the items aloud with "radio inflections" you have the experience of being spoken to, rather than of "reading" something. It should be done with verve, caring and connection. Try it. You'll find that you get much more out of it. What happens is that the "inner child" in both you and the person being read to really hears when you do this.

Working with the "Dictionaries" is very much like the motto of the 12-Step programs, in which they say something like, "Take what you need and leave the rest." The purpose of the "Dictionaries" is to provide a "translator" or a "decoder" of what the spin offs from the condition of the emotional body are saying.

As such, it is really required that you re-build the social and life history information in the items to fit the emotional/cognitive/mental/functional/soul dynamics you find or already know about the person involved.

You also need to update the data to fit the current situation and culture the individual is immersed in, especially with younger people or children, who are displaying the effects of the rapidly evolving cultural and human condition situation.

Another special consideration is when the emotional body conditions that are generating the "Dictionary" item symptoms are the resultant of a transitional and/or transformational process going on in the individual's life space, such as the healing undertaking itself.

When faced with rapidly developing change, profound healing, emerging characteristics or other change process parameters, you need to fit what you read to the situation, so that you can find the emotional body process that needs your attention and intervention right now.

In other words, it works best to place the information you derive from the "Dictionaries" on the "back burner processor," rather than going right into the "sleeve-rolling mode" or into an action-activation intervention pattern. Let it brew with the awareness process for a while.

What happens when you do this is that the information coagulates, congeals and agglutinates to lead to very helpful insights that gradually speed up the healing and/or transition/transformation process.

When working with the "Dictionaries" it is like the symptoms or problems are on one side of a mountain and your compassionate comprehension is on the other. So you handle the symptoms in a problem-solving manner, while at the same time, you "educate Rita" as to what it all means. Both processes then simultaneously bore through the mountain and meet in the middle, with no relapses.

HOW TO USE THIS "DICTIONARY"

The disorders listed below are those for which the underlying negative thought forms, emotional reactions, life histories, predispositional factors, and precipitating events-circumstances have been found in the literature and in the author's experience.

It should be noted that the life histories postulated here for the various illness and disorders represent generic dynamics-generating situation descriptions. They may or may not directly fit the situation for any given individual, which are usually much more complex and idiosyncratic in their nature than what is contained in the items.

The items are put in as an understanding device to convey a compassionate comprehension of the individual's circumstances and outcomes for purposes of amelioration and healing.

It should also be noted that the level of intensity of the symptoms implied by their title, the degree of severity of the history given, and the magnitude of the manifestation of the psychological dynamics displayed may all vary considerably from person to person and from situation to situation.

These items, descriptions and interpretations are general "ballpark estimates" of the phenomena involved, and they should be taken as the essential meanings inherent in the situation, rather than as absolutely specific, right-on descriptions of the details of the particular unique circumstances you are seeking an understanding of.

Considerable adjustments may have to be made when interpreting a given situation. In particular, there has to be major re-framing done when interpreting disorders in children. The items have to be framed and worked with in terms of the child's age, nature and situation.

One more caution. While the prototypic learning histories clearly fault the parenting that the individual received (and sometimes also the rest of the family's behavior), it should be kept in mind that this is not "parent-bashing."

The circumstances and cultural context of the isolated nuclear family of today are so antithetical to the biologic human nature outcome of our evolutionary history and our resulting needs that it is in effect guaranteed that the parenting process will falter and fail along significant dimensions almost universally. After all, if you put the screws to someone when they are forming up, they end up screwed up.

Originally, we shared a "commons" with a great deal of contact, involvement and support from the whole community in meeting the needs of the adults, the children, and the child-rearing process. We now expect spouses and parents to in effect "do the impossible with nothing" in many ways. And of course, we "fall on our faces" a lot as a result. These postulated histories are just a catalogue of the various manners in which that has happened.

In a way, this "de-coding device dictionary" is a profound call for us to "change that pattern" with regard to how we organize, prioritize and realize everything as a species and as individuals. We are now in the process of doing just that on the larger scale.

It should also be noted that for almost everyone, parenting errors of the type described in this book are on the subconscious or unconscious level. Life is rather overwhelming, especially in the isolated nuclear family in an urban environment in today's world.

So we error in our parenting. It is relatively rarely a situation of a malicious parent getting a kick out of their harm-induction, though there *are* some parents of this nature. But for the vast majority of us, it is a matter of unfortunate outcomes of in effect impossible circumstances.

It should be noted that as a result of all this, the innermost and earliest wounded part of the person will be experiencing the situation described in the item, even if the person doesn't manifest it overtly or experience it in their conscious awareness. We are formed up early on, and then we have to make corrections from then on.

One final comment about all this. At one level, this is a time-limited book. That is because we are in the midst of the greatest evolutionary change in human history. We are currently experiencing the "last grasp" of the formative process of the human race, where primitivity of consciousness has reigned supreme while we pinned down the basics of dealing with 3-D.

We have now collectively mastered that task, and we are in effect "graduating" into the full manifestation of human potential and destiny phase of our collective soul pool's development. We are now going to be coming from the heart and from wisdom -- after this transition/transformation period is completed.

As a result of this, the isolated nuclear family in a selfish world will disappear as a phenomenon, and almost all of these disorders will disappear. They will be replaced by much more subtle and refined side effects of our challenge-mastering process from then on.

And thus this book will eventually end up like an "anatomy of the Victorian Era" -- a curious historical document. Until then, however, we will still need the insights provided here about what happens when fundamental human needs go unmet or are trampled over.

The next "how to" concerns the fact that humans are highly complex beings. As a result, many of the items in this "Dictionary" have "multiple characters" associated with them. This means that you will encounter a meaning/character for an item, after which there will be a string of asterisks below it. Then there will be another meaning/character, and so on. See example below:

ABDOMINAL PAIN

"Up for grabs." They are experiencing intense survival-anxiety and concerns over whether they can really handle life. There is a strongly felt powerlessness arising from "skid row" programming and learned helplessness in the face of a severely dysfunctional family.
****

"Virgo-ism." They are trying to cover all the details, to organize and coordinate everything, to analyze the situation and meet all needs in the "right" way. The result is nit-picking perfectionism, detail-domination, and an inability to see the forest for the trees.
It is a pattern that got started in a severely patriarchal and perfectionistic family.

What you do with these is to read the "caption/quote" at the beginning of each one to get a hit as to what and who is involved. And you select the ones(s) that seem to fit for the individual you are reading about to arrive at a liberating understanding of that person.

Now for the final bit of "how to" information regarding this "Dictionary." When reading the material to yourself or to others, it should be done in a "radio reading" manner, complete with inflections, pauses, emphases, colorfulness, etc. Just reading in a monotone will not embed the information in your subconscious, where it can do its work. And for maximum effectiveness, the reading to yourself and for others should be done ***out loud***. This really takes it to the core of the subconscious.

With this as a foundation for approaching the "decoding device dictionary," we hope you enjoy Healer' Handbook *for Practitioners* and get much awareness form it.

IT WORKS THE OTHER WAY, TOO

It should be noted here that the opposite process also happens with regard to the effect of the "thought forms" and emotional contents residing in our consciousness. That is, things like reverence of self, faith in one's ability and right to survive, thrive and heal, self-love and self-acceptance, like a sense of the goodness of the self, self-commitment, trust in the operations of the Cosmos, commitment to the community, etc., are all highly effective preventatives and correctives for illnesses.

In addition, such activities as selfless service, using knowledge to help others and to thereby to increase one's own knowledge, caring for others, being a part of a social support system, developing and maintaining a God-connection, relaxation exercises, and self-hypnosis greatly strengthen the immune system and generate physical health.

Healing is "wholing" -- manifesting all of our potentials and becoming one with All That Is. It is restoring the integrated and flowing manifestational process of being "at one with" the Cosmos in your consciousness and in your way of being.

It is a process of finding what is needed and what has been systematically kept unconscious for whatever reason, and then correcting your consciousness in that area so that who you are reflects *Who You Are*.

SPEAKING OF ROSES....
A Lesson on "Labeling"

Sometimes a rose is not necessarily a rose. This is a paper about the ins and outs of "labeling," of giving a name to a phenomenon and of applying the name to specific instances and individuals.

Unfortunately, this often results in both misapplication of the labels and abuses arising from the labels themselves. What follows is a brief discussion of the nature and problems of the utilization of names for things, especially as applied to people.

A major issue that is involved here is the problem of duality, the experience of and living out of the notion that there are two distinctly different worlds in the Cosmos -- the spiritual and the material. The idea is that we need to keep these worlds separate, and that only material reality is real in any practical sense.

This generates an approach in which control of one's environment and experiences become paramount, at the expense of everything else. In this approach, labeling becomes a major tool of control, with little or no concern for the larger effects of one's utilization of labels.

This is an ancient issue, and it is related to the phenomenon of the One and the Many. We are all "chips off the Old Hologram," and so we are all One, as they say. But creation is also composed of the vast multitude of particulars that are the Many, who are here to expand their souls and the Cosmos.

In order to function in the World of the Many, we need names and identifying labels. While there are those who advocate the abandonment of labels altogether, that is a Luddite prescription that would, if actually applied, precipitate instant chaos.

The fact of the matter is that we simply have to use words to function in the world and with each other, and sometimes we have to use words to describe phenomena about ourselves and other people.

We need words and labels as the means we have to make sense of and to order our environment, experiences and responsibilities. We also need words to communicate with each other and to convey, store and retrieve fundamental information. Words and symbols are the basis of meaning and of functioning.

Unfortunately, though, as with everything else, words and symbols are a double-edged sword. In today's world of extreme materialism, cultural decline before the Great Transformation, and the resulting intense selfishness, disintegrity and sheer insensitivity, we are often subjected to the dark side of words and labels.

The worst effect of this is "reification" -- the turning of concepts into the experience of concrete, discrete, external and manipulable "things." Things with no soul, consciousness, experiences, or respectable value.

Words applied to people have this effect a great deal of the time. That in turn, has the effect of dehumanizing them, disensouling them, and depersonalizing them. Which leads to callous, calculating and cold lack of concern for anything beyond what the "cipher" can do for you or what "surfing the ciphers" can get you.

It even leads to things like drive-by shootings, torture, kidnapping and interrogating, and concentration camps. The process takes many forms. For instance, there is the "cookie cutter" phenomenon, in which integral essences and whole systems are arbitrarily "cut up" into "cipher chunks" and dealt with as if the "chunks" were the whole and the only reality there is -- with often disastrous results to both the people so dealt with and to the world at large, ultimately. Involved here are things like "welfare recipient," "student," "ex-con," "black," "employee," "customer," "voter" and "them."

Then there is the "distantiation effect" in which anyone with a label or "that" label is instantly pushed away from your heart and soul as being a "thing" to be dealt with at arm's length or not at all.

This allows other things like manipulation and exploitation to be undertaken with no qualms or even with no thought about what you are doing. It also has the effect of activating actions like not granting loans, taking people to court, sending people to jail, etc.

Another effect of labels is that they are strongly prone to be used to maintain the status quo and the system/situation as it is. Labels are powerful devices to sustain the class system and to "validate" your prejudices and expectations of privilege. They also allow, elicit and justify judgments and evaluations, with the resulting actions, labels used in this way are a highly paranoid patriarchal process.

A very common phenomenon involved in label abuse is the "blame boomerang," in which you see something in another person that you hate in yourself, and then you label them and attack them -- instead of yourself.

A closely related phenomenon is "projective identification," in which you feel an affinity-identity with someone, and then you label them on that basis and act accordingly. These kinds of responses lead to much destructive behavior and outcomes.

The most common negative outcomes of labeling are, however, the processes of control, restriction and "boxing in." We use them to "keep people in their place." And their "place" is highly subjectively and self-servingly defined.

Labels then serve as justifications for our actions, as self-reassurances, and as self-inflations. They can also operate as the tools of self-delusion, even going to the full-fledged paranoid level, as in gang turfing and national wars.

This all being the case, then, what are we to do? As was indicated, words, symbols and labels are essential to our functioning. So how do we use them without undue harm resulting?

The key on this is self-monitoring and ecological tracking. While labels are essential, they are often thoughtlessly used. So track yourself as you are using them, to see what the ultimate effects and results are.

In reality, labels are only useful when they are discerningly describing processes, rather than "tagging things." They should refer to ensouled beings living life in an intensely complex, potentially dangerous, and ever changing world.

A good way to carry this out is to work at "conscious projective identification," in which you identify with everyone you encounter as a fellow important person, so that you afford them the respect, caring and covering they deserve. In other words, reflect reality -- don't reify.

As for how this relates to how to use this book, keep in mind that the people being described in the different difficulties here are ensouled beings like you, and that compassionate comprehension, not judgments, evaluations and labels are the purpose of this "Dictionary."

It is intended to convey what is happening to and within the people so that you can understand and help them. It is a healing device. This applies especially towards yourself when you are reading about what the difficulties mean about you. Heal, don't hurt.

HOW DOES HE _DO_ IT!?

This is a discussion of how Michael J. Lincoln is able to do what he does and how he does it in arriving at the items in the numerous "Dictionaries" of the meanings of things that he has written. It is also a presentation of the thinking processes that can and if possible should be used in interpreting the items in the "Dictionaries" by the user.

It is composed of two sections. The first will trace the development of the capabilities and approach that he uses. The second will briefly discuss what the processes and parameters that are involved in arriving at a comprehensive comprehension of people.

With regard to the evolution of his approach to assessment, in addition to the particular soul, genetic and life history qualities that make up who Michael J. Lincoln is, there is a rather huge experiential history behind his work in these books.

At the beginning of the whole thing was his professional training as a clinical psychologist. It occurred in the late fifties and early sixties, and it very strongly emphasized psychological assessment practice. He worked with everything from college counseling to working with disturbed veterans, the elderly, the psychotic and the mentally challenged.

Then he commenced his professional career by serving as the clinical director of a revolutionary new approach to the treatment of emotionally disturbed children in the mid-sixties. It was the application of Skinnerian behaviorism in an open treatment program where the children went home each weekend. _(Skinnerian behaviorisms uses B.F. Skinner's work on learning from consequences with consequence-scheduling right after the behavior occurs)._

Within a few months, he found himself the clinical director of a riot. The program was just not working, despite the application of everything that had been done of this nature in the past with locked ward psychiatric populations.

This forced him to develop a brand new approach to behavioral intervention and to psychological assessment. It involved his doing "process recordings" of everything the child did, along with everything that was happening around the child. These records were then broken down into half-second segments and analyzed for what was going on for, to and within the child.

The result was an in-depth understanding of the person and their needs that was then communicated to the staff. The net effect was an almost scary effectiveness of the program. He called it the "Los Alamos of psychology" at the time, in reference to the gigantic implications of what was being discovered, and to the dangers of the misapplication of that knowledge.

Then when this was well under way, he turned the behavioral assessment process onto the child therapists as they did their work, and he co-wrote a book with the child therapy supervisor of the program on how child therapy works (_"So You Want To Work With Kids?"_), and on the components of successful child treatment by child care workers. This led to his training such child and youth workers in their profession.

He was also required by law to do full-fledged psychological assessments of all the children in the program. He did this in a manner that combined the best of his assessment training with his behavioral assessment skills. The result was profound comprehension of each person.

This led to the agency's being requested by the State of Oregon to assess the needs of all kinds of emotionally disturbed children, for purposes of designing a treatment continuum for them. Everyone from neurotics to hyperactives, to the brain-damaged the mentally disturbed chained to the walls to murderers to severely suicidal children to autistics and psychotics were in-depth assessed by Michael J. Lincoln, Ph.D. and by the entire agency, resulting in exhaustive detailing of their entire situation, nature and needs.

Out of all this evolved a number of things, two of which will be mentioned here. One was that there grew from all this experience an ability to read people's faces that was based on this intense assessment work. He went on to train people in this process.

The other thing that evolved was his coming to understand the formation and operation of the human personality. It became a two-part system -- "developmental arrests" in the first two years of life, on the one hand, and "life scripts" that were caused by the role the child played in their family, on the other.

Together, these became two books on the subject (*"A Funny Thing Happened.... On the Way To My Life"* and *"It's All In The Family"*), and they pretty much cover the nature of personality in the whole of humanity through history and across cultures.

After all this, he went on to teach assessment to future clinical psychologists at the University of Portland for some years. This led to his supervising several master's theses and Ph.D. dissertations involving in-depth assessments in a wide variety of modes and fields. He shepherded a number of Ph.D. psychologists to their licenses.

As all this was going on, he also ran a night club for teenagers during the sixties, whereupon he discovered the huge cultural and psychological evolutionary process we are undergoing. Simultaneously, he worked with very large inter-generational and inter-cultural encounter groups that further exposed him to this humanity wide consciousness-expansion process.

From this he went on to found and clinically direct a number of clinical treatment programs for everything from adolescent delinquents to drug abusers and alcoholics to dangerous and out of control children and adolescents to adult criminals. He also became involved in forensic psychology as a professional assessor and treatment intervention advisor.

Then the "Home Office" stepped in and told him that he had to become a "Q-tip" (a turban-wearing American Sikh). This led to his developing a profound understanding of the sacred and Cosmic realm. It also resulted in his integrating everything into what he calls his "sacred teacher" destiny.

Having done all this, he found himself impelled to start writing books on the psychological and sacred meanings of all manner of things. He commenced with an exhaustive examination of the implications about people arising from their preferences and rejections of over 90 common colors. It took him four years of highly intensive work to pull all this together.

This formed up his "Dictionary" approach to understanding things -- both in "getting" who people are as assessed by their responses to colors, and in writing about it so that others could understand what people's color reactions mean about the person (the book *Hue are You?*). The next development involved his reviewing the face-reading literature in order to write a "Dictionary" of the meanings of facial structure, based on his massive amount of experience in that field and upon the literature review (the book *What's in a Face?*).

This in turn led to his drawing upon his 20 years of literature examination in psychosomatics, along with incorporating with the work of others who interpreted the emotional meanings of bodily malfunctions and breakdowns (the book *Messages from the Body*). Then he turned to the psychological and symbolic meanings of animals, based on his many years of examination of the symbolic literature (the book *Animals Their Pschyo-Symbolic Meanings*).

Which in turn, led to his pulling together all his experience in the alcohol and drug abuse fields to write a "Dictionary" of addictions and cravings of all kinds (the book *Addictions and Cravings*). Then he summarized his 30 years in the mental health field to generate a "Dictionary" of Behavioral, Psychological and Psychiatric Problems (the book *Problematic Patterns*). And so it went, expanding into 14 such "Dictionaries" in all.

The point of all this is to indicate that he was in effect forced out on a limb to the cutting edge of things over and over again, with the outcome that he rose to the challenges.

This in turn resulted in his developing a highly evolved skill and form of channeling. It is not a "magical talent," on the one hand, and it is not a "fantasy creation," on the other. It is a capability derived from a lifetime of experience that became an integrated river arising from a dozen or so streams of development.

The result is a process of understanding of the meanings of things derived from systematically accumulating accomplishments of comprehension. It is in effect a combination of functional analysis, anthropological observation and interpretation, and sacred understanding.

And it is something that can be applied by others. It is to this end that we now turn to the thinking, empathic resonation and significance comprehension that hopefully will be utilized when working with the "Dictionaries."

UNDERSTANDING OTHERS

Essentially, the process of coming to comprehend who a person is from information about them involves the utilization of the laws of the Cosmos and of the resultants of our evolutionary history and our bio-psycho-social nature in the process.

The laws of physics are just beginning to tap into the interdimensional nature of the operation of everything, thereby validating the true reality of humanity and of the Universe. The systematic application of this, too, is an integral part of coming to compassionate comprehension.

So the "Dictionary" item construction and item interpretation process are an integrational multidimensional holographic comprehension, with a resulting organic and Cosmically correct intervention.

It involves a holistic pull-together of all the aspects of the situation, the person and the context of what is happening for the person when a phenomenon such as a bodily hassle, an equipment problem, or a functional difficulty occurs. This is the "streams into a river" process that led to Michael J. Lincoln's evolution into a "Dictionary-developer." This very same process is what is involved in understanding who someone is and what is happening with them from the items in one or more of the "Dictionaries."

One of the prime requirements in order to be able to do this effectively is for the "Dictionary"-user to *read the introduction* to the "Dictionary." Each "Dictionary" introduction explains how the correspondences that lie at the base of the items work, so that you can understand what things mean and how they can mean that.

The ability to interpret and understand people is not the resultant of a "talent" or a "gift." A talent is the systematic application of a "narrow-band" skill to a high degree of competence. However, in order to truly understand the meaning of someone, you have to go "broad-band" and holographic. Pulling things out of context or acting on a "narrow-band" understanding of something brings great difficulties. Context is the crux of comprehension and compassion.

So the effective way to work with the "Dictionaries" is to seek to know what the various "streams" are that make up the "river" that is the person-in-context that you are seeking to understand.

It takes a good deal of experience and practice to develop the ability to "stream-to-river" comprehend who someone is and what is happening for them. It is quite possible to have a "talent," such as face structure perceiving, without having the ability to read faces. It is also quite possible to be soul and/or life experienced enough to work holistically with information, without having much of a talent. Michael J. Lincoln is just such a person.

You don't have to have a "talent" of being able to understand people. It is not a "God-given gift." But you *do* need to be able to integrate things holistically. What has been done here is to seek to exemplify the kind of thinking and understanding that underlie Michael J. Lincoln's process of item-building and people comprehending. First "the making of the man" was described, and then the workings of "man that was made" were briefly characterized in that context. Hopefully, this will give you a better idea of "how he does it.

HEALER'S HANDBOOK

(The A-Z "Dictionary")

ABASIA (Inability to walk due to lack of coordination)

"Destabilized." They are suffering from scattered thinking, distractible trains of thought, and not being centered cognitively. They feel thrown off-base, with no sense of safety in a kind of fearful drivenness. They are "desperately seeking Susan" in an attempt to gain some sense of stability.

They are therefore always on the lookout for the "greener grass," and they are continuously in fear of missing out or of missing the "key element to things." As a result, they are often instantly pulled off balance by any passing stimulus that "might be the critical factor." It is the result of a "magical mystery tour" unstable dysfunctional family in which things never really worked, and in which there was no way to really tell what was actually going on.

(See **MENIERE'S DISEASE; PARALYSIS**)

ABNORMALLY RAPID HEART-BEAT

"False alarms." They are a "self-made person" who believes that they are all they've got. They have felt cut off from the environment and the Universe all their life, and that they therefore have to handle everything on their own hook, unassisted.

All this activates moments where things get out of control and beyond their coping capabilities. And these bring on anxiety attacks that accelerate the heart-beat. It is the result of never having received love and merging as a child.

(See **"LONG QT" SYNDROME**)

ABSCESSES (A large collection of pus that needs opening)

"Seething volcano." They are struggling with a smoldering resentment and anger that has been fermenting to a point where the situation is one where they have become irritated and inflamed to the point of an upheaval of late.

There is a feeling of restriction and over-work, of over-responsibility and deprivation. They are experiencing conflict and irritability, frustration, and rejection of their situation. They have a fulminating fury and fermenting thoughts over past hurts and slights, along with intentions for revenge.

When the resulting eruption finally occurs, it leaves them empty and exhausted, having finally blown itself out, thereby clearing the way for constructive alternatives to be formed to meet the needs of the situation.

It is a pattern that is all too familiar to them, due to the dysfunctionality of their family, where they could do nothing until things reached crisis proportions. They were also often attacked for their needs, wants and desires.

ACID REFLUX (Heartburn -- Burning distress behind the sternum, due to spasms of the esophagus or of the upper stomach, resulting in acid coming up)

"Happiness-horror." They have an intense, pervasive and clutching fear that is tripped off by their experiencing some joy or happiness. They have a horrifying sense of impending attack for "undeserved" joy.

They are getting what they want for once, and they feel that somehow they should not -- that it violates the Cosmic or the moral order somehow. They are anticipating retribution for the just rewards of their efforts and essence.

There is an intense abandonment- and betrayal-paranoia, based in part on past lives. It was generated in a severely restrictive, disapproving, moralistic and fear-inducing childhood. They came out of it with an intense fear of the Universe as a harshly judgmental and punitive place.
****

"Purple passion." They are intensely involved and activated over something -- love or anger that is very pronounced -- and it is scaring the hell out of them. They are operating with pronounced injunction not to feel, and especially not to feel strongly. It is a pattern that got started in their highly feeling-suppressing and/or denial-dominated dysfunctional family.
****

"Burning to be free." They are stuffing themselves and their feelings, out of a fear of catastrophic consequences if they let go and "let fly with themselves." They are now reaching the point where "This is an up with which I can no longer put!" It comes from growing up in a family in which it was not acceptable for them to be themselves or to threaten to grow away by becoming themselves in a destiny-manifesting manner.

ACQUIRED IMMUNO-DEFICIENCY SYNDROME (A.I.D.S)

"I don't deserve to exist!" They have a strong belief in their not being good enough, in their not deserving to manifest their selfhood. The result is auto-allergy, self-intolerance, self-hatred and the operation of self-destructive programs.

There is an inability to assimilate self-characteristics, with a resulting self-disgust and self-attack. They simply cannot love and accept themselves fully as whom they are, and they are systematically denying of their own needs.

They are self-suppressing around negative feelings such as anger and fear. They use a lot of denial of their situation, with a resulting tremendous emotional pain and blockage. There is no felt right to exist, and they are massively self-rejecting.

They are convinced that nobody gives a damn, and they therefore feel ultimately hopeless, vulnerable, defenseless and despairing. They also suffer from sexual guilt arising from self-sustaining self-gratification and indulgence. Underneath it all is an extreme deep-seated rage at themselves, the world and the Cosmos.

The whole pattern was induced by an over-possessive and rejecting mother. It is in effect a severe maternal deprivation and rejection reaction. They have a real need to become real, and to pay attention to how they live their life and who they in fact are.

ADDISON'S DISEASE (Under-active adrenals)

"What's the use?" There is an underlying rage at themselves that is resulting in and from severe emotional malnutrition. They don't understand themselves, they have little sense of selfhood, and they are unable to comprehend their feelings and reactions to things. They feel "alone on a desert island" with no support or sustenance from anyone. It has the effect of "pulling the plug" on their motivational system, and they end up effectively a "couch potato." Their family was intensely accusatory and depriving.

ADENOID PROBLEMS (Lymph nodes in the back of the nasal passages)

"There I go again!" They see everything, even arguments, as being their fault. They feel that everything that happens is somehow their doing, and they have the experience that it is as though "they caused World War II." They feel like they have no right to be here taking up resources and that they are unwelcome, in the way, and a bother, and an evil influence. It is an old, familiar feeling, as they always felt this way as a child, as a result of lack of acceptance and from sub-consciously hateful and accusatory parenting.

ADHESIVE CAPSULITIS (Joint interfaces become sticky)

"Oh no you don't!" They have a rather pronounced propensity to "hold themselves up" in their pursuit of objectives in life. It arises from a guilt-inducing childhood.

ADRENAL DEPLETION

"Emotional exhaustion." They are "running on empty," and they are in effect drained of their "life force." They have been undergoing a great deal of stress and/or over-responsibility, and they can no longer "carry that load." They are the product of a draining dysfunctional family in which they effectively played the role of the "family linchpin" and disaster-deflector.

CUSHING'S DISEASE (Over-active adrenals)

"Way out there." They are reacting to the over-production of crushing ideas that result in mental imbalance and a feeling of being over-powered. They have the experience of not being able to select or control the contents of their mind.

It comes from having had to remain continuously open to all inputs as a function of faulty cognitive structure development arising from a confusion-inducing and intrusive family.

(See **GRAVE'S DISEASE**)

ADRENAL PROBLEMS

"Resentment-rage." They are manifesting considerable anger and irritation/frustration with their life. They feel that they must constantly work at generating any form of success, recognition, influence or station in life. They were systematically prevented from having these experiences as a child, and they were programmed to be self-defeating.
****

"Blown out." They are suffering from overload, threats to their well being, fear, anxiety, and stress to the point where they no longer care for themselves. They feel like a defeated victim, and they have developed a giving up and emotionally indifferent attitude, along with a certain lack of courage and a nihilistic defeatism. Their experience is that everything is too much work, responsibility and devastation. They come from a highly dysfunctional and demoralizing family.
****

"Furiously dominating." They are manifesting pronounced "authority freak" control issues. They are experiencing intense impatience, and they are engaging in hyper-irritability and demandingness. They are also manifesting unresolved enviousness and loss-paranoia. They are essentially being abusively willful in an ecologically insensitive or even in an ecologically damaging manner. They are the product of an authoritarian patriarchal household where they had to "join the enemy."

RIGHT ADRENAL PROBLEM
"At a loss." They are intensely agitated about their relations with the world around them, including their intimate environment.

LEFT ADRENAL PROBLEM
"I can't trust me!" They are intensely agitated about their personal and inner life, including self-disgust, self-distrust and self-defeating patterns.

ADRENO-LEUKO DYSTROPHY (See **A.L.D.**)

"AGENT ORANGE" POISONING (Dioxin)
"I caused World War II!" They are suffering the effects of a profound underlying guilt/ shame complex induced by either overt and assaultive or subtle, subconscious or subterranean accusations to the effect of their having been the source of all their family's problems, especially the mother's difficulties and disappointments in life.

It arises from exploitative or unconsciously desperately needy parent(s) who reacted to their inherent qualities as the utterly fundamental resource for the parent(s) survival and/or quality of life. When they were unable to "deliver the goods" because they were only a child, the family responded with intense blame-throwing and shame-induction.

AGRANULOCYTOSIS (Loss of white blood cells resulting in no defense against infection)
"Defenseless." They feel very much "at effect" rather than "at cause." To them, it is their "just desserts" because they "don't deserve any better." They are the product of a severely accusative and exploitative family who systematically eroded their sense of worth, and who induced deep self-rejection and self-distrust.

ALCOHOLISM

"Fearful involvement-avoidance." They have a bad case of overwhelmed sensibilities and hyper-sensitivity. They are in effect a frustrated mystic trying to connect with the "Source." It arises in a super-sensitive who then has to "numb out," due to growing up in an invasive and abrasive dysfunctional family.
****

"Eeyore trip." They have strong feelings of futility, guilt and inadequacy, in a "What's the point?" giving up. They have strong feelings of having been living a lie. They have a deep self-rejection and a feeling of worthlessness, along with an intense sense of defeat and inner hostility arising from a very dysfunctional family. They are in effect immobilized by their unresolved self-undermining attitudes.

They are highly vulnerable to believing in the denigrating evaluations and characterizations of others. There are many traumatic memories of childhood, with an accompanying sense of failure. They manifest emotional weakness and inability to cope with life situations. They were subjected to "You can do no right!" and "NOW look what you've caused!" parenting.
****

"Head in the sand." They are engaged in systematic self-suppressing reality-avoidance. They are heavily into defensive accountability-avoidance, denial-domination, analysis-avoidance, perceptual emphasis, and compulsive concreteness. They are systematically feeling-avoidant, experience-dampening, and looking the other way, as they desperately fear feeling. They are the product of a severely denial-dominated dysfunctional family.
****

"Goodie-getting." They have a strong relief in a false God of "relief" in the form of artificially false pleasure-seeking. They manifest a lot of defensive dependency, and they are intensely prone to "never enough" demandingness. They also have the belief that habits can take possession of them, so that they are in effect "above accountability."

They have a profound fear of "adult responsibility" and they are continuously involved in "maturity"-avoidance because what they witnessed in their home strongly indicated that being a grown-up was a horror.

A.L.D. (Adreno-Leuko Dystrophy) [Loss of myelin sheaths in the brain in male children]

"Thinking of leaving." They have found that their needs seem to come last in the priorities of the Universe. They are feeling like they have been abandoned by the "Home Office." They feel that there are serious conflicts between their personal goals and the Divine intent, and they are very worried and anxious as a result. It is a "God is Al Capone" relational issue with the Source.

There is a profound inner conflict between the desires and intentions of their personality and their perception of their unfolding destiny. They have the feeling that the "Home Office" (All That Is) has taken the helm of their life against their will and desires. As a result, there is now a major difficulty with their "bio-computer" and communication center.

They are the product of a family who did not respond to their needs, or in which they were forced to take over the meeting of their own needs because no one else could or would. Yet there doesn't seem to be a comprehensible reason for it, and they have developed an abiding distrust of the Universe. Paradoxically enough, it is an experience their soul chose to have for the purpose of developing their soul, for Cosmic contribution, and/or for karmic compensation.

ALLERGIC SHOCK (Obstructed breathing, hives, plunging blood pressure -- it is life threatening)

"There must be some way outta here!" They are having a severe attack of self-rejection simultaneous with an intense sense of being attacked and accused by their environment. They have a great deal of guilt and shame, along with a feeling that they should be "punished for their sins."

They are functioning on the edge, due to intense emotional difficulties and to denying of their own power and self-worth. They feel threatened and they fear loss, with the result that they are dominated by anxiety, suppressed emotions and unresolved aggravations and irritations. The current circumstances are generating a "What's the use? It won't work anyway" demoralized desire to give up the ship, reflecting a sub-conscious death wish.

It all reflects unexpressed severe grief over felt rejection by an extremely "smother-loving" but cold mother. They are longing for mother's love or that of a mother stand-in. But they have suddenly arrived at the conclusion that it is useless to try any more. They are feeling that there's really no point and no winning in this business of life, so they are looking for a way out.

ALLERGIES

"Inner crying." They are experiencing the effects of suppressed grief, and they are in effect operating under the domination of a severe chronic cold. They are seeking to elicit love in an indirect manner, since they found that they did not get the love they needed as a child. They are longing for mother's love or that of a mother stand-in.

They are experiencing the effects of unexpressed grief over felt rejection by an extremely "smother-loving" but cold mother.
****

"Crushed Coke can." They feel stifled and manifestation-prevented by the world around them. They have the experience of being over-run with feelings that don't seem to have any solution or any possibility of things changing. They are in effect denying of their own power and self-worth. It came from being systematically undermined and denigrated as a child.
****

"Up against the wall." They are having an over-reaction to felt threats to their well-being, to something hostile to their welfare. They are engaged in on-the-edge functioning, due to severe emotional difficulties. They are dominated by anxiety, suppressed emotions and/or generalized dread.

They have a deep-seated fear of letting other people know what they are experiencing or who they are. They feel threatened and they fear loss, so they take a "rejecting first" approach. They are dominated by anxiety, suppressed emotions and generalized dread. There is a profound level of fear about having to participate fully in life, or about potential annihilation. They have an intense distrust of letting something or someone inside their boundaries.

They are the product of a frighteningly dysfunctional and invasive family which you could never tell when the next piece of shit was coming off the wall. You just knew it would.
****

"Suppressed rage." They are repressing rather strong anger and aggression reactions. There is an irritation reaction to life, and they are reacting to people instead of interacting with them. Who are they really allergic to?

They are laboring under the effects of an unresolved aggravation or irritant from childhood. They are the product of an intensely enraging dysfunctional family, which constantly subjected them to intolerable and insoluble situations.

(See the book *Allergies& Aversions* by the author)

ALVEOLA PROBLEMS (The air sacs in the lungs)

"I don't deserve to exist." They feel unworthy of taking up space and about having requirements and resources, and they are seriously considering "checking out" as a result. When they are vulnerable, or when they are under stress, the world is decidedly not a safe place, in their experience. They fear taking in life for fear that God will strike them dead.

It is the result of intense intrauterine and subsequent rejection and trauma. Their mother did not want them, and they got that message loud and clear from what they thought was the "Home Office" (All That Is). The outcome is existential guilt resulting in self-deprivation based on severe self-rejection.

RIGHT LUNG ALVEOLA PROBLEMS

"Guilt-grabbing." They are struggling with guilt about their actions and their environmental impacts.

LEFT LUNG ALVEOLA PROBLEMS

"Shame-frame." They have intense shame about who they are -- about their inner values, motivations and intentions.

ALZHEIMER'S DISEASE (Loss of memory and mental functioning capacity)

"Can't go on." They have a desire to leave the planet, due to an inability to face life as it is -- they are just plain exhausted from having to deal with life. They feel that they just can't face it all any more, and that they are unable to be in control in their own life.

They have intense feelings of insufficiency, inferiority, inadequacy and insecurity. They have come to a hapless, helpless, hopeless position, and they are refusing to work with the world any more. So they are now engaged in a "taking their marbles and going home" reaction. It represents a continuation of a demoralized stance they have had since their competence- and confidence-undermining childhood.

****

"Leave me alone!" They want to live in their own little world, where none of the SOB's and nincompoops can bug them. They have a lot of suppressed rage, and it comes out in continuous passive-aggressiveness and ecology-"sliming."

They are on a never-ending vengeance-vendetta, and they are indiscriminate in their victimizations. They are the product of an infuriating but implacably dysfunctional, passive-aggressive and subtly sadistic household.

(See **DEMENTIA; SENILITY**)

AMBLYOPIA (Poor refraction, leading to dullness of visual acuity)

"Awareness-avoidance." They are operating with a "Don't see!" injunction arising from a "dynamite shed" dynamic in their severely denial-dominated and dysfunctional family (they find themselves in a pitch black small space with rough-hewn square boxes, a funny smell, and skinny little ropes, and they light a match to see what it is).

When they did the "Emperor's new clothes" thing, the family about fell apart, they blew up, and/or they felt like the individual had destroyed the world. Or at least the threat that this would happen was ever-present. Furthermore, what they saw was never what they got. So they learned not to see clearly.

AMEBIASIS (Parasitic stomach disease)

"I can't take on any more!" They are intensely fearful and rageful over the experience that the world is out to get them. They feel attacked, endangered and powerless to do anything about it.

It comes from the experience that they have been "up to their eyebrows in alligators" all their life, and they just can't take any more challenges or requirements or responsibilities. They can't assimilate what is being experienced and imposed on their experience, and they are rebelling blindly in an adamant refusal to take on any more inputs and responsibilities. They are the product of a severely self-immersed and possessive family who over-loaded them with demands, and who gave them little in the way of coping capabilities.

AMNESIA; AMNESIC SYNDROME (Loss of memory)

"Damn me!" They are angry at themselves for not being able to manage and determine the outcomes of life's processes or to bring sense to their life. They feel that life is definitely not working the way they want, and they are deeply resentful at what feels like being manipulated. At the same time, they themselves are manipulative, and yet they are constantly frustrated at the way thing turn out for them all the time. They are the product of a selfish and mutually manipulative dysfunctional family.

****

"Disappearing act." They are burdened with a severe fear of life and an inability to defend themselves, which leads to a running away from life reaction. They are full of feelings of "I'm not enough," and they want to get out from under life's requirements. Their experience is that "There is no joy in Bloodville," and they are deeply worried about how things are going to go for them.

They have tremendous guilt and shame from the past. They function in a weak, unintelligent and profoundly unsafe and unequipped for survival manner, due to severely diminished self-worth and self-confidence.

It results from a severely critical and wrong-making family. There was much trauma that was over-whelming in its implications and ramifications in their formative process. As a result, they feel they have no personal potency or ability to take a stand on anything.

ANAL PROBLEMS

"Rammed up my ass." They have deep feelings of vulnerability to overwhelm, engulfment, intrusion, assault, penetration and humiliation, and they are very fearful of sexuality. They are severely self-suppressing and feeling-avoidant.

They are also highly resistive to eliminating negativity, toxins and traumas, out of a fear of what would happen if they "dumped their stuff." They have an intensely control-oriented and controlling approach, and they have a lot of contained rage over perceived survival-threats. Theirs was a severely restrictive and boundary-violating family, in a "butt-fucking" manner.

ANAL ABSCESSES

"Don't open that box!" They have a lot of anger in relation to what they don't want to release. They are greatly handicapped by fear of letting go, due to anticipated loss of vital life supports. It was learned in a highly oppressive and repressive household.

ANAL BLEEDING

"God damn God!" There is much anger and frustration about life. They are deeply distrusting of the Universe, due to a painfully paranoid household formative experience.

ANAL "BURNING"

"Fucked in the butt." They feel "royally screwed" by an authority, system or other negative father figure. It reflects a deep distrust of the Universe that was generated by highly untrustworthy parenting.

ANAL FISSURE; ANAL FISTULA (Hole in the anus)

"Won't let go." They are manifesting the effects of incomplete releasing of life's trash, and of their holding on to the garbage of the past. It is the result of a grudge-carrying, injustice-nurturing family.

ANAL ITCHING

"I'm awful!" They are suffering from guilt and remorse over the past, and from a refusal to forgive themselves. They came up in a highly uncompromising and accusative household.

ANAL PAIN

"Beat me!" They have a lot of guilt and felt need for punishment. They feel they are "bad" and "not good enough," probably arising from severely harsh toilet training that reflected a heavy-handed Calvinistic childhood.

ANORECTAL BLEEDING

"God is Al Capone!" They have a great deal of anger and frustration about life. They are deeply distrusting of the Universe, due to a painfully paranoid childhood household.

ANDROGEN PROBLEMS (Male hormone)

"Initiative issues." They are being disrupted in their ability to be effectively assertive, creatively instigating, confronting, aggressive, enduring, strong, etc. They are undergoing difficulties with these impact-making and difference-making motivations and resources. It arises from distorted and dysfunctional parenting patterns with regard to the manifestation of the creative initiative process

----

LOW ANDROGEN

They are having problems with male shame, amotivational syndrome, effective castration, or other confidence-, competence- and/or one-pointedness-undermining feelings and manifestations. They were subjected to initiative-negating and wrong-making parenting.

HIGH ANDROGEN
They are being prone to be aggressive, over-bearing, excessively willful and/or insensitive in their functioning. They were in effect overly conceded to and "privileged position" parented.

(See **HORMONAL PROBLEMS**)

ANEMIA (Shortage of red blood cells)
"There is no joy in Bloodville." There is insufficient sustaining input in their life, and they are over-loaded and drained out, due to their excessive sense of responsibility. They are suffering from intense and unresolved deprivation-grief, and they are very weak in the sense of the Spirit and in trust of the Universe. They have no joy in life, and they stay tensed for bad news or disaster in a "catastrophic expectations" orientation. They have a super-serious and "but not for me" attitude, with an "Eyeore"-type nihilism and "yes but" approach. They are afraid of life, and they can't enjoy themselves. They feel undeserving of joy and love, and that God will destroy them if they have any.

They are therefore systematically life-negating and love-refusing. They can't love themselves, let alone anyone else. They have in effect given up on life, and they suffer from feelings of total helplessness. It is the result of a severely harsh and over-responsible childhood with an unloving and aggressively attacking mother.

****

"You can't make me!" They are in effect determined to stay as sick as they are, and they utilize an invalidating, arguing for their limitations and "Yes, but . . ." process to do so. They are the product of a severely undermining dysfunctional family who only gave meager attention to them when they were behaving in a self-defeating and self-destructive manner.

****

"I'll screw it up!" They manifest constant indecision and worrying about their mistakes, and they are full of regretful ruminations as they live in the past. They can't live by their decisions, and they are unable or unwilling to use their gifts in the service of others. They don't feel "enough" to do so. They were continuously accused, abused and wrong-made as a child, and they ended up deeply self-distrusting.

****

"I let them do it again!" They are angry at themselves for not being able to manage and determine the outcomes of life's processes or to bring sense to their life. They feel that life is definitely not working the way they want, and they are angry at what feels like being manipulated. At the same time, they themselves are manipulative, and yet they are constantly frustrated at the way thing turn out for them all the time. They are the product of a selfish and mutually manipulative dysfunctional family.

ANEURISM (Bulging blood vessel in the brain)
"Serving themselves up on a platter." They are a compulsive serve-aholic who feels that they simply have to rescue any person, system or situation that needs help. The trouble is that this is so draining, depriving and derailing that their needs are not being met.

The net effect is that they are building to an explosion point in their heavily repressed resentment about all this. It is the result of being in the "family hoist" position in a significantly dysfunctional family who "put the blame on Mame," while simultaneously exploiting them.

Gerard Kite

home to self.

ANGINA PECTORIS (Severe attacks of pain over the heart due to oxygen deprivation)

"I'm late, I'm late!" They are a workaholic performance-addict who is seeking approval from withholding and disapproving perfectionistic stand-ins for similar parents. For them, ultimate failure and final irrevocable rejection are always just a breath away.

They are super time-urgent and schedule-fixated. They are always impatient and in a hurry (to accomplish the "final victory" -- the "golden orb"-winning achievement). They also have this "March Hare" worry that if they don't cover virtually all the bases in time, all will be lost. They are outwardly extremely busy, while they are ignoring their inner world and their loved ones. The attacks are a strong warning that their attention is not where it should be.

ANOREXIA (Self-starvation)

"I'm awful!" They are suffering from extreme fear, self-revulsion and self-rejection. They feel incapable of meeting the demands made on them, they feel it is completely unsafe to be themselves, and they feel totally unable to please their mother in their head. They feel nagged at, crowded in upon, and disallowed their own identity.

They have a desperate need for emotional nourishment, unconditional acceptance, and loving affection that is creating a severe emptiness inside that is demanding satisfaction. They are attempting to "starve the emptiness," in the hope that it will go away and demand less.

They have episodes of intense desires to die, due to their utter self-disgust, severe emotional deprivation, and emotional starvation. Their emotional needs are experienced as just being too great to live with.

Their mother made it crystal clear that any form of neediness or self-commitment, self-development and self-empowerment would lead to ultimate and lethal abandonment. They are therefore trying to prevent sexual maturity and growing up, and they demand exaggerated control of events.

They are trying to be "pure," non-physical, strictly mental, and ethereally spiritual, in a systematic refusal to grow up. They are attempting to remain a "genderless child" as an act of appeasement to "Godzilla" (their mother). And they systematically deny themselves the right to life in so doing.

ANTHRAX (Severe skin eruptions and boils. Caught from cattle)

"Fulminating fury." They are struggling with an intense suppressed rage and seething injustice-nurturing around deprivations and degradations that they have experienced and/or that they are experiencing.

It is a long-standing pattern that is now coming to a boil for purposes of healing, or as a result of things coming to a head in their life around this issue of being betrayed, belittled or bedeviled. It is the result of a passive-aggressive dysfunctional family.

APHASIA (Inability to form words; inability to speak)

"Struck dumb." Life has been so inhospitable that they can't find words to express their experience. They comprehend much more than those around them could handle and/or they were given a very strong "to be seen but not heard from" message as a child.

In any case, it is an annihilation-anxiety and/or a world-destruction fear that was instilled by the fact that there was a gross mis-match between what they experienced/perceived/knew and what their family could tolerate hearing about, and there was a very strongly threatening response to their attempts to speak their truth.

APNEA (Interruptions in breathing)

"Maternal deprivation." They are intensely sensitive, fearful and longing for mother love or love from someone close. They are full of family taboos, social restrictions and moral inhibitions, all learned in an intensely repressive family, which forced a pleasing/appeasing/placating "model child" adjustment on them.

There is a lot of disappointment, bitterness, unforgivingness and resentment of being over-worked. However, at the same time, they dare not express or even acknowledge these feelings, out of fear of total rejection and abandonment. They have a great deal of deep-seated guilt, shame and grief arising out of this.

They are joy-avoidant, happiness-squashing, and love-deflecting, all in the misguided hope that they will thereby finally earn the "God Housekeeping Seal of Approval." In effect, they are so self-suppressing that they are in effect suffocating themselves. They have become fatalistic, hostility-repressing, compulsively over-giving, hyper-sensitive, and lonely.

APPENDICITIS

"Raw nerves." They have lost the ability to filter and protect themselves from the impacts and imports of incoming realities. There is a lot of unrealistic fear of life and a blocking of the flow of the good things in life, due to self-hate, self-disgust and guilty self-attack.

They have a real lack of compassion for themselves and a deep dissatisfaction, with many unfulfilled desires. They are ruminating over residuals of the past with much self-recrimination. There is a good deal of emotional commotion, along with many unruly feelings that they don't know how to handle.

All of this arises from their having taken in the poisons of their intensely guilt- and shame-inducing dysfunctional family and their subsequent stand-ins. They are now poisoning themselves with the "foods" they got at home in their childhood. They feel very unsafe with their inner feelings and in the world, because their family made them so, out of their fears.

~~~~~~

APPENDECTOMY

"Cut!" The removal of the poisoning appendix marks the end of this pattern of self-poisoning, as they prepare to enter their destiny armed with the lessons, resources and wisdom generated by their experiential history. These capabilities will be used to heal, teach and liberate others from similar fates by individuals who are sufficiently evolved to manifest such contributions.

APPENDIX "BURST"

"Do it or die!" Their body has given the ultimate ultimatum. They have absorbed and self-administered so much poison into their system that it is no longer possible to continue living in this manner. It went too far, and now is the hour to terminate the pattern and remove the poisons immediately and permanently -- or else.

ARM PARALYSIS

"Hard hat." They are manifesting a certain hardness and willfulness in their functioning. They are disgusted with, and distrusting of others, and they have the feeling that they have to do everything themselves. They were the "odd one out" in their family, and they were more or less left to their own devices from a very early age.

RIGHT ARM PARALYSIS

"Island unto themselves." They are highly self-contained and self-focused, and they have real reluctance to give to others.

LEFT ARM PARALYSIS

"What are they up to now?" They are having problems in trusting and valuing what others have to offer, and they are resistant to receiving.

ARRYTHMIA (Heart rate fluctuations)

"False alarms." They are a self-made person who believes that they are all they've got. They have felt cut off from the environment and the Universe all their life, and that they therefore have to handle everything on their own hook, unassisted.

This activates moments where things are getting out of control and beyond their coping capabilities. These bring on anxiety attacks and the resulting palpitations. It is the result of never having received love and merging as a child.
****

"Fluttering infatuations." They have a fundamental inconsistency in their love nature -- it comes and goes, and they can't maintain a steady love state, input or relationship. It reflects the instability of the nature of the close relationships in their family.

ARTERIOSCLEROSIS (Hardening and fat-lining of the arteries)

"Walking the plank." There is an underlying rather severe depression, and they dread old age. They have a profound fear of accepting joy and of flowing with life, and as a result, their life flow is actually being blocked. They are incapable of expressing their feelings and emotions, and there are a lot of accumulated unresolved issues as a result. This all arose from a subtly or not-so-subtly untrustworthy early mothering and later parenting.
****

"God is Al Capone!" They have a deep distrust of the Universe and of God. They have therefore closed down and become hard-nosed and rigid, with a willful and hostile approach to the world. They believe that there is no such thing as goodness in the world, and they are rigidly closed-minded and narrow in their viewpoint. They have lost the capacity to love and be loved, as they react to a profound underlying self-dislike, with an over-criticizing, arrogant and opinionated manner.

They are intensely judgmental, and they put out a great deal of criticism. They are fiercely resistant, hardened and narrow-minded, with a great deal of tension and an adamant refusal to see good in anything or anyone.

They have a furious intent to completely control their own life, and they have no intention of letting God or anyone else have any say or influence the flow of their life. They are forever rushing, hurrying, worrying, and trying to block and outwit those who would "bleed them dry" and who would "take the fat of the land" from them. To them, love and joy are a cruel joke -- a fabrication for the foolish -- and they are the "complete Scrooge." They were treated like they were the "intimate enemy," at one level or another.

ARTERIOSCLEROTIC DEMENTIA (Progressive but "patchy" loss of mental functions)

"I can't keep up." They are engaged in a refusal to deal with the world as it is, out of an enraged helplessness and hopelessness. They feel overwhelmed by the requirements of life and that they are unable to cope any more. There is a great deal of bitterness and disgust with the Universe and the "Home Office" (All That Is). They are having an "I'm taking my marbles and going home!" reaction.

This is a pattern that got started early in life, when they had to face an uncaring and even hostilely demanding environment, which had a demoralizing effect on them. Their response to this was to set up a self-fulfilling prophecy effect in which they repeatedly found themselves in re-creations of their formative environment. They kept up as long as they could, and now they have decided that enough is enough, and they are "throwing in the towel" and exiting stage left, slowly.

ARTERY PROBLEMS

"Joyless Joe/Jo." They live out of a "Sydney Sober sides" -- "Grit and bear it" orientation. To them, life is one long problem to be solved and a very serious business, indeed. They have a rather pronounced tendency to be something of a gloom-and-doom-sayer or of a militaristic martinet. They have lost the ability to feel and express love, and they tend to be hard and bitter. It arises from a "There is no joy in Bloodville" type of dysfunctional family, where they were the one who had to maintain sanity and to deflect disaster.

ARTHRITIS (Inflamed, painful and stiff joints)

"Left in the lurch." Their experience is that they have in effect betrayed by the Cosmos, in that bad things keep happening to this good person. Their experience is that the Universe is unjust and that they in effect "bought a pig in a poke" by coming in here. There is a good deal of suppressed and restrained resentment about that, resulting in a "binding up" of their ability to take action and do things. It got started in an untrustworthy, capricious, dysfunctional family who did indeed abandon them and leave them to their own devices in a self-immersed and harmful manner.
****

"Straight-jacketed." They have a pronounced tendency to immobilization, self-criticism, lack of self-worth, fear, anger, and a feeling of being tied down, restricted and confined. They desperately want to be free to move around and to make something of themselves. They are chronically anxious and depressed, and they are afraid of being angry because it is "wrong, bad and evil."

They feel unloved, with a resulting resentful bitterness and a critical judgmentalness towards others. They are not allowing themselves to develop their full potential, due to self-distrust, leading to severe constraints. They are suffering from a lot of suppressed resentment, which tends to result in passive-aggressive behavior. They are self-suppressing and self-thwarting. They are the product of perfectionistic parenting in which in effect they could never measure up.
****

"Right and righteous." They are very blaming and critical of people, and they are convinced that others won't help them. They are quite angry that people won't "carry their load," so that they have to take on what they consider an unjust load.

They are quite fixed, rigid, intolerant and resistive in their functioning. They operate with a strong will, inflexible intentions, intense opinions, and an abiding inability to change with changing circumstances. They have a bad case of the "hardening of the attitudes," and they are highly rigid, opinionated and "hung up in principles."

There are long-standing maladjustments and stony incrustations based on internal conflicts -- often between a desire to do something and a fear of failure. They are full of projected self-disgust, finding in others what they most dislike in themselves. They have great resistance and emotional struggle, with habitual anxiety and fear, "negative faith," and expectations that of the worst case scenario. They are forcefully opinion-pushing, and they put out a steady stream of skeptical criticism. They are quite hostile, and they are always angry and tense. Calcium growths indicate the presence of hatred and a severely inflexible mind. It all came from a "vast wasteland" and "dour destiny" type of family culture in which they never knew when something would go wrong, just that it would, sure as the sun rises. It all fell to them to do the necessaries, because no one else could be trusted to do so or to do it right. No one was ever there for them, and since everything that went down was their fault, they also felt they didn't deserve anyone to be there for them, bottom line.

(See **RHEUMATOID ARTHRITIS**) [Also, see the body part(s) affected for more information]

ASBESTOS POISONING (Mesothelioma)

"Polluted environment." They are being invaded and permeated by damaging influences in their surroundings. They are being subjected to intolerable inputs and experiences. It is a repetition of their early environment, where their dysfunctional family imposed a poisonous atmosphere and contaminated their support systems. It is a message to them to the effect of "Don't pollute yourself any more!"

ASPHYXIATING ATTACKS (Sudden suffocations)

"Oh my GAWD!!" They are totally terrified of the process of life and of the world. They have a fearful distrust of just about everything, and they feel utterly unsafe in the world. The message in childhood was, "Don't you dare ever grow up and away or beyond our control!" They therefore got stuck in childhood, afraid to grow up and take the world on its own terms.

ASTHMA

"Where's Mommy!?" They are full of dependency conflicts generated by an engulfing and yet emotionally unavailable mother. They are rather intensely fearful of the world and of the demands of life, feeling that they don't have what it takes to make it. They have a lot of subconscious dependency needs, and they are hyper-sensitive to threat and to stimulation.
****

"Alone on my own." They have an overwhelming fear of God, coupled with a profound separation-paranoia. They try to take on too much and to be too much an island unto themselves. They also have a pronounced tendency to self-destructiveness arising from deep-seated guilt and shame. There is an inability to breathe for themselves and a systematic suppression of any form of crying, due to guilt-inducing "smother love."
****

"Mother-smothered." They feel suppressed and dominated by their mother, yet at the same time that it is unsafe to take charge of their own life. They are full of ideas to get ahead, but they are also afraid of pushing on against opposition, should they fail.

They are intensely inhibited against free expression, and they are plagued by the unresolved guilt and suppressed grief that got started in their childhood. They want to raise objections and to take charge of their life, but they find that they can't. They are the product of an oppressive "keep 'em around the old homestead" household.

****

"Out of sync." They are out of step and in disharmony with their environment. They are very dependent and afraid to break away from their family, yet they want to control and dominate at the same time. They are a potential leader and independent thinker who is chafing at the bit under what feels like oppressive authority-domination.

They feel held back by fools, unrecognized for their true value and talents, and not given the high place they feel they deserve. So they force themselves to "perform" to "prove themselves to the boss." They grew up in an authoritarian and simultaneously engulfing family environment.

****

"Abandonment-paranoia." They have a rather pronounced possessiveness and jealousy, so they can breathe in, but they constrict on the exhale -- they can't let go. They had to cope with a highly ambivalent mother who subjected them to intense acceptance/rejection conflicting messages and games.

****

"Mother-fixation." They have a strong ambivalence towards their mother and against mother stand-ins. They feel "left out in the cold" by such persons, in an unloved and rejected, disapproved of and shut out experience. They try to avoid and ignore that person or situation, to shut it out.

They have many unmet dependency needs induced by a domineering and rejecting mother who played upon sibling rivalry competition for her scarce love supply. As a result, they are fatalistic, hostility-repressing, compulsive, over giving, hyper-sensitive, and lonely, with a very low self-esteem.

****

"Royally pissed off." They have a lot of disappointment, bitterness, unforgivingness and over-worked resentment. There is an inability to resolve this resentment of theirs, with a resulting rejecting of the breath of life and an emotional suffocation. There is also a deep fear of letting go of childhood and a severe inner crying. They are intensely sensitive, fearful and longing for mother love or for love from someone close, because they were in effect rejected and ejected by a cold and unloving mother.

****

"Model child." They are full of family taboos, social restrictions, and moral inhibitions, all learned in an intensely repressive family which forced an inhibited/intimidated adjustment pattern on them. They are joy-avoidant, happiness-squashing, and love-deflecting, all in the misguided hope that they will thereby earn the "God Housekeeping Seal of Approval," with the result that they will then finally be allowed to grow up and away from their family.

They are full of suppressed grieving and unacknowledged mourning, and they have a dampened zest for life, due to their stifling and totally engulfing yet abandonment-threatening childhood environment. There was intra-uterine, prenatal and post-partum trauma, and when they are under stress or when they are vulnerable, they feel that the world is decidedly not a safe place to be.

EXERCIZE-INDUCED ASTHMA

"Potency-guilt." They have an uneasy feeling that it is "bad, wrong and evil" for them to be effective and impactful at a deep level.

They are the product of a "reversed role parenting" situation in which they were in effect required to mother their mother, who became paranoid of them when they invested in or manifested their personal potency and destiny.

ASTHMA IN BABIES

"There must be some way out of here!" They are suffering from a great fear of the world and of life, and they decidedly do not want to be here, and they want outta here. They feel completely unsafe, unwanted, unwelcome and intensely rejected. It is due to a hostilely smothering and/or cold and rejecting mother, or due to a situation that generates that feeling.

ASTHMA IN CHILDREN

"Ties that grind." They have many of the same dynamics as in adults, arising from a rejecting and repressive, yet engulfing and symbiotically dependent home environment, especially with regard to the mother's manner of being.

ATHETOSIS (Repetitive involuntary movements)

"Who's pulling their strings?" They were never really allowed to have a will of their own. They were subjected to severe competence- and confidence-undermining by their mother, who was either afraid of their power and/or afraid of losing them, and who also had a great deal of rage that was elicited by the individual's presence, demands, and/or characteristics.

ATHROMBIA (See INABILITY TO FORM BLOOD CLOTS)

AUTO-IMMUNE DISORDER (Immune system attacks their own body in an over-reactive manner)

"What am I *doing* here?" They are manifesting a dismayed discombobulation about the world and the way their life is going. It is the result of growing up in a vaguely overwhelmed and enmeshed family or out of being here as a "visitor" from another soul pool for soul experience and destiny-manifestation purposes.
****

"Hapless, helpless, hopeless." They have a great deal of sorrow, deep-seated grief, and despair, and they are chronically crying on the inside. They feel overwhelmed and unable to handle the requirements of life. They have in effect "thrown in the towel" on even trying to make it in life. They come from a massively dysfunctional and demoralizing family.
****

"Allergic reaction to themselves." They feel somehow responsible for all the ills of the world, which they are the cause, and they are having a "get rid of the problem" response. They have ended up with little or no ability to receive or to request or to require a return in kind.

It is a result of having "carried the world on their shoulders" all their life, starting with their dysfunctional family. They were told in effect that they were the source of all the family's problems, while they were actually the only one who was deflecting some of the disasters.
~~~~~~

AUTO-IMMUNE HYPOGLYCEMIA (Excessive insulin production due to anti-bodies, leading to abnormal insulin fluctuations to cope with the anti-bodies)

"Don't deserve it!" They are systematically engaged in resistance to the sweet part of life, resulting in a continuous ambivalent reaction to good things happening for them. They have to constantly grapple with self-rejection and guilt feelings. It comes from messaging from the most rejecting parent that they are a continuous problem, when in fact, they have always been the solution to problems in their nature and functioning. They were a threat and a guilt-induction to that parent.

AVIAN FLU ("BIRD FLU")

"Urban hermit." There is an insufficient involvement and interaction with the world, in a kind of "among us but not of us" pattern. Underneath is a buried rage and resentment about being so alone, alien and alienated. It comes from growing up in a family in which they could do no right, as the unrecognized and unacknowledged "family hoist" upon whom everyone depended and whom no one supported, sustained or validated.
****

"At their mercy." They have feelings of being under the influence of malevolent forces and of being weak and helpless. There is a good deal of internal conflict, confusion and susceptibility to suggestion, especially from the "world of agreement" or the "group mind" or "statistical proofs." It may reflect the vulnerability feelings that accompany times and processes of great change.

There is a fear of attack from others and of taking life in fully. They have a strong feeling of a lack of support and protection. They have the experience that the very worst is about to happen to them. They are the product of severely untrustworthy parenting, arising out of a deeply fearful family.
****

"Barking up the wrong tree." They tend to get into consuming passionate commitments that lead nowhere, and to get into repeated disturbing unrequited love situations. They have a sensitive mind and a very strong sense of justice, righteousness and generosity that frequently leads them into blind alleys and exploitative situations and relationships.

They are feeling that they are always in "the tie that grinds" relationships in which they feel totally stifled by over-close and/or dominating partners. They feel that they are being overwhelmed and restricted, and they are very angry about it. How, they don't feel that they can do or say anything about it, for fear of catastrophic consequences.

They come from an authoritarian, oppressive and possessive dysfunctional family in which they held a "reversed role parenting" situation that led to their repeatedly trying to rescue their family from their self-defeating patterns.
****

"Self-suppression." They are full of family taboos, social restrictions, moral inhibitions, unexpressed passions, strong desires and unexpressed intense emotions. They don't have any sense of freedom or the right or ability to communicate their feelings. This was generated by a self-immersed and dysfunctional family who were exploitative, shame-inducing and enmeshed.
****

"Suppressed grief." They are desperate and tired of life, due to generalized disturbances in their processes and situation. They are having a "salt poured into emotional wounds" experience that they are not being allowed to heal.

They are suffering under the influence of their lifelong suppressed sorrow. They are fearful and anxious to the point of being overcome with desperation and futility feelings, and they are struggling with confusion-inducing emotional conflict. There is a failure to maintain immunity to negative ideas. They are the product of a self-defeatingness-generating dysfunctional family who instilled a sense of being hapless, helpless and hopeless.

****

"Deprivation City." They have a real difficulty in taking in prana, chi, ki, élan vitale, and love or life energy, as a function of their prideful brutalizing misuse of energy in past lives. They have an inability to renew the breath of life, along with lack of enthusiasm and zeal for living. They have a real inability to take in life, and they don't feel worthy of living life fully. They are suffering from depression and chronic grief, because they are deeply afraid of taking in life energy.

They are also joy-avoidant and happiness-squashing, out of a fear of the Universe. They lack Cosmic, community and conjugal contact. They are alone, sad and non-belonging, with no sense of acceptance or approval. They feel constantly in smothering and stifling environments, with a resulting sense that life is dull and monotonous. They are the product of a severely withholding and rejecting family.

****

"My way or the highway!" The have a very strong ego that is getting in their way. They tend to believe that theirs is the only way to fly, and they are surrounded by people who not only don't understand that, but who also place restrictions on them and who "unfairly punish" them for their ways of being and of doing things. They feel that they have to handle the whole of life single-handed, with no help from any so-called friends.

While this has made for a modicum of success as a survival strategy, it has cut them off from joy and love, and they can't let people in or themselves out to merge, and that is now taking its toll. They are the product of a supremely selfish "everyone for themselves" authoritarian and patriarchal family.

****

"Bitter resentfulness." They are wasting away, due to selfishness, intense possessiveness, cruel thoughts and vengefulness. They feel that they have done their level best in a valiant effort, but that circumstances wouldn't have it so. In addition, there is also a large spiteful revenge streak playing a major part in this process. They are given to resentfully imagined guilt and remorse reactions from their people as an ego balm – "see, now they're sorry for what they've done!"

They have unhappy love affairs, resulting in disappointment, disgust, unforgivingness and clutchingness. They feel unappreciated, and they play out a "Camille" scenario in which their feeling is, "They'll be sorry when I'm gone!" They are selfishly clinging and controlling, they are slyly passive-aggressive, and they are full of "Feel sorry for me!" strategies. In the meantime, they are seeking an "easeful death." It is the result of their having had a "special" role as a child in their severely passive-aggressive dysfunctional family, and they have never gotten over or wanted to relinquish it.

****

"No right to exist." They feel unworthy of living, and they are suffocating from a chronic self-disgust reaction. They are full of angry punishment-deservingness feelings, with accompanying self-destructive motivations and manifestations. They are capitulating and giving up, in an extreme underlying abandonment depression around feeling rejected by God and of being ejected from the Cosmos.

It is the result of being massively neglected, rejected, accused and wrong-made by a severely judgmental dysfunctional family. There was a highly self-immersed, self-serving and blame-throwing mother who gave them a strong "If it weren't for you!" message. She simultaneously put

"You can do no right!" accusations out continuously, along with expecting them to "make it all better" -- an utter impossibility.

They are now having an "Enough is enough!" reaction, and they are "heading on out." They are desperately tired of life, due to life-long severe suppressed grief and emotional deprivation. They are fearful and anxious, and they are in effect too devastated to take it any more.

This all started up with an effective emotional abandonment at an early age, to which they reacted by becoming a self-contained self-made person with a "portable plexiglas phone booth" around them. So they are leaving now. Thank you and goodbye!

BACK PROBLEMS

"Utter isolation." There is a deep loneliness and sense of separation from their loved ones and from the "Home Office" (All That Is). They feel unsupported by life, and they are unwilling to trust the Universe or to cooperate with the Divine design. They feel that "God is Al Capone" and certainly not to be trusted. It started in a non-supportive and intrusive family, and it reflects a deep sense of frustration and separation from the "Source" that got started in the intra-uterine or very early infancy period.

****

"Failure-freak-out." There is a real fear of losing, on both the pragmatic and the ultimate planes. As a result, they are intensely self-determining and willful, and they refuse to give up their control or power. They are, in effect, a super-self-sustaining and self-contained "island unto themselves," and they have great difficulty and conflicts with intimates.

They feel that they have to protect themselves against threats and assaults, and they feel that have to shield off the heart area from further hurt. They also feel that they want people to get off their back. They are the product of an intensely competitive and sibling rivalry-generating family.

****

"I don't see me being it." They tend to "dump" their unacceptable qualities, feelings, functioning's and deeds "behind them," so they can't see them, and then they have the experience of having a bad back. It comes from growing up in a denial-dominated dysfunctional family.

****

"Skid Row Syd." There are often financial and worth concerns, reflecting an underlying sense of non-deservingness of support and survival resources. They have trouble dealing with emotional issues, and they feel overloaded with emotional responsibilities. They were in effect excluded from their family emotionally, while being held accountable for the emotional difficulties in their family.

****

"Will issues." They experience many conflicts of will with others and within themselves. They are either dominating of others or over-dependent on others, both of which indicate a poor self-image and a sense of not being deserving of support. There is a conflict between their conscious and their unconscious, originating in conflicts with their parents or parent stand-ins.

~~~~~~

LOWER BACK PROBLEMS

"Overloaded." This is their pivotal point for all body movements, their leverage fulcrum for strength and the anchoring area for action -- it's the balance beam for the body.

It is also the foundation floor on which everything is built in the way of being in the world. Their basic emotional support, financial sustenance and physical subsistence and sense of security are located here.

When problems develop in this area, it means there is an imbalance of power, an unequal exchange of energy, an experience of interfering interventions, a sense of things being out of harmony. There results a feeling of injustice and of being overburdened and under-supported. Indeed, there is a strong sense of insufficient support and a great deal of agitation over finances, with a considerable resentment over that. There is a notable amount of grief over lack of basic support, both currently and in their childhood.

There is a significant need for nurturance being displayed with lower back problems. They were in effect abandoned at an early age emotionally. Incidentally, this pattern can also develop or be precipitated or activated in response to growing older.

****

"Financial freak-out." There is a fear of financial failure and about money, and they have a deep insecurity over basic support. They feel at risk on the survival level, and there are concerns about the need for protection.

They are full of self-doubt, competence-anxiety and worth concerns, and they are having problems with the lack of the will or strength to overcome the obstacles they face. They are success-avoidant, out of fear of abandonment-annihilation that was built in during their early childhood. They feel at risk on the survival level, because their home was not supportive, and it was overloaded with excessive demands in their childhood.
****

"Run amok-anxiety." They find their situation of lack of connection and support painful and heavy, and they want to run away, as they suppress a desire to attack. They are therefore into over-control for fear of release of aggression and of the misuse and abuse of power. They come from a family who was into blame-throwing and accusation as an accountability-avoidant strategy.
****

"Sexual shame." They are guilt-ridden about sexuality, due to sex-ploitative parenting and to demands that they never commit to themselves or to anyone or anything outside the family. They are over-responsible, self-condemning, depressed and despairing.

RIGHT LOWER BACK

"But not for me." They are having conflicts over the nature and/or availability of environmental support systems and supplies. The feeling is that there is not what is needed by them out there in one form or another, and there is little or no trust of the environment to provide for their fundamental needs. It arose in a dysfunctional family who were not able to provide their basic life support systems and resources much of the time.

MIDDLE LOWER BACK

"God's gonna kill me!" There is a considerable amount of annihilation-anxiety and of survival concerns. Their feeling is that they are here on "borrowed time," and there is the real possibility of being "found out" in this.

There is also their "run amok-anxiety," the fear that they may "lose it" over their situation of non-support and deprivation. It derives from strong experiences of unacceptability or unwelcomeness from very early on.

LEFT LOWER BACK

"Leave me alone!" They have an inability to accept or to utilize intimate emotional support and basic need-meeting. They are excessively self-sufficient, in an "island unto themselves" pattern. They have a significant trust of the Universe problem, due to early deprivation and untrustworthiness of their maternal and intimate environment.

~~~~~~

CANCER OF THE LOWER BACK

"Atlas trip." They feel responsible for the well-being of the world around them, and they are a "serve-aholic." They carry the load of care-taking everything and everyone.

As a result, they have a lot of inner conflict and strife all the time, but they seek to hide that from others by "putting on a happy face." They are burdened with continuous emotional issues about which they feel they are in no position to do anything. They were the "family hoist" in their dependent and dysfunctional family.

~~~~~~

(See **CANCER**)

MIDDLE BACK

"What will people think?" This is the fulcrum of actions, and it sensitively reflects the individual's evaluations of their intentions and impacts. It is a highly attuned response system around implication readouts. When trouble develops here, it indicates that they fear environmental reactions and play-outs to their release of themselves in a kind of "How will the world react?" response.

It reflects catastrophic expectations about what would happen if they "let themselves go," in a kind of fundamental environmental fear. They are afraid at some internal level that they are going to be "stabbed in the back," like they often were as a child.

****

"Perfectionistic standards." They are intensely upright and uptight about moral issues. They have considerable guilt over past actions, reactions, intents and impacts, as they get stuck in all that "stuff" back there.

This reaction leads to "Get off my back!" feelings. It also involves a fear of moving forward, and simultaneously of being "trapped in the past." Still a third response contained here is anxiety over lack of coping capabilities, and about not having what it takes to handle the demands of life. It reflects survival issues and fear about what might happen to them.

In addition, it is a manifestation of issues with personal power -- either suppressed power or the abuse and corrupt use of power. Still another issue is that they have difficulty in validating themselves, and in trusting themselves to have what it takes to make it.

At base, problems here often reflect a need for reassurance of one type or another. This whole pattern got started in an exploitative, oppressive and/or dysfunctional family in which expressivity, responsibility, and personal potency were systematically distorted and/or suppressed, with the result that they have trouble in taking initiative action.

RIGHT MIDDLE BACK

"Can I pull it off?" Difficulties here reflect competence concerns, issues with regard to their survival strategies, and problems with their defense mechanisms. It has to do with questions concerning the adequacy of their functioning. These problems usually reflect a fair amount of competence- and/or confidence-undermining as a child.

MIDDLE MIDDLE BACK

"Implication-anxiety." They experience that "You never know what will happen when you take action!" and their tendency is to take a basic "Lewella" ("Leave well enough alone!") stance. They grew up in a dysfunctional and "magical mystery tour" unpredictable environment.

LEFT MIDDLE BACK

"Self-distrust." Problems here center around their trust of themselves and their motivations. It has to do with their relationship with their personal potency, along with guilt complexes over past, current, intended, or probable outcomes. Here, the family induced deep concerns about their inner intentions.

~~~~~~

UPPER BACK

"Self-love issues." This area reflects self-acceptance issues that have not been resolved over a number of lifetimes that must be resolved now. It involves self-disgust, guilt, and felt responsibilities.

Problems here represent a felt need to "earn" love, a feeling that they don't deserve love, and a feeling that they don't dare let love out or in. So they hold back love and vulnerability to love. They feel unloved, unsupported emotionally, while also simultaneously feeling over-loaded with responsibilities.

They were placed on a highly conditional love basis, and they ended up feeling that they don't deserve love -- that they have to earn it.
****

"Alone and alien." There is stored anger and bitterness over unexpressed feelings here, as well as feelings of being unlovable. They lack self-approval, and they don't have the feeling of Cosmic acceptability. They also have a way of withholding and placing conditions on their love.

They were subjected to a lack of love and a lot of wrong-making, while at the same time, they were being subjected to demands for the provision of support for their family, in a kind of "Cinderella/Cinderfella syndrome."
****

"Over-responsible depressive." They have an over-developed sense of accountability and responsibility, and they take on excessive responsibilities, while they are suppressing themselves and deflecting vulnerability to love and support, in a "work-aholic"-- "serve-aholic" pattern.

They have a good deal of frustration and irritation over not doing what they really want to do, out of their over-developed sense of responsibility and their under-developed sense of deservingness.

There may also be deep-seated resentment over thwarted ambitions, aspirations, or desired achievements, arising from having "buried them behind them" early on in life. They grew up in an excessive responsibility-demanding family.

RIGHT UPPER BACK

"I'm doing it wrong." The issue here is guilt over their methods of dealing with life. They are in conflict about the manner in which they meet their responsibilities and about how they express themselves. They were constantly wrong-made as a child, and they ended up deeply concerned about not doing things "right."

MIDDLE UPPER BACK

"*Weltschmerz*." (Sadness over the evils of the world) They have pronounced a sense of universal responsibility for everything, including themselves, and they feel a lot of pain over all that is not right with the world.

Their experience is that it is somehow "all their fault" and that they are responsible for World War II, and potentially for World War III. They were held accountable for everything that went wrong in their family, in response to their "better than the average bear's" personal resources.

LEFT UPPER BACK

"I don't deserve." Here they are deeply concerned over the nature of their needs, desires and ambitions. They feel they don't have the right to these, or they are guilty about their "failure to carry out their responsibilities" because they have these needs, wants and desires. They feel they should be "clear" of such "immoralities" or "impurities" or "impediments to their role manifestations."

They are in effect putting up a "protective shield" over their heart chakra (intake point from behind the back for Cosmic love energy) as a vulnerability- and "undeserved nurturance"-deflecting defense. It is the result of numerous messages that they have no right to have needs when they were a child.

~~~~~~

BROKEN BACK

"Change it!" They are being given the message in no uncertain terms that their take on life and their manner of dealing with things is not working any more.

They were programmed to feel unsupported or competence-anxious, they were undermined in their coping capability or in their ability to take life on their own terms, or they were trained to operate in an accountability-denying manner.

(See **SPINE PROBLEMS** for information on the particular vertebrae involved)

STABBING JABS OF PAIN IN THE BACK

"Tit for tat." There are detrimental events that are going on "behind their back," along with nasty and nefarious thoughts and deeds on their part, often as a result of the felt necessity for retribution. This is a pattern that grew out of a mutual mayhem-exchanging hostile dysfunctional family.

BALANCE PROBLEMS

"Teetering." They are suffering from severe disorientation and feelings of being thrown off base. They have a strong sense of being at risk in a confusing and potentially dangerous world. They don't have a clear sense of direction or of the nature of what is happening around them, they are manifesting scattered thinking, and they are not at all centered.

They are sick and tired of all this and they aren't willing to put up with demands for more responsibility and accountability. They are the product of a "magical misery tour" chaotic dysfunctional family in which they were expected to be the "sane one," but where sanity was not attainable.

(See **ABASIA**)

BELL'S PALSY (Facial paralysis)

"Super-suppressed." They are manifesting an extreme control over their anger and a total unwillingness to express their feelings, arising out of an intense "run amok-anxiety" -- the fear of "losing it" and of ecological calamity at their hands. They are intensely judgmental towards themselves, with little tolerance or compassion being manifested. It is in response to an underlying fulminating fury generated by a severely invasive and oppressive family.

RIGHT FACE PARALYSIS

"Blank slate." They refuse to let people know what they feel, for fear of the environmental results.

LEFT FACE PARALYSIS

"Feeling-avoidance." They have an inability to feel what they experience, out of catastrophic expectations about what the feelings are, and out of what the feelings represent about who they are.

BERYLLIUM POISONING

"What's the use?" They are harboring deep grief and a sense of underlying despair and demoralization. They have an unnerved resignation attitude in the making or in their manifestation. They are overwhelmed by too much sorrow, and by the "running on empty" effect of a severe inequality of energy exchange with the world, whereby they put out much more than they get back.

They have effectively given up on life, feeling that they have no ability to determine or control anything. They feel that they are just simply insufficient to the cause, and they can't care any more.

It is a result of having carried the world on their shoulders all their life, starting with their dysfunctional family, with little or no ability to receive or to request or to require a return in kind. They were told in effect they were the source of all the family's problems while actually being the only one deflecting some of the disasters.

BILE IN THE BLOOD (Liver secretion)

"Forget it!" They are strongly given to cynical pessimism and nihilism. They are deeply disappointed, discouraged and disgusted, and they are handicapped by an unbalanced reason that is dominated by negative internal and external prejudices.

They are condescendingly contemptuous, and they have an intense resentment over lack of recognition of who they are and what they contribute. They manifest a notable lack of love, compassion and tolerance. It derives from an intensely injustice-nurturing and nihilistic dysfunctional family.

BLADDER PROBLEMS

"Down-loading time." There is a need to get rid of something in their life -- they are desperately trying to clear the toxic things, situations and people out of their life. They feel the necessity for the release of pressure. However, their lack of self-love makes this a quite difficult undertaking. They came up in a rigidly domineering family who allowed them little room for self-manifestation or relief from their suppressive restrictions.
****

"I can't expect any better." They have a fair amount of guilt and grief arising from a severely suppressive and non-supportive childhood. It led to suppressed resentment over vulnerability and abandonment-anticipation. They feel tired and that they are "running on empty," and there is poor endurance and a considerable amount of inner agitation and irritation. Their family intended to "keep them around the old homestead" as their "private preserve" and their "whipping kid."

****

"I don't dare." There is a certain lack of inner direction arising from the fear that if they have any hopes, they will prove to be false and blow up in their face. They have a fearful orientation towards the world, along with a cautiously conservative approach which results in their hanging on to old ideas and being afraid of letting go. They are lacking in adaptability, and they have a fear of change, with the result that they are prone to depression.

They have the feeling that their need for love is unfulfilled and unfulfillable, and they have a strong underlying abandonment-anxiety, with a resulting tendency to dependent attachment and to vulnerability-avoidance.

It is a pattern that got started in rigidly denial-dominated and bitter dysfunctional family who would systematically see to it that anything they got would be destroyed or removed, out of a generalized envy and alarm reaction to the individual's (to them) incomprehensible capabilities and potentialities.

****

"Deeply unhappy." There is very little basic trust that things are going to go well for them, and they are just miserable about that. They have a lack of self-confidence, and they feel insufficient and cope-ability-anxious. They are deeply survival-anxious in all arenas, and they have a great need for order and predictability in their life. They come from an alarmingly and implacably dysfunctional family who were themselves quite fearful of life.

****

"Piss off!" They are thoroughly resentful about their life, and they are looking for who is responsible for it. They are intensely angry and blame-throwing, and they feel betrayed and victimized. Much of their venom is directed to their intimates, especially those of the other gender. They feel the parent of the other gender is the cause of all their problems.

They have significant problems in the sexual arena, including suppression of their sexual identity and repression of their sexuality. Underneath all this is the uneasy feeling they are really getting their "just desserts." This whole pattern came about as a result of their being sexualized and sex-ploitative in a seductive-destructive "tantalizing tarantula"-- "seduce-slap" guilt-inducing and accusatory manner in the context of a severely dysfunctional family.

CYSTITIS; INFLAMMATION OF THE BLADDER

"Chronically pissed off." They are perennially angry at the world, and everything sets them off. They are intensely irritable, and they impose their negative take on everyone and everything. They are, in effect, addicted to being unhappy and to negativity. They are the product of a seethingly resentful injustice-nurturing family system.

BLANCHING

"Freak-bleach." They are prone to sudden fear episodes arising from the approach of what are to them unstoppable disasters. It is a pattern learned in a severely dysfunctional family, where they developed an intense learned helplessness, at least in some situations.

****

"Losing it." They have rushes of overwhelming rage and readiness to engage in direct combat. It is the result of having come up in an emotionally explosive dysfunctional family.

BLEEDING

"Seething leakage." They have a lot of undirected anger that is draining out the joy of life. They seem to be in an angry Universe full of nasty people who are inflicting losses and putting them in danger. It feels like they feel singled out for singularly unpleasant experiences by the indifferent vagaries of the Universe.

It comes from having experienced a lot of "They're so good with their stiletto, you don't even mind the pain" treatment in their childhood. In other words, they were surrounded by people who were intensely angry and slyly effective with subtle and indirect passive-aggressive behaviors for which there was no recourse.

BLINDNESS

"Martian anthropologist." Their essence chose to have the experience of being a "sidelines participant-observer" for this lifetime. They wanted to both learn from this experience, to teach from the wisdom this life experience generates, and to share the wisdom that they brought with them.

****

"I can't deal with this!" There is an inability to handle all the realities of their situation. They are in effect overwhelmed, demoralized or terrified by what they experience happening around and within them. So they have had to "turn away from it all" to "keep on trucking." It is the product of a severely dysfunctional and destructive family system and/or family circumstances.

RIGHT EYE BLINDNESS

"Ostrich." They are "tuning out" what is happening in the world around them, due to its being too much to handle.

LEFT EYE BLINDNESS

"Self-revulsion." They are suffering from severe self-rejection arising from massive messaging to the effect that they are a "sight to make eyes sore" from their family and/or from their mother in the womb.

"BLOATED" (Abdominal distention)

"Creature from the Black Lagoon." Something in their current situation is generating a gripping fear and as yet undigested ideas, along with a sense of responsibility-overload and the associated resentment.

There is a considerable amount of anxiety and agitated anticipation of aggravating developments. They are implication-catastrophizing and generalized dread, and there are vague and intangible fears about things that "go bump in the night," the nameless terrors of which they dare not speak. It came from a "magical misery tour" family experience in which they could never tell when and what piece of excrement would come off the wall at them, just that it would.

"BLOATED" (Body-wide water-retention)

"Holding on." They are not letting go of something or someone, out of resistance to changes. They are hanging on to the past for fear that if they let go, something awful will happen.

They feel like they are carrying a heavy load on their shoulders, an overload of responsibility. They want to share the load, but they are afraid to ask for fear of alienating and losing what support they do have.

It's a "Cinderella" pattern in which they were held accountable and responsible for the needs and situations of everyone and everything in their family. Their only support came from just that "unsung hero(ine)" role, in a "serve-aholic" situation.

They are therefore desperate for love and afraid of the loss of love, with an associated intense underlying chronic grief. (Water retention is stored grief from this whole situation and life history) It comes from a fear that any change will result in the loss of even more in their life.

They'd rather keep things as they are than take a chance they will end up with nothing, which is what they fully expect is their "just desserts" for all the "failures" of their care-taking represented by the negative events in their family's history.

BLOOD CLOTS

"Pulling the world in over their heads." They have an intensely conservative and restrictive reaction to life. They are resisting change and expansion, closing down on the flow of joy and growth in their life. Change usually meant things got considerably worse when they were a child, and their subsequent experience has done little to change that impression.
****

"Love Ret ard." There is a blocking off of self-love, the ability to express love to others, and the capacity to receive love. They are feeling neglected, abandoned and/or unacceptable, due to the lack or loss of love in their life. They cling to or to hold on to love for fear of its moving away. It is the result of an emotionally depriving early environment.

BLOOD POISONING

"Dark shadow." They have an intense negativity in their mind in the form of rage, conflict, resistance and fear. It results in abuse of the body by neglect, carelessness and/or dissipatingly self-destructive self-indulgence. It arose from an enragingly dysfunctional family that engendered a strong self-rejection and a nihilistic resignation about ever being able to do anything worthwhile with their life.

BLOOD PRESSURE -- HIGH

"Look out!" They have a feeling of being threatened in some vague but very important high stakes manner, with a resulting intense sense of endangerment. They feel ready for virtually anything to happen. There is stress and conflict, shocks and tension in their situation. It is the result of a long-standing emotional problem that hasn't been worked out, a deep resentment over the past that is eating at them. They come from an unpredictably violating dysfunctional family.
****

"Going down." They are severely depressed and demoralized, and they are giving up on life. They feel powerless regarding their situation and with respect to their coping capability, and they feel that their situation is hopeless, with the result that they are "throwing in the towel." They are the product of a devastatingly dysfunctional family who undermined all possible out routes.
****

"Seething rage." They are intensely angry and resentful about just everything. They have a great deal of suppressed rage and hostility over the felt external control of their lives. They are afraid of their anger, and they feel that they can't handle it, so they stuff it. They suppress their negative emotions with intimates for fear of hurting their loved ones.

They tend to be over-compliant and anger-avoidant to mask their intense feelings of betrayal-rage. They are bitterly negative about everyone and everything, and they always have been. They are a seething volcano who "makes mountains out of molehills." They grew up in a hostile and severely dysfunctional patriarchal family.
****

"Sealed unit." They are hyper-self-responsible, and they feel that they can't count on anyone or anything. They feel they have to do it all themselves. They have an abiding inability to relax, they tend to overeat and to be over-weight. Their love nature is unresolved and reserved for only a few. They won't allow themselves to feel love, affection or compassion for many, and they operate with highly conditional love habits.

They have never had a childhood, and they were never given the message that who they are is enough, and that what they accomplished filled the bill. They were effectively "abandoned at an early age" and left more or less to their own devices throughout their childhood, resulting in an "island unto themselves" self-made person.
****

"Perfection-expecting." They have a profoundly frightening dread of failure that was produced by their parents making them into an "ego extension" -- "vicarious accomplisher" for them. They are tremendously parent-admiring, especially of their father, and they are an "achieve-aholic" hard-driving competitor for paternal validation. They are a "work-aholic" -- "number-addict" and "coup-seeker" who wants to "make a killing," and they are perfectionistically disappointed in themselves.
****

"This is MY show!" They won't accept help or delegate responsibility, and they are an aggressive dominator, with a deep need to be in control, arising from an underlying dependent passivity and fear of domination. They have an underlying deep distrust of the universe, and they feel that they have to personally determine everything, lest all hell break loose. They were the "sane one" in their severely dysfunctional and patriarchal family.
****

"I'm all I've got, and one strike and I'm out!" They are spirituality-denigrating and love-suppressing, and at base they are shy, with a poor sex adjustment, as they seek satisfaction within themselves only. They are anxious about money, they are time-urgent, they are insecure about life, and they are stress-sensitive. They are impatient, angry, and wanting to live life in the moment, as they try to pound away too quickly at life. All of which arises from their having had to take on their parent(s) ambitions for them from far too early an age.

BLOOD PRESSURE -- LOW
"Eeyor." They are experiencing a "What's the use? It won't work anyway" demoralized defeatism resulting in a giving up on life and in a "settle-for" lifestyle. They tend to get into doing a sacrificial pattern, followed by unconscious deep-seated resentment. There is a feeling of purposelessness, along with a letting go of a sense of meaningfulness, both of which reflect a subconscious death wish. There is a good deal of anxiety, insecurity and frustration that have led to their becoming nihilistic. They have withdrawn their energy from the process of living.

It all got started in a family who operated in the same manner and simultaneously demanded that they be the "pillar of strength," and the one who tries to keep things together and cleans up the mess. Theirs was a loveless and joyless family experience. At the same time, their family was completely unable to give them any love or hope as all this was going on. The individual ended up feeling that there's really no point and no winning in this business of life, and so they are marking time and "*waiting for rigor mortis*" as they experience the feeling, "There must be some way out of here."

BLOOD PROBLEMS
"Going down." They are severely depressed and demoralized, and they are giving up on life. They feel powerless regarding their situation and with respect to their coping capability. They feel that their situation is hopeless, and they are "throwing in the towel." They are the product of a devastatingly dysfunctional family who undermined all possible out routes.
****

"Seething rage." They are intensely angry and resentful about just everything. They have a great deal of suppressed rage and hostility over the felt external control of their life. They are afraid of their anger, and they feel that they can't handle it, so they stuff it.

They suppress their negative emotions with intimates for fear of hurting their loved ones. They tend to be over-compliant and anger-avoidant to mask their intense feelings of betrayal-rage. They are a seething volcano who "makes mountains out of molehills." They are bitterly negative about everyone and everything, and they always have been, and there are deep-seated thoughts and feelings of unwillingness to go on with life. They grew up in a hostile and severely dysfunctional patriarchal family.
****

"Investment-avoidant." Their "emotional body" is deeply troubled, and there is a real lack of joy. There is no circulation of new ideas, information and possibilities. There is also an absence of love in their heart. They have difficulties in how well they are taking care of their own needs and getting nurtured. There is also a diminution of life energy and little vitality-replenishment, and their thinking is redundant, repetitious, stagnant and going nowhere.

They have intensely negative feelings about themselves arising from a profound buried guilt over a felt impeding of someone else's life, an existential guilt about "being a burden." They have a rigid, somber and disaster-deflecting orientation that got started in a severely dysfunctional and ferociously closed-mindedly denigrating family in which nothing ever worked, and in which they were held accountable for everyone's misery. There was no room for their having any needs of their own or for any form of hope or joy.

~~~~~~

PLATELETS, LOW (Difficulty clotting blood)

"Over-responsibility." They have a sense that they are here to make the world all better, and that they should care-take everything and everyone. It comes from having grown up in a situation of many unmet needs for everyone, and they rose to the challenge to the point where they have some difficulty limiting demands made on them or in taking care of their own needs.

BLURRED VISION

"I don't want to see that." Their version of reality is not meshing with the realities that confront them. They have a real difficulty with focusing, with being clear, and with accepting what they see. They don't want to accept what their eyes are telling them. They are the product of a demoralizingly dysfunctional and denial-dominated family.

BOILS

"Roiling turmoil." They are having problems with deprivation-resentment, along with a seething fury. They are "boiling over" with anger at their whole situation. It also represents a feeling of being betrayed and sabotaged. They were denied love and joy as a child, they deeply resent it.

This can come from:

1) an indeed depriving and undermining family,

2) an imperious expectations-generating capitulating family, and/or

3) a current situation in which they are in fact being frustrated, deprived and harmed.

(See **CARBUNKLE** and/or the part(s) of the body affected for more information)

BONE PROBLEMS

"Vulnerability-anxiety." They are having real problems with mental or emotional feelings of weakness and defenselessness. They feel that they are not strong enough to meet the requirements of life, and that they are unable to protect themselves. They grew up in an aggressive, self-immersed and uncaring family who rode rough-shod over them.

****

"Moral cretins." They feel a real lack of the fulfillment of their standards and norms in their life. Their experience is that they are surrounded by fools and "moral monsters" that could care less about values, ecological impact and standards. They also feel no sense of support or commitment from the universe in this matter. They are the product of a highly morally-oriented family who expected perfection of them. It is probable that this is a multi-life issue for them.
****

"I ain't enough." They had and have a tremendous sense of accountability and responsibility for the state of their ecology, along with a simultaneous feeling of "faking it to make it," of being a "fraud," and of "in way over their head" -- like they were when they were a child.

They feel that they are the only one who can even try to pull anything out of the fire, but they don't know if they have the strength or firmness to pull it off. They feel very much alone on their own, inadequate to the cause, and deserving of the negative outcomes that they generate for themselves. They grew up in a demoralizingly dysfunctional family in which they were the "sane one," but in which they had little or no power, and in which they were blamed for all that went wrong.

They were placed in a parental role from a very early age in their dependent and enmeshed family. On top of which, they were also feeling endangered, because they were indeed potentially in great trouble, due to being required to do far more than a child should and could do.
****

"Losing it." Life's vicissitudes and difficulties have undermined or overwhelmed the depths of their sense of sanity. They have the feeling that they are losing their mind, and they have severe doubts about their ability to handle the situation. They come from a crazy-making and confusion-inducing family.
****

"No support." There is a strong experience of a lack of validation and assistance from their loved ones -- a feeling that they are out on a limb with no back-up. Indeed, they have the impression that they are actually being actively undermined and invalidated by those close to them. It is an old, familiar experience for them, in that their family consistently denigrated and disrespected them as a child.
****

"Mr./Ms. Nobody." They feel a real loss of standing in the world, and there is deeply hurt pride in them. They feel under-rated, invisible, unappreciated and exploited. They are very angry about this, and it gives them the pronounced sense that the Universe is unjust and indifferent. It all got started in their family, where they were dealt with in this manner.

~~~~~~

BONE MARROW PROBLEMS

"Cope-ability problems." They have a deep sense of being insufficient to the cause of living life, of being unable to support and care for themselves. They feel that they are in way over their head and thoroughly unsafe in an uncaring and overwhelming Universe. It arose from being thrown into self-care at a very early age, due to familial overwhelm and/or dysfunctionality.

BONES – BROKEN, FRACTURED

"Sharp break." There has been an abrupt shattering of the foundations of their life and in the structure of their Universe -- significant losses or great failures in their life. They are experiencing profound inner conflict in the depths of their being.

They are reacting to experiences that run contrary to their deepest beliefs -- moral, spiritual, ethical, social and/or scientific/pragmatic -- as in a "paradigm problem."

There is a definite break from the past, along with an accompanying desire to quickly change circumstances to compensate for their dissatisfaction with their personality and/or with their situation.

****

"There must be some way outta this!" They are desperately needing a radical change in their circumstances, and in a way, it is a cry for help, a giving in to the need for assistance, and/or a dire necessity for a significant change in direction. However, they are too rigid or frightened to acknowledge this need.

They have an underlying feeling that they aren't allowed to be their own authority, and there is even a sense that authority figures are doing their thinking for them. They are apt to have had a strict and authoritarian upbringing, with a resulting resentment of and rebellion against authority.

****

"Here it comes!" There is a fair amount of fear and/or a belief in violence happening to them. They are the product of at least a "flying emotional bodies" and perhaps a literal "flying bodies" type of virulent and violent dysfunctional family.

(See **"BRITTLE BONE" SYNDROME; OSTEO-MYELITIS; OSTEO-POROSIS; PAGET'S DISEASE**)

BOTULISM (The most dangerous form of bacterial food poisoning)

"Sitting duck." They are feeling defenseless, and like they have to allow others to take control and run their situation. It is a learned helplessness reaction and a feeling that they don't have the right to protection, support or nurturance. They simply expect to "eat shit" as a part of living. It is a pattern that arose in a family where they had few, if any rights, and in which much anger and negativity took place over which no one seemed to have control.

BOWEL PROBLEMS

"No dumping." They have a fear of letting go of the past, the old and no longer needed -- the waste products their learning history. They have a rigid and intensely conservative, cautious and controlling approach to life, in which they are deeply afraid to let go of the "tried and true" to take on the new and renewing. It is the result of an intensely entrenched and past-fixated family.

****

"Jealous possessiveness." They are deathly afraid of losing their intimates, and they are in effect horrified at the prospect of finding themselves homeless with no resources. They are madly restricting of their intimates as a result. At the same time, they are terrified of alienating their loved ones, and they bend over backwards to please them. They were threatened with abandonment and told that they are "unfit for human consumption" by their mother.

****

"Control freak." They are hell bent for leather to stay in control of every situation they encounter. They are totally resistant to any form of delegation or release of the throttle in any situation. They have the experience that at base they can't control their situation, so they are frantic/fanatic to try to control something or someone. They are the product of an out-of-control dysfunctional family, in which they tried desperately to impose some sort of sanity on the scene.

(See **COLON PROBLEMS; LARGE INTESTINE PROBLEMS; SMALL INTESTINE PROBLEMS**)

"BRAIN FOG" (Clouded thinking, memory problems, confusion, disorientation, fatigue, etc.)

"Self-worth issues." They are experiencing excessive guilt, self-doubt and self-image problems. They feel unappreciated, and they are also unsure of their capability and value. They need appreciation, love, and understanding of the kind they never got as a child in their accusatorially invalidating family.

****

"Assimilation problems." They are having absorption difficulties and problems in separating the wheat from the chaff, so to speak. They are having problems with analysis and with processing things. They are being hampered by distorted discrimination and disturbing distrust generated by a dysfunctional family's "magical mystery tour" pattern, and by their being subjected to systematic invalidation then and ever since.

****

"What am I doing *here*!" They are manifesting a dismayed discombobulation about the world and the way their life is going. It is the result of growing up in a vaguely overwhelmed family, of being the product of a severely enmeshed and incompetencing family, or of being a "visitor" from another soul pool who came here to learn and/or teach.

BRAIN PROBLEMS

"In over their head." They are feeling drained and over-demanded, like they are being abandoned by the "Home Office" (All That Is). There are serious conflicts between their personal goals and the Divine intent, and they are very worried and anxious as a result. It is a "God is Al Capone" relational issue with the "Source."

They have the feeling that the "Home Office" (All That Is) has taken the helm of their life against their will and desires, and that they are unable to manage their life. They have a great deal of anxiety and nervousness as a result.

As a result, there is now a major difficulty with their "bio-computer" and "communication center" in either the belief systems or the "Executive Officer" or both. There is a profound inner conflict within the operational ego and/or between the desires and intentions of the personality and their perception of their unfolding destiny.

This developed as a result of a family history in which a lot didn't make sense, and yet it was justified as being "God's Will" or the equivalent. They are the product of a significantly dysfunctional family who did not respond to their needs or in which they were forced to take over the meeting of their own needs because no one else would. As a result, they developed an abiding distrust of the Universe.

RIGHT HEMISPHERE (Perceptual, spatial and holographic processing)
"No comprehension." They have handicaps in the handling of perceptual integration, emotional/experiential processing, and intuitive functioning. They were not supposed to "get" what was going on in their severely dysfunctional family.

LEFT HEMISPHERE (Conceptual, logical and verbal processing)
"Irrational." They are suffering from a befuddlement of the ability to conceptualize, to interpret, and to apply logical analysis. They got a strong "Don't think!" injunction.
~~~~~~

CORPUS CALLOSUM (Rich highway of fibers connecting the hemispheres)
"I went thata way" (pointing in two opposite directions). There is a disruption of their action-integration, of their programming, and of the initiation of strategies. They were impeded in their development of the ability to take initiative action.

FRONTAL LOBE (Behind the forehead – the interpreter and decision-maker)
"Can't make sense of things." They are having difficulties in the integration and interpretation of information that are disrupting the decision-making process. It is the result of confusion-inducing parenting.

TEMPORAL LOBE (The temples -- auditory and information-processing center)
"Disc failure." There are disruptions of their ability to accept, organize and store information, along with problems in the verbal encoding and processing of experiences. They were subjected to very rigid restrictions on what was and what was not acceptable.

RIGHT TEMPORAL LOBE
"World-confusion." They are having difficulties processing environmental events.

LEFT TEMPORAL LOBE
"Self-chaos." They are encountering problems dealing with the qualities of their personal situation.
~~~~~~

OCCIPITAL LOBE (Back of the head – the visual projection center)
"Can't see it." They are being hampered by distortions and derailments of their ability to organize visual inputs and to form images. They were given a strong "Don't see!" injunction.

CEREBELLUM (Motor control center)
"Action disruption." There has been a derailment of their ability to coordinate and carry out intentions and actions. They were systematically incompetenced as a child.

MID-BRAIN (Emotional manifestation system)
"Meaning confusion." They are having difficulties in the management of their feelings and in the process of evaluation and application of decision criteria. They were not supposed to arrive at their own conclusions, and they were programmed to be emotional-commotional and/or emotionally illiterate as a child.

There are four major structures in the mid-brain that handle the meanings of things:

The first is the **_hippocampus_**, located at the back end of the corpus callosum. It is sort of crescent-curved and ends out in a form like the paw of an animal such as a cat.

Its function is continuity and coherence, in the sense of sequence of events, memory of things, the experience of one's self, the sense of time, history, tradition and how everything fits together, etc. It is the understanding function, so to speak.

When things break down here, the result is a lost in the moment non-comprehension of what things signify and where everything fits into the scheme of how everything works and what it all means.

The second major structure is the **_thalamus_**, which is a lemon-sized cluster of nuclei located in the center of the brain. It processes almost all information prior to its entrance into the cerebral cortex.

It screens out stuff via repression, and it prepares the cortex to receive the information via activation of the cortex. It is essentially the "control center for consciousness." Things like, "I am aware . . ."

Trouble here results in their functioning in a "brain-dead" manner -- operating without awareness on "automatic pilot," systematically screwing up due to lack of tracking or comprehension, "lost in space," etc.

The third significant structure here is the **_hypothalamus_**, which is a dime-sized structure located at the base of the mid-brain underneath the thalamus. It handles emotional responses, sexuality, stress-management, and a number of other activities related to the emotional system.

It orchestrates and activates the cortex via the meaning implications, indications and interventions that are involved in the significations of things. "I feel. . ." is the generic reaction occurring here.

Trouble here takes the form of deranged, demoralized, delusional, defiant, depressed, devastated and/or emotional-commotional functioning, or in other ways disrupted emotional functioning.

The fourth major structure in the mid-brain is an almond-shaped little structure called the **_amygdala_**. This is one of the oldest parts of the brain, and it handles the importance question. That is, it asks, "How serious, significant, immediate action-requiring, dangerous, survival-threatening, etc. is this?" It's primary operational impact is anxiety/fear/panic-induction, but it also mediates all "gut level" emotions, significances, and action-imperative implications of things. Most conditioned anxiety, fear, panic and blind self-protective stuff emanates from here.

When it goes off strongly, it throws the whole system into emergency mode. In more run-of-the-mill things, it runs our impulses, inclinations, leanings, attractions and aversions, impetuses to explore further or to back away, etc. Trouble here shows up as either "frayed nerves" over-reactivity to things or as stuporous and unresponsive under-reactivity, as if they had no idea of the significance of things.

~~~~~~

AMYGDALA PROBLEMS

"Emotional overwhelm." They are having problems with the intrusion into their consciousness, experience and functioning of massively traumatic emotions from severely damaging experiences in their past. Things like "burst-outs," self-hatred, sexual shut down, etc. are occurring.

They underwent a great deal of emotional trauma in their childhood, and current events are re-activating those and associated experiences.

HIPPOCAMPUS PROBLEMS

"I don't remember . . .." They are having trouble with their sense of continuity of their self and with their experience of the continuum of events and reactions over time, such as amnesia, fugue states, multiple personality alters sub-routine take-overs, senility, etc. They are the product of a severely denial-dominated dysfunctional and destructive family.

HYPOTHALAMUS PROBLEMS

"Emotionally disrupted." They are prone to deranged, demoralized, delusional, defiant, depressed, devastated and/or emotional-commotional or in other ways disturbed emotional functioning. They grew up in a severely emotionally damaging dysfunctional family.

MEDULLA/BRAIN STEM (Back base of the skull "instinctive system" center)

"Self-endangering." There are seriously threatening disruptions of the life maintenance systems. They received a "Don't be!" injunction.

THALAMUS PROBLEMS

"Brain-dead." They are prone to functioning without awareness on "automatic pilot," to systematic screw-ups due to lack of tracking or comprehension, to being "lost in space," etc. Their family was intensely awareness-avoidant and automated in their functioning.

BRAIN TUMOR

"Demoralization-despair." There is a deep mental conflict about being fully in the world and concerning dealing effectively with reality. They are withdrawing in confusion and disoriented devastation. They are manifesting incorrect beliefs and interpretation systems, along with a stubborn refusal to change old patterns. They are unable to "reprogram the bio-computer" of the mind, with a resulting pessimistic depression and nihilistic worry. A major issue is growing to unmanageable proportions, because they are unable to revise their views of things. It is the result of highly rigid rearing in childhood.

BREAST PROBLEMS

"Maternal conflicts." They are having deep conflicts over their maternal attitudes, home and motherhood. They feel unable or unwilling to be loving, nurturing and supportive, due to never having been nurtured or due to having the maternal denigrated in their family.
****

"Slave feelings." They feel exploited, unappreciated and oppressed in response to a patriarchal environment. They grew up in just such a family, and they have consistently drawn to themselves repeats of that pattern.
****

"Serve-aholic." They are over-nurturing, self-denying and insufficiently nourished, refusing to nourish themselves and putting everyone else first. They are also conflicted about their ability to be nurturing. It is a function of having been totally defined as a source of nurturance as a child.
****

"Allure issues." They have deep conflicts over their sexual attractiveness, sexuality, seductive projection and/or erotic sensitivity and receptivity. They feel insufficiently feminine or attractive, due to devaluing by their family.
****

"Erotic rejection." They feel sex-ploitative and they deeply resent it. It is s a function of having encountered such treatment a lot in their family.
****

"Tripod-rage." They have a significant case of the irresistible urge to kick anything with three legs arising from a patriarchal family, from a dysfunctional father, and/or from maternal programming.
****

"Gender role problems." They feel too feminine, in the sense of feeling like a second class citizen, because they were treated as such at home.
****

"Womanhood issues." They have many conflicts over their femininity. They feel "masculine" or "unfeminine" because of the strong forcefulness of their personality and/or because of intense devaluation by their family on the grounds of their gender.
****

"Potencylessness-resentment." They feel powerless and unable to cope with life on their own two feet, and they resent it. It is a pattern which comes from being competence-undermined and power-prevented as a child.
****

"Love-avoidance." They have deep conflicts over the role of love in their life. They feel unable to be loving, as a result of never having been loved themselves.
****

"Forget it!" They feel that love is a "poison apple," because that's what it was as a child.
****

"Love-aholic." They are starved for love, and they are not finding it because they imprinted on unloving people.
****

"Unfit for human consumption." They feel they don't deserve love, as a result of a severely shaming and denigrating family.
****

"Self-rejecting." They have a profound sense of worthlessness, and they are intensely self-belittling. They were systematically denigrated and rejected as a child.

RIGHT BREAST PROBLEM
"How do I do it right?" They are encountering issues over their preferred forms, means of expressing and/or recipients of their nurturance, sexuality-manifestation or love.

LEFT BREAST PROBLEM
"Where do I get it?" They have issues over their preferred sources of nurturance, sexuality or love.
****

"How dare I?" There are issues over felt deservingness of nurturance, sexual support and expression and/or love and caring.

~~~~~~

BREAST CANCER

"Sucked dry." They are struggling with feelings of being "eaten out of house and home." They have a lot of exploitation-resentment and a strong rejection of motherhood or the maternal role. They are deeply in conflict about the whole feminine role and what it means to be a woman in society vs. her own needs, desires and qualities, as she sees it. Usually, this development represents the culmination of a co-dependent lifestyle generated in a dysfunctional family. They finally have reached the point where "This is an up with which I will no longer put!"

RIGHT BREAST CANCER

"Enough already!" They are fed up with the way in which they are being utilized, the types of resources and responses they are required to produce. They are also ashamed and self-disliking.

LEFT BREAST CANCER

"This is an up with which I will no longer put!" They are sick and tired of being everyone's "tit," and they are not willing to have it continue. They feel that their acceptance has been solely on this basis, and they now insist on recognition, validation and appreciation for who they are.

~~~~~~

(See **CANCER**)

BREAST CYSTS; BREAST LUMPS

"Sexual rejection." They are feeling or being rejected sexually by their partner or the world at large. Or they are resentful of the sexual attentions they get. In either case, it is reflective of an underlying sense of worthlessness or unacceptability except through their sexual appeal. They grew up in a conditionally-loving household that was also sex-ploitative in their approach.

****

"Hyper-maternal." They are engaged in over-mothering, in excessive nurturing output. In the process, they are cutting off nourishment to themselves. There is a real inability to be themselves, and they are "serving themselves up on a platter" to others. They have insufficient self-respect and self-commitment -- a "Me last!" orientation, derived from an exploitative, dysfunctional and/or denigrating family.

****

"Mama knows best!" They have over-protective and over-bearing attitudes. They are infantilizing and maturity-derailing "smother-mothering." They refuse to allow others to be themselves, and they are feeding wrong ideas to those being "ministered to." It arose from their being the only "sane one" in a dysfunctional family.

RIGHT BREAST CYST

"Cut it out!" They intensely dislike the realms and manners in which they are being drawn upon and "drained."

****

"One and only way." They have rigidly fixed ideas of how things need to be done.

LEFT BREAST CYST

"Drained out." They are becoming exhausted and depleted by all their self-denial and co-dependent "serve-aholic" output.

****

"Mama knows best!" They are imposing their values, assumptions and priorities on those around them in a "dominatrix" manner.

~~~~~~

BREAST DISCHARGE

"Frustrated motherhood." They are not being able to manifest their maternal principle effectively. It is a situation where either:

1) their actual mothering process is being painful and/or unsuccessful, or

2) they are being prevented from manifesting their maternal qualities and/or their generativity, or

3) they are not manifesting the children and/or child-rearing they need to do.

It is a pattern that got started in their exploitative and denigrating patriarchal household, in which the feminine and the maternal were devalued, distorted and/or exploited.

RIGHT BREAST DISCHARGE

"Derailed." They are frustrated over the blockage of their ways of nurturing, generative expression, and care-taking by the environment or by circumstances.

LEFT BREAST DISCHARGE

"Prevented." They are experiencing a sense of non-fulfillment arising from being prevented from manifesting their generative/maternal capacities and motivations.

~~~~~~

BREAST INFAMMATION

"Burned up." They are sick and tired of all the sorrows of womanhood. They deeply resent the restrictions, over-requirements, exploitation, sexualization, and on, and on, and on. They may also have a strong case of "tripod-rage"- the irresistible urge to kick anything with three legs. She is either the product of a patriarchal household and/or of a tripod-raging mother.

BREAST SORENESS

"Sexual rejection." They are feeling or being rejected sexually by their partner or by the world at large. Or they are resentful of the sexual attentions they get. In either case, it is reflective of an underlying sense of worthlessness or unacceptability except through their sexual appeal. They grew up in a conditionally-loving household that was also sex-ploitative in their approach.
****

"Over-mothering." They are putting out excessive nurturing and cutting off nourishment to themselves. There is an inability to be themselves, they are serving themselves up on a platter to others. They have insufficient self-respect and self - commitment. It is a "Me last!" orientation derived from an exploitative, dysfunctional, and/or denigrating family.
****

"Over-protective and overbearing attitudes." They are engaged in an infantilizing and maturity-derailing "smother-mothering" pattern. They refuse to allow others to be themselves, and they are feeding wrong ideas to those being "ministered to." It is a "Mama knows best!" attitude arising from being the only "sane one" in a dysfunctional family.

RIGHT BREAST SORENESS

"Enough already!" They have an intense dislike of the realms and manners in which they are being drawn upon and "drained."
****

"My way or the highway." They have rigidly fixed ideas of how things need to be done.

LEFT BREAST SORENESS

"Drained out." They are becoming exhausted and depleted by all their self-denial and co-dependent "serve-aholic" output.
****

"Mama knows best!" They are imposing their values, assumptions and priorities on those around them.

~~~~~~

BREAST TUMOR

"Destiny-derailment." There is a frustrated desire to grow and be fulfilled through home and/or children. They put all their eggs in this basket, and it came up empty. They were over-restricted in their outlook on possibilities for themselves as a child.
****

"Love-aholic." They are looking for love in all the wrong places. They imprinted on a dysfunctional family and intimates and are trying to put a new ending on the old story with the same type of people -- with the predictable results.
****

"In their face." They are experiencing having their "conditional nurturance" backfiring on them, in the sense that they intended to guarantee love and/or control via generating an obligation to them in others, and instead it has resulted in negative consequences. It is a continuation of a pattern established in a manipulative and exploitative family.

RIGHT BREAST TUMOR

"Wrong recipients." They are feeling little or no fulfillment in or from the recipients of their maternal feelings in their life.
****

"Wrong choices." They are deeply frustrated with the type of people they give their love to.
****

"Wrong ways." They are conflicted over the methods they use to garner love or control.

LEFT BREAST TUMOR

"Vast wasteland." They are finding insufficient joy and fulfillment in their expression of their maternal capacities.
****

"Love-starved." They are realizing that they aren't getting the love they need.
****

"Down the drain." They are demoralized over their failure to get the return on their investment that they intended.

"BRITTLE BONES" SYNDROME (Extremely vulnerable to breakage)

"Cosmic abandonment." They have a profound feeling that nobody cares. The feeling is that there is no longer (or there never was) any foundation to build on. They feel abandoned by the "Home Office" (All That Is), and that there is nothing out there to sustain them. Their experience is that they are "alone on their own," that they have been in effect "left to their own devices," and that they are therefore highly vulnerable and feeling continuously endangered. They feel totally betrayed by the Cosmos.

They have a good deal of fear, anger and frustration with the very structure of the Universe and with the fundamental nature of life. They feel absolutely unsupported, with no sense if safety. They feel that there is just no love for them from God.

Their interpretation of it is that they live in a heartless "random Universe," and that they lost out in life this time around. In reality it is a situation in which their Destiny is designed to expand their soul, and to serve the Cosmos with their life experiences and contributions.

The experiential basis of all this was a family in which their needs were not comprehended or met enough in a "raising themselves by their own bootstraps" situation. The whole thing may be reflective of previous incarnations in which they themselves "betrayed their contract" and the Universe, which now requires restitution.

BROKEN BLOOD VESSELS

"Self-rejection." They are operating out of an underlying assumption that there is something fundamentally wrong with them. They therefore feel that it is unjustified for them to experience love, joy and abundance in their life. As a result, they have guilt feelings when any of these arise or arrive. They are also prone to attack themselves in the areas and arenas where they experience such inputs. It comes from neglectfully rejecting early experiences that lead to a chronic low level depression and dejection.

"BROKEN HEART SYNDROME" (Stress cardiomyopathy) [Pseudo-heart attack] (Much more frequent in women, particularly older women)

"Oh my God, NO!!" They end up showing all the symptoms of a heart attack in response to some profound loss or threat, such as the end of a profoundly important relationship or a serious threat to their child.

It occurs in the context of a sense of overwhelmed powerlessness due to the nature of the precipitating circumstances. It usually happens after a lifelong history of having been able to keep such traumas and threats at bay with their competence and control. There is a sense of there being no support system in this crisis, with an accompanying feeling at some level of abandonment by the "Home Office" (All That Is). They grew up in a "the buck stops here" situation in which they were the only one capable and committed enough to prevent disaster in their dysfunctional family.

BRONCHIAL PROBLEMS; BRONCHIAL SPASMS

"God must be Al Capone!" They have an underlying distrust of the Universe and God. They live in a lot of betrayal-fear, implication-anxiety, and insecurity in the world. They feel unsafe and unprotected, and they live in an "emotional foxhole."

They are out of sync with the environment with a skeptical, "I'll believe it when it works for me!" attitude. They are an ejectee-rejectee-dejectee who feels unwanted, with a lot of separation-anxiety that is actually a separation from God experience. Their underlying deep despair and depression arises from anger with themselves, guilt, shame, and a felt need for punishment for their "sins."

They grew up in an angry, rejecting, yelling, inflamed dysfunctional family, or who were silently seething volcanoes. They "force fed" and "smother-loved" the individual out of their own needs, rather than out of those of the individual.

BRONCHITIS (Inflammation of the windpipe)

"What the hell's going on here!?" There is fear, tension, anxiety, and a feeling of things being very unsettled. When they are under stress or vulnerable, they feel that the world is not a safe place. They feel that they will be betrayed and attacked, even by friends and family. They feel somehow responsible for all the ills of the world, and that they are alone in the world. There are many deep despair and depression feelings to get off their chest, along with anger or rage. They are suppressing screams of grief and rage as they live life in an "emotional foxhole."

They are deeply rejecting of what is happening inside, of their feelings about themselves, and of how they are doing. They are intensely frustrated and angry with themselves, but they are afraid to express or let go of it. This is all the result of an inflamed family environment that was saturated with silent or not-so-silent yelling and arguments. They got lost in the belligerence, and they felt severely rejected, with a resulting grief-strickenness. They have incorporated their conflictual environment, and they are at war with themselves.

BRONCHIAL OBLITERATIVE OBSTRUCTIVE PNEUMONIA (BOOP) (Severe blockage of breathing leading to threatened or experienced suffocations)

"God must be Al Capone!" They have an underlying distrust of the Universe and God. They live in a lot of betrayal-fear, implication-anxiety, and insecurity in the world. They feel unsafe and unprotected, and they live in an "emotional fox-hole." They are out of sync with the environment with a skeptical, "I'll believe it when it works for me!" attitude.

They are an ejectee-rejectee-defectee who feels unwanted, with a lot of separation-anxiety that is actually a separation from God experience.

They grew up in an angry, rejecting, yelling, inflamed dysfunctional family, or who were silently seething volcanoes. They "force fed" and "smother-loved" the individual out of their own needs, rather than out of those of the individual.
****

"Tie that grinds." They are feeling totally stifled by an overly close and/or dominating relationship. They are being overwhelmed and restricted, they are very angry about it. However, they don't feel they can do or say anything about it, for fear of catastrophic consequences. It is the result of an authoritarian and oppressive and possessive family.
****

"Suppressed grief." They are desperate and tired of life, due to generalized disturbances in their processes and situation. They are having an "salt poured in emotional wounds" experience that is not being allowed to heal. They are suffering under the influence of their lifelong repressed sorrow, grief and despair.

They are fearful and anxious to the point of being overcome with desperation and futility feelings. They are struggling with confusion-inducing emotional conflict, and there is a failure to maintain immunity to negative ideas. They are the product of a self-defeatingness generating dysfunctional family who instilled a sense of being hapless, helpless and hopeless.
****

"Self-revulsion." They are "choking to death" on their own guilt and shame. They feel that they should be thoroughly punished or even destroyed for their "sins." It comes from a severely accusatory, blame-throwing, moralistic and punitive family.

SUDDEN SUFFOCATION EXPERIENCES

"Refusing to grow up." They are totally terrified of the process of life and of the environment around them. They have a fearful distrusting of just about everything, and they feel utterly unsafe in the world.

On top of which, the message in childhood was, "Don't you dare ever grow up and away or beyond our control!" They therefore got stuck in childhood, afraid to take the world on its own terms.

BRONCHIAL DRYING, BURNING AND PAIN

"No right to life." There is no "juiciness" in their life, and there is insufficient life fluid in their body. They believe at the deep gut level that they should not have needs, wants and desires, and their life experience reflects that. There is profound self-rejection and hurt, in the form of severe suppressed grief. It comes from "NOW look what you've done!" parenting. They feel that they have no right to experience, express, relieve or release. There is also a great deal of repressed rage at their life history and experience, along with unexpressed outraged indignation at the Cosmos for allowing all this to happen.

The result is effective systematic self-deprivation as atonement and as fusion with their severely rejecting mother in a childhood fixated belief that they somehow deserve what has happened and what continues to occur. This often takes the form of "one way street" compulsive giving and unrequited love/caring/commitment/ contribution in their life.

77

There was active hostility for their existing, for their being a "demand," and for their being a threat/rival to their mother. They were treated as the "intimate enemy" and as the source of all their family's problems, often in a paradoxical outcome of their unusually potent and resourced nature. Their mother's unconscious feeling being that they had the power to "make it all better" and instead they generated threats, all her problems and humiliation.

BUBONIC PLAGUE (Swollen lymph glands, severe fever and delirium)

"Return of the repressed." They are experiencing a "bursting out" of "shadow-shoved" and suppressed desires, dreads and destructive motivations. They have been "keeping on trucking and never looking back" all their lives, and by now they have a very impressive "gunny sack of emotional monsters" in there.

The result is that they have been "running on empty" so long that their "emotional body" has broken down, and they therefore have no immunity to external or internal attacking agents. And now it is all "coming to roost" on their head, and it is spewing out all over their body. They are unable to process or release past wounds, and they are now consumed by them.

It is the result of a massively repressive, suppressive, oppressive and aggressive paranoid patriarchal family who "shoved it all into the sub-basement" while they kept up a self-deluding persona of "normalcy." The family relied extremely heavily on intense shame-inducing and subterranean threats and assaults in a highly pathologically dysfunctional manner.

BULIMIA (Compulsive food bingeing and then vomiting)

"What a disaster!" They have a hopeless terror of life, along with a frantic stuffing and purging of their self-hatred and self-disgust. They are a profoundly self-rejecting "love-aholic" who has no hope whatsoever of ever getting the love they need for reasons they can never fathom. They are suffering from a deep depression and desperation.

Theirs is a "magical misery tour" and "nameless terror of which they dare not speak" experience of life. So they turn to self-solace in the form of "controllable" love-substitutes in the form of food binges. But then their self-hatred surfaces again, and they "punish" and "purify" themselves with purging, which is also a way of keeping their "terrible secret."

It was generated by a horrifyingly dysfunctional and rejecting family who, however, assiduously disguised their hatred with seeming lovingness, so that the individual took on all their hatred and rejection as deserved "punishment."
****

"Run amok-anxiety." They have the feeling that they are unable to regulate themselves effectively, and that they have no control over themselves. They feel that their needs are never met, and that they can't measure up to people's expectations of them. They erroneously see themselves as effectively not up to snuff or up to meeting the demands of life. They were consistently undermined in their ability to cope with things in their possessive and dysfunctional family.

BURSITIS (Inflammation of the joints)

"Unfit for human consumption." They are feeling rejected for what they are, in the sense of being totally unappreciated. They are feeling very victimized and put upon, and they experience a lack of love. They feel somehow that they will never receive the acceptance, validation and affection they need. They are the product of a systematically rejecting family system.
****

"Repressed rage." They are full of suppressed resentment and anger and they have a strongly squashed desire to hit someone. They continuously ruminate and recriminate over their "indignities," and they cling to every item like "super-glue." They have a chronic bitterness and resentment, they are forever sending out arrows of hatred, jealousy, general discord and other negative vibrations. Their mind is wound up so tight in their hostile preoccupations that it grinds their whole system to a halt, and they are constantly suppressing their desire to strike out and hit people. At this point, they are pushing another person around, or they being pushed around by another person. They are the product of an intensely hostile home.
****

"Will of iron." They have a rigid will and very strong opinions that they will not and probably cannot change. They are unbending in their expression and self-manifestation. They never let go of anything, as they try to be the "boss of the Universe" in an effort to make life just the way they want it. They grew up in a highly inflexible patriarchal and perhaps authoritarian family, and they "identified with the aggressor."
****

"Fight or flight." They are immersed in a strong reaction to their situation, and they are chronically anxious. They feel that things have gotten out of hand, and that they can't regain control.

They feel that they can't do anything to change their circumstances, and they are utterly frustrated with the way their life is going. They have no trust of the "Home Office," (All That Is) and they feel that "It is botching the job." Underneath all this is a feeling of utter powerlessness and a severe self- and other-rejection arising from their being treated as the "intimate enemy" by their family.

CALCIFICATION (Deposits of calcium in the body)

"Hardening of the attitudes." They are rigidly adhering to standards and patterns that are unrealistic, outdated, and self-defeating. They have to rely on them to provide themselves a sense of security in a highly insecurity-generating world. They feel that they are in over their head, and that they have to handle it by strictly adhering to the tried and true. It is the resultant either of a highly regimented and perfectionistic family and/or of having had to serve as the "sane one," the "Rock of Gibraltar," in a severely dysfunctional family.

CANCER

"Potencylessness-rage." They feel overwhelmed and devastated, with a sense of intense emptiness in their life. There has been many years of inner conflict, guilt, hurt, grief, despair, resentment, confusion and/or tension surrounding their deepest personal issues. It is connected with feelings of hopelessness, inadequacy, helplessness and self-rejection. They see no possibility of relevance or effectiveness from the Cosmic realm.

They have disharmonious attitudes towards parts of themselves that they don't want to deal with. They are consciously very loving, supportive and kind, but they repress their personal feelings, in a long-suffering low self-esteem pattern. They are a conservative controller and feeling-avoider/denier "serve-aholic" who is suffering with deep emotional disappointment while being systematically self-sacrificing. They give too much, and they don't take care of themselves, as they play out the "Rock of Gibraltar" pattern that got started as they became the "family hoist" in their dysfunctional family.

They carry all the problems and never complain, believing that they deserve this fate. They seek to ignore their inner pain by attending continuously to others' needs. In effect, they don't want to live any more, and they are manifesting a death wish. They are the product of a rejecting yet exploitative dysfunctional family who made them feel responsible for all that went wrong in the family, about which they were unable to do anything.

****

"Futility feelings." They have strong feelings of failure and incompetence, with little sense of self-accomplishment. They believe others are right, and that they are wrong. They have a deep sense of inner worthlessness that they compensate for with unstinting service while they bury their profound rage at their whole life pattern. They repress their negative feelings, especially their anger.

There is deep hurt and long-standing resentment arising from frustrated plans and felt blockages by other people or circumstances. There have been great troubles and sorrows that they have had to suffer silently and stuff. They have a deep secret or heavy grief eating away at the self in a "What's the use?" orientation. They come from a demoralizingly dysfunctional family.

****

"Hot hates." They are carrying deep-seated hatreds of the world around them and of the people in it. They feel they are in a rotten situation, and that they always have been. They hate it, and they see no way out of it. But they are afraid to express their rage about it or to find an outlet for their creative energy. There is considerable unresolved hate, revenge desires, envy, jealousy and anger that is expressed subtly, subterraneanly and subconsciously in such things as passive-aggressiveness, errors of omission, self-inconveniencing and guilt-induction. They were subjected to systematic subtle and subterranean attack by a hostile family.

****

"Love-aholic." They are an ambivalent love-seeker who never really is able to connect or to let love in. They are suffering from a deep loneliness which, however, they repress, for fear of "going down the tubes."

They are self-chastising and alone-feeling, due to severely critical parenting and systematic victimization in childhood. They are suffering from loss and hopelessness, morbid fears, abandonment-depression and deprivation-resentment.

Not uncommonly, the illness is precipitated by the loss of a loved one on whom they were very dependent, and on whom they waited hand and foot, sometimes years previously or symbolically. It trips off a sense of loss of purpose and a deep sense of despair.
****

"Seething volcano." They are sitting on a lot of fulminating fury, and they have made a lifestyle of acting on these feelings. They are a "long-suffering victim" a "cruel world," a "pseudo-saintly sufferer," and/or an "avenging angel" who is just giving people "what they deserve" because "they have asked for it."

They are completely identified with their "suffering succotash" persona, and they are unaware of their rage and revenge pattern -- except as it fits in with their rationales and justifications for their passive-aggressive vengeance orchestrations. They feel "at the so-called mercy" of a grossly unjust world, and they hate it. They are the product of an "apprenticeship training" parenting pattern in a similar family culture.

CANDIDA (Systemic yeast infection)

"Flying off in all directions." They are feeling very scattered and discombobulated. They just can't seem to get it together to run their life effectively. They come from a chaotic dysfunctional family who undermined their capacity to cope.
****

"Tie that grinds." They are entrapped and engulfed in an imposed symbiotic relationship with their mother that allows no independent life or self-manifestation. They feel very scattered and non-productive, and they are not able to own their own power.

They have a lot of unresolved negative feelings floating throughout their system, and they have a pronounced propensity to be blame-throwing regarding all this at the unconscious level.

They are demoralized and debilitated over the sealed unit *folie a deux* externally enforced life plan play-out. They were in effect not allowed to carry out their destiny or to connect or commit elsewhere -- only with Mom.
****

"Forget it!" They have a "love is a poison apple" -- "urban hermit" distrust of and in relationships. There may be sexual guilt and deep conflict with an intimate. They have been systematically prevented from manifesting any creativity, sexuality, capacity for generating for the future, or bonding in intimacy. They are the product of an engulfing, enmeshed and untrustworthy relationship with their mother.
****

"Fuming fury." They are full of frustrated rage at the futility of their life and situation. They seem to be going up the down escalator -- and losing in the race. As a consequence, there is lots of resentment-rage that results in their being untrusting and bitterly resentful in relationships. Underneath, they are infuriated at their inability for meaningful contribution, connection and commitment. Their family was intensely enmeshed, engulfing and competence-undermining, out of a "keep 'em around the old homestead" motivational system.
****

"One way street -- in." They are highly demanding and exploitative in their relationships, in a chronic taker pattern. They are untrusting and bitterly resentful in their relationships. They can also be care-coercing and severely draining. It is a case of a "whim of iron meets will of spaghetti" parenting outcome.

CANKER SORES
"Back talk." They are full of blaming, angry and judgmental attitudes, and festering words that are held back and unexpressed. They are feeling frustrated, criticized from all sides, and picked on in a situation in which they do not feel free to talk back.

They are also overburdened with excessive responsibilities and requirements that are loaded with emotional stress. They are detail-fixated, anxiously hovering, and emotionally upheavaled.

It is a pattern that got started in a family in which they were frequently "constructively criticized" in a manner that was really coming from the family's dysfunctionality.

RIGHT MOUTH CANKER SORE
"Sealed lips." They are engaged in suppression of expression of their feelings regarding how they must do things.

LEFT MOUTH CANKER SORE
"Squashed and mad." There is a lot of seething frustration over not being allowed to express or to manifest their true feelings and identity.

CENTER MOUTH CANKER SORE
"Royally pissed off." They are caught up in a generalized resentment reaction to everything in their life.

CAPILLARY PROBLEMS
"Agitated anxiety." They are immersed in conflicts over their services to others or over services they are receiving from others. It is the resultant of a "never good enough" messaging parenting pattern.

CARBUNKLE (Cluster of boils)
"Festering fury." They full of poisonous anger about personal injustices that happened long ago and/or that are happening now. It represents a long-standing suppressed intense resentment over past pains and anticipated attacks. It is a pattern that reflects an injustice-nurturing family culture.

CARDIAC ARREST (Heart-stoppage -- sudden)
"Death implant." They have just violated the ultimate taboo of really beginning to have success in work and/or love, and the result is that they have been given a clear message that it is absolutely not allowed. They were told in no uncertain terms in effect that if they ever cross the line to self-manifestation and destiny-playout, they are to "stop dead in their tracks."

It is the resultant of a severely possessive "Don't sit under the apple tree with anyone else but me" parenting pattern from the mother. Her intention was, "If I can't have you, nobody can!" at base.

****

"Cold-hearted." They are trying to squeeze all the joy out of their heart in favor of money, power, position, prestige or the like. They are not expressing and manifesting love with others -- now and/or before. They operate out of scarcity assumptions and the belief in constricting limitations.

They tend to judge themselves a failure and therefore work furiously to accomplish on the job and to dominate others. They are full of tension, anxiety, resentment and suppressed aggression. Underneath, they are a frightened child who is full of regrets, sorrow and remorse for a life wasted and a "vast wasteland" experience.

They are the product of highly judgmental and demanding parenting that never gave them the message that they were good enough.

CARDIAC ARRHYTHMIA [Irregular heartbeats] (See **ARRHYTHMIA**)

CARDIO-VASCULAR PROBLEMS
"Big Daddy." They are hyper-achievement-motivated, and they have feelings of having to "take care of the world" (either gender). They also feel that they are in a never-ending competition in which they simply must come out the winner. They are highly materialistic, impatient and agitated, and they want things done yesterday.

There is an underlying lack of self-acceptance and a felt need to "atone" or to "make up for" their personal lacks and their prior "letdowns" and "betrayals" of those people and things which are important to them.

It comes from their having been in a "family hoist" position in which the family depended on them to be the one to come through for them, and who made it very clear to them every time something went wrong that they "should have handled it."

~~~~~~

CARDIO-VASCULAR ACCIDENT (CVA) [Broken blood vessel in the heart]
"Death wish." This is the resultant of a subconscious desire to get out of here. They have a "No one cares" attitude and an intense resistance to people and things. They are rejecting life, and they would rather die than change.

They tend to become engaged in compulsive and "co-dependent compassion" and in taking on the problems of the world in a "serve-aholic" --"unsung hero(ine)" pattern. They then get burned out and resentfully burned up about the lack of recognition and support in their lives. Now they have finally reached the point where they are giving up and trying to put an end to it all.

It is the resultant of their being the "family hoist" in a severely dysfunctional, exploitative and self-immersed family.

CARPAL-TUNNEL SYNDROME (Painful nerve pain, numbing, tingling/burning in the hands/ wrists, and wrist-weakening, due to inflammation of the nerves in the wrist)
"Cope-ability anxiety." They are handicapped by a sense of learned helplessness and felt powerlessness in the face of the difficulties of the world. They end up in a situation where they are afraid to manifest their own potency, for fear of what might happen if they did.

There is a lot of anger and frustration at life's seemingly injustices, deprivations and degradations. It's a "God is Al Capone" distrust of the Universe reaction. They have the profound conviction that anything they want will be taken away from them or that it will lead to punishment/ attack of some sort.

It comes from being betrayed by the family in a "love is a poison apple" type of situation, where the original "local representatives" of the "Home Office" (All That Is) played havoc with their welfare, and they could do nothing about it. They were subjected to a "look but don't touch, much less take or partake" formative process.

CATALEPSY (Unable to move muscles)
"Immobilized." They have an overwhelming fear and terror, a feeling of utter helplessness. They feel that they are under attack from the Universe and that nothing is trustworthy. They are mentally and/or emotionally confused, they feel overwhelmed and inadequate, and they lack self-control at this point.

They are in a thorough-going escape mode, and they are doing all they can to avoid an unwanted task or experience and/or to escape a situation or person. They are experiencing an intense resistance to life, people and things, in a "super-stubbornness" reaction.

It is the resultant of having come up in an irrational and/or chaotic family in which there was nothing they could do to change the course of events, improve the situation, or provide themselves a better experience.

CATARACTS (Clouding of the eye lens)
"Walking the plank." They are seeing a dark future ahead in which there is no joy and no end in sight. They desperately want to control their future and to impose their will, but they have learned that there is no way they can do that.

As a result, they systematically seek to avoid looking at the future. There is a real fear of what lies ahead for them, along with a lack of nourishment in their experience. It is the resultant of a grimly dysfunctional family culture in which there was no way out.

RIGHT EYE CATARACT
"Ostrich." They are avoiding seeing what is coming up in their environment and in the world around them.

LEFT EYE CATARACT
"I don' wanna know me!" They have a fear of what is going on inside themselves or of what is happening or of what is going to happen to them.

CATARRH OF THE EAR (Inflammation of the mucous membrane and the hyper-section of the glands in the area)
"Feeling-avoidance." There is an emotional suppression pattern in which they try to avoid dealing with deep feelings that alarm them intensely. They tend to react to things in a hyper-sensitive manner, and they are prone to take a vaguely persecutory stance about things. Their approach tends to emphasize closing off from and not wanting to hear the "bad news" of life, especially around emotionally sensitive issues.

It is a pattern that got started in their denial-dominated dysfunctional family in which all emotional matters tended to be "swept under the rug." And yet, there were a great many emotional commotional events constantly going on. Everyone tended strongly to try to "fix the blame on Mame," to hear no evil, and to look the other way.

CELIAC DISEASE (A genetically influenced allergy ailment whereby the inside lining of the small intestine is damaged by gluten intake, often leading to arthritis, fibromyalgia, multiple sclerosis, kidney disease, lupus, hypothyroidism, osteoporosis, epilepsy, psychiatric problems, brain disorders, attention deficit and other learning disorders, and over 130 other severe disorders.)

"Assimilation problems." They are having absorption difficulties and problems in separating the wheat from the chaff, so to speak. They are having problems with analysis and with processing things. They are being hampered by distorted discrimination and disturbing distrust generated by a dysfunctional family's "magical mystery tour" pattern, and by their being subjected to systematic invalidation then and ever since.
****

"Self-worth issues." They are experiencing excessive guilt, self-doubt and self-image problems. They feel unappreciated and also unsure of their capability and value. They need appreciation, love, and understanding of the kind they never got as a child in their accusatorially invalidating family.
****

"Forget this!" They are engaged in life-rejecting fertility-, creativity-, productivity- and responsibility-avoidance, along with the denigration of the feminine and of the sacred at a very deep level. It is the resultant of extremely harsh and rejecting parenting at some level, especially from the mother.

CELLULITIS (Inflammation under the skin)
"Blame-frame." They are harboring a lot of stored anger and self-punishment over past events. They are unable to forgive and forget or to accept themselves, people and life. It got started in a severely blame-throwing family.

CENTRAL NERVOUS SYSTEM ("C.N.S.") PROBLEMS
"What's the point?" They have a profound ambivalence about being here, and it is showing up in a disruption of the intention-application system. They have had a life of disappointments, discombobulations and disagreeable experiences, and they are now seriously questioning whether to continue or not. It is the resultant of a severely dysfunctional family of origin having imprinted and programmed them with self-disruptive patterns of motivation and manifestation.

"CEREBRAL ALLERGY" (Loss of brain functions)
"God must be Al Capone!" They are feeling betrayed by the "Home Office" (All That Is). It is due to conflicts between their personal goals and desires and their Divine destiny, with a resulting disgust/distrust reaction that makes them totally unwilling to let anything within their boundaries. They feel that God has taken over their life, and they feel drained and over-demanded.

They are reacting with great repressed rage and fear to all this, and they have a deep distrust of the Universe. They have the feeling that they are being asked to "do the impossible with nothing," and they are systematically denying their personal power and self-worth in response. They are now staging a "sit down strike" by disrupting the "bio-computer's" functioning. There is much unexpressed grief about all this, and they are "desperately seeking Susan" -- the nurturing maternal love they never got as an infant.

CEREBRAL PALSY (Impaired functioning or paralysis due to congenital nervous system problems)

"Stopped in their tracks." They are getting stuck, due to paralyzing thoughts. They are fixated on a particular mind-set, mental approach and paradigmatic model. They want to "make things all right" out of a feeling of having to be the one who is responsible for everything that happens. However, they are extremely rigid in how they think that should be.

They have an intensely anxious relationship with the Universe that is full of fear, uncertainty and insecurity. They are trapped in implication-terror at the thought of things being different from what they imagine or of their having to try a new approach to things. They are also full of guilt and rejection of life, and they are not able to forgive others or themselves. They have a "God will KILL me if I do anything different!" feeling.

It is the result of a very rigid adaptation to a severely dysfunctional and frightening family who themselves manifested a very fearfully narrow viewpoint and lifestyle. They played the role of the "family hoist" who was the pivot point and support system of everything. Underneath it all, they have a desperate need to unite their family in love and acceptance.

CERVIX PROBLEMS

"Self-suppression." They feel that it is not safe for them to manifest their creativity or their generativity. They fear rejection, abandonment and attack, along with envy, jealousy and retaliation.

It comes from their experience in a patriarchal and dysfunctional family in which the feminine and the creative were greatly feared and devalued.
****

"Self-belittling." They are hassled with worries over not being good enough, along with self-denigration and self-disgust. They don't trust their feminine receptivity, and they won't surrender to themselves. They also have a fear of sex and sexual desire, along with a fear of procreativity and vulnerability. It is the resultant of an intrusively controlling, sex-ploitative and "never good enough" withholding and judgmental father -- or a similar, "animus-dominated" mother.
****

"Tripod-rage." They are operating out of intense and irresistible impulse to kick anything with three legs. It was generated originally by an equally misanthropic mother. It was then re-validated by an abusive and sex-ploitative father, along with a patriarchal culture.
~~~~~~

CERVICAL CANCER

"Powerlessness feelings." They feel overwhelmed and devastated. It is connected with feelings of hopelessness, inadequacy and self-rejection. They have disharmonious attitudes towards their personal potency -- they don't want to deal with it.

They have strong feelings of failure and incompetence, with little sense of self-accomplishment. There is deep hurt and long-standing anger arising from frustrated plans and felt blockages by other people or circumstances. They were programmed to be exaggeratedly feminine, "cute," powerless and functionally dependent, so that they could never "grow away."
****

"Fuck you all!" They are carrying deep-seated hatreds of the world around them and of the people in it. They also feel very resentful of their being a woman, of the patriarchy, and of the masculine, but they repress awareness of this.

They feel that they are in a rotten situation and always have been. They hate it, and they see no way out of it. However, they are afraid to express their rage about it or to find an outlet for their creative energy. It is the resultant of a sex-ploitative and intensely possessive misanthropic mother and a distant, absent, sex-ploitative and/or abusive father in a dysfunctional family who relied on them intensely.

CESSATION OF OVULATION (Premature)

"Destiny-protection." They have work to do in this life that does not permit the limitations and demands of motherhood.
****

"Femininity-rejection." They deeply resent being a woman, and they want to terminate the marker of womanhood. They are the product of a patriarchal family.
****

"Peter Panella." They are an "eternal girl" who wants no part of adult responsibility. It is the resultant of possessive and maturity-preventing parenting.
****

"Self-rejection." They are so disgusted with themselves that they can't allow the possibility of "passing it on," and they therefore cease the process. They come from a severely rejecting and/or neglectful family.
****

"Refusal to mother." They want no part of motherhood, period. They are repelled by their mother's example and/or life history.
****

"Mother-rejection." They are so angry at their mother that they deny her the possibility of grandmotherhood. It comes from any number of negative mothering and/or devastating childhood experiences for which they blame their mother.

CHAMEROID (Painful dime-sized ulcers on the penis or clitoris)

"Worthlessness feelings." They are suffering from feelings of inferiority, low self-esteem, ostracism and obstruction. They are ashamed of themselves, and they are troubled by their unlovely thoughts about other people that have arisen out of their life history. To make matters worse, they have strong longings which can't be realized at present.

At the base of all this is a conflict between their desire for affection and their fear of being hurt if it is sought. There is also a felt need for punishment arising out of sexual guilt. They have a lot of anxiety and fear from old, buried "gukky stuff," including from past lives.

They have the gut-level belief that the genitals are sinful or dirty, due to a sexually suppressive and shame-inducing and yet simultaneously "tantalizing tarantula" seductive-destructive sex-ploitative dysfunctional family.

CHARLES BONNET SYNDROME (C.B.S.) [Non-psychotic hallucinations caused by impaired vision sensory deprivation effects]

"I'm lonely." They are prone to being emotionally and/or socially isolated. They don't trust the world enough to form sufficient meaningful relationships and emotional contact/support/ enrichment environment. They come from an untrustworthy early family environment.

CHEMICAL POISONING

"Polluted environment." They are being invaded and permeated by damaging influences in their surroundings. They are being subjected to intolerable inputs and experiences. It is a repetition of their early environment, where their dysfunctional family imposed a poisonous atmosphere and contaminated support systems. It is a message to them to the effect of "Don't pollute yourself any more!"

"CHICKEN POX"

"Regimentation blues." They are experiencing restriction-resentment and simultaneous guilt, abandonment-anxiety, and self-disgust about their violations of the rules and regulations. They are also concerned about their resentment of the suppressive environment around them.

They are the product of an authoritarian patriarchal household in which there was an undercurrent of collusion from the mother.
****

"Waiting for the other shoe to drop." They are manifesting a "generalized dread" response. They have a lot of fear and tension, as they anticipate disaster. It results in their being hyper-sensitive, in the "finding the cat is stomping loudly" fashion. It comes from their having been buffeted about helplessly by the self-destructive lifestyle of their dysfunctional family.

"CHILBLAINS" (Painful swelling of fingers and toes caused by extreme cold)

"Et tu, Brute?" They are feeling betrayed and sabotaged by those who are close to them or who are in positions of influence over their situation. It comes from never knowing when this would happen in their family.

CHLOASMA (Brown patches on the skin, not uncommon in pregnant women)

"Going through it again." They are immersed in over-involvement and emotional commotion of an enmeshed and co-dependent nature. They are looking for the nurturance they never got. It is the resultant of a self-immersed or in other ways non-available dysfunctional and emotional-commotional family.

The frequent co-presence of pregnancy with this phenomenon is reflective of the developmental recapitulation that we go through when we raise children. We re-experience what happened to us at the same stage all the way along.

CHOLERA (Intestinal disease -- often fatal)

"Off-the-wall attacks." They fear being struck down and/or attacked from any quarter in an unpredictable and unpreventable manner. It is a feeling of being in a pervasively hostile environment which arose in a family where they were treated and regarded as the "intimate enemy."

CHOLESTEROL PROBLEMS

"Sydney Sobersides." -- "Grit and bear it" orientation. Life to them is one long problem to be solved and it is very serious business, indeed. They have the distinct impression that joy is evil, and that they are not supposed to be happy or content.

They are afraid that "God will strike them dead" if they accept joy and happiness in their life. They therefore have a tendency to be something of a "gloom-and- doom-sayer" or of a "militaristic martinet."

They may also tend to compensate with a superficial, self-indulgent, comfort-concerned, and luxury-loving lifestyle in a "live now, pay later (if ever)" pattern. It arises from a "There is no joy in Bloodville" type of dysfunctional family, where they had to maintain sanity and deflect disaster, at the expense of any form of enjoyment.

CHOREA (Involuntary movements due to central nervous system disease)

"Vast wasteland." They have had a severe sense of deprivation and degradation all their life. It results in a "self-fulfilling prophecy effect" driving away of those who might support and love them. It got started in a severely rejecting family, and they took it all personally, so that underlying this is a basic assumption that they and everybody else are no dammed good.

(See **HUNTINGTON'S CHOREA**)

CHRONIC DISEASE

"Hell no, I won't grow!" They are manifesting a refusal to change and expand, arising out of a fear of the future. They don't feel safe in the world, they don't trust the processes of the world and they operate out of catastrophic expectations. They would rather stick with the unpleasant present than to take a chance on the unknown future.

It comes from a "Leave well enough alone!" attitude inducing severely dysfunctional family system in which any intervention or change was very likely to make things considerably worse than they already were.

CHRONIC FATIGUE SYNDROME; CHRONIC FATIGUE IMMUNE DYSFUNCTION SYNDROME; C.F.I.D.S (Exhaustion and irritability that can lead to gland problems, meningitis, and immune system breakdown)

"Crushed talent." They are undergoing unfulfilled giftedness-suppression, resulting in severe despair-rage, along with emotional commotional episodes of almost psychotic-seeming proportions, and utter exhaustion comparable to Epstein-Barr.

They also find themselves being "used" by their gifts, in the form of uncontrollable outbursts and breakouts of their talents in a non-functional and often highly detrimental manner. In addition, they also go into experiences and expressions of intense mental and emotional distress and distortion that are extremely alarming and alienating. They feel possessed by these explosions, and they become quite "run amok-anxious" about it all. In addition, they often are possessed by their family, by institutions and/or by spouse figures.

They are the product of extremely possessive and oppressive parenting that got started intra-uterine. They were forbidden and prevented from doing their own thing and/or from developing their own capabilities, identity and destiny. They were instead forced into playing out their parent(s) (usually the father's) unexpressed destiny.
****

"Pooped out." They are pushing beyond their limits, and they have a dread driven fear of not being good enough, leading to an exhaustion reaction. They were draining all of their inner support, and a stress virus took hold. They are "running on empty," due to overwhelm and deprivation-exhaustion.

They have lost their sense of purpose and direction, of the desire for life, and the wind has gone out of their sails. They have developed a deep fear of life, of taking further responsibility, and of coping with any further demands. The illness can become a safe place to be, a retreat from confrontation and action. They are the product of perfectionistic parenting.
****

"Overwhelmed." They are into a hapless-helpless-hopeless victimization experience. There is an inability to self-nurture, self-appreciate and self-soothe. As a result of all this, they can sometimes end up being care-coercing of the environment, in a very belated attempt to get the fundamental nurturing they never received. But in general, they compulsively seek to minimize further damage, and to try to earn some semblance of acceptance.

The family was highly authoritarian, non-supportive and repressive-suppressive from the beginning. Often there was also physical and sexual abuse, along with the intense emotional abuse and deprivation. They were subjected to highly conditional, demanding and self-immersed parenting, and "there was no joy in Bloodville." The whole pattern could be summarized in the phrase, "*It's not allowed*!"
****

"I stink!" There is a programmed self-rejection that has resulted in a "belly up" of the immune system. It in effect works against them, as if they were allergic to themselves and to the world.

They were placed in the "family hoist" position of over-responsibility, and they were targeted with the attributed accountability for everything that went wrong in the family -- as if it was a motivated let down betrayal or a personal failure on their part.

This came about as a function of their being a gifted child living in a dysfunctional family who expected them to be able to handle all the family's problems. They played the "hero(ine)" role in the family, and they turned into a work-aholic -- achieve-aholic contribution-freak. They operated in a chronic flight-fight system arousal in childhood, in a context of continual rejection, blame-throwing, and impossible demands.

They became very accomplished and independent, with perfectionistic standards around worth-earning arising from unpleasable parenting -- they could never, ever measure up. They ended up validation-starved as a result.
****

"Hands on rescue efforts." They have a huge control trip that doesn't work that arises because they have no sense of their personal worth or value. They have no sense of entitlement, along with a tremendous over-responsibility pattern about "saving" others as their justification for existence.

There is a severe "family betrayal" delusion and a guilt-grabbing propensity, due to their being told in effect that they caused World War II. It was a "Cinderella/Cinderfella syndrome" where, due to their gifts, they actually tried to "go for the gold ring" of healing their family.

There was little nurturance, compassion or protection in infancy, which resulted in very heavy self-numbing and frantic-fanatic efforting to "make up for what they have caused." They were, in effect, abandoned at an early age by expectations of perfection and miracles.

In the meantime, the family was severely exploitative and betraying, as they overwhelmingly expected of and over-utilized them. No one taught them self-care or self-soothing in their first year of life. They were expected to care for the parents instead. They are now collapsing, out of a sense of non-deservingness and from having run out of inner resources to pull of the "rabbit in the hat" trick any more.

CHRONIC OBSTRUCTIVE PULMINARY DISEASE (C.O.P.D) [Blockage of alveoli in the lungs]

"Where's the EXIT?" They feel unworthy of taking up space and requiring resources, and they are seriously considering "checking out" as a result. When they are vulnerable or when they are under stress, the world is decidedly not a safe place, in their experience. They fear taking in life because "God will strike them dead."

It is the resultant of intense intrauterine and subsequent rejection and trauma. Their mother did not want them, and they got that message loud and clear from what they thought was the "Home Office" (All That Is). The outcome is existential guilt resulting in self-deprivation based on severe self-rejection, of potentially lethal proportions.

RIGHT LUNG C.O.P.D

"Blast from the past." They are struggling with guilt about their actions and their environmental impacts.

LEFT LUNG C.O.P.D

"Moral monster." They have deep-seated shame about who they are -- their inner values, motivations and intentions.

CHRONIC REVERSED POLARITY (Of the body's magnetic field, resulting in cognition problems, distractibility, inattention, impulsivity, hyperactivity, etc.)

"Self-alienation." They feel somehow responsible for all the ills of the world, and that they are the cause. They have "carried the world on their shoulders" all their life, starting with their highly stressful dysfunctional family.

They were in effect told that they were the source of all their family's problems, while they were actually the only one who was deflecting some of the disasters. They are an emotionally sensitive soul who was in effect overwhelmed by their super-stressed out family.

CIRCULATION PROBLEMS

"Emotional suppression." They feel that they dare not experience or express feelings such as joy, love and fascination, and that it is not right or safe to feel their feelings. They have a low interest in life, and they are feeling no reason to go on. It arises from a sense of separation from the "Source," and of abandonment by the "Home Office" (All That Is) Their experience is that "there is no joy in Bloodville," and that joy, pleasure, and love are non-existent.

They have little capacity for hope or forgiveness or to feel and express the emotions in positive ways. So they take an observing rather than a participatory role, and they are distantiated and disengaged from life. It is the resultant of an "abandonment at an early age" experience in which they have had to fend for themselves in what has been an indifferent world from very early on.

****

"Dreary destiny." They feel that they are over-burdened with responsibilities and requirements in a non-fulfilling life. They have the experience of being caught in a job they hate that they can't let go of or quit.

They have the feeling that they have to "prove themselves," but they haven't the foggiest notion how, really. They are intensely tense and deeply discouraged with their whole life.

They got started in this pattern in a family in which they had to take on responsibilities and roles for which they were ill-equipped, and which were exploitative and competence-development undermining in their nature.

~~~~~~

(See the body parts affected for more information)

BAD CIRCULATION IN THE EXTREMITIES

"Connection-prevention." They are engaged in withdrawing of involvement, vulnerability and expression of love. They are refusing to meet other people.

"CLUSTER HEADACHES" (They occur in clusters)

"Yellow alert." They have a disturbed mental condition, due to a subconscious shock or to a chronic state of guarded vigilance that has been "emergency preparation" activated by current circumstances. They labor under a great deal of guilt and fear over imagined failures and their consequences, arising from their having been the "sane one" in a dysfunctional family.
****

"Red-orange alert." They are on intense vigilance, with "hair-trigger" reactivity. They don't dare to relax because they don't trust the process of life. They have a "Stop the world!" feeling, blocking the flow of life and of their process, as a distraction or an escape operation. They are trying not to experience what is happening at this time. It is reflective of a deep distrust of the Universe that was generated by untrustworthy mothering.
****

"Out of synch." Their "internal clock" is in effect at odds with the world, resulting in their being either awake at night and sleepy during the day, or disorganized in their sleep need, or changeable in their sleep pattern.

There is much resentment-rumination and many angry thoughts about why they are angry, while not doing anything about it. They also have a lot of anxiety about things that aren't handled, including their anger. Some circumstance, relationship, situation, issue, pressure, individual or whatever that they dislike intensely but which they feel they have to put up with, to live with, is really bugging them. They have a strong habit of generating such situations and of negativity and resentment.

It comes from having been in a dysfunctional family in which much that was frustrating and insoluble occurred, in which unusual life schedules and/or disrupted internal rhythms were generated by their dysfunctional family lifestyle, and in which they were made to feel accountable and responsible for it all as a child

----

(See **HEADACHES; HEADACHES-COLDNESS PRODUCED; MIGRAINE HEADACHES**)

COLD EXTREMITIES -- CHRONIC

"Sealed off." They have a good deal of vulnerability-resentment and reachability-avoidance. They are an "urban hermit" contact-disliking people-avoider who is reticent with strangers and a poor circulator who tends to agoraphobia (the fear of going out of their home).

They are rejection-paranoid, and they are retreating into their core. They feel rejected and not understood, and that any reaching out to touch someone would result in rebuff or worse reactions. They feel like an "ugly duckling" who elicits rejection everywhere they go.

It all got started when their parents punished and rejected them for being different and formidable, because they were frightened by the individual's potency.

****

"Lost in confusion." They feel cut off from understanding their life circumstances or their direction, in a learned helplessness situation and reaction. Their family was a chaotic, repressive and power-preventing dysfunctional system.

The individual felt no recourse, and, at the same time, they deeply resented the treatment they were getting. They want to hit or strangle someone as a result, and they want to take any sort of hostile physical action against them.

But they don't want others to know how they feel, so they get "cold feet." Ultimately, however, they took it all to heart, and they have sadly settled into a resignation apathy, as an overlay on their intense desire to strike out.

COLD EARS, CHRONIC

"Awareness-avoidance." They are avoiding tuning into what is really going on in their life and in the world around them.

COLD FEET – CHRONIC

"Commitment-avoidance." They don't want to move forward and *prove* that they don't have the wherewithal to stand on their own two feet to deliver the goods. They take a conservative not-making-a-move approach.

RIGHT FOOT CHRONIC COLDNESS

"Forget it!" They are not wanting support from others or from the environment, out of a deep distrust.

LEFT FOOT CHRONIC COLDNESS

"Disaster-deflection." They are systematically vulnerability-avoidance and involvement-deflecting, in order to prevent their engaging in mayhem, they fear.

COLD FINGERS, CHRONIC

"Destiny-implementation avoidance." They feel that they are over-burdened with dreary responsibilities and/or they feel overwhelmed by life's demands. They were either effectively ignored or engulfed and competence undermined by their self-involved family.

COLD HANDS, CHRONIC

"Backed off." They are systematically disengaging themselves from the world around them. They find that being involved and vulnerable leads to too many untoward consequences.

They are the product of a severely dysfunctional, non-supportive and perhaps untrustworthy family, from whom they originally backed off.

RIGHT HAND CHRONIC COLDNESS

"Involvement-avoidance." They are avoiding contact with the world for fear of what it would do to them.

LEFT HAND CHRONIC COLDNESS
"Run amok-anxiety." They have a deep fear of their own hostile impulses and what they would do to the world.
~~~~~~

COLD NOSE, CHRONIC
"Potency-distrust." They are afraid of their personal potency and its potential consequences for them and for the ecology.

COLD TOES, CHRONIC
"Destiny-implementation difficulties." They are essentially ungrounded and/or amotivational regarding carrying out the details of their destiny. They in effect feel that they don't have the wherewithal to pull off the job of doing what is necessary to take on their destiny requirements. It is the resultant of insufficient support and preparation for life by their intensely selfish family.

"COLD SORES" (Virus-caused blister(s) inside or outside the mouth)
"Festering fury." They are suppressing angry words, and they have a real fear of expressing them. The issue is grief-rage and an underlying sense of deservingness of the loss of resources they have experienced and the ones they are undergoing now.

They are being severely bothered by the irritations, frustrations and annoyances in their surroundings. It re-activates early deprivation reactions from a time when to object to losses only made it worse, in their self-immersed or dysfunctional family.
****

"Over-burdened." They feel that they are being required to do too much, and that they are under pressure to perform. They have the experience that they are in over their head, and that they just can't meet the requirements of life. They are resentful over their situation, but they are unable to do anything about that either. They are the product of a suppressive, demanding and non-nurturing family.
****

"Love-hunger." They are feeling deeply deprived of emotional support, acceptance and love in their life. Their experience is that there is nothing they can do to improve the situation. It reactivates early deprivation reactions from a time when to object to losses only made it worse in their self-immersed or dysfunctional family.

RIGHT MOUTH COLD SORE
"Injustice-hating." They have a lot of resentment about how the world functions, and about how they were treated.

CENTER MOUTH COLD SORE
"Vast wasteland." They are experiencing despair-rage over what they can expect out of life.

LEFT MOUTH COLD SORE
"It's all my fault." They are suffering from shame and self-blame around their deprivation experiences.
~~~~~~

UPPER LIP COLD SORE

"This is an up with which I will no longer put!" They have been rescuing and care-taking for love all their life -- and they are now arriving at the conclusion that they neither deserve nor need to do this any more. They are the product of an exploitative, depriving dysfunctional family.

LOWER LIP COLD SORE

"Lucy and the football." They have the underlying conviction that any love or other support will be yanked over and over again. Their family was highly depriving in a forever promising and gamy manner.

COLIC

"Red alert." They are picking up mental irritation, impatience, annoyance, emotional upset and tension from their parents and/or their surroundings, and it is alarming and upsetting them. They are becoming irritable, angry and impatient with everything as a result. They feel like they are in a "bed of prickles."

COLLAPSED LUNG

"Deprivation city." They have a real difficulty in taking in prana, chi, ki, élan vitale, love or life energy, as a function of their prideful brutalizing misuse of energy in past lives. They have an inability to renew to the breath of life, along with a lack of enthusiasm and zeal for living. They have a real inability to take in life, and they don't feel worthy of living life fully.

They are suffering from depression and chronic grief, because they are deeply afraid of taking in life energy. They are joy-avoidant and happiness-squashing, out of a fear of the Universe. They lack Cosmic, community and conjugal contact. They feel unworthy of living fully, and they are alone, sad and non-belonging, with no sense of acceptance or approval. And they are once again in a smothering and stifling environment, with a resulting sense that life is dull and monotonous. They are the product of a withholding and non-accepting family.
****

"Barking up the wrong tree." They tend to get into consuming passionate commitments that lead nowhere, and to get into repeated devastating unrequited love situations. They have a sensitive mind and a very strong sense of justice, righteousness and generosity that frequently leads them into blind alleys and exploitative situations and relationships. They come from a dysfunctional family in which they held a parental role that led to their repeatedly trying to rescue them from their self-defeating patterns.
****

"Self-suppression." They are full of family taboos, social restrictions, moral inhibitions, unexpressed passions, strong desires and emotions. They don't have any sense of freedom or the right or ability to communicate their feelings. This was generated by a self-immersed and dysfunctional family who were exploitive, shame-inducing and enmeshed.
****

"Done in." They are engaged in a collapsing, giving up, or loss of control, due to there no longer being sufficient energy to maintain their "elasticity." There is a mental prostration, devastation and deactivation. They suffer from an inner hopelessness, depression, and a sense of no longer having control of their life. It is a reactivation of an old, familiar feeling, arising from having grown up in a hopeless and helpless position in their severely dysfunctional family.

RIGHT LUNG COLLAPSE

"Exploitation-paranoia." They are struggling with guilt over real and/or imagined abuses of energy and resources, to the point where they feel they just can't do it any more.

LEFT LUNG COLLAPSE

"Don't need!" They have shame over having needs for energy and resources, and they are prone to severe self-deprivation. It has now reached the point where they are arriving at the end of their rope.

COLON PROBLEMS (The "garbage disposal" of the digestive system)

"Processing problems." They are not being very successful in handling their personal "shit." They are experiencing an overload of side-effects, waste products, and distortions of their functioning, arising from their dysfunctional childhood. It is a healing crisis effect, in which they are being required to "clear their tubes," so that they can effectively channel their energies, resources and intentions.
****

"Won't let go." They are holding on to and refusing to let go of injustices and abuses of the past. They are being plagued by exasperated doubts, skepticism, cynicism and nihilism. They manifest over-criticality and a strong inclination to "throw the baby out with the bath." They are holding on to and refusing to let go of injustices and abuses of the past. It arises from a supremely fault-finding and dysfunctional family history.
****

"No place to put it." They are having real difficulties handling their deeper emotional issues and their side effects. They don't seem to be able to find a time or a place or a way to process and clear them. They are the product of a distorting dysfunctional family.
****

"Blast from the past." They are being inundated with emotional issues, experiences, and processing from very early in their formative period. They are in effect finding themselves caught up in their unexpressed and suppressed grief reactions to what happened at the deepest level of their emotional wounds. The foundational basis of this is their devastation from being "rejected by God" (their mother, in the very beginning of their formative process).
****

"In their face." They are being "nose-rubbed" in the effects of their self-defeating and alienation-inducing patterns trained in by their enmeshed and/or dysfunctional family.
~~~~~~

COLON CANCER

"Misery Maude." They are not happy with their life or with the world around them. "There is no joy in Bloodville!" is their continuous experience. They were subjected to continuous abuse, exploitation, wrong-making and suppression by their severely domineering and dysfunctional family.
****

"Annihilation-anxiety." They are in effect terrified of the universe, due to being attacked from conception on. They have the deep-seated conviction that they deserve all this assault, as a result of karma, because of the continuousness of the pattern in their life. They were also programmed to bring upon themselves further attacks from the environment, so that all their life they have been under siege.
****

"Broken record." They are severely closed-minded, with a very poor ability to learn life's lessons. They are the "universal expert" who won't listen to counsel, in a "My mind's made up -- Don't confuse me with facts!" attitude. They literally can't let go of yesterday's wastes, and they are full of backed up hatred. It came from an equally dogmatic, authoritarian, dominating, patriarchal and "sealed unit" cognitive system family who treated them as the "intimate enemy."
****

"Massive materialism." There is a constant demanding search for more possessions, more pleasures, and more satisfactions. They are forever striving to achieve, only to find out that achievements don't do it either. They feel that they have been denied their rightful happiness and position. They are the product of a power- and position-conscious patriarchal family who felt the same way.

(See **CANCER**)

COLITIS (Inflammation of the colon)

"Self-deprivation." They have a guilty feeling of unlovability and a great need to be loved that is prevented fulfillment by self-punishing self-denial for presumed transgressions that the outside world is unaware of. There is desperation for affection they never got that results in self-denigration and pessimism. They are apt to go off into a frenzy of self-recrimination in reaction to rejection of love from a dear one. They are over-conscientious and hyper sensitively over-conscious and conscientious, with false feelings of accountability and moral culpability. They tend to be a self-defeating loser out of an emotionally immature attitude of self-destruction.

There is a considerable feeling of undue burdens, emotional strain and loneliness. They are very insecure, and they have a very difficult time letting go of that which is over and done with.

It came from over-exacting parents who imposed an experience of intense oppression, over-responsibility, and defeat.
****

"Done in." They feel injured and degraded by some external malignant force. They want to eliminate the responsible agent. They feel they are being humiliated, and they want to dispose of it now! They are bursting with unexpressed rage, and they are super-self-suppressing. At the same time, they are fulminatingly furious about both their incapacity and their situation.

They are in perfectionistic denial of the realities that they are maintaining a "conspiracy of silence" about, and which they studiously avoid looking at. They are a basically sensitive, bright, timid, dependent, Pollyanishly denying, and passive person who is reluctant to take life on. They are indecisive, ingratiating, immature and impotent.

They are the product of a dysfunctional family in which the mother was dominating and repressive and the father was passive and jealous. There were many miseries and health hassles in the family, and yet it was a "tight little island" from which there was no escape.
****

"Ambulatory paranoid." They have an organized suspiciousness orientation derived from persecutory parenting. They believe that virtually everything is dangerous and double-dealing. They feel that they have the right to eliminate the causes of their presumed persecution.

They display extreme distrust, security-freak, and stability-seeking behavior. They are actively suspicious of the environment, and they are intensely control-imposing. They have great rageful resentment, feeling like they have received something poisonous. They want to get rid of it, to dispose of it and its source.

They come from an overtly paranoid and hostile family who hid none of their embittered, extremely suspicious and rage fully vengeful attitudes. They treated the individual as the "intimate enemy" as well.

ILEECTOMY (Removal of the colon)

"Universal expert." They are severely closed-minded, with a very poor ability to learn life's lessons. They won't listen to counsel, in a "My mind's made up -- don't confuse me with facts!" attitude.

They literally can't let go of yesterday's wastes, and they cling to the "bad old ways" intensely, with much resentful rumination about yesterday's hurts. They are not happy with their life or with the world around them, and there is a constant demanding search for "more" -- more possessions, more pleasures, and more satisfactions.

They constantly strive to achieve, only to find out that achievement doesn't do it either. "There is no joy in Bloodville!" is their experience. It all came from an equally dogmatic, authoritarian, dominating, patriarchal and "sealed unit" cognitive system family, who treated them as the "intimate enemy."

INFLAMMATION OF THE COLON

"Self-rejecting affection-desperation." They have a guilty feeling of unlovability and a great need to be loved that is prevented fulfillment by self-punishing self-deprivation for presumed transgressions that the outside world is unaware of.

Their constantly thwarted efforts to achieve affection that never get results end up in intense self-denigration and severe pessimism. They are apt to go off into a frenzy of self-recrimination in reaction to rejection of love from a dear one. There is a considerable feeling of undue burdens, emotional strain and loneliness.

They are over-conscientious and hyper-sensitively over-conscious, with a false feeling of accountability and moral culpability. They tend to be a self-defeating loser, out of an emotionally immature attitude of self-destruction. They are very insecure, and they have a very difficult time letting go of that, which is over and done with. It came from over-exacting parents who imposed an experience of intense oppression, over-responsibility and defeat.

****

"Ambulatory paranoid." They have a generalized suspiciousness orientation that is derived from persecutory parenting. They believe that virtually everything is dangerous and double-dealing. They feel that they have the right to eliminate the causes of their presumed persecution.

They display extreme distrust, security-freak, and stability-seeking behavior. They are actively suspicious of the environment, and they are intensely control imposing. They have great rageful resentment, feeling like they have received something poisonous. They want to get rid of it, dispose of it, and to destroy its source. They are the product of a rather severely paranoid patriarchal and authoritarian family who treated them as the "intimate enemy."

MUCOUS IN THE COLON

"Blast from the past." There are layered deposits of old, confused thought that are clogging the channels of elimination. They are in effect "wallowing in the gummed mire" of the past.

It is the resultant of their having had to try to make sense of the nonsensical lifestyle of their dysfunctional family. They haven't found out yet that "the war is over," and that the world is not their family.

COMA

"Lem' me outta here!" They are engaged in fearful escaping from something or someone. They are "checking out" rather than "facing the music." There is a profound sense of endangerment and of a hostile environment. They don't want to stay, but they are afraid to die. They can also be being kept here by the fears of their intimates about losing them. Their sense of lack of safety got started in their family, which conveyed to them that the world is not a safe place for them.

CONCUSSION (Stunned, dizziness, confusion, unconsciousness)

"Brain bruise." They are feeling traumatically over-demanded, over-burdened and overwhelmed. They feel at some level that they no longer have the wherewithal to rise to the requirements of the situation, and they are unwilling to continue with the impossible responsibilities they face. They therefore have "staged a walkout."

This is a new development for them, in that heretofore, they have always considered it their somehow deserved deprivation and punishment for being a "moral cretin." It is a pattern that got started when they were left to their own devices from the very beginning.

Theirs was a significantly dysfunctional and self-immersed family, and they had to fend for themselves and later to take care of and to make up for the incompetence, inconsiderateness, and irresponsibility of the parent(s). There may also have been an accusatory and/or denigrating parent, most likely the father. This developed into a lifestyle, and they are now saying, "This is and up with which I will no longer put!" It is part of a clearing out of this whole pattern.
****

"Space case." They have been living too much in their head in a high-flying idealist or ungrounded impractical manner. They need to get back to earth and deal with reality more responsibly. They were systematically under-required and over-indulged by their "keep 'em around the old homestead" family.

CONDOLYMATA (Non-contagious herpes -- viral polyps on the genitals)

"Unfit for human consumption." Their feeling is that there is something inherently "bad, wrong and evil" about them that makes them unacceptable in God's eyes, and *persona non grata* with other people. They expect rejection, and they feel in their inner core that it is somehow deserved. It got started when their mother became enraged when they weren't able to live up to her rescue expectations.
****

"Cosmic contrition." They have a massive belief in sexual guilt and the need for punishment. They are full of public shame, and they are convinced that God is going to punish them for being who they are. They are intensely rejecting of their genitals and of themselves.

It all comes from a "tantalizing tarantula" seductive-destructive entice-arouse-attack and sex-ploitative/punitive parenting pattern. They were made to feel like an utter "moral cretin" for being a sexual being.

CONGESTION

"Inner crying." They are having a reaction to an experienced rejection from someone they love, or they are undergoing an exacerbation or return of their long-standing feeling that they have never had the love they needed from someone they loved very deeply.

They feel they have somehow caused the abandonment, rejection or loss, and they are trying to "put a new ending on the old story" with "stand-ins for the original cast." They feel like they are trying to "squeeze blood from a turnip," and they deeply resent it. The whole thing got started and maintained by an intense "never good enough" parenting pattern.

CONSTIPATION -- CHRONIC

"No shit!" They are engaged in stubborn resistance to working on a problem, and they are refusing to relate to it. They have a desire to slow up or stop a condition, experience or requirement. They are intensely refusing to the flow of life and to the way things work.

They have a possessive, controlling, angry retentiveness, a pronounced tendency to refuse to release old ideas, and to end up stuck in the past. They have poverty consciousness that sometimes leads to stinginess and Scrooge-like behavior, such as grasping and hoarding of money, people or property. They grew up in a rigidly restrictive and conservative patriarchal family.
****

"No way, Jose!" They are self-suppressing, withholding, resentful and self-contained. There is a fundamental lack of trust, along with an accompanying and resulting anxiety and fearfulness. There are thoughts of restriction, bondage and immobilization or inaction. They come from an authoritarian, suppressive and untrustworthy family.
****

"Grit and bear it." They are in a situation where nothing good will come of it, but they keep grimly on with it without saying anything about it. They feel stuck permanently in the patterns of the past, and that they might as well accept that fact.

They are basically defeatist and convinced that nothing will ever work, and they fret constantly. In effect, they are "hunkering down in the bunker" and refusing to let go of the "good old ways" and the ideas of the past. Out of all this comes an embittered lack of compassion and an associated pessimism and cynicism. They feel unloved, rejected and persecuted, and they are deeply distrustful and disgusted. It all resulted from their getting into a power struggle with the mother that they have never won over or let go of.

CONSTRICTIONS (Limitations on movement possibilities)

"Holding back." They are exercising excessive self-control, and they have a real fear of letting go. The fear is of falling in love, of losing touch with reality, of losing consciousness, of being rejected, of being abandoned, of being taken advantage of, of loss of support, of loss of self, of running amok, and/or of annihilation. They are freaked out for dear life by "dangerous environment" perceptions and equally powerful self-distrust, both of which were generated by a deeply distrusting and distrust-inducing family.

CONTACT DERMATITIS (Rashes arising from coming in contact with irritants)

"Polluted environment." They are being invaded and permeated by damaging influences in their surroundings. They are being subjected to intolerable inputs and experiences. It is a repetition of their early environment, where their dysfunctional family imposed a poisonous atmosphere and contaminated support systems. They ended up believing that they deserve no better. It is a message to them to the effect of "Don't pollute yourself any more!"
****

"I hate my life!" They are in the grips of suppressed irritation or repressed anger trying to find expression. The anger is often more towards themselves than towards others. Someone or something is getting under their skin, irritating and frustrating them, upsetting them, and alarming them. It brings up old fears and insecurities that are reinforcing their repression. It also has the effect of putting a barrier between them and others. It is a pattern that got started as a child in their wrong-making and chronically dysfunctional family.
****

"Suppressed rage." They are repressing rather strong anger and aggression reactions. Who are they allergic to? There is an irritation reaction to life, and they are reacting to people instead of interacting with them. They are laboring under the effects of an unresolved aggravation or irritant from childhood. They are the product of an intensely enraging dysfunctional family which constantly subjected them to intolerable and insoluble situations.
****

"Crushed Coke can." They feel stifled and manifestation-prevented by the world around them. They have the experience of being over-run with feelings that don't seem to have any solution or any possibility of things changing. They are in effect denying of their own potency and self-worth. It came from being systematically undermined and denigrated as a child.
****

"Up against the wall." They are having an over-reaction to felt threats to their well-being, to something hostile to their welfare. They are engaged in on-the-edge functioning, due to severe emotional difficulties. They feel threatened and they fear loss, so they take a "rejecting first" approach.

They are dominated by anxiety, suppressed emotions and generalized dread. They have a deep-seated fear of letting other people know what they are experiencing or who they are. There is a deep level of fear about having to participate fully in life or about potential annihilation. They have an intense distrust of letting something inside their boundaries. They are the product of a frighteningly dysfunctional and invasive family in which you could never tell when the next piece of shit was coming off the wall. You just knew it would.

CONVERSION DISORDER (Odd physical symptoms like hysterical blindness and glove anesthesia)

"Perennial infant." They are engaged in responsibility and accountability-avoidance. They effectively refuse to "grow up," and they are an imperious demander who will not contribute. They come from a family in which they were systematically sex-ploitated. In effect, they were turned into the infantile "spouse" of the parent(s).

CONJUNCTIVITIS (Inflammation of the cornea)

"I *hate* it!" They have a good deal of anger and frustration at what they are looking at in life. There is a sense that there is no solution, that it is a "lose-lose" situation. They see no point in all of it, not to mention seeing the cosmic perfection in things.

This is not an unfamiliar situation for them, as it harks back to a lot of times when as a child they faced just such "double bind" circumstances in their dysfunctional family.

RIGHT EYE CONJUNCTIVITIS
"What am I supposed to do!?" They feel powerless in an insane world.

LEFT EYE CONJUNCTIVITIS
"I don't have what it takes." They are feeling overwhelmed and unable to cope with their personal situation.

~~~~~~

PTERIGIUM (Growth on the cornea)
"Nursing old wounds." They feel victimized and trapped in the past, as a result of their being forced to live with painful and destructive situations as a child in their intractably dysfunctional family.

RIGHT EYE PTERIGIUM
"Learned helplessness." They feel unable to cope with the requirements of life.

LEFT EYE PTERIGIUM
"Just desserts." They feel that somehow it is their "earned fate" to suffer.

~~~~~~

BLUISH CORNEAS
"Harm-anxious." They are worried and frightened, as they expect unpredictable calamities like those which occurred in their childhood in their severely dysfunctional family.

REDDISH CORNEAS
"All out." They are high-strung and passionate, and they feel everything strongly. They are also inclined to be emotional-commotional, like their family was.

YELLOWISH CORNEAS
"Running on empty." They are melancholy and depressed. They are now "reaching the end of their rope." It is the resultant of an exploitive and demoralizingly dysfunctional family.

CORONORY THROMBOSIS (Clots in heart blood vessels)
"I'm not good enough." They are feeling alone and scared, in an "I don't do enough -- I'll never make it!" feeling. The experience is that it's all on their shoulders, and, like "Atlas," if they even shrug, all hell will break loose and it will all be their fault. They are bottom line convinced that they don't have what it takes. It comes from their having been the "family hoist" in a dysfunctional family who depended on them to be the one to pull it all out of the fire.

(See **HEART ATTACK**)

CORTISOL PROBLEMS (Adrenal hormone)

"Effectance issues." They are having difficulties in dealing with the world in a functional manner. Their orientation and approach is getting in their way as they seek to make an impact and to contribute. Their family was highly disruptive in the formative process regarding their environmental interface.

~~~~~~

LOW CORTISOL

"Blown out." They are suffering from overload, threats to well being, fear, anxiety, and stress to the point where they no longer care for themselves. They feel like a defeated victim, and they have developed a giving up and emotionally indifferent attitude, along with a certain lack of courage and a nihilistic defeatism. Their experience is that everything is too much work, responsibility and devastation. They come from a highly dysfunctional and demoralizing family.

HIGH CORTISOL

"Furiously dominating." They are manifesting pronounced "authority freak" control issues. They are experiencing intense impatience, and they are engaging in hyper-irritability and demandingness. They are also manifesting unresolved enviousness and loss-paranoia. They are essentially being abusively willful in an ecologically insensitive and even in an ecologically damaging manner. They are the product of an authoritarian patriarchal household.

(See **HORMONAL PROBLEMS**)

COUVADE (The expectant father experiences pregnancy side effects, such as nausea, mood swings, weight gain and bloating) [It is French for "to hatch" or "to brood"]

"Boundaryless anticipatory joy." They are so excited about what's happening that they emotional fuse with their wife, and they experience what she is experiencing to a point. They either had a truly loving childhood or they were rather neglected, rejected and/or deprived as a child and they are eagerly looking forward to make up for all that.
****

"Frustrated futility feelings." They are intensely troubled that they can't participate and ameliorate more. They have a deep-seated need to help and desire to "make it all better." They were the "family hoist" who held everybody up in the background when they were a child.
****

"Precipitation-guilt." "I've caused World War Three!" is the feeling they are having. It is especially pronounced if they are not fully welcoming of this huge change in their life. They were always being turned to with accusations like, "Now look at what you've done!" as they grew up.
****

"Envy over her ability to bear a child." They are having something of a "male shame" reaction over the enormity of what child-bearing is. It makes them feel inferior and perhaps useless or a burden. They were made to feel somehow wrong, bad and evil for being a male, or it could be an instance of a rather universal male feeling.
****

"Look at me!" They are feeling shoved to the sidelines by this "pas de deux" relationship that is going to be around for the rest of their life. This is also a rather universal male feeling, though it could also be caused by an over-indulgent and male privilege child-rearing.

(Some of this information came from an article called "Why do some expectant fathers experience pregnancy symptoms?" By D. Barbara in Scientific American, October, 2004)

COXSACKIE VIRUS (Intense tension and pain in the upper shoulders and lower neck, along with flu symptoms)

"Straw that broke the camel's back" reaction. It is a response to having to handle too much for too long -- a responsibility overload stress symptom. Life is being intensely demanding of their system, and it produces a kind of "just barely there" functioning -- able to handle only the pressing demands of life. They feel the heaviness of life, and they have a problem carrying their responsibilities in a joyful manner. Life is a very serious business to them, and they have real difficulty "lightening up."

They tend to take on too many responsibilities and/or to feel responsible for handling everything personally. They feel that they dare not relinquish their control of themselves, the environment and the events around them, lest all hell break loose.

They operate out of a very strong sense of "Papa/Mama knows best," and they feel that no one else knows how to do things the way they simply have to be done. So "the buck stops with them," and now they are breaking down under the load.

When they finally do succumb to exhaustion, they spend a lot of time in a heap or staring at the wall or like a lump, complete with phone phobia, and amotivational syndrome for anything but the most immediate needs. The pain and tension in the neck and shoulders tends to immobilize them and make them painfully aware of their down time while everything is going to hell in a bread basket situation. All of this makes them highly susceptible to infection and re-infection with this stress-related virus.

There are, of course, a number of situations where that can happen. Here are three:

"Life calamities." The Universe has dealt them some hard cards of late and/or they live a crisis-hopping lifestyle. In either case, it is proving to be too much for them to handle right now, and it activates an underlying sense of being insufficient to the cause of living.

"Future shock." "Stop the world, I want to get off!" This reaction happens when life is laying massive amounts of change on them recently. It's a "One more change and I'll go off the deep end!" type of reaction. It tends to evoke a sense of having too much asked of them all their life.

"Healing crisis." They are manifesting high stress-vulnerability, due to emotional exhaustion connected with an intensely accelerated and deep-reaching healing process in which they are on down time while they re-program their whole "bio-computer."

This virus attack involves re-contacting very deep emotional wounds and early deprivations and degradations, with a surfacing and releasing of long-suppressed grief and mourning. It also involves re-vamping their entire belief system, emotional meaning readings, and operational functioning processes.

On top of which, it also often involves a good slug of "the hair of the dog that bit them," in the form of representations of situations that are prototypic and that evoke the same devastations as the original imprinting events. It is indicative of significant progress towards liberation from the patterns that are being cleared out in this process.

"CRABS" (Venereal disease)

"Moral cretin." They suffer from sexual guilt and they are engaged in self-punishment for sexual pleasure. Very often, this will be precipitated and/or accompanied by a feeling of engaging in and enjoying of what feels like an incestuous relationship.

It is caused by having come up in a repressive, denial-dominated, accusatory family in which there is a good deal of "shadow sexuality" going down in the form of sex-ploitative parenting or even incestuous practices of one form or another.

CREUTZFELDT-JAKOB DISEASE (Virus-caused deterioration of the brain)

"Left on a desert island." They feel that they have been abandoned by the "Home Office" (All That Is), and there have been serious conflicts between their personal goals and the Divine intent. They feel drained and over-demanded, and that their life is on a path that is completely against their will and desires. Now they have "given up the ghost," and they are full of anxiety, worry, agitation and deterioration.

It is the product of a significantly dysfunctional family in which a lot didn't make sense and yet it was justified as being "God's Will" or the equivalent. The family also did not respond to their needs, and they were forced to take over the meeting of their own needs because no one else would. As a result, they developed an abiding distrust of the Universe.

"CROUP" (Childhood cough and difficulty breathing)

"NOW look what's happening!" They are experiencing guilt and shame, as well as anxiety and tension about how unsettled things are around them. They feel they are somehow the cause of it all and that the world is an unsafe place. They feel alone in the world and responsible for all that happens. They are suppressing their feelings of anger and grief in response to the emotional tension in the family.

(See **BRONCHIAL PROBLEMS**)

CRYING -- EXCESSIVE OR CHRONIC

"Fail-wailing." They have a strong feeling of despair and pain arising from a sense of not having what it takes to make the thing work. It can also represent a sense of being overwhelmed by the environment and/or of being unfairly restricted, deprived and/or attacked by the unmodifiable environment.

It is the feeling of being at the mercy of the world of the infant, and it derives from growing up in a demoralizingly dysfunctional family in which nothing worked and nothing could be done about it.

FREQUENT CRYING

"Hapless, helpless, hopeless." They are having an impotent rage and despair reaction to what feels like a terminal or at least a permanent or long-lasting dreadful situation. It is a resignation reaction to having grown up in a thoroughly dysfunctional family in which there was nothing that could be done to make things sane.

INEXPLICABLE TEARS

"Back burner processing." They are engaged in working through of very old and unresolved grief arising from early deprivation, degradation and/or humiliation. It is now recognized by the "wounded child" within that this was not deserved after all, and that mourning for their "childhood lost" is required.

CUMULATIVE TRAUMA DISORDER (Job-related)

"Recognition-deprivation." They have an inner conflict between their felt responsibility and need to be of service vs. their need for self-commitment and enlightened self-interest. They don't know how to integrate altruistic concern and selfless service with personal need-meeting and self-advancement.

They are not able to carry on with a "What other people think of me is none of my business!" attitude. Instead, they are hyper-sensitive to criticism, and they crave recognition, appreciation, and response from the world around them.

This situation makes for considerable resentment, frustration and anger, and they are therefore very irritable and quite alienated towards the daily responsibilities they perform. There is also a considerable amount of disappointment over the lack of recognition for their performance.

The net effect is that they grudgingly carry out their responsibilities -- in a kind of "unsung hero(ine)" manner -- and they quietly fervently wish that their efforts were more appreciated.

This all arose from an exploitative and self-immersed dysfunctional family who relied on them heavily, with little realization or recognition of their life-necessity-supplying support.
****

"Competence-anxious." They have difficulty in articulating and carrying out their intentions, and they are concerned about their ability to move through life with ease and skill. They are cope-ability-concerned and lacking in confidence. As a result, they are quite uptight and rather ungraceful in their execution of things. It arises from "You can do no right!" messaging from a rejecting and demanding family.

CUSHING'S DISEASE (See ADRENAL DEPLETION)

CYSTIC FIBROSIS (Fiber in the internal organs, particularly in the form of sticky mucous in the lungs)

"Things just aren't going to work out for me." They have a thick belief that life is going to be a "downhill run." They are suffering from chronic grief and depression because they are deeply afraid of taking in life energy. They are joy-avoidant and happiness-squashing, out of a fear of the Universe generated by their misuse of life energy in their past lives. They feel unworthy of living fully, and they are forlornly alone, sad and non-belonging, with no sense of acceptance. They tend to be life-rejecting and self-disgusted.

It arose in a family in which nothing worked, especially for them. This pattern will be particularly pronounced in people who were put into a "family hoist" position or who feel they have to rescue their family to "justify their existence" or to "atone for" their "evilness."

CYSTS (Fluid-filled sacs in their body)

"Poor me." They are running the same old painful scenario in their head, and they are heavily into self-pity. They are nursing old hurts and current examples, as they are unable to heal their hurt feelings. Underlying the pattern is a guilt-based self-rejection that was generated in a blame-throwing and shame-inducing family.

DEAFNESS

"Martian anthropologist." Their soul chose to have the experience of being a "sidelines participant-observer" for this lifetime. They wanted to both learn from this experience and to teach from the wisdom it brings and from that they brought with them.

****

"Rejecting urban hermit." They have an intensely self-isolating orientation along the lines of "Don't bother me!" There is a strong stubborn streak and an isolated rejection of inputs that raises the question, "What don't they want to hear?"

They are into bull-headed stubbornness and insisting on "marching to their own drummer." It's a case of "hardening of the attitudes" and a "firmly sealed unit" pattern. They are rigidly insisting on doing things their own way -- ignoring advice and going it alone. They are intensely, self-isolating, self-centered and self-complacent. In the extreme case, self-deluding behavior can lead to paranoia.

In addition to the impact of the handicap the deafness creates, their "urban hermit" orientation arose from being regarded by their family as the cause of all their problems, so they feel that involvement and vulnerability is dangerous, destructive and very painful. They are also likely to have a serious problem of worthlessness feelings and a lack of self-love.

It is the result of unresolved past life issues that need to be examined this time. They are trying to avoid dealing with these issues again because the issues are so loaded. There is a deep distrust of the Universe for setting their life up this way and for running things the way it does.

RIGHT EAR DEAFNESS

"Take it and shove it!" They are manifesting a refusal to hear what the world is saying.

LEFT EAR DEAFNESS

"Shut up in there!" They are turning a "deaf ear" to their own "inner voice."

DEGENERATION OF THE SPINAL CORD AND MUSCLES; DEGENERATIVE DISORDERS

"I don't *DARE*!" They have severe annihilation-anxiety around the issue of seeking, manifesting and especially acknowledging success. They have the utter conviction they are "turd of the Universe," and that they have no worth whatsoever. They deny their success, and they are totally unwilling to accept their self-worth.

They are completely immobilized by "betrayal avoidance," in that the family, the mother in particular, conveyed to them very clearly that any form of self-manifestation, success in the world, and commitment elsewhere would destroy the family.

It started at a time when there was in their experience no difference between their mother and the Universe, so that in effect, they would be committing "Deicide" if they seek success or recognize their worth -- they would be destroying God and all of its creation. So to avoid that ultimate calamity, they are sacrificing themselves on the alter of "filial piety."

DEGENERATIVE JOINT DISORDER (DJD) [Arthritis-like]

"Straight-jacketed." They have a pronounced tendency to immobilization, self-criticism, lack of self-worth, fear, anger and a feeling of being tied down, restricted and confined. They are self-suppressing and self-thwarting. They are not allowing themselves to develop their full potential, due to self-distrust, leading to severe constraints. They desperately want to be free to move around and to make something of themselves, but they won't let themselves.

They feel unloved, with a resulting resentful bitterness and a critical judgmentalness towards others. They are suffering from a lot of suppressed resentment, which tends to result in passive-aggressive behavior. They are chronically anxious and depressed, and they are afraid of being angry because it is "wrong, bad and evil." They are the product of perfectionistic parenting in which in effect they could never measure up.
****

"Unfit for human consumption." They are feeling rejected for what they are, in the sense of being totally unappreciated. They are feeling very victimized and put upon, and they experience a lack of love. They feel somehow that they will never receive the acceptance, validation and affection they need. They are the product of a systematically rejecting family system.
****

"Fight or flight." They are immersed in a strong reaction to their situation, and they are chronically anxious. They feel that things have gotten out of hand, and that they can't regain control. They feel that they can't do anything to change their circumstances, and they are utterly frustrated with the way their life is going. They have no trust of the "Home Office" (All That Is), and they feel that "It is botching the job." Underneath all this is a feeling of utter powerlessness and a severe self- and other-rejection arising from their being treated as the "intimate enemy" by their family.
****

"Repressed rage." They are full of suppressed resentment and anger and they have a strongly squashed desire to hit someone. They continuously ruminate and recriminate over their "indignities," and they cling to every item like "super-glue." They have a chronic bitterness and resentment, and they are forever sending out arrows of hatred, jealousy, general discord and other negative vibrations.

Their mind is wound up so tight in their hostile preoccupations that it grinds their whole system to a halt, and they are constantly suppressing their desire to strike out and hit people. They are pushing another person around, or they are being pushed around by another person. They are the product of an intensely hostile home.
****

"Will of iron." They have a very strong will and very strong opinions that they will not and probably cannot change. They are unbending in their expression and self-manifestation. They never let go of anything, as they try to be the "boss of the Universe" an effort to make life just the way they want it. They grew up in a highly inflexible patriarchal and perhaps authoritarian family, and they "identified with the aggressor."
****

"Rigidly fixated." They are manifesting intense and resistance to change in the direction of their life. They are unbending, locked in their position, and unable to move, out of a fear of what lies ahead and out of a refusal to surrender to the processes of life. They have a basic distrust of themselves and/or of the Universe, and they decidedly do not like the way things are headed.

As a result, there is no ease of movement in their functioning or in their moving through the changes in their life. Their force-flows of life are not fluid or flexible, and there is a lack of presence and gracefulness in their functioning.

However, the changes in direction of their life are in response to multi-life issues that they haven't been able to handle, and that now must be handled. Their reaction to this situation is based on having come up in a rigidly patriarchal and conservative family.
****

"Right and righteous." They are very blaming and critical of people, and they are convinced that others won't help them. They are quite fixed, unbending, intolerant and resistive in their functioning. They are quite angry that people won't "carry their load," so that they have to take on what they consider an unjust load.

They are full of projected self-disgust, finding in others what they most dislike in themselves. There are long-standing maladjustments and stony incrustations based on internal conflicts -- often between a desire to do something and a fear of failure. They have great resistance and emotional struggle, with habitual anxiety and fear, "negative faith," and expectations that of the worst case scenario.

They operate with a strong will, inflexible intentions, intense opinions, and an abiding inability to change with changing circumstances. They have a bad case of the "hardening of the attitudes," and they are highly rigid, opinionated and "hung up in principles." They are forcefully opinion-pushing, and they put out a steady stream of skeptical criticism. They are quite hostile, and they are always angry and tense. Calcium growths indicate the presence of hatred and a severely inflexible mind.

It all came from a "vast wasteland" and "dour destiny" type of family culture in which they never knew when something would go wrong, just that it would, sure as the sun rises. It all fell to them to do the necessaries because no one else could be trusted to do so or to do it *right*. No one was ever there for them, and since everything that went down was their fault, they also felt they didn't deserve anyone to be there for them, bottom line.
****

"Super-glue injustice-nurturing." They are feeling rejected for what they are, in the sense of being totally unappreciated. They are full of repressed resentment and anger, and they have a strongly suppressed desire to hit someone. They continuously ruminate and recriminate over their "indignities," and they cling to every item. They come from a severely injustice-nurturing dysfunctional family.
****

"Ambulatory paranoid." They are forever sending out arrows of hatred, jealousy, general discord, and other negative vibrations. Their mind is wound up so tight in their hostile preoccupations that it grinds their whole system to a halt. Underneath all this is a feeling of utter powerlessness and a severe self- and other-rejection arising from their being treated as the "intimate enemy" by their family. They are the product of an intensely hostile home.

(Also see **JOINT PROBLEMS**)

DELIRIUM (Loss of reality contact to the accompaniment of great agitation)
"Spring-release." They are engaged in a sudden outburst of repressed or suppressed deep desires or dreads. They are in the grips of that which they have systematically shoved into their "shadow" or "sat on." It is being triggered by a situation which contains elements of the circumstances which led to the repression or suppression in the first place. They are the product of an oppressive and/or denial-dominated dysfunctional family.

110

DELIRIUM TREMENS ("D.T.'s" -- Alcohol withdrawal symptoms of anxiety, sweating, hallucinations, trembling, etc.)

"Run amok-anxiety." They are afraid of "losing it" in such a way as to result in catastrophic acting out and its results. They are also accessing their "shadow" and their subconscious/unconscious/collective consciousness -- particularly the terrible/terrifying aspects thereof -- and they are overwhelmed with implication reactions.

It is the result of a severely dysfunctional addictive family system in which there was a great deal of denial, suppression and repression required in order for everyone to continue functioning.

DEMENTIA (Loss of mental functions)

"Take this job and shove it!" They are manifesting a refusal to deal with the world as it is, out of an enraged helplessness and hopelessness. They feel overwhelmed by the requirements of life and unable to cope any more.

There is a great deal of bitterness and disgust with the Universe and the "Home Office" (All That Is). There is a good deal of anger, resentment and bitterness involved here. They are tired of the fight, and they are having an "I'm taking my marbles and going home!" reaction. They kept up as long as they could, and now they have decided that enough is enough.

This is a pattern that got started early in life, when they had to face an uncaring and even hostilely demanding environment, which had a demoralizing effect on them. Their response to this set up a self-fulfilling prophecy effect in which they repeatedly found themselves in repetitions of their formative environment.

(See **ALZHEIMER'S DISEASE; SENILITY**)

DEMENTIA DUE TO H.I.V. VIRUS (Deteriorating and slowing of mental functions)

"Gradually leaving." They have a strong belief in not being good enough, with much self-intolerance, self-rejection and self-destructive potentials. There is also sexual guilt imposed by an over-possessive yet simultaneously rejecting and wrong-making mother. It is in effect a severe maternal deprivation and denigration reaction. They therefore are "following orders" and leaving the planet by self-harming degrees.

DENGUE (Yellow fever-like tropical disease carried by mosquito)

"Enough, already!" They are "blown out" and "blown away" by life's tribulations and traumas. They have the pronounced feeling that they just can't take it any more. They feel that they have been constantly attacked, accused and abused all of their life.

They have withdrawn into themselves with a "Wall of China" around their heart and their "emotional body." They have reached the point where they are rejecting their situation and life's requirements and responsibilities. They are deeply resentful of the way their life has gone, and they are on the verge of "bowing out." It is the result of having been the "family hoist" in a rejecting, wrong-making and exploitative dysfunctional family, with a resulting propensity to take on too much responsibility and to be targeted for blame and exploitation.

DERMATITIS (Skin inflammation)

"I hate my life!" They are in the grips of suppressed irritation or repressed anger trying to find expression. The anger is often more towards themselves than towards others. Someone or something is getting under their skin, irritating and frustrating them, upsetting them, and alarming them. It brings up old fears and insecurities that are reinforcing their repression. It also has the effect of putting a barrier between them and others. It is a pattern that got started as a child in their wrong-making and chronically dysfunctional family.

DETACHED RETINA

"Retinal retaliation." They are experiencing a "backlash" for insisting on seeing clearly despite severe "Don't see!" injunctions from their intensely dysfunctional and denial-dominated family. They have crossed a "taboo line" into forbidden territory of clarity of comprehension and perception in areas they were supposed to never see, and an "implanted booby trap" has gone off.

RIGHT EYE RETINA DETACHED

"I see, I see!" They saw too much of the realities of the world that was in direct contradiction of their family's world view.

LEFT EYE RETINA DETACHED

"NOW I know who I am!" They found out the truth about what and who they are, and about what their role and destiny is.

DEVIATED SEPTUM (The cartilage divider between the nostrils)

"Awareness-avoidance." They are coming from "Keep your nose out of other people's business!" programming. They found out early on that any exploration of the whys and wherefores of things led to "dynamite shed explosion" reactions when they tried to "strike a match of enlightenment" in their denial-dominated family.

They are of an intensely inquiring mind by nature, which has caused them great internal conflict, all of their life. It has also caused the deviation of their septum from its normal location and nature.

DEVIATED TO THE RIGHT

"Mind your P's & Q's!" They were given strong injunctions not to know their own inner life and nature, to focus unduly on their role in the world at the expense of their true nature.

DEVIATED TO THE LEFT

"Mind your own business!" They were not to rock the boat by noting what was happening around them, so they were in effect driven into introverted and introspective functioning to an unnatural degree.

DHEA PROBLEMS (Dehydroepiandrosterone) [Precursor or pro-hormone that triggers, buffers, interacts with, and regulates other hormones. It is a key chemical for the life process.]

"What's the use?" They are harboring deep grief and a sense of underlying despair and demoralization. They have a demoralized resignation attitude in the making or in their manifestation. And are overwhelmed by too much sorrow, and by the "running on empty" effect of a severe inequality of energy exchange with the world, whereby they put out much more than they get. They have effectively given up on life, feeling that they have no ability to determine or control anything. They feel that they are just simply insufficient to the cause, and they can't care any more.

It is a result of having carried the world on their shoulders all their life, starting with their dysfunctional family, with little or no ability to receive or to request or to require a return in kind. They were told in effect they were the source of all the family's problems while actually being the only one deflecting some of the disasters.

DIABETES – TYPE I (Pancreatic problems and insufficient insulin production)

"Boulevard of broken dreams." They are longing for what might have been in their life, and they are in a state of emotional shock. They have a deep dissatisfaction with their life, and an accompanying self-dislike. There is intense sorrow, and a sense of starving to death in the midst of plenty, of being surrounded by most of the things that have meaning without their being available to them.

They have a great deal of despairing desperation, depression and demoralization. It's a . . "but not for me" attitude that is often accompanied by a fair amount of feeling very sorry for themselves. There is no sweetness left in life for them, and there is insufficient joy in their life. They are stuck on an ideal image of what life should be like, and they feel that their quality of life has been taken away from them. They are the product of a demoralizingly dysfunctional and depriving environment.
****

"One strike and I'm out!" They have a great need to control, arising from feeling alone and on their own in an indifferent/hostile world. They operate out of fatalistic expectations of further complications and debilitations in their life.

At base, they feel they don't deserve to have their needs met, which reflects past life issues that have to be examined. They are joyless and super-serious/somber in their orientation, with a lot of worry, anxiety and fear about survival. They feel that there is an insufficiency of emotional support and/or a loss, deprivation or non-requiting of love, with a resulting starvation for affection and a suppressed grief.

This all got started when they experienced being an ejectee-rejectee-dejectee "Martian" who was a very different soul from their mother. They were at best ambivalently accepted from conception onward. They came into the world and found they had to rear themselves because no one else could or would. They became a "self-made person" who found little of relevance, nurturance or validation for them.
****

"Feel bad about my situation!" They have a need to be a "martyr," in a "share the misery" process. They utilize guilt-induction and bringing out other people's insecurities through condemnation of themselves and others in a hyper-critical stance.

They are deeply disappointed with their life, and they feel that things should not have gone the way they have. They have become rather intensely embittered and cynical in their orientation. The result is a self-rejecting and rather scathingly angry individual who now needs to re-examine assumptions about who they are and what life and the Universe are all about. They were subjected to repeated traumatic shocks in a severely self-immersed, dysfunctional and abusive/invasive/ violating family.

DIABETES -- TYPE II (Elevated insulin and insulin-resistance, with elevated glucose)

"Love-starvation." They have a desperate longing to belong, yet they are intensely emotionally insulated. They also experience much social isolation, with a resulting self-sustaining self-nurturance pattern. They are a severely self-protective "urban hermit" who was continuously blamed, in an, "If it weren't for you . . .!" pattern.

They ended up believing that they don't deserve any better, so they have withdrawn into themselves and away from emotional/social involvement on any close or vulnerable level. They have turned to self-maintaining love-substitutes such as carbohydrates, sugars and pasta and/or their body has become insulin-resistant.

DIAPHRAGM PROBLEMS (Breathing difficulties, pain on breathing, etc.)

"Lying low." There is intense self-repression and fear of expression. In addition, they have a pronounced tendency to reject reality out of a fear of what would happen if they allowed the facts of their situation to penetrate to their inner core.

They are rather shallow and lacking in depth of manifestation, due to dread of what would happen if they were to go with the flow of life. They operate in an intensely self-restrictive and self-immersed manner. It comes from having grown up in a denial-dominated dysfunctional family in which it was literally dangerous to be themselves or to experience reality.

DIGESTIVE SYSTEM PROBLEMS

"I can't take that in." There are difficulties with assimilation of experiences and inputs, due to generalized dread, repressed rage and/or despairing depression. They are the product of a family who in effect placed their needs last, and who were up to their eyebrows in continuous stress.

(See COLON PROBLEMS; ILEITIS; ILEOCECAL VALVE PROBLEMS; SMALL INTESTINE PROBLEMS; STOMACH PROBLEMS; ULCERS)

DIPTHERIA (Swollen nose and throat -- often occurring in childhood)

"In over their head." They are suffering from felt helplessness, along with a sense of powerlessness to do anything about their significant close relationships. They have much frustration over restrictions, requirements and rejections, along with abandonment-anxiety. They feel that they can't be themselves without losing the love-line support they need.

In an adult, this represents a lifelong issue that started in childhood in a suppressive and demanding family. In a child, it represents their currently living in such an environment.

DISCOLORATION OF THE SKIN (Due to blood seepage under the surface)

"Bad, wrong and evil." It is a self-accusing and self-denigrating self-rejection. They are harsh on themselves, and they feel that "There is something wrong with this picture – I'm still in it." It is the result of intensely neglectful and rejecting parenting from the very beginning.

DISSEMINATED SCLEROSIS (Patches of hard tissue throughout the central nervous system)

"I don't *DARE*!" They are experiencing severe annihilation-anxiety around the issue of seeking, manifesting, and especially acknowledging success. They have the utter conviction they are the "turd of the Universe," and that they have no worth whatsoever. They deny their success, and they are totally unwilling to accept their self-worth.

They are in effect completely immobilized by "betrayal avoidance," in that the family, the mother in particular, conveyed to them very clearly that any form of self-manifestation, success in the world or commitment elsewhere would destroy them.

It started at a time when there was in their experience no difference between their mother and the Universe, so that in effect, they would be committing Deicide if they seek success or recognize their worth -- e.g., destroying God and all Its creation. So to avoid that ultimate calamity, they are sacrificing themselves on the alter of "filial piety."

DISRUPTION OF MOTION

"Oh no you don't!" They are experiencing the effects of a severe injunction against taking action in the world. It came in early in their childhood, and it remained in force throughout their formative process.

DIVERTICULITIS (See **LARGE INTESTINE PROBLEMS**)

"DIZZINESS"

"Flying off in all directions." Reality has become overwhelming, and they have lost their sense of center, stability and groundedness. There is no feeling of balance and harmony, and mental confusion and flighty, scattered thinking due to outside pressures has resulted.

They are refusing to look things squarely in the eye, and they don't want to have to deal with things as they are. They feel threatened by life's demands and realities. It feels very unsafe to them, and that it is impossible for them to have joy in their life.

Now they are faced with a high intensity and/or high stakes decision, commitment, undertaking or experience, and they are feeling overwhelmed, overloaded and unable to cope.

It is a pattern that got started in a denial-dominated dysfunctional family in which they were required to function in the face of chaos and the refusal to deal with reality.

"DROP-FOOT" (Unable to raise their foot, due to paralysis of the calf muscles)

"Catastrophic expectations." They have a "Leave well enough alone! – It's bad enough as it is without making any further trouble!" attitude. They are immobilized with implication-paranoia. They fear taking any action, lest all hell break loose.

They are intensely growth-avoidant and excessively conservative, with a sense that their basic values and beliefs are being betrayed. They are so entrenched in their stance that they have literally paralyzed themselves.

It is the result of their having come up in calamity-courting dysfunctional family who were constantly bringing the roof down on their own heads. They found they could do nothing to deflect disaster, so they took the position that "no news is good news," and they have dug in for the long haul in a "trench warfare" experience of life.

"DROPSY" (Fluid in the abdomen)

"Holding on." They are not letting go of something or someone, and they are engaged in resistance to changes. They are hanging on to the past, for fear that if they let go, something awful will happen.

It comes from a fear that any change will result in the loss of even more in their life. They'd rather keep things as they are than take a chance they will end up with nothing -- which is what they fully expect is their "just desserts" for all the "failures of their care-taking" represented by the negative events in their family's history. The water retention is stored grief from this whole situation and life history.

****

"Over-burdened." They are carrying a heavy load on their shoulders, an over-load of responsibility. They want to share the load, but are afraid to ask for fear of alienating and losing what support they do have. They are therefore desperate for love and afraid of the loss of love.

It's a "Cinderella/Cinderfella" pattern in which they were held accountable and responsible for the needs and situations of everyone and everything in their family. The only support they got came from just that "unsung hero(ine)" role in a "serve-aholic" situation.

DYSENTERY -- AMOEBIC (Severe diarrhea caused by amoeba)

"What NEXT!?" They have a lot of anxiety about their current situation, and they are very fearful of the world. They have a lot of fear and intense anger over the "fact" that "They are out to get me." They feel attacked and endangered, and they feel powerless to do anything about it. They feel they have no authority and no clout in their world. It is a feeling that they have had all of their life, starting in a self-immersed and seemingly indifferent or even hostile family.

DYSENTERY -- BACILLARY (Severe diarrhea caused by bacteria)

"Hapless helplessness." There is a feeling of utter oppression and hopeless overwhelm. Their experience is that it is a very unjust world in which they are constantly dealt with unfairly. They feel that there is no point to trying to make things any better, because nothing ever works anyway. It is a demoralized "Why bother? It won't make any difference anyway attitude" derived from a similarly nihilistic family culture.

DYSKINESIA (Uncoordinated involuntary movements)

"Oh no you don't!" They have "crossed the forbidden line" into self-commitment and destiny manifestation, and a long-ago implanted injunction to the effect of "If you ever violate this taboo, a hex on you!" from their family has gone off. They were to never abandon the family by bonding with relevant others, developing their capacities, or moving into manifestation of their purpose.

DYSLEXIA (Inability to read -- inability to perceive written material correctly)

"Street smart." They are too concerned with pragmatic survival to pay attention to the abstract world. They were left to their own devices emotionally and/or physically as an infant and child, and the result are that they never had the leisure or the stimulation to develop their symbolic perception function adequately. The outcome is a developmental deprivation effect that results in difficulty in learning to read. They don't care whether the ball or the stick comes first -- whether it's a "b" or a "d."

RIGHT HEMISPHERE (PERCEPTUAL) DYSLEXIA [Accurate but slow]

"Canny comprehension." They had to be responsible for accurate readouts of what was going on emotionally and practically in a kind of emotional survival situation. They are intensely emotionally attuned and concerned with handling things "right."

LEFT HEMISPHERE (CONCEPTUAL) DYSLEXIA [Quick but error – prone]

"Street survivor." They learned early on to make the right moves with other people, to "fake it to make it" in a kind of handling situations any way that "got them through the night" or out of the pickle. They are intensely tuned in on the situation-handling level, including emotional issues that have to be "handled."

DYSTONIA (Slow, repetitive, sustained muscle contractions that often lead to "freezing" in the middle of an action via twisting, turning and torsion movements. It is the result of genetic problems in most cases, though some have had lack of oxygen at birth or later in life.)

"They'll KILL me!" They have a real fear of the consequences of putting it out there, involving anticipation of attack, and expectation of harmful events on the environment of the output, catastrophic predictions about what will happen within or to them, and/or a conviction that to become successful will betray their family.

Their attempt to restore some semblance of success in their life has activated an "Oh no you don't!" sub-routine designed to prevent them from ever engaging in self-committed destiny-manifestation. It is the result of the "dynamite shed effect" (where they find themselves in a pitch black space with rough-hewn boxes, skinny ropes and a funny smell, and they light a match to see where they are . . .).

They became afraid of "putting it out there" when they were a child in their denial-dominated "keep 'em around the old homestead" possessive family, in which they were never to succeed their way away from home. "So you think you got away, do you?" They were severely programmed by their family to fail in all attempts at effective functioning.

EAR PROBLEMS

"*I* know what's going on!" They have a hypersensitivity to the "music" under what's happening and/or of not being understood. They have intense receptivity and a fear of not being able to hear what the true nature of the situation is. They are carefully attuned to hear any and all information and "secrets."

They were shoved to the sidelines of their dysfunctional family early on because of their perceptivity. There they became the "objective observer," the "mediator," and the "comprehender" for the family.

****

"Don't you hurt me!" They are permanently traumatized by the nasty words they have heard, and they are fearful of criticism. They are also intensely resentful of all that rejection, negativity and pain. They therefore tend to focus on the negative, and to be unsupportive and a gossip-monger.

They are firmly fixed in their belief in their utter separateness and their "deservingness" of rejection by God because of their "negativity" and "disobedience." They are in a self-rejecting and self-isolating, in an "alone and alien" pattern. They are separately alone, alien and alienated in what feels like an unsupportive environment. This pattern got started in a family in which they could do no right and yet which looked to them to be the answer to all their problems.

****

"Forget it!" They don't want to hear any more, and they are systematically understanding-avoidant. They also want to have their outlook heard -- they want to coerce others to agree with them. They are the product of a severely denial-dominated dysfunctional family.

RIGHT EAR PROBLEMS

"I don't want to hear it!" They have a fear of and/or hypersensitivity to environmental inputs.

LEFT EAR PROBLEMS

"I don't want to know about me." They have a fear of and/or hyper-sensitivity to their personal characteristics or inner inputs.

~~~~~~

EAR PROBLEMS -- EAR CANAL

"Unclear channel." They are prone to distortions, selectivity, "creative hearing" and obstructions to their ability to comprehend what is happening around and within them. They are tending to become alarmed, enraged, disgusted or even paranoid about their role in the world and in the Cosmos. Their experience is that things are not going right, and it is significantly upsetting them.

They have had a considerable history of thwarting, deprivation, exploitation, abuse and accusation in the past, and they are afraid that it is coming back. They are the product of an ambivalent, rejecting and/or abusive dysfunctional family who programmed them to bring all manner of difficulties down upon themselves.

RIGHT EAR CANAL

"What was that!?" Their experience is that things are going awry in their world, and it is deeply alarming them.

118

LEFT EAR CANAL.

"There I go AGAIN!" They are finding that they are becoming detrimental to their own best interests of late.

~~~~~~

EAR PROBLEMS -- EXTERNAL STRUCTURE

"Conform -- or else!" They are having conflicts with the structure of society, in the form of feeling pressured to not be who they are. It's an old, familiar theme to them, since this has been the basis of much of their learning history.

RIGHT EXTERNAL STRUCTURE EAR PROBLEM

"Rebellious child." They are manifesting control-avoidance and unwillingness to "march to other people's drummers."

LEFT EXTERNAL STRUCTURE EAR PROBLEM

"Sealed unit." They are engaged in withdrawal within and vulnerability-avoidance in a retreat from involvement.

~~~~~~

EAR PROBLEMS -- INNER EAR STRUCTURE

"Inner mis-directedness." They are finding themselves engaged in self-deluding, disoriented, and/or misguided self-regulation. They are "missing the mark" rather consistently, and they are increasingly agitated about it. It reflects an intense need for re-prioritizing and re-evaluation of their life direction and manifestation. The underlying cause is a self-misleading self-direction system implanted at an early age by a possessive and simultaneously rejecting family.

RIGHT INNER EAR STRUCTURE PROBLEM

"Self-misdirection." They are being self-misleading in the manner in which they manage their life and in which they make interventions. They have the right formula for every situation -- only it isn't really right.

LEFT INNER EAR STRUCTURE PROBLEM

"Self-deluding." They are reality-redefining in a manner that is detrimental to their functioning. They are bound to beliefs learned early in life in their family.

~~~~~~

EAR WATER PROBLEMS (Water in the ears)

"Repressed grief." They are sitting on long-standing mourning for losses and deprivations from gestation, infancy, childhood and beyond. They have the belief that it is wrong, bad and evil to mourn for their hurts, pains and emotional starvation.

Or they are afraid that they would cry themselves to death or that some other calamity would result if they got in touch with the deep-seated grief. It is the result of emotional neglect, deprivation or nurturance-withholding.

****

"Great white hopes." They are in effect giving up love in their life or from some one dear to them for what they think are greater things. They are intensely ambitious, prestige-conscious, driven by inner self-rejection and/or poverty conscious. It arises from a family experience that put the fear and dread of "Skid Row," due to emotionally depriving and/or rejecting parenting -- often at the subtle and subterranean level.

****

"I don' wanna know!" There is an inhibition of the ability to develop any breadth of understanding and comprehension -- a pronounced propensity to reject wisdom. They are doing a systematic refusal to know or understand.

There is also a frustrated inability to translate their feelings and intentions into effective action. Their determination has found no place to go, and it therefore has turned into resentment, and they are rather prone to blame.

This whole pattern arises from their having been in an "associate parent" position in a denial-dominated dysfunctional family who would likely explode and "blow apart at the seams" if the individual noted or expressed any patterns, any understanding, or tried to make things work.

RIGHT EAR WATER

"Pain-avoidance." They are engaged in efforts to not experience their underlying grief about how things went and are going in the world around them.

****

"Pass." They are giving up love for external gains and concerns, due to their finding that love is a four-letter word.

****

"Pissed off." They have a lot of resentment of the way things work in the world. They have a grim determination to make things happen THEIR way. This came about when they found if they did things in the right way in their family, they could make some progress.

LEFT EAR WATER

"Pain-avoidance." They are engaged in efforts to not experience their underlying grief about their deep inner wounds.

****

"I don't need it." They are giving up love for hoped for internal benefits such as guilt-relief, expectations of inner comfort, etc., because love only led to internal pain.

****

"I'll get mine!" They have a lot of resentment about unmet needs and a fierce determination to get their needs met, come what may. Their experience was if they went after their needs in this way, sometimes it would work.

~~~~~~

EAR WAX PROBLEMS

"Self-shielding." They are backing away from vulnerability and involvement with the social environment because it is too irrelevant, painful and/or dangerous. Their experience is what is being said and what is going on with others is detrimental to their health and best interests.

They are much more comfortable with their own interpretations and way of doing things than in allowing the environment to have an impact on their lifestyle or belief system. They are a "sealed unit" who is self-determining and a "self-made person."

It is a pattern that got started when they were very young in a family in which they were the "oddball" or the "odd one out." They found that much of what went on in the family was either irrelevant or detrimental to them. Their family, in turn, often criticized and blamed them when anything went wrong, and the result is they developed an "urban hermit" lifestyle.

RIGHT EAR WAX PROBLEM

"Forget it!" They are in disengagement from the world around them on the grounds that it hurts too much to be vulnerable to the processes going on out there.

LEFT EAR WAX PROBLEM

"Plexiglas barrier." They are pulling into themselves, and they are putting up a wall around themselves to prevent any further invasions and violations of their self-system.

~~~~~~

ITCHING EARS

"Urban hermit blues." They are intensely involved in a deep-seated sense of separateness and isolation, and they feel rejected by God because of their negativity. As a result, they try to suppress or to take care of any and all of their needs, wants and desires entirely on their own.

They have a great deal of guilt and shame for having these wants, and that is now becoming quite intense as an issue. They feel that "God is not pleased" with them because they are encountering needs and desires to connect and form intimate relationships. Their experience is that this is "am strengsten verboten," (*most strictly forbidden*) yet they can't continue to suppress this growing motivation and manifestation. It is a matter of considerable conflict for them at the present time.

This whole complex developed as a function of being relied upon exploitatively as the "family hoist" while simultaneously being blamed for everything that went wrong in the family. This occurred as a function of being sufficiently superior in some way to their parents that they were subconsciously placed in the "in loco Deity" position by their family. They were literally unconsciously experienced as a "little God" who was betraying the family when they "allowed" negative things to happen.

RIGHT EAR ITCHING

"Leave me alone!" They are being bothered by inputs from the environment concerning their needs, wants and relationship-interest.

LEFT EAR ITCHING

"Vulnerability-alarm." They are being alarmed by their inner thoughts and feelings concerning the possibility of forming relationships.

~~~~~~

MIDDLE EAR PROBLEMS

"I don' wanna hear it!" They feel beset by unwanted and unwarranted criticism, judgments, prescriptions, proscriptions, interpretations, recommendations, etc. They experienced (or are experiencing) just this situation as a child in their perfectionistic, rejecting, convenience-concerned or social acceptance-focused family.

RIGHT MIDDLE EAR PROBLEMS

"Shut up!" They are systematically shutting out critical comments from the environment.

LEFT MIDDLE EAR PROBLEMS

"Tuning out." They are refusing to listen to their own inner critic.

~~~~~~

"PLUGGED" EAR(S)

"I don' wanna know!" There is an inhibition of the ability to develop any breadth of understanding and comprehension -- a pronounced propensity to reject wisdom. They are doing a systematic refusal to know or understand of late.

There is also a frustrated inability to translate their feelings and intentions into effective action. Their determination has found no place to go, and it therefore has turned into resentment, and they are rather prone to blame.

This whole pattern arises from their having been in an "associate parent" position in a denial-dominated dysfunctional family who would likely explode and "blow apart at the seams" if the individual noted or expressed any patterns, shared any understanding, or tried to make things work.

RIGHT EAR "PLUGGED"

"Reality-resentment." They have a lot of resentment of the way things work in the world. They have a grim determination to make things happen THEIR way. This came about when they found if they did things in the right way in their family, they could make some progress.

LEFT EAR "PLUGGED"

"I'll get mine!" They have a lot of resentment about unmet needs and a fierce determination to get their needs met, come what may. Their experience was if they went after their needs in this way, sometimes it would work.

~~~~~~

RUPTURED EARDRUM

"Blown up." They have been severely traumatized by what they have heard. They feel that the negativity experienced is thoroughly deserved, and that they are totally demoralized by their sense of shame and accountability, not to mention their utter rejection by God, as they experience it. It comes from being severely overloaded with responsibility and accountability as a child in their severely dysfunctional, abusive and denial-dominated family.

RIGHT EARDRUM RUPTURED
"Environmental distrust." They have the experience they can't believe what they have heard about how the world works.

LEFT EARDRUM RUPTURED
"Self-rejection." They feel that they caused World War II, and they are taking the information they have heard as validation of that.

(See **EAR PROBLEMS -- EAR CANAL; EAR PROBLEMS -- EXTERNAL STRUCTURE; EAR PROBLEMS -- INNER EAR**)

EATING DISORDERS
"Turd of the earth." They are utterly disgusted with themselves, and they are convinced in their guts they are utterly worthless, evil and deserving of severe rejection punishment. There is an intense emptiness inside that reflects a desperate need for the maternal nurturance they never got.

They are strongly self-rejecting, punishment-seeking and "self-purifying" in a desperate effort to "balance the moral budget" and to "earn the God Housekeeping Seal of Approval." They are a love-aholic who is deeply depressed and desperately despairing. There is an accompanying overwhelmed fear of life and an underlying desire to die.

They are the product of severe "smother-mothering" and "keep them around the old homestead" massive possessiveness. This was coupled with intense sex-ploitativeness, deprivation and denigration disguised as great affection.

(See **ANOREXIA; BULIMIA**)

"E-BALL VAPOR" POISONING
"Oppression." They are being subjected to external domination to which either they are either surrender in fear or they are violently resisting. They are suffering from vulnerability to negative suggestions from others. It is the product of their having been reared in an oppressive and invasive family.

~~~~~~

POISONED TO DEATH
"Snuffed out." They were so crushed by the environment that they were driven over the edge by it.

****

"Shit happens." Sometimes things just show up. It's the result of the "random generator," which sets off events that are neither the result of the Divine Intent nor of the play-outs of our will. The purpose is to continuously challenge us with growth-generating events. It should be noted in this regard that "shinola happens" too.

ECLAMPSIA (Internal poisoning and possibly convulsions late in pregnancy)
"Second thoughts." They have an extreme ambivalence about or an out-and-out rejection of this pregnancy. It is a profound refusal of motherhood, arising from their own severely rejecting and abusive mothering, especially during infancy. It may also involve a rageful rejection of this particular individual as an additional aggravator.

E. COLI [Escherichia Coli] (Bacteria from drinking water producing inflammation of the stomach and intestinal lining that is potentially lethal)

"Hemmed in." They feel over-demanded of, exploited and prevented from doing what they want to do with their life. They are afraid to refuse the demands for fear of rejection or abandonment, so they grudgingly carry out their imposed responsibilities.

But they dearly wish they could express their true feelings and selfhood. In the more severe cases, it involves so much self-rejection that they end up in effect sacrificing themselves to it as the seemingly only way out of their misery. It comes from having had their "love-line" contingent upon their performing "up to snuff," and upon their meeting their family's needs first.

ECZEMA (Itchy rashes on skin)

"You-eschewing." They have a lot of hurt individuality which was caused by a "Don't be you!" injunction imprinted by an ambivalent mother who was narcissistic, exploitative, punitive and possessive. They are attacking themselves before the anticipated external attack comes. They have guilt for manifesting their individuality, the feeling being that they are destroying the family who are dependent on them by doing so.
****

"Moulting." They are releasing their old thought patterns, like a snake shedding its skin. They have an "old personality" that needs to be released. However, they are having difficulty doing so, and they are tending to hang on to the past, with a resulting frustration and irritation arising from the conflicts involved. They fear the future and they expect that things will only deteriorate, due to the way things went in their dysfunctional family.
****

"Royally pissed off." They are full of suppressed resentment, breathtaking antagonism, and mental eruptions. They feel frustrated by external events, and they have a feeling of powerlessness to do anything about them.

They feel people are not helping, and that they are not being handled correctly. They feel interfered with, blocked and prevented from doing something, and they are very irritated about it. Their experience is that they can't make themselves understood, and that they probably shouldn't even try, given the stakes involved. In their experienced frustrated helplessness, they take it out on themselves instead. It is the result of having been constantly constricted as a child or conversely of not having had enough training in ecological cooperation.
****

"Alienation-starvation." They have a pronounced sense of isolation and deprivation. There is an underlying stroke-starvation and excessive need for physical contact, due to early emotional deprivation. They are super-sensitive to any loss of love, and they have a lot of hurt feelings from the past. They are repressing all negative emotions, due to fear of alienating and disapproval-eliciting. Also operative here is a strong sexual guilt that arose from "tantalizing tarantula" sex-ploitation in the context of systematic punishment for any affection-seeking or sexual activation.
****

"Persona problems." They are experiencing deep discomfort with themselves and the image they project. They are reacting by not wanting to deal with the issues involved. They want to withdraw into themselves and to just close up inside. They are hypersensitive to their environment and about themselves. They were massively messaged that what they are is "unfit for human consumption."

EDEMA (Body-wide water retention)

"Holding on." They are not letting go of something or someone, and they are resistant to changes. They are hanging on to the past for fear that if they let go, something awful will happen. They are repressing, denying or clutching to inner feelings and urges. They feel emotionally trapped in the direction they are going in, and they feel unable to emotionally assert themselves to bring any release. They had to grit and bear it in their rigidly restricting dysfunctional family.
****

"Over-burdened." They feel like they are carrying a heavy load on their shoulders, an overload of responsibility. They want to share the load, but they are afraid to ask for fear of alienating and losing what support they do have. It's a "Cinderella/ Cinderfella" pattern in which they were held accountable and responsible for the needs and situations of everyone and everything in their family, while the only support they got came from just that "unsung hero(ine)" role in a "serve-aholic" situation.
****

"Love-starved." They are desperate for love and afraid of the loss of love. It comes from a fear that any change will result in the loss of even more in their life. They'd rather keep things as they are than take a chance that they will end up with nothing, which is what they fully expect is their "just desserts" for all the "failures" of their "care-taking," as represented by the negative events in their family's history.
****

"Clutching/clinging." They have a great fear of losing something vital to their survival and acceptability as a human being. They are intensely abandonment-paranoid and approval-enslaved, and they are into severe self-suppressing and pleasing-appeasing patterns as a rejection-deflection strategy. They are also prone to highly possessive and jealous patterns in their relationships.

It is the result of being placed on very conditional acceptance from very early on. They had to earn their "love-line," which of course "meant" that "God said" that they don't deserve love, -- they "earn" it by "selling out," and then hating themselves for it.

ELEPHANTIASIS (Severe swelling of extremities and genitals, with skin-thickening)

"Shut down." They desperately need to re-center on the essentials of life, namely the need for love and joy in their life. They are handicapped by an inability to release past memories and other wastes, such as harmful habits and traits, or to defend themselves against negative thoughts. They are enormously defended against external or internal attacking agents, and they have an insulated/isolated attitude.

They are therefore "running on empty," and they have become inadequate to the cause, with the result that they have no felt need or motivation in a lazy, being-tired-of-it-all reaction to some one or some situation or some set of circumstances.

Their emotional body is in severe disrepair, and they are having real difficulties in how well they are taking care of their own needs, getting nurtured, and handling their negative feelings about themselves. They are the product of an attacking and intensely shame-inducing dysfunctional family who conveyed very clearly to them that they have no right to love and joy, and that "There's no joy in Bloodville."

EMBOLISM (Floating blood clot in their circulation system)

"Overwhelmed and immobilized." It is a feeling of being asked to do far too much. They feel inadequate to the cause and/or that the world has no right to demand so much of them. It comes from having been the "family hoist" for a dysfunctional family all through their childhood.

EMPHYSEMA (Degeneration of the lungs)

"No right to exist." They feel unworthy of living, and they have the belief that they are somehow violating the Cosmic order by being here. When they are vulnerable or under stress, the distinct impression is that the world is decidedly not a safe place. They fear taking in life, for fear that "God will strike them dead."

It is the result of intense intrauterine and subsequent rejection and trauma. Their mother did not want them, and they got that message loud and clear from what they thought was the "Home Office" (All That Is). The result is existential guilt, resulting in self-deprivation based on severe self-rejection.

RIGHT LUNG EMPHYSEMA

"Ecological concerns." They have great guilt about their actions and their environmental impacts.

LEFT LUNG EMPHYSEMA

"Shame-frame." There is profound guilt and self-disgust about who they are -- their inner values, motivations and intentions.

ENCELUCIALGIA (See PAIN IN THE ABDOMEN)

ENCEPHALITIS (Inflammation of the brain)

"God is Al Capone!" They are enraged at the Universe for the "dirty end of the stick" they have gotten since the beginning. They have always felt like a misfit, that they somehow don't belong here. As a result, their needs have not been met, and they in turn have been unable to fit in, with the outcome that they have gotten a lot of "You don't belong here!" messages from the environment. They feel totally betrayed by the "Home Office" (All That Is). It all got started in their dysfunctional and exploitative yet wrong-making family.

ENDOCRINE SYSTEM PROBLEMS

"Careening cannon." Their life is massively out of balance and out of control. Their functioning is disrupted, disoriented and discombobulating to them and to the surrounding ecology. They are the product of a subtly or overtly chaotic dysfunctional family.

ENDOMETRIOSIS; ENDOMETRITIS (Inflammation of the womb lining)

"She-jection." She is involved in alienation from her femininity and her personal power in reaction to a patriarchal family's denigration and devaluation. She is insecure and deeply disappointed in herself, with a notable inability to manifest self-love. There is also a great deal of sorrow and grief going on that is not being handled, dealt with or acknowledged.

However, underneath all this is a great amount of frustration and a raging resentment over being dealt with in the manner she has been, and there is a great deal of frustration and blame-throwing that she tries to keep to herself. The trouble is- she ends up turning it on herself. It is the result of both the patriarchal society and a highly chauvinistic household.

****

"Blame-throwing." She is being royally screwed over, as far as they are concerned. She feels that she is being discriminated against, exploited and abused. She is the product of an accusatory and accountability-avoidant dysfunctional family.
****

"Non-self-loving." They feel that she doesn't deserve love, and that she has to make do all by herself. She therefore goes for all king's of love-substitutes like sex and sugar. She was more or less left to her own devices from the very beginning in a neglect and perhaps rejection pattern.

ENTERITIS (Inflammation of the intestinal tract)
"Going up in flames." They are intensely enraged at the world and at their life. Nothing seems to be working right, and they are infuriated about it. Everything is irritating and frustrating them, due to their having absorbed a nihilistic and embittered attitude from their family. Their attitude is poisoning them, yet they hold on to it because it seems the only realistic response to reality. It got started in a dysfunctional family where nothing DID go right.

SMALL INTESTINE ENTRITIS
"Where am I?" They can't tell which end is up, due to the distortions of their discrimination generated by their dysfunctional family.

LARGE INTESTINE ENTERITIS
"Ambulatory paranoid." They are deeply suspicious and across-the-board skeptical and critical about everything, due to having come up in a highly dysfunctional, distrusting and untrustworthy family.

ENVIRONMENTAL ALLERGY (Allergic to just about everything)
"Total control." They are completely blown out by their mania for total hands-on determination of everything. They simply have to take charge of the critical parameters of every situation. Their feeling is that if they don't, all hell will break loose. They were the "sane one" in a dysfunctional family who placed them in a parental role from very early on.
****

"Pissed off." They have an intense irritation reaction to life, and they react to people instead of interacting with them. They are utterly enraged and frustrated at their situation and at the world for making them this way. They were programmed to be self-defeating and alienating by their injustice-nurturing dysfunctional family.
****

"Suppressed feelings." They are dominated by anxiety, repressed emotions, and unexpressed rage from their childhood. They are sitting on severe emotional difficulties, and they are massively denying of their own power and self-worth. They feel that bottom line they don't deserve and can't expect any love or validation in their life. They were severely rejected by their self-immersed dysfunctional family.
****

"Arrested mourning." They have a great deal of unexpressed grief and despair over felt rejection by their parents, their mother in particular. Although their family was intensely involved with the individual, they were effectively doing it all on their own terms, not in response to the individual's characteristics and needs. So the individual is now longing for mother's love or for that of a mother stand-in.

****

"Their majesty." They have the feeling that they are very special and requiring of super "special" treatment. They were intensely "smother-loved" and sex-ploitatively "spoiled" by severely dysfunctional parents who were addicted to them.

This placed them in a position of power for which they were totally unprepared, with the resulting sense of responsibility for all that happens on the one hand, along with the pronounced tendency to abuse the power as a child, on the other. This effectively arrested their development to the point where they are now incapable of coping, and they feel completely frustrated.

EPILEPSY

"Fear-freakout." They have a sense of persecution and pressure from the environment, along with a feeling of great struggle. They are being overloaded in what they can handle, and they want to opt out. However, a considerable amount of this overload is due to their exaggerating events in their mind. They are displaying a rejecting of life and certain violence towards themselves. They are also very agitated about what they regard as the "ship of fools" surrounding them, and they tend to become arrogant and think they know more than anyone else. They have a good deal of rage about all they encounter.

There is also a hidden fear amounting to severe "run amok-anxiety" and agitated anticipation of a potential homicidal rampage from themselves. There is an extreme need to escape from the experiences of life, along with a great fear of the expectations of society. They have tremendous competence-anxiety and profound cope-ability-anxiety. There is a pronounced sense of being out-classed and overwhelmed by the world, along with a tremendous resentment of their situation. The convulsions are fear paroxysms and intense resentment-energy releases.

It came from having too much expected of them, either for what they were capable of or for a child. There was much performance-conditional love and a resulting rejection. In the more intense cases, the mother operated as a "psychic vampire" who sucked their juices all the time. If the epilepsy appeared in childhood, it added to the sense of their being incapable and "broken brained," which only fueled the flames of the situation.

****

"Self-punishing." They have an inordinate need to flagellate, castigate, and castrate themselves. They therefore consistently engage in various forms of violence against themselves. They want to get the hell out of here, or at least to withdraw from the fray so they don't have to be required of any more. They come from a severely undermining, negating and punitive family who convinced them that they "caused World War II."

(See **SEIZURES**)

EPSTEIN-BARR VIRUS (Continuous exhaustion)

"Crushed talent." They are experiencing unfulfilled giftedness-suppression, resulting in severe despair-rage, along with emotional commotional episodes of almost psychotic-seeming proportions, and utter exhaustion comparable to Chronic Fatigue Syndrome.

They also find themselves being "used" by their gifts, in the form of uncontrollable outbursts and breakouts of their talents in a non-functional and often highly detrimental manner. They go into experiences and expressions of intense mental and emotional distress and distortion that are extremely alarming and alienating.

They feel possessed by these explosions, and they become quite "run amok-anxious" about it. In addition, they often are possessed by their family, institutions, groups, "friends," and/or by spouse figures.

They are the product of extremely possessive and oppressive parenting that got started intra-uterine. They were forbidden and prevented from doing their own thing or from developing their own capabilities, identity and destiny. They were instead forced into playing out their parent(s) (usually the father's) unexpressed destiny.

****

"Pooped out." They are pushing beyond their limits, and they have a dread-driven fear of not being good enough, leading to an exhaustion reaction. They were draining all of their inner support, and a stress virus took hold. They are "running on empty," due to overwhelm and deprivation-exhaustion.

They have lost their sense of purposes and direction, of the desire for life, and the wind has gone out of their sails. They have developed a deep fear of life, of taking responsibility, and of coping with any further demands. The illness can become a safe place to be, a retreat from confrontation and action. They are the product of perfectionistic parenting.

****

"Moral monster." There is a programmed self-rejection that has resulted in a "belly up" of the immune system. It in effect works against them, as if they were allergic to themselves and the world. They were placed in the "family hoist" position of over-responsibility, and they were targeted with the attributed accountability for everything that went wrong in the family -- as if it was a motivated let down betrayal or a personal failure on their part. This came about as a function of their being a gifted child living in a dysfunctional family who expected them to be able to handle all the family's problems. They played the "hero(ine)" role in the family, and they turned into a work-aholic -- achieve-aholic contribution-freak.

They became very accomplished and independent, with perfectionistic standards around worth-earning arising from unpleasable parenting -- they could never, ever measure up. They ended up validation-starved as a result.

****

"Desperate vindication-seeking." They have a huge control trip that doesn't work that arises because they have no sense of their personal worth or value. They operated in a chronic flight-fight system arousal in childhood, in a context of continual rejection, blame-throwing, and impossible demands.

There is a severe "family betrayal" delusion and a guilt-grabbing propensity, due to their being told in effect that they caused World War II. It is a "Cinderella/ Cinderfella" syndrome where, due to their gifts, they actually tried to "go for the gold ring" of healing their family. In the meantime, the family was severely exploitative and betraying, as they over-whelmingly expected of and over-utilized them.

No one taught them self-care or self-soothing in their first year of life. They were expected to care for the parents instead. They therefore have no sense of entitlement. There was little nurturance, compassion or protection in infancy, which resulted in very heavy self-numbing and frantic-fanatic efforting to "make up for what they have caused." They were, in effect, abandoned at an early age by expectations of perfection and miracles.

They are now collapsing, out of a sense of non-deservingness and from having run out of inner resources to pull of the "rabbit in the hat" trick any more.

****

"At effect." They are into a hapless-helpless-hopeless victimization experience. There is an inability to self-nurture, self-appreciate and self-soothe. As a result of all this, they can sometimes end up being care-coercing of the environment, in a very belated attempt to get the fundamental nurturing they never received.

The family was highly authoritarian, non-supportive and repressive-suppressive from the beginning. Often there was also physical and sexual abuse, along with the intense emotional abuse and deprivation. They were subjected to highly conditional, demanding and self-immersed parenting, and "there was no joy in Bloodville." The whole pattern could be summarized in the phrase, "It's not allowed!"

ESOPHOGUS PROBLEMS

"Self-protective self-starvation." They are having real difficulties with their food intake control system. They are deeply conflicted about whether and what to take in, in the way of nutrients. They are having a severe "love is a poison apple" deep distrust reaction to all that the Universe provides them. Yet at the same time, they need to eat, and they are in constant conflict about this issue. It got started when they encountered rage/hate-contaminated nourishment and nurturance in the beginning of their life as a function of severe ambivalence or rejection by their mother.

ESTROGEN PROBLEMS (Female hormone, particularly in regard to the sexual system)

"Femininity issues." They are conflicted or having difficulties in the manifestation of their female nature. They are either rejecting the feminine or they are feeling unfeminine or unable to manifest the feminine. They are the product of a patriarchal feminine-rejecting family.

~~~~~~

LOW ESTROGEN

"Yang-banging." They have a rather pronounced propensity to suppress the feminine and/or to over-manifest the masculine in their approach and orientation. They come from a feminine-denigrating and power-abusing patriarchal and perhaps authoritarian family.

HIGH ESTROGEN

"Over-receptive." They tend to be too easily influenced, persuaded or intimidated into accommodating to what is being desired, suggested or imposed in their functioning. They may also be excessively sexually active or accommodating. Their family was rather exploitative and sexualizingly dysfunctional.

EUSTACHIAN TUBE PROBLEMS

"Belongingness issues." They have deep concerns about their right to be here, taking up resources and space, and about fitting in, finding a niche and being relevant. It is the result of being more or less left to their own devices from infancy onward, emotionally and perhaps even physically.

EXHAUSTION

"Walking zombie." It reflects that a great deal of "back burner processing" of a healing and/or re-organizational nature is going on. In this situation, the pattern is one of being able to rise to the demands of situations as they arise, but then there is a "collapse into a limp noodle" like a puppet with its strings cut, when the situation no longer requires their resources. In such a situation, it could be characterized as being "emotional exhaustion."

****

"Wiped out." They are experiencing depleted resources arising from having committed all available reserves to the situation. If this is a chronic pattern, it represents frantic avoidance of dealing with what ails them, due to a denial-based dysfunctional family history.

OR: It is indicative of a "serve-aholic" lifestyle arising from feelings of having to "make up for" something "missing" or "wrong" with them, an impression that came from a shame-inducing family. In any case, they need to work on being able to receive help, and on being able to engage in co-creative endeavors.

(See **FATIGUE**)

EXOSTOSIS (See **SPINE PROBLEMS**)

EYE PROBLEMS

"Unable to see the truth." They are having difficulty in seeing clearly the nature of reality. They are wearing distorting filters and lenses that make it hard to see the world. They have self-protective screens so the world can't see their soul or who they are and what they see.

In short, they are lacking insight into the realities of things, and they don't see the truth. They also fail to see their own personal worth, nature and potency. It stems from their not liking at all what they see in their life, and from their fear of the future.

It is denial-domination -- systematically avoiding seeing something they need to see and that they need to take action on in regards to their life -- they don't want to comprehend what they are witnessing. All of which, stems from a highly dysfunctional family that literally forced them to adopt the strategy of not seeing clearly in order to survive.

****

"I" problem. It is hard for them to see themselves clearly, and that leads to either inflation and arrogance, or to deflation and self-denigration. They are apt to demonstrate blind prejudices, self-aggrandizement and insensitive egocentricity, or to be constantly facing situations of infidelity, betrayal, exploitation, losses, deceptions, devastations and degradation.

They are also apt to be prone to self-belittling, to being hyper-humble, and to find themselves in demeaning situations, with a striking lack of self-protection. The net effect is that they lose sight of where they are going in their life. They also don't see things in the same manner as others, which often results in conflicts.

They have little or no insight or understanding, and they have to operate under a cloud of confusion -- the "magical mystery tour" pattern, as in "I just don't see why. . ." There results a bondage to fixed ideas and a reluctance to see the true nature of things.

One outcome of this is that they are prone to be non-comprehending and non-forgiving of others. They are fearful, agitatedly nervous and awareness-avoiding, which leads to limited vision, self-masking and "mental squinting" -- with all the attendant events. They are the product of an incomprehensible and reality-distorting severely dysfunctional family.

RIGHT EYE PROBLEMS

"Things are awful!" They have deep conflicts about what they see going on in the world around them.

LEFT EYE PROBLEMS

"Oh my Gawd!" They are involved in intense emotional reactions to what they see happening to and within themselves.

~~~~~~

"BLOODSHOT" EYES

"Overload." They are under a lot of pressure. They are over-worked, exhausted, handling high stakes requirements, processing very deep issues, facing a heavy situation, or any combination of such circumstances. They are apt to become careless and accident-prone under these conditions. It is a re-run of an old, familiar pattern, as they were the "sane one" in their dysfunctional family.

****

"Grief-relief." They are processing deep grief that is being set off by current circumstances. It is a clearing out of some of the early devastation generated by neglect, ejection and/or rejection in childhood.

RIGHT EYE "BLOODSHOT"

"How'm I doin'?" They are having issues with how they are handling things. This often arises from a history of wrong-making from their family.

LEFT EYE "BLOODSHOT"

"Internal schisms." They are wrestling with conflicts about their inner feelings, commitments and motivations. They were often made to feel shame or guilt for their experiences and intentions.

~~~~~~

"BURNING" EYES (Due to internal toxin release)

"Emotional exhaustion." It is arising from processing very early foundational ego damage. The individual is now clearing out the earliest self-relationship-distorting experiences, and they are changing their entire operational system as a result. This depletes almost all available energy.

****

"Over the top." They are having a "straw that broke the camel's back" resentment reaction. They are a "serve-aholic" co-dependent who is going over the top in intolerance for any further exploitation, deprivation and humiliation. It got started in a severely dysfunctional family in which they learned that the only way they could meet their needs was to serve to survive.

****

"Depths of depression." The present situation is activating their underlying anaclitic depression (due to emotional abandonment in infancy). They are dealing with severe deprivation-grief and rejection-pain. It arises from having been functionally neglected as an infant.

RIGHT EYE "BURNING"

"Oh my Gawd!" They are encountering despair, depression and/or resentment over what they see going on in the world around them and its implications.

LEFT EYE "BURNING"

"Where is this taking me!?" They are undergoing despair, depression and/or resentment about what has happened to them, what is happening to them and/or the impacts and implications of either.

~~~~~~

"DRY EYE" (Disruption of the tearing process in they eyes)

"Denied broken heart." They are out of touch with their feelings. Indeed, they have in effect turned their emotions off in reaction to all the hurts they have experienced. They avoid and are in effect unable to contact or express their considerable grief.

They systematically misperceive their early life, so as to not activate their great sorrow and pain. They are the product of a depriving and demoralizingly dysfunctional family.

****

"Hate-spate." They are engaged in a highly spiteful refusal to see with love. They would rather do anything than to forgive or forget anything, and they have very angry eyes. They are incapable of compassion or comprehension, and they are full of rage and judgmentalness.

They are the product of a hostile and self-serving family in which they were treated as the "intimate enemy."

RIGHT "DRY EYE"

"Baleful glare." They have a hateful orientation towards the world around them.

LEFT "DRY EYE"

"You're gonna pay for this!" They are having a rageful reaction to what is happening to them.

~~~~~~

"EYE FATIGUE"

"Constraint-fighting." They are operating out of resentful rebellion and refusal to restrict themselves to an over-narrow point of view or range of reaction and manifestation. It is often a response to an oppressive situation and system, in their present external situation and/or within themselves and in their lifestyle and life history. It is a "This is an up with which I will no longer put!" reaction.

The pattern got started in their overly demanding and restrictive family system. They did not have the right to self-determination and self-expression to a significant degree, and this was placed in the context of moral imperative, intense responsibilities, perfectionistic expectations and/or intensely intrusive/invasive parenting.

EYE PROBLEMS IN CHILDREN

"I don' wanna know!" They are harm-alarmed about what is happening in their family. They are afraid of the implications and ramifications, and they are tending to use their imagination to conjure up the worst case scenario. They do not want to see what is going on in the family and in their life, because it's too overwhelming for them. It occurs when there are chronic or situational stresses happening in their family.

"EYE STRAIN" (Fatigue generated by restricted range or amount of fixation and/or movement)

"It's being done to me!" They are trying too hard to find answers outside themselves, rather than looking inwards for resolution. They are avoiding their inner core, and they are seeking to locate their resources externally. It is a self-avoidant pattern that got started in their rejecting and denial-dominated dysfunctional family.

****

"Constraint-fighting." They are engaged in resentful rebellion and refusal to restrict themselves an over-narrow point of view or range or reaction and manifestation. It is often a response to an oppressive situation and system either in their present external circumstances and/or within themselves and their lifestyle and life history. It is a "This is an up with which I will no longer put!" reaction.

The pattern got started in their overly demanding and restrictive family system. They did not have the right to self-determination and self-expression to a significant degree, and this was placed in the context of moral imperative, intense responsibilities, perfectionistic expectations and/or intensely intrusive/invasive parenting.

EYE "TWITCHES"

"Attack anticipation." It represents a fear of the return of the kind of emotional and/or physical assaults they experienced as a child in their authoritarian and/or dysfunctional household.

RIGHT EYE "TWITCHES"

"Duck!" They are helplessly anticipating the return of the environmental assaults they had as a child.

LEFT EYE "TWITCHES"

"Mea culpa." They are re-experiencing the internalized emotional attacks they developed in childhood.

~~~~~~

INFLAMMATION OF THE EYEBALL

"Right and righteous." They are engaged in an outraged indignation stance of anger and frustration with the "moral cretins" around them. They do not want to see what is happening around them.

Underneath all this approach is a deeply disturbing questioning of their self-worth. They are the product of wrong-making and judgmental parenting.

RIGHT EYEBALL INFLAMMATION

"Outraged." They have a lot of rage at the state of the world.

LEFT EYEBALL INFLAMMATION

"Grudge-grinding." They are outraged at how they are being treated by the world.

~~~~~~

ITCHING EYES

"Ostrich response." They are engaged in awareness-avoidance and denial-domination, as they become threatened by the prospect of fully seeing their life history, current situation and intended destiny on their way to enlightenment. There is a lot of fear, grief and guilt coming up as an impending breakout from self-limitations looms on the horizon.

They were never supposed to get this far, and there is a feeling of family-betrayal, self-endangerment, and oceanic grief as they progress along.
****

"Outta my sight!" There is a deep sense of irritation by what they see, and they want to rub it out of sight. They find what they are encountering utterly intolerable, and they react to their indignation by trying not to see the full implications and ramifications of what is happening. They are the product of a demoralizingly dysfunctional family where looking the other way was the only way to survive the tumult and torture of their experiences.

RIGHT EYE ITCHING

"I don' wanna know." They have a big fear of seeing too much about the world around them.

LEFT EYE ITCHING

"Let's pretend." They are avoiding knowing their personal characteristics and their situation.

~~~~~~

MACULA PROBLEMS (The yellow spot on the retina which is the optic nerve exit)

"Retinal retaliation." They are experiencing punishment for insisting upon seeing clearly despite severe "Don't see!" injunctions from their intensely dysfunctional and denial-dominated family.

They have crossed a "taboo line" into forbidden territory of clarity of comprehension and perception in areas they were supposed to never see. An "implanted booby trap" has gone off.

RIGHT EYE MACULA

"That's enough out of you!" They saw too much of the realities of the world in contradiction of their family's world view.

LEFT EYE MACULA

"Future-fear." They found out the truth about who they are, and about what their role and destiny is, and it is greatly alarming them.

~~~~~~

"PINK EYE" (Inflammation of the eye ball)
"Right and righteous." They are engaged in an outraged indignation stance of anger and frustration with the "moral cretins" around them. They do not want to see what is happening around them.

Underneath all this approach is a deeply disturbing questioning of their self-worth. They are the product of wrong-making and judgmental parenting.

RIGHT "PINK EYE"
"Outraged." They have a lot of rage at the state of the world.

LEFT "PINK EYE"
"Fed up." They are enraged at how they are being treated by the world.

~~~~~~

PRESSURE BEHIND THE EYEBALLS THAT THREATENS THEIR EYE-SIGHT
"Hardening of the attitudes." They are having a problem with exacerbating pressures from long-standing hurts. They are having a difficult time being tender, loving and trusting of themselves and others as a result of a harsh and judgmental patriarchal family. They are therefore losing sight of the Truth of things and of the Divine design.

RIGHT EYE PRESSURE
"Hard-hearted." They have developed a rather cold and uncaring approach to the world.

LEFT EYE PRESSURE
"Self-blaming." There is an underlying relentless unforgivingness towards themselves.

~~~~~~

READING VISION PROBLEMS WITH ADVANCING AGE (Presbyopia-- increasing difficulty seeing things close up)
"Implication-anxiety." Because of the increasing sophistication and world-wisdom associated with being older, the ramifications and indications of whatever is examined in detail range far and wide, often in threatening implications. The result is a "too much to handle" reaction.

In addition, a "mental squinting" process develops in which "I don' wanna know!" becomes their motto. They seek to avoid knowing too much in detail about anything as a self-reassurance strategy. They have a severe fear of losing control and a pronounced propensity to avoid trauma, such as becoming aware of an incestual history.

The tendency for this defense to show up was programmed in their denial-dominated dysfunctional family when they were growing up.

~~~~~~

RED-RIMMED EYES
"Overload." They are under a lot of pressure. They are over-worked, exhausted, handling high stakes requirements, processing very deep issues, facing a heavy situation, or any combination of such circumstances.

They are apt to become careless and accident-prone under these conditions. It is a re-run of an old, familiar pattern, as they were the "sane one" in their dysfunctional family.
****

"Grief-relief." They are processing deep grief that is being set off by current circumstances. It is a clearing out of some of the early devastation generated by neglect, ejection and/or rejection in childhood.
****

"Victimization-resentment." They feel inexorably done to by their environment, and there is a great deal of rage about that. There is a strong element of resignation-despair involved here, the feeling that nothing is going to get any better, and that there is nothing to do to make it any different. It was an exploitative, accusatory and disempowering household.

RETINA PROBLEMS
"Retinal retaliation." They are experiencing physical problems for insisting on seeing clearly despite severe "Don't see!" injunctions from their intensely dysfunctional and denial-dominated family.

They have crossed a "taboo line" into forbidden territory of clarity of comprehension and perception in areas they were supposed to never see. And an "implanted booby trap" has gone off.

(See **CATARACTS; CORNEA PROBLEMS; GLAUCOMA**)

RIGHT EYE RETINA
"Don't see!" They saw too much of the realities of the world that is in contradiction of their family's world view.

LEFT EYE RETINA
"Aha!" They found out the truth about who they are and what their role and destiny is.

(See **DETACHED RETINA; INFLAMMATION OF THE RETINA**)

137

FACIAL "TIC" (Involuntary movements of the facial muscles)

"Faltering persona." They are sitting on a good deal of repressed "violation-rage." They feel invaded by the environment. They have a bad case of "run amok-anxiety" and an equally intense fear of the world knowing what they feel and want to do. They are deeply afraid of being seen for who they really are.

They have a history of being wrong-made, rejected and judged. They are the product of a subtly but inexorably intrusive, invasive, oppressive and emotionally abusive dysfunctional family.

RIGHT SIDE FACIAL "TIC"

"Wizard of Oz." They are afraid of being found out a "fraud" who is "faking it to make it" as a function of their competence- and confidence-undermining family.

LEFT SIDE FACIAL "TIC"

"Just desserts." They feel as if something is fundamentally wrong with them that will lead the world to become invasive.

~~~~~~

RIGHT EYE "TIC"

"Don't get caught!" They are afraid that they will be discovered looking at or seeing what is happening around them.

LEFT EYE "TIC"

"Cover-blow." They are deeply alarmed at the possibility of being "discovered" for "who they are" at base.

RIGHT MOUTH "TIC"

"Social anxiety." They are intensely competence-anxious about social situations and interpersonal inter-relations.

LEFT MOUTH "TIC"

"Keep your mouth shut!" They have real difficulty dealing with their fear of expressing their feelings about their life and the world around them, especially regarding other people.

(See "TICS")

FALLOPIAN TUBE PROBLEMS (Particularly blocking)

"Intense tension." They are "up tight, out of sight" a lot of the time. They have a high-strung temperament that drives them to freak out and over-react to things. They live in constant agitation and "red alert" alarm and vigilance. They come from a fear-inducing dysfunctional family in which they had to fend for themselves in the midst of chaos and discombobulation all the time.

"FALSE PREGNANCY"

"Frustrated generativity." They feel thwarted in their capacity, need and/or desire to create for the next generation. There is a sense of being prevented from manifesting their destiny. It is an old, familiar story, in that their life has been devoted to the care and maintenance of others at their own expense. It got started in a suppressive and exploitative family.
****

"Yes-No!" They are intensely ambivalent about sexuality and motherhood -- they both want them and are afraid of them. They don't want the responsibility of motherhood at some level, and they don't want to be sexual and a mother at the same time. It is a result of intensely possessive mothering as a child.
****

"I want out!" They are intensely determined to "opt out of the fray," to withdraw into "kids and kitchen" as an escape from the demands and threats of involvement in the community. It is a play-out of an underlying "perennial child" pattern that got started in an over-indulgent and under-requiring family, so that they never learned the art of coping effectively. They want to be "taken care of," with no responsibilities to speak of.

FATIGUE

"Down-timing." They leave the clock and the refrigerator running while they shut down everything else and they re-vamp the entire program through internal processing that takes up all their energy and leaves them emotionally exhausted.
****

"Why bother?" They are dealing with resistance, boredom and lack of love for what they are doing with their life. They have opted for disengagement, accountability-avoidance and responsibility-deflection, in a kind of burnout reaction. It arose from a family system in which they received a "Don't be you!" injunction, and in which anything they did led nowhere.
****

"Struggle-addict." They are constantly over-extending, over-exerting, and putting themselves through deprivation, prolonged worry, tension and stress and strain. This pattern got its start in a similar household.
****

"I'll try anything!" They have a self-destructive susceptibility to suggestion, dissipation and repeated shocks to the system. They came up in a neglectful, perhaps chaotic dysfunctional family, and the only way to get any support was to do something self-destructive.
****

"Wiped." They are wrestling with weariness with life and inner tiredness, because of having to cope or keep going. There is a sense of being inadequate, incompetent, and ultimately uninterested. They have lost their sense of purpose, and they have gone into an amotivational syndrome. It comes from having grown up in a chronically severely dysfunctional family. They have reached the point where their experience is, "Enough, already!"

(See **EXHAUSTION**)

FATTY TUMORS (Fatty deposits and growths)

"Protective padding." They are feeling a need for a buffer to absorb the "slings and arrows of outrageous fortune." They feel unduly vulnerable and unable to do anything directly about it, so they are "padding up" to weather the storm. It arises from a history of feeling powerless in an irrational and assaultive environment, as a function of their highly dysfunctional family.
****

"Preventive medicine." They have a bad case of "run amok-anxiety," the fear that they will somehow "get out of hand." They have a deep distrust of their personal power, of their motivational system, and of their environmental impact. It is the result of a "NOW look what you've done!" and "Can't you do ANYTHING right!!??" parenting pattern.

"FEMALE PROBLEMS"

"She-jection." They are denying of their self, and they are rejecting their femininity and the feminine principle. It comes from their having been shamed for being female by their family, due either the mother's self-shame, the father's rejection, and/or their wanting a male child.
****

"Father-fury." They are full of resentment over felt betrayal by their father. Her experience was that he was never there for her, that he promised and reneged, that he was hopelessly inadequate, that he was abusive and/or incestual or he put her through other experiences of betrayal. She might also have picked up her mother's "tripod-rage" (the irresistible urge to kick anything with three legs). In any case, she has real problems dealing with the concept of having a mate.
****

"Self-suppression." She is into power-avoidance to appease their mother, to reassure her that she will not abandon her. Her mother had become symbiotically attached and dependent on her, and she programmed in a strong "Don't leave me!" injunction.
****

"Abandonment-paranoia." They are having attachment problems and abandonment-anxiety issues arising from being threatened with abandonment, as either a disciplinary technique and/or as a means of preventing her from "growing away."
****

"Slave-rage." She has a lot of resentment over her "serve-aholic" pattern that was generated in a dysfunctional family who placed them in the "family hoist" position, or who fostered a rescuing pattern.
****

"Running on empty." They are having endurance problems arising from the feeling that they have to "sell themselves out" to survive. This pattern developed in a household who made it very clear to her that if she intended to have any support, she was going to have to "pay for it in spades."
****

"Sexual competence-anxiety." They are hung up and obstructed in their ability to relate to their sexuality. They feel insufficient to the cause in their ability to function and perform in the sexual arena.

It arises from a considerable amount of fear and/or guilt about sexuality. They are the product of a sexually denigrating and inhibiting family, or they are the victim of excessive and invasive sexualizing parenting.

FEMALE SEXUAL AROUSAL DISORDER

"Dry river bed." She can't lubricate or she can't enjoy it. It comes from possessive imprinting and "tripod-rage" induction from her mother and/or from a history of aversive experiences in the sexual arena ("Tripod -rage" is the irresistible urge to kick anything with three legs).

FETAL ALCOHOL SYNDROME (Severe birth defects due to alcohol ingestion during pregnancy)

"Time out." They are manifesting a "forced vacation" life involving their having to be in effect completely taken care of. The intention of the soul is to use this life as one in which they assimilate what has gone on before in preceding lives. It is probable that there is also some karma with alcohol.

FEVER

They are "burning up" with intense anger and stored resentments. They have a lot of agitated worry and hurry in fear of anticipated outcomes. There is a severe lack of harmony and internal conflict.

They are highly resistant to the processes of life, and they are hung up in the past. They have a fear of or reaction to loss of friendships, and they suffer from abandonment feelings.

It represents an experienced return to the uncertainties and frustrations of their dysfunctional and abandonment-threatening family.

FIBRILLATION (Abnormally rapid heartbeat)

"False alarms." They are a self-made person who believes that they are all they've got. They have felt cut off from the environment and the Universe all their life, and they therefore have felt that they have to handle everything on their own hook, unassisted.

This activates moments where things are getting out of control and beyond their coping capabilities. And these bring on anxiety attacks -- complete with heart palpitations. It is the result of never having received love and merging as a child.

(See **"LONG QT" SYNDROME**)

FIBROIDS (Benign tumors and cysts in the womb)

"She-jection." They are caught up in rejection of their femininity, sexuality, womanhood and/or motherhood. They are manifesting accumulated or unexpressed guilt, shame, inner confusion or past hurts and abuse that they attribute to their being female. They are the product of a patriarchal and/or misogynistic household.

****

"Betrayal reaction." They are nursing a hurt from a partner, in what feels like a repeat of the devastations of her childhood. There has been a blow to the feminine ego that represents to her a re-run of her experience with her father and/or "proof positive" of the accuracy of her mother's "tripod-rage" (the irresistible urge to kick anything with three legs).

Michael J. Lincoln, Ph.D.

FIBROMYALGIA

"Pooped out." They are pushing beyond their limits, and they have a dread-driven fear of not being good enough, leading to an exhaustion reaction. They were draining all of their inner support, and a stress virus took hold. They are "running on empty," due to overwhelm and deprivation-exhaustion. They are the product of perfectionistic parenting.
****

"Self-distrust." They have great difficulty coordinating the execution of things, integrating ideas of what is wanted to be accomplished with the pragmatic results they are getting, and dealing with the feelings and issues associated with success.

They have little sense of competence and confidence, and they are having significant problems in mobility, flexibility and activity. They have to be extremely inhibited and careful in all they do, or they become immobilized and unable to take action.

It arises from an intensely self-distrust-inducing "keep them around the old homestead" family, who programmed them to be super-successful (for the family only), and to otherwise fail. They have "come up a cropper" in reaction to the re-emergence or continued confrontation with this dilemma, and it has effectively immobilized them.
****

"Hunkering down in the bunker." They are resistant to new experiences and they are refusing to move on in life. Unsettling memories are surfacing, and they must confront issues that have been long put off.

There is either guilt-based self-punishment and atonement-seeking or a belief in bondage, victimization and victim-tripping. In any case, they have a deep feeling of separation and sinfulness, arising from massive guilt-induction their family for who they were, what they needed, what they did, and what went down in the family.

FIBROUS GROWTHS

"Self-disgusted life-rejection." They have an intense feeling that "Things just don't work out for me." They have a jaundiced feeling that the Universe is biased against them, partly arising from their misuse of life energy in past lives. Underneath, they have the rueful feeling they are getting their "just desserts."

It arose in a highly dysfunctional family in which things never worked, especially for them. It is also probable that they have had to rescue their family and family stand-ins to "atone" for their "evilness."

"FIFTH SYNDROME" VIRUS (Dry red rashes. Highly contagious)

"Resentful resignation." They are having the experience that life is being quite difficult, and they are feeling very little, if any joy. To them, it feels like everything is one long series of responsibilities, traumas and drudgeries of late. It is a result of a "grimly getting through the night" dysfunctional family.
****

"Roughed up." They feel that they are being rubbed the wrong way. There is a sense of being attacked, a fear of harm, and an abiding insecurity. They are the product of a wrong-making family, especially by their mother.
****

"Off with their heads!" There is a chronic intense irritation over delays of gratification, along with a notable lack of patience. They have a pronounced tendency to "infantile tyrannosaurus" tactics. They are simply unable to be cooperative, to be respectful, to be considerate or to go with the flow of life.

They were not allowed to differentiate and to individuate as a child, and they are still symbiotically attached to the "tie that grinds" with their mother, with mother-substitutes and with mother stand-ins.
****

"Unfit for human consumption." They are plagued by embarrassment and shame for who they are. There is considerable guilt about their feelings, intentions, motivations, actions and/or thoughts. It is the result of having been made to feel "bad, wrong and evil" for having wants, needs and desires as a child.

FISTULA (Hole from surface to an inner organ)

"Slow DOWN!" There is a blockage in the letting go process, due to a great deal of fearfulness. They have no trust in the flow of the Universe, and are trying to put the brakes on things. Theirs was a singularly frightening family in which nothing was as it seemed, and in which much that was horrifying happened in a "happenstance" manner.

"FLESH-EATING VIRUS;" "FLESH-EATING BACTERIA"

"Bad, wrong and evil." They have a very strong belief in being somehow "negative," "immoral," and "unclean." They also feel that they aren't good enough, and that they deserve just punishment for their "wrong-being." They have a "rotten" self-image that is massively self-rejecting. They believe that God hates them. They are immobilized by their limitations, both genuine and imagined, and they can't handle life at all.

They are the product of a devastatingly destructive and denigrating dysfunctional family who were abusive, sex-ploitative and shame-inducing. There never was any love in their life.

"FLOATERS" (Free-falling dark bits in the ocular fluid)

"Obfuscating issues." Their perceptions, experiences and reactions are being distorted by residual vestiges of unresolved traumas and conflicts. They are the product of a severely dysfunctional, traumatic and/or rejecting family.

FLU; INFLUENZA (Virus infection)

"At their mercy." They have feelings of being under the influence of malevolent forces and of being weak and helpless. It may reflect the vulnerability feelings that accompany times and processes of great change. There is a fear of attack from others and of taking life in fully. They have a strong experience of lack of support and protection. They have the experience that the very worst is about to happen to them.

There is a good deal of internal conflict, confusion and susceptibility to suggestion, especially from the "world of agreement" or the "group mind" or "statistical proofs." They are the product of severely untrustworthy parenting arising out of a deeply fearful family.
****

"Urban hermit." There is an insufficient involvement and interaction, an "among us but not of us" pattern. Underneath is a buried rage and hatred for their being so alone, alien and alienated. It comes from a family in which they could do no right as the unrecognized and unacknowledged "family hoist" upon whom everyone depended and whom no one supported, sustained or validated.

FLUCTUATING ILLNESS (It comes and it goes)

"Magical misery tour." They live with chronic uncertainty and confusion as to the nature of reality arising from a "magical mystery tour" family experience. It led them to "dance with the second" as the "only way to fly," with the result they are highly susceptible to momentary variations in stimulation and situation.

FRACTURED SKULL

"Shattered paradigm." Their entire framework about who they are, what things mean and what it's all about has been massively assaulted. They feel that they are "adrift without a rudder," and they have no guidelines regarding where things are going or what's important. They have lost their sense of direction and values, and they feel betrayed by the "Home Office" (All That Is).

They don't have the wherewithal to rise to the responsibilities of their situation, and they want to "abdicate their position." It arises from finding that the fundamental premises of their life were founded on the "shifting, drifting sands" of a dysfunctional family's value and operational system, and they want out of it.

FREQUENT ILLNESSES

"Taking their marbles and going home." They feel completely outclassed and overwhelmed by life, and that they simply don't have what it takes. This results in across-the-board stress reactions covering virtually all the bodily systems, which then sound off the signal that something has to be done. So they are going with the "pulled out of the action" strategy fulltime.

They are the product of a severely dysfunctional family which generated overwhelmingly stressful situations continuously, and that was so self-immersed and chaos dominated that they couldn't or wouldn't pay attention to the individual unless they developed an illness. As a result, they have taken this on as a lifestyle.

"FROST BITE" Damage to extremities caused by freezing)

"Done in." They feel severely betrayed and sabotaged by those who are close to them or in positions of influence over their situation. They have been seriously damaged and/or endangered by the significant others in their life. There is even the possibility of having been lethally dealt with by such individuals. It comes from never knowing when this would happen in their severely dysfunctional and potentially dangerously destructive family.

"FROZEN SHOULDERS"

"Hell not, I won't go!" They have reached the point where "This is an up with which I will no longer put!" regarding the responsibilities and requirements of life. They feel that they have been over-loaded and under-supported and unappreciated, and that they are in effect doing a "sit down strike"

The problem is that they can't opt out of service, in addition to which the cumulative damage to the shoulders has reached severe physical form. They therefore find themselves in deeper water than ever.

There simply HAS to be a reasonable solution worked out so that they don't undo the physical healing, and to avoid re-plunging themselves into their over-responsible role any more. It all got started when they were placed in the "family hoist" and the "sane one" position in their severely dysfunctional, self-immersed and at-risk family.

FUNGUS

"Swamp growth." They are refusing to release the damages of the past, thereby letting their formative traumas dominate their life. They are immersed in stagnating beliefs and stationary strategies. The feeling is, "The war is *not* over," that nothing has substantially changed since they developed their ways of being and doing things in a dysfunctional family.

That, in turn, is a self-fulfilling prophecy effect generated by the assumption that nothing has changed, so that there is continuous re-validation of the assumptions and strategies of the past. They are the product of a severely self-defeat-programming and demoralizingly dysfunctional family who were effectively intractable and unstoppable in their patterns.

GALL BLADDER PROBLEMS.

"Implied opposites." They are seeking to project the opposite of what they are feeling inside, as a survival compensation strategy, so they have a way of being rather arrogant and seemingly prideful. They tend to be rather strong to a certain inflation of their self-importance, and to a pronounced propensity to be judgmental. They have a pronounced tendency to be power-seeking, dominating and intensely expecting in their relations with the world.

They are intensely inclined to feel that they are surrounded by a ship of fools, and that they are not in a position to do anything about it, with a great deal of resulting resentment. They are apt to be rather self-immersed, willful and indignantly outraged at the way the world treats them. They have also ended up systematically grudge-holding and injustice-nurturing. They come from a patriarchal, position-conscious and supercilious family.

****

"Relationally shut down." They don't trust love, and they have had a history of deeply disappointing relationships. They are rather insulated and isolated in their relations with other people. They have retreated within themselves to a state of sad solitude and loneliness.

They were systematically held accountable for things that went wrong in their dysfunctional family, and they were accused and blamed a lot. They reacted with an over-compensating self-defensiveness, resulting in a lot of quiet or overt discord in their family. They felt effectively totally rejected.

****

"I wanna go home!" They have a "beset" experience of life, and they are greatly agitated about the ways of the world. They find other people frustrating, disgusting and untrustworthy. They feel that things are just totally unjust. They just want to get the hell out of here, pronto. They were rejected from the womb on, and they have a profound self-rejection and self-revulsion at base as a result.

GALL STONES

"Bitterness." These stony encrustations are due to "stony thinking," and they are rigidly unyielding in their orientation. They are apt to be prideful, judgmental and full of hard thoughts and condemning attitudes. They have real difficulty in being flexible in their thinking, and they emanate a certain compulsive contemptuousness.

They are rather bitterly resentful, they are compassionless and unforgiving, and they are holding back their love from their intimates. They have gone within into a state of intense solitude and loneliness, self-sorrow and self-pity. Underneath all this is a severely suppressed intense depression and grieving, in reaction to a severely depriving, rigid, "right and righteous" wrong-making family.

GANGRENE

"There is no joy in Bloodville." They are laboring under mental morbidity and poisonous thoughts that are often arising from guilt or shame over illicit intentions or actions. They have a severe lack of self-love, sense of security and felt right to move forward.

It arises from an intensely disintegritous and dysfunctional family who both generated gross situations and then blame-threw and guilt- and shame-induced intensely. It was a continuously poisonous environment.

GIARDIA (Toxic parasite that induces nausea, vomiting and diarrhea)

"I should have . . ." They feel personally accountable for everything that happens, particularly the negative outcomes. Their family held them accountable and responsible for all that took place. All eyes turned in their direction when anything ever went wrong -- which was frequently. They were made very aware that they had no right to commit to anyone or anything but continued maintenance of the family.

They therefore have a great deal of guilt about sexuality, success and intimacy, as if these were "evil deeds." Any move towards independence, self-empowerment and significant involvement/contribution/commitment activates annihilation-anxiety and betrayal-guilt.
****

"At effect, not at cause." They feel dominated by the world, and they are therefore feeling dominated, as they let their emotions run them, rather than taking charge of their reactions to thing. They also tend to give their power to others, letting them take over everything in their life.

It is a pattern that got started with "never good enough" parenting, to which they reacted with frantically tying over and over again to get the "God Housekeeping Seal of Approval" -- and they forever failed to do so, of course.
****

"Run amok-anxiety." They are deathly afraid of their own personal power at the deep subconscious level. They are in effect terrified of releasing themselves in their internal resources and potency.

They were the reversed role parent, the "Sane One" and the "family hoist" in their severely dysfunctional family, who became extremely dependent upon and afraid of them. They were therefore subjected to much fear-induction about owning their own potency and about committing to their own destiny. It operates as an embedded "foreign body" that leads to delusional self-destructive stuff induced from the environment, as they experience it.
~~~~~~

PRECIPITOUS EXTREME AND DEMORALIZING NAUSEA, VOMITING AND DIARRHEA FROM GIARDIA (Potentially lethal)

"Facing the dragon." They are clearing the poisons from their system and purging the devastating early programming that generated deep-seated self-hatred for their potency and positivity, along with severe self-paranoia that leads to chronic underlying fear/dread. This cleansing/healing process therefore precipitates a very dangerous implication-panic reaction and a potential death-out.

"GAS;" "GAS PAINS"

"Creature from the Black Lagoon." Something in their current situation is generating a gripping fear and as yet undigested ideas, along with a sense of responsibility-overload and the associated resentment. They have a considerable amount of anxiety and agitated anticipation of aggravating developments. They are full of implication-catastrophizing and generalized dread. They have vague and intangible fears about "things that go bump in the night," the nameless terrors of which they dare not speak. It came from a "magical misery tour" family experience in which they could never tell when and what piece of excrement would come off the wall at them, just that it would.

GASTRIC BY-PASS (Stapling off part of the stomach to lower food intake)

"Emotional starvation." They have a deep-seated desperation for love that leads to excessive "soul-solace" type food intake, which results in overweight and the resulting operation to inhibit over-consumption.

In a substantial proportion of cases, their emotional issues were not healed before the operation, resulting in their reacting to the loss of food with a profound sense of deprivation, of nurturance and of soul-fulfillment. They can't satisfy their profound hunger for love, and intense depression is the likely result. It is the result of early and subsequence emotional abandonment in childhood.

GASTRO-INTESTINAL PROBLEMS (See **DIGESTIVE SYSTEM PROBLEMS**)

GENITAL PROBLEMS, FEMALE

"Moral cretin." They have worries over not being good enough, along with self-denigration and self-disgust. They don't trust their feminine receptivity. They also fear of sex and sexual desire, along with a fear of procreativity and vulnerability. It is the result of an intrusively controlling, sex-ploitative and never good enough withholding and judgmental father.
****

"Tripod-rage." They are operating with an intense irresistible urge to kick anything with three legs. It was generated originally by an equally misanthropic mother but revalidated by an abusive and sex-ploitative father, and by the patriarchal culture.

(See **OVARY PROBLEMS; REPRODUCTIVE ORGAN PROBLEMS; UTERUS PROBLEMS; VAGINAL PROBLEMS**)

GENITAL PROBLEMS, MALE

"Insufficient to the cause." They are hampered by worries about not being good enough, of not being masculine enough, of not being enough of a man, along with a fear of sex and self-distrust about their impact-intending, initiative and innovation motivation. There is also the issue of whether it's safe to be a man.

They were subjected to excessively spousal treatment by their mother, including expectations of perfection and to be the man of the house, along with significant sex-ploitation. She was domineering, possessive and wrong-making. She was afraid to express her animus, of being a man. Her father was essentially ashamed of being a man.
****

"Moral monster." They are into intense self-indulgence and self-centered "infantile tyrannosaurus" coercion or "slick dick" sleazy and sly manipulativeness. They put out continuous intrusive demandingness, instability of functioning and irresponsibility.

It arose from a severely sex-ploitative "special" relationship treatment by an intrusively possessive, over-indulgent and interference-running mother. But regardless of how and why it occurred, what goes around comes around, and the karma has now come to roost.

(See **PENIS PROBLEMS; PROSTATE PROBLEMS; REPRODUCTIVE ORGAN PROBLEMS; TESTICLE PROBLEMS**)

GENITAL "WARTS"

"Self-revulsion." They are full of guilt and self-disgust, and they believe in ugliness, especially with regard to themselves. They believe they are utterly unlovable. They have a generalized hatred, especially of themselves.

They are forever letting out little expressions of hate as they experience a spreading frustration about the future. They are bitterly cynical and angry about virtually everything at the gut level (though not necessarily consciously). They also have a felt need for punishment arising out of severe sexual guilt arising from sexually suppressive and simultaneously sex-ploitative "tantalizing tarantula" parenting.

This was part of the slyly exploitative and negative assumptive dysfunctional family system which systematically trained them to have a narrow-eyed and jaundiced view of everything, but especially of themselves.

G.E.R.D. (Gastro-Esophageal Reflex Disease [Heartburn] -- Burning distress behind the sternum, due to spasms of the esophagus or of the upper stomach, resulting in acid coming up)

"Happiness-horror." They have an intense, pervasive and clutching fear that is tripped off by their experiencing some joy or happiness. They have a horrifying sense of impending attack for "undeserved" joy.

They are getting what they want for once, and they feel that somehow they should not -- that it violates the Cosmic or moral order somehow. They are anticipating retribution for the just rewards of their efforts and essence.

It was generated in a severely restrictive, disapproving, moralistic and fear-inducing childhood. They came out of it with an intense fear of the Universe as a harshly judgmental and punitive place. There is an intense abandonment- and betrayal-paranoia based in part on past lives.
****

"Purple passion." They are intensely involved and activated over something -- love or anger that is very pronounced -- and it is scaring the hell out of them. They are operating with a pronounced injunction not to feel, and especially not to feel strongly. It is a pattern that got started in their highly feeling-suppressing and/or denial-dominated dysfunctional family.
****

"Burning to be free." They are stuffing themselves and their feelings, out of a fear of catastrophic consequences if they let go and "let fly with themselves." They are now reaching the point where "This is an up with which I can no longer put!"

It comes from growing up in a family in which it was not acceptable for them to be themselves or to threaten to grow away by becoming themselves in a destiny-manifesting manner.

GERMAN MEASLES (Mild fever and skin rash)

"They don't like me." They feel they are being excluded and picked on by their intimate circle. They feel misunderstood and unappreciated. It is a reaction to being regarded as something of an irritant or problem by their family.

GIARDIA LAMBIA (Parasitic protozoa that lodges in the intestinal lining, producing immune disorder-like symptoms)

"Self-rejection." They are having difficulties in receiving and feeling deserving. They tend to be something of a "serve-aholic" who puts their own needs last in their list of priorities. They feel that they are somehow "not good enough." It is in effect a maternal non-commitment, deprivation or rejection reaction, along with having subsequently been subjected to perfectionistic expectations.

"GLANDERS" (Swollen mucous membranes in nostrils and jaw. It comes from horses.)

"Power-paranoia." They have a fear of the responsibilities and potentials for abuse of their personal potency arising from a father-fixation. It is a reaction to being made to expect that exercise of their potentials will lead to rejection and attack by their patriarchal family, and later by the male race.

GLANDULAR FEVER (See **MONONUCLEOSIS**)

GLANDULAR PROBLEMS

"Deep-seated self-distrust." They are out of balance and in disharmony, due to their holding onto past traumatic events. They are not able to cleanse their thoughts and to purify their feelings so as to get on with life's processes.

They have difficulty integrating the significance of things, and they are in a state of continuous alarm. Their creative processes have been severely curtailed, and their self-image and ability to express their identity have been disrupted.

Their "get up and go" has "gotten up and gone" -- derailed by self-distrust and uncertainty of what to do or where to go. They are holding back for fear of setting off World War III. It is the result of a severely demoralizingly dysfunctional and perhaps dangerous family.

GLAUCOMA (Fluid pressure increase and the resulting hardening of the eyeball)

"Hardening of the attitudes." They are operating with a certain stony unforgivingness and lack of compassion for themselves and others. They are greatly alarmed by what they see coming for them as they get older and they are refusing to see accurately. They only want to see what is right in front of them.

There is an embittered reaction to their life that is being activated by exacerbating pressures from long-standing hurts. They are manifesting a long-standing generalized hostility towards the world. They have an inability to be tender and loving, due to their distrust and disgust. They are the product of a harsh and judgmental patriarchal family.
****

"Despairing disappointment." They have the distinct experience that life is one long downhill slide. They have a rather embittered and disgusted reaction to much of what happens to them. Their life seems to be a kind of treadmill in which they are slowly losing ground.

They are the product of a highly enmeshed and engulfing but simultaneously subtly rejecting dysfunctional family who did not want them to grow away. They were therefore programmed to be systematically subtly self-defeating and self-undermining in their functioning, in a success-avoidant pattern.

This, in turn, generates increasing suppressed depression and refusal to directly look at their patterns. The basic fears are that if they become aware of their situation, they will "betray" their family, and that if they self-commit, they will be ostracized or struck dead by God.

RIGHT EYE GLAUCOMA
"Hard-hearted." They are taking a cold, calculating and perhaps even cruel approach to the world, in a self-protection strategy.

LEFT EYE GLAUCOMA
"Moral monster!" They have relentless unforgivingness towards themselves.

GLUCOSDE SENSITIVITY (Abnormal immune system reaction to gluten that leads to things like asthma, auto-immune disease, cancer, chronic fatigue syndrome, dementia, diabetes type I, heart disease, hepatitis, kidney disease, liver disease, psychiatric problems, thyroid diseases, ulcerative colitis, vitiligo and over 170 other serious disorders)
"What am I *doing* here!" They are manifesting a dismayed discombobulation about the world and the way their life is going. It is the result of growing up in a vaguely overwhelmed and enmeshed dysfunctional family or of being a "visitor" from another soul pool who came here to learn and/or teach.
****

"Allergic reaction to themselves." They feel somehow responsible for all the ills of the world, that they are the cause. They are having a "get rid of the problem" reaction. It is a result of having "carried the world on their shoulders" all their life, starting with their dysfunctional family.

They ended up with little or no ability to receive or to request or to require a return in kind. They were told in effect that they were the source of all the family's problems, while they were actually the only one who was deflecting some of the disasters.
****

"Hapless, helpless, hopeless." They feel overwhelmed and unable to handle the requirements of life. They have in effect "thrown in the towel" on even trying to make it in life. They have a great deal of sorrow, deep-seated grief, and despair, and they are chronically crying on the inside. They come from a massively dysfunctional and demoralizing family.
****

"Bitterly disgusted patriarchalness." They are manifesting a life-rejecting creativity-, productivity-, fertility-, and responsibility-avoidance pattern, along with a denigrating attitude towards the feminine and the sacred. It is the result of an intensely rejecting maternal parenting pattern, with or without an accompanying severely patriarchal family culture.

"GOITER" (Enlarged thyroid gland)
"Destiny-derailed." They are feeling thwarted in life and prevented from growing. They feel totally unfulfilled and non-manifesting of their potentials and purpose. They are plagued by powerlessness feelings, and by the conviction that they are never going to be allowed to contribute what they came here to contribute. They are the product of a severely self-immersed, enmeshed and undermining family.
****

"Seething volcano." They have a hatred arising from being victimized and inflicted upon, as well as used and exploited, with the result that they feel that their purposes have been prevented.

They are operating out of and intensely rageful resentment of restriction. They would dearly love to explode all over the place, but they are terrified of doing so. It arose from an oppressive and abusive patriarchal and dysfunctional household.

(See **GRAVE'S DISEASE**)

GONORRHEA

"Shame-frame." They have a severe felt need for punishment for being a *bad* person. It comes from guilt and shame about their sexuality, and from generalized guilt and shame about themselves. It is the result of a shame-inducing and simultaneously sex-ploitative and sexually stimulating household.

GOUT (Uric acid retention, resulting in swollen hands and feet and/or sharp pains in the legs, due to uremic poisoning)

"Hopelessness-rage." They feel trapped, with no escape from a dreary life and outcome, and they profoundly resent it. They are manifesting impatience, anger and temper, along with emotional imbalance. They are holding in negative emotions and reactions that should be released.

It is a "learned helplessness" reaction to an overwhelmingly dreadful and dreary life history, especially in their formative period. It as resulted in a consistent pattern of being "at effect" rather than "at cause" in their functioning. They are the product of a rejecting, neglectful and self-immersed family.
****

"My word is your command!" They are into fearful greediness and the need to dominate. They are fixated in a negative thought patterns and attitudes and there is a notable lack of love in their make-up. They are intensely judgmental, condemnatory and rejecting.

They are likely to be compulsively engaged in undisciplined eating, drinking and rich living, resulting in self-poisoning from a "debauchment debacle" outcome. It arises from severe "scarcity" feelings and insecurity, which they are seeking to compensate for with greedy consumption and compulsive control. They are the product of a highly authoritarian, massively selfish, and hostilely controlling paranoid patriarchal family.

GRANULOCYTOPENIA (Reduced defensive white blood cells)

"Valueless." They are suffering from loss of self-commitment, due to a sense of worthlessness being activated by current circumstances, which replay in updated form the experiences of childhood. It's an old, familiar theme or a return of the repressed. In either case, it is the result of being given the message by the way they were raised that they aren't worth a hill of beans.

GRAVE'S DISEASE (Hyper-thyroidism)

"Shining light." There is a felt need to perform, contribute and be creative, and to be a source of continuous inspiration to others. So they are compulsively communicative, excessively expressive, and frantically manically driven. They were put on contradictory conditions for love as a child -- to super succeed and yet to never grow away. They vacillate between meeting this awesome criterion and retreating from it, in a constantly agitated hyper-active performance pattern.
****

"Perform -- or else!" They are desperately afraid they will lose something or someone they love, in a frenetic abandonment-anxiety pattern. They feel that they have to super-perform for their "love-line." They are engaged in a panicky effort to speed up in order to prevent the anticipated catastrophic loss.

There are underlying profound feelings of non-deservingness of love, there is a tremendously over-developed sense of responsibility and a co-dependent care-taking compulsion. They are the product of a severely conditionally loving family in which they had to constantly "earn" their love.
****

"Rejection-rage." There is a tremendous anger at being left out, and being made to feel that they have to constantly contribute and to suppress their own needs. This drives them to a huge output of activity and energy, in a frantic/manic effort to meet criteria and to deflect rejection. They were required to be the "linchpin" for their severely dysfunctional and rejecting/neglecting family.

"GRIPPE" (See FLU)

"GULF WAR SYNDROME" (Fatigue, allergies, asthma, etc., due to chemical, radiation and extra low frequency (ELF) exposure)

"Alone on their own." They have an overwhelming fear of God, coupled with a profound separation-paranoia. They have the experience that they are all they have, in a cold, hostile and attacking world. They have no sense of connection to the Cosmos. There was intrauterine, perinatal, and post-partum ambivalence, and they feel that when they are under stress or vulnerable, the world is decidedly not a safe place to be.
****

"Under fire." They are over-reacting to felt threats to their well-being, to something that is regarded as being hostile to their welfare. There is a deep level of fear about having to participate fully in life or about potential annihilation. There is also an intense distrust of letting something inside their boundaries. They are the product of an untrustworthy and invasive dysfunctional family.
****

"Frayed nerves." They are driven by anxiety, suppressed emotions and unresolved aggravation or irritants from childhood. They are engaged in on-the-edge functioning, due to severe emotional difficulties, and due to denying of their own potency and self-worth. They feel stifled and yet at the same time that it is unsafe to take charge of their own life. They grew up in a devastatingly dysfunctional family who totally dominated and exploited them.
****

"Thwarted leader." They are very dependent and afraid to break away, yet they want to control and dominate. They often are possessed by their family, by institutions and by spouse figures. They are a potential leader and independent thinker who is chafing at the bit under what feels like oppressive authority-domination.

They feel held back by fools, unrecognized for their true value and talents, and not given the high place they deserve, so they force themselves to perform to prove themselves to the "boss."
****

"Not allowed!" They are full of ideas to get ahead, but they are afraid of pushing on against opposition, should they fail. They are intensely inhibited against free expression, and they are full of unresolved guilt and suppressed grief. Their family was highly enmeshed, selfish, dysfunctional and suppressive.
****

"Generalized disgust." They have a lot of disappointment, bitterness, unforgivingness and over-worked resentment. They are out of step and in disharmony with their environment. They feel threatened and they fear loss, so they take a "rejecting first" approach.

There is an inability to resolve their resentment, with a resulting rejecting of the breath of life and an emotional suffocation. There is also a deep fear of letting go of childhood and an intense inner crying. They have a strong ambivalence towards their mother and against mother-stand-ins.

They are being plagued by unmet dependency needs induced by a "smother loving" yet rejecting mother who systematically undermined their capacity for independence, identity and destiny-manifestation.

****

"Abandonment-paranoia." They are intensely sensitive, fearful and longing for mother love or for love from someone close, and they have a rather pronounced possessiveness and rejection-anxiety.

As a result, they are fatalistic, hostility-repressing, compulsive, hypersensitive and lonely, with a very low self-esteem. They have a dampened zest for life due to their stifling, engulfing and yet abandonment-threatening mothering.

****

"Wind has gone out of their sails." They have lost their sense of purposes and direction, along with their desire for life. They have developed a deep fear of life, of taking responsibility, of coping with any further demands. The illness can become a safe place to be, a retreat from confrontation and action. They are the product of a destiny-undermining possessive mother who generated a sense of overwhelm and futility in them.

"HANTA-VIRUS" (Quickly precipitated lethal respiratory failure) [Transmitted by fleas]

"Throwing in the towel." They feel highly unsafe in the world, and they fear taking in life as a result. They feel unworthy of living fully, and they are alone, sad and non-belonging, with no sense of acceptance. They are joy-avoidant and happiness-squashing, out of a fear of the Universe. They can't let people in or themselves out. This has cut them off from joy and love, and it is now taking its toll.

They are having an "Enough is enough!" reaction, and they are heading on out. They are desperately tired of life, due to life-long suppressed grief. They are fearful, anxious and too devastated to take it any more. It came about from effective emotional abandonment at a very early age, to which they reacted with becoming a self-made person with a "portable Plexiglas phone booth" around them.

HARDENING OF THE ARTERIES

"Island unto themselves." They are hyper-self-responsible, and they feel that they can't count on anyone or anything. Their deep experience is that they have to do it all themselves. They are perfectionistically disappointed in themselves, and they won't accept help or delegate responsibility. They were left to their own devices from very early on in their effectively neglectful family.

****

"Intimacy-rejecting." They are spirituality-denigrating and love-suppressing, and at base they are shy, with a poor sex adjustment. Their love nature is unevolved and reserved for only a few. They won't allow themselves to feel love, affection or compassion for many people, and they operate with highly conditional love habits. They come from an unloving and ferociously self-immersed family.

****

"Here it comes!" They are dealing with a feeling of being threatened in some vague but very important and high stakes manner, with a resulting intense sense of endangerment. They feel ready for virtually anything to happen. Their family was notorious for their off-the-wall calamity-production arising out of their severe dysfunctionality.

****

"Thwarted." They feel prevented and blocked in their life, and that they aren't being allowed to manifest themselves. It is the result of a long-standing emotional problem that hasn't been worked out, a deep resentment over the past that is eating at them. They are the product of a feeling-avoidant dysfunctional and patriarchal family.

****

"Seething volcano." They are prone to "make mountains out of molehills" in an intensely rageful manner. They are impatient, angry and wanting to live life in the moment, and they are prone to try to pound away too quickly at life.

There is a great deal of suppressed rage and hostility over the felt external control of their life. As a result, there is a resistance to their emotional energies and a "hardening of the attitudes," with a hard-nosed and authoritarian approach. They are an aggressive dominator who has a deep need to be in control.

It all arises from an underlying passive dependency and a fear of domination that came from an authoritarian household.

****

"Perfectionistic performance." They have a profoundly frightening dread of failure produced by their parent(s) making them into an "ego extension" vicarious accomplisher for them. They are tremendously parent-admiring, especially of their father. They are an achieve-aholic hard-driving competitor for paternal validation. They are a work-aholic number-addict and "coup-seeker" who wants to "make a killing." They could never measure up, in their father's eyes.
****

"Feeling-suppressing." There is stress and conflict, shocks and tension in their situation, and they are afraid of being "over-the-top" disappointed again. They are afraid of their anger and they can't handle it, so they stuff it.

They suppress their negative emotions with their intimates, for fear of hurting their loved ones, and they are over-compliant and anger-avoidant to mask their intense feelings of hostility. Their family made it very clear to them that they were to be seen and not heard.
****

"On the go." They are anxious about money, time-urgent, insecure about life and stress-sensitive, all of which arises from their having had to take on their parent(s) ambitions for them from far too early an age.

They have never had a childhood, and were never given the message that who they are is enough or that what they accomplished filled the bill. They are deeply resentful about that.

(See **ARTERY PROBLEMS**)

HAY FEVER

"Woe is me." They are suffering from emotional congestion -- they are hung up in the hurts of the past, in the form of chronic grief. They believe that time is passing them by, and that things are only going to get worse.

They feel unsafe and unloved, yet they don't feel they have the right to release their grief and sorrow, so they repress it and they suppress their tears. This all arose out of a shame-inducing and punitive family.
****

"Resentment-rage." They are plagued with the effects of their repressed anger and desires for aggression. They want revenge for all the pain they have experienced, but they deeply fear the implications and ramifications should they ever act on this.

They come from a virulently but subtly invasive and abusive family in which to do or say anything about what was happening would have led to disastrous results.
****

"Persecution trip." They are convinced that the world is out to get them and to torture them. Their experience is that things are forever working against them in a maleviolent manner. They are the product of an essentially slyly sadistic family who really did subtly persecute them.
****

"Guilt-grabbing." They feel responsible for everything that goes wrong, that has gone wrong, or that will go wrong. Their experience is that "I caused World War II," and their fear is that they will cause World War III. Their family was intensely accusatory, accountability-attributing and blame-throwing.
****

"Season-fearing." They are enslaved to the calendar, in the sense that they so expect the congestion that they precipitate it right on schedule. Their family was full of such expectations, attributions, interpretations and elicitations.

HEADACHES

"Feeling overwhelmed." They are under a lot of stress, and they are feeling quite tense about it. Their fear and anxiety are alarming them to the point of threatening to upset their whole apple cart.

They are having strong experiences of internal pressures rising to the point of getting out of control. There is an intense need for them to be able to get on top of their situation so they can problem-solve and issue-resolve.

This is an old, familiar feeling for them, because they were the "pivot person" in their dysfunctional family, the only "sane one" in a potentially catastrophically ineffectual family.
****

"Stop the world!" They are blocking the flow of life and of their process as a distraction or escape operation. They are trying not to experience what is happening at this time, and they are being unable to deal with or face the issues that are causing distress right now. It is reflective of a deep distrust of the Universe generated by untrustworthy mothering.
****

"Hot hurts." They are into resentment-ruminations and angry thoughts about why they are angry, while not doing anything about it. They have anxiety about things that aren't handled -- including their anger. They have a strong habit of generating such situations and of negativity and resentment.

Some circumstance, relationship, situation, issue, pressure, individual or whatever that they dislike intensely but which they feel they have to put up with, to live with, is really bugging them.

It comes from having been in a dysfunctional family in which much that was frustrating and insoluble occurred.
****

"Fuck-up feelings." They are highly prone to self-invalidation and self-criticism. They are a perfectionist who is feeling frustration at missing their mark. They are full of self-disapproval and self-disgust. They may desire to be the "head" of a home or business situation.

It comes about as a function of having had to be an "associate parent" when they were a child in a dysfunctional and perfectionistic family.
****

"Dumbo-head." They are being hampered by competence-anxiety, self-doubt and feeling stupid -- by cope-ability-anxiety. There is much worry, anxiety and tension, bringing congestion in the head.

They are manifesting confusion and mental knots that have to be untied. There is suppressed emotion or extreme excitement over something -- or over nothing. They are full of hurt feelings, emotional upsets, and uncertainty as to what is happening. It is the result of a "magical mystery tour" dysfunctional family environment.
****

"Does not compute!" They are trying to integrate incompatible-seeming ideas and information. They have a lot of implication-anxiety about what would happen if they don't succeed in coming up with a meta-interpretation that pulls it all together in a cohesive context. It is the result of having been the reality-interpreter for their rather chaotic meaning-challenged family.
****

"Trying too hard." They are "going for the brass ring" all the time, and it is creating stress and tension. They are something of an achieve-aholic, and they are always seeking to get ahead. They had to "perform for their breakfast" as a child.
****

157

"Sitting on it." They are suppressing negative feelings and thoughts for fear that they are inappropriate or unacceptable, or because they are afraid of voicing them. They are avoiding expressing or acting on their pain and hurt feelings. They tend to get locked inside with nowhere to go, and it hurts. Their family was highly repressive.

****

"Relationship problems." They are feeling trapped in unpleasant and inescapable issues and processes in one or more of their relationships at the present time. It is causing them a great deal of alarm and distress, but they don't see any effective ways to deal with the problems.

It is an all-too-familiar experience for them, as they are tending to attract and elicit the kinds of phenomena, processes and people that they grew up with, in an attempt to "put a new ending on the old story."

****

"Joy-avoidance." They are systematically somber and serious to the point of not allowing themselves to experience or express the up and sillier side of life and themselves. They have a need to enjoy life more -- to laugh, to praise people, to express their gratitude, to sing and dance, and to just plain have a good time. They are the product of a "nose to the grindstone" work ethic family.

RIGHT SIDE HEADACHES

"Gestalt-fearing." They are experiencing conflicts over their perceptions, intuitions and overview comprehensions of things. These were not acceptable to their family.

LEFT SIDE HEADACHES

"Don't know!" There are issues regarding their interpretations, conceptualizations and cognitive understandings of what's happening. Their family "didn't want to know."

~~~~~~

BACK OF THE HEAD HEADACHES

"Don't see!" They have issues about implications and images that they are experiencing. They weren't supposed to see what was going down when they were a child.

FOREHEAD HEADACHES

"Walking cerebrum." They are given to hyper-rationality, leading to muscle contractions. They think too much, in a feeling-suppressing manner, resulting in a chronic anger reaction. They have a need to "blow their top." They weren't allowed to experience or express feelings in their home.

SINUS HEADACHES

"Suppressed mourning." They are suffering from suppressed grief over abandonment-anxiety and frustration with their intimates about insufficient support and love.

It is an issue dating back to childhood, when their family kept them on highly contingent and conditional acceptance.

(See **SINUS PROBLEMS**)

TEMPLE HEADACHES

"Understanding-avoidance." They are caught up in obsessional thinking, or they are suppressing thinking about something. It is the result of a "Don't know!" injunction from their family.

(See **"CLUSTER HEADACHES;" HEADACHES -- COLDNESS-PRODUCED**)

HEADACHES -- COLDNESS-PRODUCED (e.g. cold air, cold drink intake, etc.)

"Suppressed mourning." They are experiencing suppressed grief over abandonment-anxiety and frustration with their intimates about insufficient support and love, an issue dating back to childhood.

In effect, they are a self-made person who tends very strongly to believe that there is no one out there for them, and even that "God might be Al Capone." They are a "sealed unit" -- "island unto themselves" -- "urban hermit." It is the result of pervasive and persistent lack of support throughout their infancy and childhood.

HEAD TRAUMA

"Who's in charge here!?" They are in deep conflict with their Higher Self and/or with the Divine authority, a conflict in which THEY want to be the one running the show. They feel denied, humiliated and undermined/prevented.

They are full of rage and despair about everything involved in this. They have had authority conflict problems all their life, either internally and/or externally/behaviorally. It has now "come to a head." It got started with a great deal of conflict with a dominating parent or with parental conflict about who was in charge.

(See **BRAIN PROBLEMS**)

HEART ATTACK

"Broken hearted." They are an "urban hermit" who has never really had any form of emotionally close relationships -- a "sealed unit" who takes care of business single-handedly and in an emotionally shielded or shutdown manner.

They were in effect rejected from the very start, and they were shoved to the sidelines of their family. They therefore ended up with the profound conviction they don't deserve love, and that others are untrustworthy.

****

"Scrooge." They are squeezing all the joy out of the heart in favor of money, power, position, prestige or the like. They are not expressing and manifesting love with others, now and/or before. They operate out of "scarcity assumptions" and the belief in constricting limitations. They judge themselves a failure, and they therefore work furiously to accomplish on the job and to dominate others. They are full of tension, anxiety, resentment and suppressed aggression.

Underneath, they are a frightened child full of regrets, sorrow and remorse for a life wasted and a vast wasteland experience. They are the product of highly judgmental and demanding parenting that never gave them the message they were "good enough."

(See **CORONARY THROMBOSIS**)

HEART-BEAT SLOWED

"Alone on their own." They have been "taking care of business" with in effect no help from their friends since infancy. They were expected to meet their own needs in a "Child, PLEASE, I'd rather you do it yourself!" parenting pattern. The result is a chronic low-key depression that is reflected in their slowed down heart rate.

"HEARTBURN" (Burning distress behind the sternum, due to spasms of the esophagus or of the upper stomach, resulting in acid coming up)

"Happiness-horror." They have an intense, pervasive and clutching fear that is tripped off by their experiencing some joy or happiness. They have a horrifying sense of impending attack for "undeserved" joy.

They are getting what they want for once, and they feel that somehow they should not -- that it violates the Cosmic or moral order somehow. They are anticipating retribution for the just rewards of their efforts and essence.

It was generated in a severely restrictive, disapproving, moralistic and fear-inducing childhood. They came out of it with an intense fear of the Universe as a harshly judgmental and punitive place. There is also an intense abandonment- and betrayal-paranoia based in part on past lives.

****

"Purple passion." They are intensely involved and activated over something -- love or anger that is very pronounced -- and it is scaring the hell out of them. They are operating with a pronounced injunction not to feel, and especially not to feel strongly. It is a pattern that got started in their highly feeling-suppressing and/or denial-dominated dysfunctional family.

****

"Burning to be free." They are stuffing themselves and their feelings, out of a fear of catastrophic consequences if they let go and "let fly with themselves." They are now reaching the point where "This is an up with which I can no longer put!"

It comes from growing up in a family in which it was not acceptable for them to be themselves or to threaten to grow away by becoming themselves in a destiny-manifesting manner.

HEART BY-PASS OPERATION

"Heartless." They are operating in a cold manner, in the sense of not allowing or believing in the flow of love. They have to "hands on control" everything or "it will all go to Hell in a bread-basket." They are functioning like an "over-extended octopus," trying to do it all single-handedly, with no help from friends.

They are operating with the underlying conscious or unconscious assumption that they are alone on their own, an ejectee-rejectee-dejectee from the Cosmos, because either there is no God or they blew it royally with the "Home Office" (All That Is), and they are getting their "just desserts."

It is the result of "Never good enough!" parenting in a family in which they were nevertheless regarded as the "linchpin" of the system whose fault everything is.

(The more valves to be by-passed and the more frequent the operation, the more intense this dynamic is.)

"HEART FAILURE"

"Died with their boots on." They had been "in the saddle" since early infancy, when they found out that there was no one there to meet their needs or those of the situation. So they rose to the challenge and became the "buck stops here" person everywhere they went. Now the buck has stopped for them.
****

"Shit happens." Sometimes things just show up. A small percentage of events are indeed accidental for purposes of constantly creating new situations for us to handle that are the result of neither our will nor the Divine Design. The purpose is to continuously challenge us with growth-generating events. It should be noted in this regard that "shinola happens" too.

"HEART MURMUR"

"Heart-hurt." They received an at best ambivalent reception in the womb, and they are resigned to a life with little or no love, or to one in which there is much ambivalence. They just don't expect much in the way of love in their life.

HEART PROBLEMS

"Broken-hearted." They are abandonment-paranoid and rejection-expecting. They are desperately dependent and rescuing in the hope that someone will rescue them. They have little or no sense of personal worth or deservingness of love, as if they lost out in the "love sweepstakes" altogether. They feel they are "unfit for human consumption," and that no one could, would or should ever be there with and for them. Yet hope springs eternal, and they constantly put out reams of heart energy and service in the heart of their hearts dream that some day their prince(ss) will come.

It is the result of a loveless, shame-inducing and exploitative dysfunctional family who gave them no support, nurturance, acceptance or fulfillment.
****

"Home is where the hurt is." They are trapped in an ungiving, rejecting and harmful relationship. To them, it is all they can expect, and they have a history of such relationships. Their mother and later their family held them responsible and accountable for all of their experiences, particularly the negative ones. They therefore feel that they have to take on the responsibility for trying to "get the God Housekeeping Seal of Approval" from disapproving intimates.
****

"Hardening of the heart." They have a bad case of "heartless" attitude. They are joyless, and they have the intense belief in the necessity of stress and strain. They feel that they have never experienced any approval from others, and they have become embittered and encased as a result.

They have lost their capacity for compassion, and they are unable to manifest *agape* and universal love or acceptance, and they are unable to process love. They are feeling-suppressing, cut off from any form of love, and hung up in principles. They are also repressing their reaction to being rejected in childhood.

There is a distinct resemblance to "Scrooge" in their workaholic, achieve-aholic intimacy-avoidance, along with a certain "Type A" drivenness. There is a great deal of extremely suppressed grief and pain that they simply will not get in touch with at all costs. They are totally self-immersed, input-deflecting, hard-hearted, rejecting, vengeful, unforgiving, and hateful, as a manifestation of long-standing emotional problems.

It arose as a function of being treated in the same manner as a child, as well as from their finding that "giving it back harder" worked.

****

"Stress and strain." They have long-standing emotional problems that lead to constant upheaval, difficulties, discombobulation and trauma. Their experience is that they can expect nothing different, and that they deserve no better.

They are the product of a severely dysfunctional and blame-throwing family. They harped on how "You asked for it, asshole!" to such a degree that the individual now believes it in their heart.

HEART VALVE PROBLEMS

"Can't let love in." They are something of an "urban hermit" whose experience is either that "love is a four letter word" and/or that they don't deserve and they can't count on love. They are the product of an untrustworthy early emotional environment, and they ended up doing a "one man band operation" on the emotional level, in essence working to provide themselves whatever love they can manage to muster all by themselves.

"HEAT PROSTRATION" (Complete overwhelm by high temperature environments)

"Fried." They feel overloaded with demands, expectations and responsibilities with very high stakes, and they can't take it any more. It is a bad case of a "the buck stops here" syndrome. It got started in their severely dysfunctional, demanding and denigrating family, where they were expected to be the "family hoist" while simultaneously being blamed for everything that went wrong.

Now they are on the verge of "checking out" because they have reached the point where "This is an up with which I will no long put!"

"HEAT-STROKE" (Dizziness, nausea, spots before their eyes)

"Get me outta here!" They are feeling overwhelmed and very oppressed by their current circumstances. They are highly co-dependent and over-responsible for everyone in their life's problems, and they hate it. They are disgusted and revolted, and their feeling is that "This is an up with which I will no long put!"

It came from out of nowhere in a "return of the repressed" fashion as their situation reactivated their childhood experiences in spades. They were systematically suppressed, exploited and blamed by their dysfunctional family.

(See **HEAT PROSTRATION**)

HEEL SPUR (Calcification growths on bottom of the heels and at the Achilles heels)

"Go ahead -- everybody else does!" They have a way of wearing a "Kick me!" sign that elicits rejection and abuse. The have the bottom line feeling that somehow they deserve it, and they are into intense resignation and resentment about it all. They were the scapegoat and "identified problem" in their severely dysfunctional family, who blamed them for everything that went wrong.

RIGHT HEEL SPUR
"NOW what have I done?!" They have grave concerned about their ecological impact.

LEFT HEEL SPUR
"There I go AGAIN!" They have deep self-distrust and self-disgust.

HEMATOCHEZIA (See **ANORECTAL BLEEDING** in **ANAL PROBLEMS**)

HEMOPHILIA (Defective blood-clotting)
"Drain out." They have serious boundary problems, and they feel that they have to "caretake" the world. They were never allowed to have their own needs or any limits on the demands that were made of them. It is the ultimate co-dependency pattern. At the soul level, this situation was chosen as a karma payback, as an experience-expansion, or as an example-provider.

HEMORRHAGING (Uncontrolled outpouring of blood)
"Blown away." They are experiencing profound emotional trauma or upsets, resulting in uncontrollable emotional outbursts. Their experience is that they have been completely devastated by what is happening, and that they are totally unable to handle it.

This can either reflect a truly overwhelming set of circumstances or it can be reflective of a sense of having been driven "over the line" in a life pattern that has been consistently painful and difficult. Even in the circumstantial case, the situation reflects their life pattern of being in over their head in emotional difficulties.

HEMORRHOIDS (Enlarged protruding and painful veins around the anus)
"Self-squashing." They are deathly afraid to let go, in a kind of "run amok-anxiety" reaction to their whole life. They are highly restricted and restrained in their functioning, and they are terrified of generating rejection, retaliation or remorse. They are the product of a severely suppressive/oppressive household.
****

"Over-burdened." They are carrying the world on their shoulders, as they experience it. Their feeling is that the buck always stops with them, and that they have to rise to the challenge, lest all hell break loose. They were the "family hoist" in their severely dysfunctional system, and they functioned as the disaster-deflector and the "sane one."
****

"I'm late! I'm late!" They have a dread and great fear of deadlines, because they are forever running late and coming up a day late and a dollar short. They have the overwhelming pattern of not being able to say no, and of over-committing, so that they are always strung out 16 ways to breakfast and effectively letting people down one way or another. They are intensely rejection-abhorrent, and they are also rather massively over-responsible.

It comes from being blamed for everything that went wrong in the dysfunctional family, so that they ended up seeking to atone and to make up for their being "bad, wrong and evil."
****

"Repressed resentment." They are "sitting on" a lot of anger and anxiety over their quality of life and about the potential threats of serious calamities hanging over their head. Their experience is that they just have to "bite the bullet" and to "make lemonade" out of the "lemons" that life hands them so often. They feel rather largely "at effect" rather than at cause. Indeed, intervention rather frightens them because it has so often "blown up in their face" in the form of "lash-backs," accusations, punishments and "escalating disasters."

They were intensely programmed to be systematically self-defeating, and at the same time, they were forced to be self-suppressing in a severely patriarchal, oppressive, exploitative and overtly or covertly abusive family.
****

"Bile-blowout." They are full of fear, anger and hatred about the past, and they have a lot of explosive rage. There is also fear of exploitation, and they are afraid to let go. They have numerous other anxieties, worries and irritations, particularly around money.

There is intense exertion expended over control of the environment. They are in a continuous conflict between trying to get something out and holding on for dear life. They engage in a "zipper-lip" closed-mouthedness and non-expression of their feelings of being over-burdened.

There is a carefully hidden guilt and spite reaction that got started during a very harsh toilet training, and that was consistently and continuously reiterated throughout their childhood, in a highly oppressive and distrustful household.

HEPATITIS (Inflammation of the liver)

"Competence-anxiety." They have great fear arising out of experienced powerlessness, self-doubts and guilt. They that they are totally overloaded with demands, and that they are unable to deal with them. It arose in a highly dysfunctional and enraging family who demanded far too much, and who instilled deep-seated self-doubt and cope-ability-anxiety.
****

"Volcanic fury." They are sitting on a lot of seething resentment of the past, and they are full of anger and hatred. All of which is projected out as accusations of corruption and exploitation. They come from a highly patriarchal, exploitative, abusive, accusative and accountability-attributing family.
****

"No way, Jose!" They are manifesting an intense resistance to change. In their experience, new means trouble, loss, pain, frustration and even disaster. Theirs was a severely self-defeating, chaotic, out of control dysfunctional family. They reacted by disengaging as much as possible, and by setting up rigidly adhered to routines and resources as a safety-seeking strategy.

HERNIA (Internal organ protruding through the muscles)

"Serve-aholic." They are forever over-burdened, under severe strain, and involved in inappropriate applications and expressions of their creativity. They feel that they have to continuously "atone for" and to "make up for" their being "bad, wrong and evil." They feel like they caused World War II, and they are intensely guilt-grabbing, shame-framing and self-denying/self-punishing. They are the product of a severely blame-framing, enmeshed, exploitative, punitive and rejecting family.
****

"Ruptured relationships." It seems that every time they get into any kind of close or important relationship, it ends up erupting, ripping apart or rupturing. They are a work-aholic who is so endlessly busy and emotionally unavailable that they become maddening to their intimates.

It is the result of being shoved to the sidelines of their family early on, in an "odd one out" and "family freak" pattern. They reacted by trying to prove their worth and acceptability by compulsive contribution.
****

"Hands on domination/determination." They are super-self-suppressing and manically controlling of the environment. They try to pin everything down -- especially themselves -- in a "Lilliput-like million little ropes" pattern. They rupture all their relationships, as they struggle under the strain of enormous burdens, as they experience it.

Much of what they do is incorrect manifestation of creative expression in the direction of trying to "hands on" determine everything. They are also prone to feel that they deserve punishment for what they are, and they are apt to be quite self-punishing. They are the product of an oppressive/suppressive and exploitative family.
****

"Powder keg." They are a compressed container of rage about to go off, and they are engaged in a frantic effort to control their anger. They do so by pretending it isn't there in an ostrich-like manner, which only generates events and outcomes that feed the volcano inside. They feel that life is "so pressing," and they try to ignore it all, resulting in self-violence and self-injury.

They have a considerable amount of "run amok-anxiety" and guilt arising from an extremely punitive and controlling upbringing.

HERNIATED DISC (Torn-apart platelet between the vertebrae)
"Cop-out artist." They are engaged in chronic problem-avoidance, as they try to put it behind them whenever they can. It is an "ostrich approach" that they learned in their denial-dominated and accountability/responsibility-ducking dysfunctional family.

(See **SPINAL DISC PROBLEMS** for what it means to have the particular disc involved rupture)

HERPES; HERPES GENITALIS (Viral blisters on the sexual area)
"Mea culpa." They have a massive belief in sexual guilt and the need for punishment. They are convinced that God is going to punish them for being who they are. They are full of public shame, especially around their sexual nature. They are intensely rejecting of their genitals and of themselves.

They are angry and anxious about themselves and their situation. They have a rather strong "alone and alien" loneliness, along with the feeling they are "unfit for human consumption." It all comes from a "tantalizing tarantula" seductive-destructive, entice -- arouse -- attack, sex-ploitative/ punitive parenting pattern. They were made to feel like an utter "moral cretin" for being a sexual being.

HERPES SIMPLEX; HERPES LABIALIS (Blister clusters on the mouth)
"Vast wasteland." They are experiencing intense grief-rage over the lack or loss of support and resources. They also feel underneath that they deserve it somehow. At the same time, they are quite bitter and resentful underneath, with a raging desire to complain and expound on it all. However, they are too afraid to say anything about it, and they are full of unspoken bitter words.

This whole thing re-activates early deprivation reactions, from a time when to object to losses or lacks only made it worse in their self-immersed dysfunctional family.

HIATAL HERNIA (Internal organ protruding above the stomach, producing excess bile, sour stomach, and much belching)

"Paranoid hostility." They are sitting on an intensely suppressed sub-conscious vengeful viciousness. They are highly judgmental and resentful of everyone and everything. They are feeling over-burdened with having to track everything, and they are experiencing a deep sense of deprivation and frustrated dependency needs. The result is a great deal of "run amok-anxiety" arising from their unconscious hatred over this life experience.

They are the product of a severely dysfunctional family in which there was a great deal of subterranean sabotage and hateful hostility towards the world and towards each other. They can't imagine ever truly trusting anything or anyone -- least of all themselves -- as a result.

H.I.V. POSITIVE (Human Immuno-deficiency Virus)

"Worthless turd." They have a strong belief in not being good enough. There is much self-intolerance and self-rejection, resulting in self-destructive potentials. They are feeling defenseless and that nobody cares. They have considerable sexual guilt imposed by an over-possessive and yet simultaneously rejecting and wrong-making mother. It is in effect a severe maternal deprivation and denigration reaction.

"HIVES" (Red and itchy small eruptions on the skin)

"Abandonment-anxiety." They were subjected to intense ambivalence and to severe acceptance/rejection games by their mother. They are too terrified of being "abandoned on a desert island" (which they assume they deserve) to do anything to change their situation or the nature of their relationships.
****

"Punching bag." They feel endangered and unfairly attacked, particularly by their family, intimates or close relationship people. They feel they are taking a beating, and that they are helpless to do anything about it. They experience being knocked around, hammered on, mistreated, betrayed or subjected to injustices.

They also feel personally persecuted for everything that happens. When attacked, they take it out on themselves rather than risk the losses involved in standing up for themselves or attacking back. They are the product of an abusive, accountability-attributing and blame-throwing family.
****

"Harm-avoidance." They are very fearful, and they have many small "molehill" hidden fears of which they "make mountains." Underlying this is a feeling of being personally responsible for everything that is -- a feeling that arises from the conviction they are the center of their universe.

Their family responded to them by expecting them to take care of everything, and they therefore took an unconscious accusatory stance towards the individual when anything went wrong. This generated a very deep and pervasive abandonment-anxiety in them, and they now personally take charge of everything as an acceptance-earning and a rejection- and abandonment-deflecting or abandonment-delaying tactic.
****

"Root of all evil." They have a kind of inverse megalomania, in that they have come away from their formative process with the unconscious conviction they are responsible for everything that goes on, especially that which goes wrong.

They were responded to as being capable of "making it all better," due to some inherent or apparent superiority. However, when they, being only a child, could not live up to such high expectations, their family became enraged at them, and they pounded in that they were the cause of everyone's problems.

HODGKIN'S DISEASE (Enlargement of lymph glands and spleen -- cancerous)

"Not good enough." They have a virulent self-blame and a tremendous fear of not being sufficient to the cause. They are engaged in a frantic race to prove themselves over and over, in a desperate attempt to be accepted -- until finally their blood has no substance left to support itself.

The joy of life is forgotten in the desperate struggle for acceptance by "stand-ins for the original cast" of totally unpleasable parent(s). They end up with no self-validation capacity, and with no ability to express themselves or to receive anything.

"HOOF AND MOUTH" DISEASE (Severe skin eruptions and boils, caught from cattle)

"Fulminating fury." They have an intense suppressed rage and seething injustice-nurturing around deprivations and degradations they have experienced and/or are experiencing. It is a long-standing pattern that is now "coming to a boil" for purposes of healing or as a result of things coming to head in their life around this issue of being betrayed, belittled or bedeviled. It is the result of a severely passive-aggressive dysfunctional family.

"HOOK WORM" (Small intestinal parasite)

"Massive competence-anxiety." They are terrified to strike out on their own or to stand on their own rights, their own ground, and their own two feet, for fear of the "ultimate blow-it." They have no trust of themselves, and they are convinced that there is an answer that they don't have and that others do. It's a pattern that got started in a "never good enough" parenting situation in which they frantically tried over and over and over to get the "God Housekeeping Seal of Approval" -- and they forever failed to do so.

The result is that now they feel that they lack the "secret for success and worth" that everyone else has, and have to keep trying with "stand-ins for the original cast" in reruns of the original scenario until they "get it right," finally, they hope.

So they keep on trying to "find the key," and in the meantime, they turn everything over to those in the know or to those they think hold the "Golden Orb of Final Validation." As a result, they give their power to others, letting them take over everything in their life. They end up having to deal with constant interference and exploitation in their life.

HORMONAL PROBLEMS

"Heavy issues." They are experiencing intense lack of resolution, conflicts, inundations, and/or severe threats regarding deep matters that stem from very early emotional damage. They need to come to some clearing of these issues now.
****

"Emotional-commotional." They are on an "emotional roller coaster" regarding their relationship with themselves, with others, with the world and/or with the Universe. They grew up in a disruptively dysfunctional family, and they ended up at the mercy of their reactions instead of using them as information for coping and problem-solving.
****

"Unbalanced." They are operating like a "careening cannon," with the associated ecological impacts and self-damaging. They are the product of a severely destructive and demoralizing family who had the effect of programming them to be systematically self-destructive.

HOT EXTREMITIES, CHRONIC

"Poor boundaries." They have a pronounced propensity to get over-involved in, impacted upon and over-heated by things. They are a "serve-aholic" and a "rescue-tripper" who can't keep their hands off of things. They feel that it is up to them to meet all needs and to deflect all disasters. They were the "family hoist" person in their family who was expected to "make it all better."
****

"Right and righteous." They are highly judgmental and negatively assumptive, and they act on their takes on things in an invasive manner. They are chronically infuriated at everything, and they have the resulting absolute imperative to intervene.

They are the product of a severely and implacably dysfunctional family who held them responsible and accountable for everything that went wrong -- which it almost always did.

HOT FEET – CHRONIC

"Silently seething." They feel both powerless in and victimized by the world. They tend strongly to life "at effect" rather than "at cause," and it greatly irritates them. They are the product of a passive-aggressive and suppressive household.

****

"Steamed up." They are forever fuming over the frustrations and set backs of life. Their experience is that they are being constantly thwarted by the course of events, systems and priorities of the world. They are intensely willful and one-pointed in their functioning, and they are always running into conflicts between their priorities and those of the surrounding environment.

They are the product of a patriarchal family who either capitulated to their demands and/or encouraged their river-pushing style.

RIGHT FOOT CHRONIC HOTNESS

"Blocked action." Their experience is that they are continually being prevented from making the kind of impact on things that they want.

LEFT FOOT CHRONIC HOTNESS

"Self-frustration." They have the experience of "I have met the enemy, and it is me." It seems that every time they set out to do something, they get into their own way.

CHRONICALLY HOT TOES

"Ill-executed moves." They have a tendency to botch up their intervention efforts.

HOT HANDS, CHRONIC.

"CHARGE!" They have this intensely driven need to intervene and to "set things right." They are something of a serve-aholic who feels that it is imperative that they correct situations. They were the "family hoist" for their severely dysfunctional family.

****

"What's good for General Bullmoose is good for EVERYBODY!" They are convinced that their way is the only right way. They are intensely self-referencing and judgmental, and they impose their evaluations, interpretations and intentions on the environment everywhere they go. They are the product of an intensely patriarchal and authoritarian dysfunctional family.

RIGHT HAND CHRONIC HOTNESS

"Frustrated re-former." They are forever feeling that they are being prevented from "making it all better."

LEFT HAND CHRONIC HOTNESS

"Always outraged." They take the stance that the world is going to hell in a breadbasket, and they are utterly disgusted and enraged by that.

~~~~~~

CHRONICLY HOT EARS

"Embarrassment/shame." They labor under a constant feeling that they are not doing enough about things.

CHRONICLY HOT FINGERS

"Hot head." They are always itching to grab hold of things to "make things right."

CHRONICLY HOT NOSE

"Helmsman." They have the intense feeling that it is their duty to intervene whenever things start going wrong, as they experience it.

"HPV" (HUMAN PAPILLOMA VIRUS) [Genital warts, often sexually transmitted.]

"Mea Culpa." They have a strong belief in sexual guilt and the need for punishment. They have the feeling that God is going to punish them for who they are. They have a good deal of shame, especially about their sexual nature.

They are angry and anxious about themselves and their situation. There is a rather strong "alone and alien" loneliness, along with the feeling that they are somehow "unfit for human consumption." It all comes from a "tantalizing tarantula" seductive-destructive, sex-ploitative and punitive parenting pattern. They were made to feel like a "moral cretin" for being a sexual being.

HUNTINGTON'S CHOREA (Involuntary muscle spasms, constant tremors, mental deterioration)

"Why don't you listen to me?!" They are intensely resentful at not being able to change who others are and how they operate. They have a feeling that it is their personal responsibility to hold up the whole Universe and to "make it all better."

They feel like a horrible failure when their efforts to handle everything don't do the trick. They then go into a profound self-attack mode, along with feeling utterly hapless, helpless and hopeless. They are deeply depressed, and they have a great deal of irresolvable sorrow. It came from being the "family hoist" in a severely self-destructive dysfunctional and vampirishly dependent family.

HYPER-GLYCEMIA (Excess blood sugar)

"Strung out." They are so busy taking care of the world that they don't know how to take care of themselves. They are forever on the go trying to coverall the bases single-handed. Their family relied heavily upon them as the behind-the-scenes "pivot person" and they learned a rescuing and self-depriving lifestyle from it.
****

"Over-amped." They are being flooded with energy and the goodies of life -- too much for their own good. They are enslaved to the hedonic value of whatever they are involved in, due to over-indulgent and under-requiring parenting.

HYPER-PARATHYROIDISM (Excessive calcium secretion, leading to passive reactivity and/or an amotivational syndrome)

"Serving themselves up on a platter." They are giving their power away in a continuous process of shoring up others' power, rather than manifesting or taking care of themselves. They are always fulfilling others -- and ending up in effect giving themselves away. They have extreme disappointment at not being able to do what they want to do with their life, and at their life circumstances of the moment.

It comes from a family that put them on a "Cinderella/Cinderfella" pattern in which they sustained and supported everyone else for meager bare sustenance maintenance. Meanwhile, their family gave the continuous message that "They had damn well better be grateful for what they got because Heaven knows they didn't deserve it," and besides, "You are the cause of all our problems."

HYPER-SOMNIA (Constant sleepiness or sleep attacks)

"Escape hatch." They want to escape their life and/or they are bored to death with their life. It comes from having had to "sleepwalk" their way through their childhood, because their family would not let them be themselves. Now they find they can't "wake up and smell the coffee."

HYPER-TENSION (High blood pressure)

"Look out!" They have a feeling of being threatened in some vague but very important high stakes manner, with a resulting intense sense of endangerment. They feel ready for virtually anything to happen. There is stress and conflict, shocks and tension in their situation. It is the result of a long-standing emotional problem that hasn't been worked out, a deep resentment over the past that is eating at them. They come from an unpredictably violating dysfunctional family.
****

"Going down." They are severely depressed and demoralized, and they are giving up on life. They feel powerless regarding their situation and with respect to their coping capability. They feel that their situation is hopeless, and they are throwing in the towel. They are the product of a devastatingly dysfunctional family who undermined all possible out routes.

****

"This is MY show!" They won't accept help or delegate responsibility, and they are an aggressive dominator, with a deep need to be in control, arising from an underlying dependent passivity and fear of domination. They have an underlying deep distrust of the universe, and they feel that they have to personally determine; everything, less all hell will break loose. They were the "sane one" in their severely dysfunctional and patriarchal family.

****

"Seething rage." They are intensely angry and resentful about just everything. They have a great deal of suppressed rage and hostility over the felt external control of their lives. They are afraid of their anger, and they feel that they can't handle it, so they stuff it. They suppress their negative emotions with intimates for fear of hurting their loved ones.

They tend to be over-compliant and anger-avoidant to mask their intense feelings of betrayal-rage. They are bitterly negative about everyone and everything, and they always have been. They are a seething volcano who "makes mountains out of molehills." They grew up in a hostile and severely dysfunctional patriarchal family.

****

"Sealed unit." They are hyper-self-responsible, and they feel that they can't count on anyone or anything. They feel they have to do it all themselves. They have an abiding inability to relax, they tend to overeat and to be over-weight.

Their love nature is unevolved and reserved for only a few. They won't allow themselves to feel love, affection or compassion for many, and they operate with highly conditional love habits.

They have never had a childhood, and they were never given the message that who they are is enough, and that what they accomplished filled the bill. They were effectively "abandoned at an early age" and left more or less to their own devices throughout childhood, resulting in a "sealed unit self-made person"

****

"Perfection-expecting." They have a profoundly frightening dread of failure that was produced by their parents making them into an "ego extension" -- "vicarious accomplisher" for them. They are tremendously parent-admiring, especially of their father.

They are an "achieve-aholic" hard-driving competitor for paternal validation. They are a "work-aholic" -- "number-addict" and "coup-seeker" who wants to "make a killing," and they are perfectionistically disappointed in themselves.

****

"I'm all I've got -- and one strike and I'm out!" They are spirituality-denigrating and love-suppressing, and at base they are shy, with a poor sex adjustment, as they seek satisfaction within themselves only.

They are anxious about money, they are time-urgent, they are insecure about life, and they are stress-sensitive. They are impatient, angry, and wanting to live life in the moment, as they try to pound away too quickly at life. All of which arises from their having had to take on their parent(s) ambitions for them from far too early an age.

HYPERTHERMIA [Overwhelmed with heat] (See **"HEAT PROSTRATION"**)

HYPER-THYROIDISM (Over-active thyroid gland)

"Shining light." There is a felt need to perform, contribute and be creative, and to be a source of continuous inspiration to others. So they are compulsively communicative, excessively expressive, and manic-frantically driven.

They were put on contradictory conditions for love as a child -- to super-succeed and yet to never grow away. They vacillate between meeting this awesome criterion, in a constantly agitated hyper-active performance pattern.

****

"Perform -- or else!" They are desperately afraid they will lose something or someone they love, in a frenetic abandonment-anxiety pattern. They feel that they have to super-perform for their "love-line." They are engaged in a panicky effort to speed up in order to prevent the anticipated catastrophic loss.

There are underlying profound feelings of non-deservingness of love, there is a tremendously over-developed sense of responsibility and a co-dependent care-taking compulsion. They are the product of a severely conditionally loving family in which they had to constantly "earn" their love.

****

"Rejection-rage." There is a tremendous anger at being left out, and being made to feel that they have to constantly contribute and to suppress their own needs. This drives them to a huge output of activity and energy, in a frantic/manic effort to meet criteria and to deflect rejection.

They were required to be the "linchpin" for their severely dysfunctional and rejecting neglecting family.

HYPER-VENTILATION (Excessive inhalation)

"Freaked out intake." They are in the grips of a generalized fear and dread, and of a deep distrust of the process of the Universe. There is great resistance to change and newness, and they hate life's unpredictability, uncertainty and requirements. They have a tremendous underlying self-rejection generated by a frighteningly dysfunctional and shame-inducing family.

HYPO-GLYCEMIA (Insufficient blood sugar)

"What's the use?" They feel overwhelmed by the requirements of life, and by what they feel are their excessive burdens. They feel that there is an insufficient input of support, nurturance and resources. Or that there is no allowance for such input, with the result that they are drained dry and "running on empty." Their experience is that "There is no joy in Bloodville."

There is an attitude of nihilistic resignation that got started in childhood in an overwhelmingly dysfunctional family, in which they were the ones that had to hold the ship together "with spit and bailing wire," while being told they were the only one who had to do so because they were a "moral cretin" who had to "atone."

HYPOTHALAMUS PROBLEMS (The governing gland for the pituitary and pineal glands -- the endocrine gland/orchestrators)

"Emotionally devastated." They are overwhelmed with anxiety, insecurity, frustration, resentment-rage, disgust, grief and despair. They feel that there is no point or possibility of continuing. They are the product of a massively demoralizingly dysfunctional family who in effect derailed any and all hope of a workable life.

HYPO-TENSION (Low blood pressure)

"Eeyore." They are experiencing a "What's the use? It won't work anyway" demoralized defeatism resulting in a giving up on life and in a "settle-for" lifestyle. There is a feeling of purposelessness, along with a letting go of a sense of meaningfulness, both of which reflect a subconscious death wish. There is also a good deal of anxiety, insecurity and frustration that have led to their becoming nihilistic. They have withdrawn their energy from the process of living.

Their family was completely unable to give them any love or hope, due to their being intensely nihilistic and pessimistic. The individual ended up feeling that there's really no point and no winning in this business of life, so they are marking time and "waiting for *rigor mortis*" as they have the feeling, "There must be some way out of here."
****

"Keeping things afloat -- at their own expense." They tend to get into a sacrificial pattern, followed by unconscious deep-seated resentment. It all got started in a family who operated in the same manner and simultaneously demanded that they be the "pillar of strength," and the one who tries to keep things together and cleans up the mess. Theirs was a loveless and joyless "Cinderella/ Cinderfella" family experience.

HYPO-THYMUS PROBLEMS (Under-activity of the thymus gland)

"I have no right." They are having difficulty with their desires, arising out of a generalized shame and guilt over having needs, wants and wishes. They are convinced that not only do they not deserve to have requirements, they actually cause the environment harm by doing so.

It is a pattern that got started in an extremely self-immersed, exploitative, blaming and shame-inducing family.

HYPO-THYROIDISM (Insufficient secretion of the life-sustaining growth hormone)

"Giving up the ghost." They are manifesting stagnation, lethargy, ennui and nihilism. They have a hopeless and defeatist personality, with a felt uselessness of effort and an obsessive rumination about how nothing ever works. They are given to intense pessimism, demoralization, and a feeling of being hopelessly stifled, all of which result in their "throwing in the towel."

It is the result of a thoroughly defeating dysfunctional family. It is also indicative of past life issues that have to be worked out.

HYSTERECTOMY (Removal of the uterus)

"She-jection." There is intense repudiation of their femininity and creative powers. They feel it is not safe for them to manifest their creativity or their generativity. They fear rejection, abandonment and attack, along with envy, jealousy and retaliation. It got started with a severely ambivalent mother who was also envious and possessively engulfing.
****

"Run amok-anxiety." There is a strong streak of fear of their going out of control, and they are self-suppressing and fearful of their personal power. It arises from their "tripod-rage" (the irresistible urge to kick anything with three legs), their patriarchy-paranoia, and their father-fury.

They are systematically self-denigrating and ashamed of their feminine role, situation and nature. They don't want to release their creativity for fear of exploitation by the patriarchy as well. They have a strong "Take this job and shove it!" feeling and they would just as soon "take their marbles and go home."

It is the result of a direct infusion of self-rejection and "tripod-rage" from their mother, with subsequent intense experiential validation from their father's behavior and from the patriarchal society.

IATROGENIC ILLNESS (Caused by treatment procedures -- e.g., staph infections, antibiotic reactions, surgical problems, medication side effects, chemotherapy effects, drug side effects, etc.)

"Parental violation -- repeated." They are manifesting their underlying unconscious expectation of being betrayed and invaded. It arose from a childhood experience of being repeatedly violated by their dysfunctional and self-serving family.

Their experience now is that they are still feeling the effects of destructive and self-sabotage-inducing "implants" from their invasive family. They also find that the environment has a way of reproducing their home environment -- complete with all the destructive invasions and violations.

I.L.C. [Idiopathic Lympho-Cytopenia -- an AIDS-like pattern without H.I.V.] (See **ACQUIRED IMMUNO-DEFICIENCY SYNDROME**)

ILEITIS (Inflammation of the opening to the large intestine)

"Freaked out." They have a lot of worry about not being good enough, along with a fearfulness about what that might bring. There is much self-disapproval and insecurity generated by a capability-undermining and shame-inducing family.
****

"Resentful resignation." They have the feeling that things are not going to get any better. The trouble is, thing suck, as far as they are concerned, and they are very angry about that. It got started in their implacably dysfunctional family, in which they could do nothing to improve things.

ILEOCECAL VALVE PROBLEMS (Leading to back-flow of fecal matter from the large to small intestines)

"Self-poisoning." They hold on to old patterns in a rigid and self-destructive manner. They are refusing to let go of the past and of rancorous bitterness, and they are taking a highly conservative approach to things. They are the product of a highly authoritarian household.

IMMUNE SYSTEM PROBLEMS

"What's the use?" They are harboring deep grief and a sense of underlying despair and demoralization. They have a demoralized resignation attitude in the making or in their manifestation. They are overwhelmed by too much sorrow, and by the "running on empty" effect of a severe inequality of energy exchange with the world, whereby they put out much more than they get. They have effectively given up on life, feeling that they have no ability to determine or control anything. They feel that they are just simply insufficient to the cause, and they can't care any more.

It is a result of having carried the world on their shoulders all their life, starting with their dysfunctional family, with little or no ability to receive or to request or to require a return in kind. They were told in effect they were the source of all the family's problems while actually being the only one deflecting some of the disasters.

IMPETIGO (Contagious virus-based skin lesions)

"Why me?" They have the feeling that they are being in effect "singled out for shit" by the "Home Office" (All That Is). They are the product of an abusive, rejecting and dysfunctional family who did indeed single them out.
****

175

"Despair-rage." They are experiencing a great deal of inner anger at the way that their life is going, and they have a pronounced sense of helplessness to do anything about it. They feel trapped in a careening truck that is heading for the cliff, and they are utterly and desperately infuriated by the whole situation. So much so that it is creating a skin-burn.

It is the result of a highly possessive, engulfing and yet simultaneously rejecting and punitive dysfunctional and oppressive family.

****

"JAP-out" (Jeweled American Prince(ss))." There is an intense internal conflict going on between wanting to please everyone at any cost and a "whim of iron" that wants everything to go exactly their way.

It is a result of having become their mother's "special relationship," in which she indulged them profusely, but in which she also demanded they be totally there for her. The resulting internal conflict generates so much cell electricity that it literally burns the skin.

IMPOTENCE

"Walk-out." It is a manifestation of an "I'm not interested in this relationship because it is just not meeting my needs" message and/or experience (though not necessarily the reality of the situation). They don't want to surrender to a woman. It's based primarily on fear of and rage at their mother, possibly accompanied by spite against their former mate(s).

****

"Sexual shut-down." There is a great deal of grief, felt rejection, fear of loss and confusion that is permeating their relationship at present. There is also the possibility of their seeking to gain power by withholding sexuality from their partner. Sometimes it reflects intense stress and/or pressure in their life. It is the result of an intense abandonment-anxiety and castration-anticipation in reaction to felt sexual performance pressures.

****

"Sexual shame." There is a pronounced sense of inadequacy, guilt and tension in the sexual arena that was generated by excessive self-expectations based on social beliefs and maternal intrusions and demands. The result is that they in effect "go numb," and they can't "keep it up."

They had to be "Mommy's little man," often in a sex-ploitative manner, while simultaneously being subjected to engulfing and ensnaring mothering and her intense "tripod-rage" (the irresistible urge to kick anything with three legs). The result is a mother-fixation in which he is unable to truly connect, commit, be passionate or be vulnerable.

INABILITY TO ABSORB NUTRIENTS

"Forget the whole damned thing!" There is a simultaneous profound self-rejection and distrust of the Universe. Their experience is that anything the environment has to offer is going to be "poison apples" because "that's all they can expect." It is the result either of some sort of karmic issue or of extreme rejection and accusation by their family or both.

INABILITY TO COMPREHEND SPEECH

"Tuning out." They are ignoring the environment and verbal inputs, because such inputs are either traumatic, associated with trauma, or inconsistent with what have been found to be more reliable nonverbal indicators of true feelings and intents by their care-takers.

They come from a family where what was said did not match reality and where "what you sees is not necessarily what you gets."
****

"I'm not listening!" They are manifesting a refusal to be influenced by or to take inputs from their care-takers due to rage at their treatment. They may be developing a control-avoidant, rebellious and/or authority-freak approach. They come from a severely dysfunctional family in which there was a great deal of passive-aggressiveness.

INABILITY TO CRY (Emotional)

"What, *me* worry?" It is an intense feeling-avoidance based on profound vulnerability-anxiety and fear of being out of control. They have a deep distrust of the Universe and other people. It is due to severely dysfunctional and dependently demanding parenting and/or a massively repressive and denial-dominated dysfunctional family and/or a severely male role-enforcing family.

INABILITY TO CRY (Genetic)

"Karmic re-balance." They are operating under the requirement for a rectification for having been intensely repressive, oppressive, suppressive, and femininity-purse cutting in former lives. The lesson is the importance of fluid flowingness, vulnerable involvement, and compassionate comprehension.

INABILITY TO DISCERN EMOTIONS

"Feeling-phobia." They were so devastatingly but super-subtly trained to avoid awareness of the emotions as a child that it has resulted in a breakdown of the physical system for doing so. They come from a severely denial-dominated and/or repressive dysfunctional family in which any contact with what people were really feeling would have resulted in a calamitous collapse of the whole family.

INABILITY TO FORM BLOOD CLOTS

"Drain out." They have serious boundary problems, and they feel that they have to care-take the world. They were never allowed to have their own needs met or to have limits on the demands that were made of them. It was the ultimate co-dependency pattern. At the soul level, this situation was chosen as a karma payback, an experience-expansion, or an example-provider.

INABILITY TO FORM WORDS

"Struck dumb." Life has been so inhospitable that they can't find words to express their experience. Either they comprehend much more than those around them can handle and/or they were given a very strong "to be seen but not heard from" message as a child.

In any case, it is an annihilation-anxiety and/or a world-destruction fear that was instilled by the fact that there was a gross mis-match between what they experienced/perceived/knew and what their family could tolerate hearing about, and there was a very strongly threatening response to their attempts to speak their truth.

INABILITY TO PERCEIVE THINGS

"I don wanna know!" They are manifesting an information-avoidant approach. It was generated by a severely denial-dominated dysfunctional family in which it was disastrous to perceive what was really going down. It was literally "world destruction" for them to comprehend what was happening to, within and around them.

INABILITY TO PHONETICALLY SOUND OUT WORDS

"Ball and stick problem." They are too concerned with pragmatic survival to pay attention to the abstract world -- including whether the ball or the stick comes first (the difference between a "d" and a "b").

They were left to their own devices emotionally and/or physically as an infant and child, and the result is that they never had the leisure or the stimulation to develop their symbolic perception function adequately. The result is a developmental deprivation effect that results in difficulty in learning to associate sounds with symbols.

(See **DYSLEXIA**)

INABILITY TO PRODUCE MILK

"Subtle selfishness." She is experiencing rather intense ambivalence about motherhood. She has a lot of resentment of the demands and drains of mothering, and she is subconsciously looking to the infant for the succorance she never got. It's a case of not being able to do for others what was never done for her. (The key factor here is the nurturing attitude was missing, regardless of the history of breast or bottle feeding).
****

"Ostracism-fear." She has a strong fear of rejection and abandonment because of her having become an "asexual object" for her family. This arose out of a "romancing the stone" relationship with her father, in which he was very conditional in his functioning with her so that she got the loud and clear message that she is acceptable ONLY IF. . .
****

"Not YOU!" She has an ambivalent or rejecting attitude towards this particular infant, as a function of a clash between the infant's characteristics and the mother's life history and dynamics and/or because of the circumstances surrounding this child's being in her life.

INABILITY TO RECOGNIZE FACES

"Who am I?" They have been forced to the realization they have never effectively formed an identity/destiny of their own. They were either prevented from doing so as a function of being born with this disorder (in which case it is a karmic or special experience destiny) or by being required to become a chameleon by their demanding, domineering and dysfunctional family.
****

"Who are you?" They are overwhelmed, outclassed and in over their head with their important people, and they have "pulled the plug" on having to meet the requirements of being in relationship. They are the product of an extremely severely emotionally abusive and draining family.

178

INABILITY TO SLEEP

"Red-orange alert." They are on intense vigilance and "hair-trigger" reactivity. They don't dare to relax because they don't trust the process of life. They have a disturbed mental condition, due to a subconscious shock and/or due to their being in a chronic state of "red-orange alert."

There has now also been an "emergency preparation" activated by current circumstances. They labor under a great deal of guilt and fear over imagined failures and their consequences. It arises from their having been the "sane one" in a severely dysfunctional family.

INABILITY TO SMELL

"Anhedonism." It is a manifestation of the inability to experience or value pleasure. It is a karma-paying or experience-expanding decision by the soul to cut off the ego from the primary grounding and/orienting sense, as well as from the major source of aesthetic experiences.
****

"No discernment." They have an inability to "smell a rat" or to tell that "something's rotten in the state of Denmark." It is the result of a highly collusive and denial-dominated dysfunctional family who required that the individual to not look below the surface of things, and to not tap into their intuition and subconscious perceptivity.

INABILITY TO SNEEZE

"Grief-suppression." It can happen temporarily, as in a situation where the individual is afraid to mourn due to external situational factors, or it can be chronic due to internal emotional factors.

In either case, it represents a pronounced resistance to sadness or to the acknowledgment of sadness as an emotion, due to anticipated dire consequences associated with contacting sadness. It was generated by a family who was denial-dominated, dysfunctional and repressive.
****

"Grief-avoidance." This can represent past life holdovers and/or a learning history in which it was highly traumatic to access grief. It often reflects severe underlying depression or fragmented ego development.

When it is a chronic condition, it reflects a severe self-rejection and the feeling that they have absolutely no right to mourn, as if they would be "wallowing in self-pity." This, in turn, is the result of intensely depriving and denigrating treatment from their family to the accompaniment of "You asked for it, asshole!" messages in large doses.

INABILITY TO SPEAK; INABILITY TO TALK

"Speak no evil." They are in the process of karma-paying for negative utilization of the capacity for speech in their past lives. They are "making an inspirational point" with their handling of their situation, as in the case of Helen Keller.
****

"Seen but not heard." Their family system was so destructive that it made it very clear to them that to speak out about anything that was going on was the occasion for annihilation and/or world-destruction.

INABILITY TO SWALLOW

"Poison apple reaction." The feeling is that nothing can be trusted to be what it appears to be, and that everything is potentially dangerous. They can't accept anything at face value, and they won't swallow anything without a thorough checkout. It arises from an intensely untrustworthy formative environment.

INABILITY TO TASTE

"Repressive shut-down." They are self-protectively into intensity-avoidance, predictability-addiction, and self-suppression. They have a deep-seated fear of the unknown and the unexpected arising from an annihilation-anxiety-inducing childhood in which it was never clear when and whether the end would come.

****

"Balancing the moral budget." They are paying past karma for over-indulgence or utter immersion in the realm of the senses and in hedonic pleasures.

INABILITY TO URINATE

"Pissed off." They are intensely angry at their life, and they are looking for who is responsible for it. They feel betrayed and victimized, especially by their intimates of the other gender. They feel the parent of the other gender is the cause of all their problems. Underneath all this, they have the uneasy feeling that they are really getting their "just desserts."

This whole pattern came about as a result of their being sexualized and sex-ploited in a seductive-destructive and guilt-inducing manner in a severely dysfunctional family.

INABILITY TO WALK

"Teetering instability." They are suffering from scattered thinking, distractible trains of thought, not being centered cognitively. They feel thrown off-base, with no sense of safety, in a kind of fearful drivenness. They are "desperately seeking Susan" in an attempt to gain some sense of stability.

They are therefore always on the lookout for the "greener grass," and they are continuously in fear of missing out or of missing the "key element to things." As a result, they are often instantly pulled off balance by any passing stimulus that "might be the critical factor."

It is the result of a "magical mystery tour" unstable dysfunctional family in which things never really worked, and in which there was no way to tell what was really going on.

(See **BALANCE PROBLEMS; MENIERE'S DISEASE; PARALYSIS**)

INCURABLE DISEASES

"Dead end script." There is lethal programming playing out or an inner decision by their soul to leave. They are chronically disgusted and judging of themselves and others in a "No point staying" manner. They utterly refuse, and they are in effect unable to forgive and forget anything -- they are a grudge-nurser from way back.

It is usually the result of "Don't be!" or "If you commit anywhere, you're going to die because you have killed me!" scripting. It can't be cured by external means, only by going within and re-programming the "bio-computer," and then only if their inner soul is willing to continue here.

INFECTION

"Flare-up." There is irritation, annoyance and anger arising out of a chronic resentment of their situation that has now "gone over the top." There is an intense inner conflict and generalized hostility has taken on physical form.

They are being stressed by current circumstances, and this has resulted in their becoming very angry at their lot in life, particularly around the issues tapped into by their present situation. They are full of annoyance, fury and suspiciousness about everything that is happening to them at this point. It got started in a dysfunctional family in which nothing worked right, and nothing could effectively be done about it.

INFERTILITY

"In over their head." They are experiencing great fear and resistance to the process of life. There is a considerable amount of tension, anxiety, emotional conflict and traumatic shock involved in their life history. They are heavily into competence-anxiety, self-distrust and self-inhibition. It arises from a "blame-throwing" dysfunctional family.
****

"Cold-hearted." It is a case of egotism, selfishness and dishonest feelings being expressed in an ignorant manner. In effect, they don't *want* to be a parent for all the wrong reasons (or maybe for the right reasons, given who they are). They are hard, harsh, cold, judgmental, negative assumptive, angry and blaming. They are manifesting a primitive manner of functioning learned in a similar family.
****

"Not this time around." They don't need to go through the parenting experience, and they are therefore are unconsciously choosing not to sustain the procreation process.
****

"Not time yet!" The child's soul intends to come in, but the circumstances are not appropriate at the moment, for whatever reason.
****

"Are you kidding?!" They have had a long-standing pattern of monastic celibacy in past lives, and they intend to continue the tradition.
****

"Karma." They have a past life history of severe abuse and even murder of children. They are being required to work off that karma before they will be allowed to parent again.
****

"More than one way to skin a cat." The parents are destined to express their generativity in other ways that would prevent, derail or distort proper parenting.

(See **MISCARRIAGE**)

INFLAMMATION

"Flame-throwing." They are caught up in inflamed thinking, and they are fearfully enraged and "seeing red." There is also intense implication-anxiety and implication-anger about everything that is going on in their life.

The experience is of being beset on all sides by inexorable and continuously irritating and threatening forces. They also have the experience of constantly "shooting themselves in the foot," and they are disapproving of and disgusted with themselves.

It all got started in a dysfunctional family in which things were always in an uproar and nothing worked very well.

(Also, see **INFECTION**)

INFLAMMATION OF THE ABDOMINAL CAVITY LINING

"This is an up with which I will no longer put!" They are fed up with the "slings and arrows of outrageous fortune." They have a deep-seated resentment of their lot in life, the hard knocks they have experienced (or are experiencing).

They feel they have assimilated far more than their share of negativity, and they are putting up a protective shield of vulnerability- and involvement-avoidance as a result. It reflects an underlying distrust of the Universe generated by a "poison apple"-dispensing dysfunctional family.

INFLAMMATION OF THE BONES

"Asleep at the wheel Up There." They have a good deal of fear, anger and frustration with the very structure of the Universe, and with the fundamental nature of life. They feel totally unsupported with no sense of safety.

It is a continuation of a feeling they have had all their life, starting in a depriving infancy and childhood in a dysfunctional family where they had to be the tower of power, the "Rock of Gibraltar," the "pillar of strength," the "family hoist."

INFLAMMATION OF THE BRAIN

"God is Al Capone!" They are enraged at the Universe for the "dirty end of the stick" that they have gotten since the beginning. They have always felt like a misfit, that they somehow don't belong here. As a result, their needs have not been met, and they in turn have been unable to fit in. They feel totally betrayed by the "Home Office" (All That Is).

It is the result of their having gotten a lot of "You don't belong here!" messages from the environment. It all got started in their dysfunctional and exploitative yet severely wrong-making family.

INFLAMMATION OF THE CHEEK(S)

"Get out of my face!" They have a fulminating fury about having to suppress their emotional experiences and expressions. Yet they are too inhibited to express it directly. It is the result of an oppressive and accusative family.

RIGHT CHEEK

"Conformity-rage." They have intense irritation over how they have to persona-project, and about how they have to suppress their feelings with other people.

182

LEFT CHEEK

"Moral cretin." There are deep issues of self-rejection and self-rage over their having "unacceptable" feelings and emotions.

INFLAMMATION OF THE MAMMARY GLAND(S)

"This is an up with which I will no longer put!" They are experiencing inflamed thinking, and they are fearfully enraged and "seeing red." There is intense implication-anxiety and implication-anger. The feeling is that they are being beset on all sides by inexorable and continuously irritating and threatening forces. They are the product of an implacably dysfunctional and infuriating family.
****

"Shooting themselves in the foot." They experience constantly getting in their own way, and they are disapproving of and disgusted with themselves. The issues revolve around their maternal manifestation, their sexual attractiveness, and their femininity, along with the role and nature of love in their life. They feel boundary-invaded, exploited and patriarchally harassed.

It all started in an exploitative dysfunctional family in which things were always in an uproar, where nothing worked very well, and in which they were the "sane one" and their only source of feminine resources.
****

"Infernal maternal." They have intense conflicts over their maternal attitudes, home, and motherhood. They feel unable or unwilling to be loving, nurturing and supportive, due to never having been nurtured or due to having the maternal denigrated in their family.

OR They feel exploited, unappreciated and oppressed in response to a patriarchal environment. OR They are over -nurturing, self-denying and insufficiently nourished, refusing to nourish themselves and putting everyone else first, as a function of having had to do so as a child.
****

"Erotic issues." There are conflicts over their sexual attractiveness, their sexuality, their seductive projection and/or their erotic sensitivity and receptivity. They feel insufficiently feminine or attractive, due to devaluing by their family.

OR They feel sex-ploitated, and they deeply resent it, as a function of having encountered such treatment a lot in their family. OR There is a significant case of "tripod-rage" (the irresistible urge to kick anything with three legs) arising from a patriarchal family, from a dysfunctional father, and/or from maternal programming.
****

"Female competence concerns." They are enmeshed in conflicts over their femininity. They feel "masculine" or "unfeminine" because of strong forcefulness of personality or because of devaluation by their family.

OR They feel too feminine, in the sense of feeling like a second class citizen, because they were treated as such at home. OR They feel powerless and unable to cope with life on their own two feet, and they resent it. It is a pattern which came from being competence-undermined and power-prevented as a child.
****

"Love questions." They have conflicts over the role of love in their life. They feel unable to "be loving" as a result of never having been loved themselves. OR They feel that "love is a poison apple," because that's what it was as a child. OR They are starved for love, and they are not finding it because they imprinted on unloving people. OR They feel they don't deserve love as a result of a severely shaming and denigrating family.

RIGHT MAMMARY GLAND
"Conformity-demand resentment." They have a lot of anger over the world's reaction to their preferred forms, means of expressing and/or recipients of nurturance, sexuality-expression or love.

LEFT MAMMARY GLAND
"Emotional deprivation." They are angry over their felt inability to manifest their preferred sources of nurturance, sexuality or love. OR They have issues over felt deservingness of nurturance, sexual support or expression and/or love and caring.

INFLAMMATION OF THE MASTOIDS (The bone behind the ear)
"Tuning out." They have an intense desire not to hear the hostility, conflict and aggression that is going on around them (it usually occurs in children). Their fear is infecting their understanding, and their anger and frustration with the situation has become acute.

It is, of course, the result of a dysfunctional family, in which their needs are often overlooked or belittled, or in which their needs become the grounds for blame and accusation.

RIGHT MASTOID
"Implication-anxiety." There is much fear and anger over the indications for future developments of the hostility in their environment.

LEFT MASTOID
"Abuse-resentment." They have much fear and anger over the treatment that they are receiving, and its implications for their future.

INFLAMMATION OF THE PALATE
"Life sucks!" They have intense resentment of their lot in life. They do not find what has been dealt to them at all to their taste. They feel they should be experiencing a far more palatable fare, and they find their whole situation totally distasteful.

It is the result of their being over-indulged in a highly dysfunctional family, leading to elevated expectations and continuously disappointing servings.

INFLAMMATION OF THE RETINA
"Outraged witness." They are inflamed by what they are seeing going down around them. They feel powerless to do anything about it, and they find the whole situation utterly enraging. It is highly reminiscent of their severely infuriatingly dysfunctional family background.

INFLAMMATION OF THE STOMACH LINING
"Over-burdened." There has been prolonged uncertainty about how things are going to come out, along with a pronounced feeling of doom and disaster in the making. They also have an inability to say "No" to demands, with the result that they "sell themselves out."

It's due to a fear of rejection and abandonment, with an associated grief, despair, guilt and self-disapproval about the loss of their "self-values." They are a perfectionistic workaholic who is trapped in inescapable overwhelming responsibilities in which they are expected to "do the impossible with nothing." They are the product of perfectionistic, judgmental, wrong-making and extremely demanding parents.

INFLAMMATION OF THE TONSILS

"I don't have the right." They have a strong belief that they can't speak up for themselves or ask for their needs. They believe that they don't deserve to have their needs met or to seek any form of gratification. They have an "atonement" approach to life. It is the result of an oppressive and shame-inducing family.

INFLUENZA (See FLU)

INHIBITED ORGASM -- FEMALE

"Can't come." It reflects either a generalized repressive family system and/or a specific programming against sexual passion by one or both possessive parents.

INHIBITED ORGASM -- MALE

"Won't go off." They can't "come" inside a woman. It is the result of possessive and probably sex-ploitative maternal parenting.

INNER EAR PROBLEMS

"Inner mis-directedness." They are finding themselves engaged in self-deluding, disoriented, and/or misguided self-regulation. They are "missing the mark" rather consistently and they are increasingly agitated about it. It reflects a re-prioritizing and re-evaluation of their life direction and manifestation. The underlying cause is a self-misleading self-direction system implanted at an early age by a possessive and simultaneously rejecting family.

RIGHT INNER EAR PROBLEMS

"Self-misleading." They are engaged in self-misdirection in the manner in which they manage their life and in which they make interventions. They feel have "the right formula" for every situation -- only it isn't really right.

LEFT INNER EAR PROBLEMS

"Self-deluding." They are reality-redefining in a manner that is detrimental to their functioning. They are bound to beliefs learned early in their family.

185

INFLAMMATION OF THE INNER EAR

"Angrily self-misguiding." They are very disturbed with, agitated about and resentful of their situation in life. As a result, they are interpreting things from an anger distorted orientation that gets them into trouble. They are the product of a competence-undermining and self-sabotage-inducing dysfunctional family.

INSANITY

"Lost in space." This is a situation in which there is too large a mismatch between the Higher Self and the ego capabilities. There is an overload of Universal energy and Cosmic consciousness for their ego in this life to handle.

The result is that the Higher Self can't help them in mental processing, due to unfinished past life stuff, and that leads to things like fetal malformation, severe physiological limitations or overwhelm, etc., in reaction to the difficult and hostile training environment they chose for their purposes in this life. They have lost or were never able to make connection with the "Home Office" (All That Is).

They end up driven from the pragmatic world, and they are consequently stuck in the dysfunctionality and despair of their past lives, for whatever purposes.

****

"Distorted perceptions." They have much confusion and delusion about what's happening which is generated by perceptual distortions and disorders created by their severely dysfunctional family.

It is reflective of an inability to handle the demands of consensual reality and of pragmatic coping generated by intensely confusing strongly ambivalent parenting very early in life, so that the perceptual/conceptual processes are prevented from developing effectively. It also often involves a body that is genetically restricted in its ability to handle stress.

****

"Shattered, scattered ego." The contents of their experiences reflect the rejection at a very early age. They have no idea who they really are, and their identity is thoroughly fragmented. Their operational ego is a shambles, and it is highly primitive in its nature. They have an inability to disengage from their early formative period and its events.

They have settled upon a violent separation and a thorough-going withdrawal from life, in a totally giving up in the face of overwhelming odds. Escapism, withdrawal and the desire to run from their family are the result. It is the result of a cognitively confusing, severely ambivalent and intensely dysfunctional and operational ego-devastating family.

****

"Past life processing." It reflects a life goal of re-evaluation in which they seek to process the meanings and implications of the last several lives. The soul chooses to have this experience for purposes of consolidating and integrating its previous experiences, so as to eliminate the overload of Universal energy and Cosmic consciousness. The soul may also on rare occasions seek to communicate what it has learned from this process.

(See the book *"Problematic Patterns"* by the author for information on the particular mental illnesses and other psychological disorders)

INSOMNIA

"Yellow alert." They are into chronic vigilance and implication-anxiety, and they are full of tension and negative expectations. They have a deep fear of letting go and surrendering, and they don't dare to relax because they don't trust the process of life.

There is an inability to release the affairs of the day, in a feeling that they have to have hands on control of everything or all hell will break loose. They have a disturbed mental condition, due to subconscious shock, grief and despair arising from a rather severely dysfunctional family.
****

"In-over-their-head effects." They labor under a great deal of guilt and fear over imagined wrong-doings and failures and their consequences. They are forever experiencing potentially intensely threatening situations. They have an inability to love themselves, to trust love, and to trust life.

It's a function of having been the "sane one" in their family during childhood. They were therefore in effect overwhelmed at all times, along with being targeted for the blame for all the misery -- and they bought the guilt.

INTERMITTENT BLEEDING ("Irregular Menstruation")

"She-jection." She has a lot of ambivalence about her femininity or her feminineness. She is angry or ashamed about being a woman in part, and that is acting up now. It comes from having been made wrong for being a woman -- "We (I) wanted a boy." -- "Isn't that just like a woman?" -- "God dammit, why can't you think like a man?!" -- "Women are the cause of all the world's troubles." -- "It's a man's world." etc.
****

"No way, Jose!" She is into intense fertility/creativity-avoidance. She is afraid of or resistant to the generative function -- with all its responsibilities and ramifications. Something in her current life is activating this issue at the present time.

It arises from being made to be afraid of her intuition, creativity, and/or generativity by her family OR from being over-indulged and under-required as a child.
****

"Peter Panella." She is refusing to grow up and become a woman, wanting to remain a little girl who is "taken care of" all of her life. This imprinting is now surfacing in her life. It is the result of over-indulgent and under-requiring parenting, or of being given the message that to grow up and grow away is total family-betrayal.

INTERSEX (Born with both gender characteristics, usually with a surgical decision early on. It frequently leaves the person very confused about gender identity issues.)

"Experience-expansion." Their soul opted for a truly challenging and broadening experience for this lifetime. They will add it to their whole soul history in a manner that is designed to increase their capacity to teach and heal.
****

"Karmic balancing." They now have to learn from the consequences of their abusive patterns in past lives. They will honor the First Law of the Cosmos, the Equal Exchange of Energy, by this process. They will also come out of it a much richer soul in experience.

INTESTINAL CRAMPS

"Dodge ball." They are engaged in a fearful refusal to flow with experiences, and they are stopping the process in its tracks. They fear assimilating negativity. They have learned that nothing can be counted on, and that all good things are "poison apples." It is the result of an underlying distrust of the Universe generated by a dysfunctional family.

INTESTINAL FLU

"Damned if I do, damned if I don't." They have a fear of attack from others and taking life in fully. There is a feeling of lack of support and protection. There is an insufficient involvement and interaction, an "among us but not of us" -- "urban hermit" pattern.

They are subject to conflict, confusion and susceptibility to suggestion, especially from the "world of agreement" or the "group mind" or "statistical proofs." Underneath is a buried rage and hatred for their being so alone, alien and alienated.

It comes from a family in which they "could do no right" as the unrecognized and unacknowledged "family hoist" on whom everyone depended, and whom no one supported, sustained or validated.

"INTUITION HEADACHES" (That come on whenever they exercise their intuition)

"Not allowed!" They are experiencing intense conflicts over their perceptions, intuitions and gestalt comprehensions of situations and processes. These were not acceptable to the family in a BIG way.
****

"Direct perception-deflection." They are systematically suppressing their intuition and psychic capabilities. They are heavily into imaginization-avoidance, and they are detached and intellectually stagnant.

They have difficulty in discrimination and in focusing in life in the form of perceptual problems. They are lost in projections of their negative feelings, and of feared "distorting lens" effects. It came about as a function of their being in a family in which any form of intuitive or imaginative activity was either the basis of disaster in the family's functioning or the grounds for severe rejection and assault.

INVOLUNTARY TREMOR

"Responsibility-immobilization." They are getting stuck, due to paralyzing thoughts, and they are fixated on a particular mind-set, mental approach and paradigmatic model. They want to "make things all right," out of a feeling of having to be the one responsible for everything that happens.

They were placed in a position of excessive and parental role responsibility from a very early age, with the result that they were in over their head from the very start. Their family was highly dysfunctional, and they felt it was their fault.
****

"Rigid rejection." They are full of guilt, and they are not able to forgive others or themselves. They are extremely rigid in how they think that should be, and they are rejecting of life. They are trapped in implication-terror at the thought of things being different from what they imagine, or of their having to try a new approach to things. They are the product of a perfectionistic and inflexible family culture who blamed them for all that wasn't "up to snuff."
****

"Cosmic calamity." They have an intensely anxious relationship with the Universe that is full of fear, uncertainty and insecurity. They have a "God will KILL me if I do anything different!" feeling. It is the result of a very rigid adaptation to a severely dysfunctional and frightening family who themselves manifested a very fearfully narrow viewpoint and lifestyle. They played the role of the "family hoist" who was the pivot point of everything.

"IRRITABLE BOWEL SYNDROME" (See "SPASTIC COLON")

"IRRITABLE STOMACH SYNDROME" (Pains, upsets, nausea, etc.)

"I can't *stomach* this!" They are encountering experiences that are all too evocative of the feelings and events of their dysfunctional childhood, where they were helplessly entrapped.

ITCHING

"Scratch attacks." They are having desires that "go against the grain," in the form of guilt and shame over their wants, needs and desires. There is something "getting under their skin," and they are greatly irritated by it. They want to get away from it, to "scratch it out of their life," and they are most unhappy with where they are in life. There is an intense dissatisfaction with their situation, along with numerous unfulfilled needs, wants and desires.

This is an old, familiar feeling for them, as they come from a severely dysfunctional family in which nothing ever really worked or worked out for them.
****

"Chronic remorse." They have a lot of sorrow and regret over past intended interventions, actions and/or events. There is a torturing sense of "evilness" for having needs, wants and desires, and over their particular wishes and requirements. They are systematically joy- and positivity-avoidant, out of a deeply ingrained sense of somber morality towards themselves.

They have a pronounced feeling of non-deservingness of having their needs met, and an intense fear of and shame for their own desires. Their creative nature seems to be all dried up, because of sudden self-disgust and self-distrust and they are heavily into self-punishment and guilt. It is the result of severe wrong-making, accusation and rejection, starting in infancy.
****

"Stroke-starved." They are experiencing steadily mounting emotional problems in intimacy, or they are deeply troubled by their intimacy-inability. They are "itching" to get out or to get away. Yet they feel they don't have the right to do so. They are resenting having the need for stroking and having to do it for themselves. They are the product of a withholding and untrustworthy family.
****

"Sexual shame." There is a lot of sexual guilt, due to a sexploitive smother-mothering and a shame-inducing history. They have a desperate desire for affection, and a deep fear of being hurt for it. The end result is an inability to let love, affection, and erotic contact in, and they are deeply hurting and hurting themselves for it. It also results in touch-starvation, with a simultaneous vulnerability-paranoia.
****

"Urge to merge." They are experiencing a profound and deep-seated need for "Cosmic fusion" and some sort of ecstatic experience. They feel utterly isolated and cut off, and they long for a truly meaningful connection with something larger than themselves. It is the feeling of being desperately separate from God, along with anxious and self-accusatory concerns about why they are that way.

It is the result of an intense "urban hermit" reaction to being held accountable and responsible for everything that went wrong in their family, along with consistent rejection, starting in the womb.

****

"Experienced rejection." Someone is projecting their irritation at the individual. They have become an irritant to this person, and they are feeling the effects of the anger the other person has towards them. This is not an unfamiliar experience for them, as they were told all their childhood that they were a constant source of irritation.

ITCHING EARS

"Urban hermit blues." They are intensely involved in a deep-seated sense of separateness and isolation, and they feel rejected by God because of their negativity. As a result, they try to suppress or to take care of any and all of their needs, wants and desires entirely on their own. They have a great deal of guilt and shame for having these and that is now becoming quite intense as an issue.

They feel that "God is not pleased" with them because they are encountering needs and desires to connect and form intimate relationships. Their experience is that this is *am strengsten verboten*, (most strictly forbidden) yet they can't continue to suppress this growing motivation and manifestation. It is a matter of considerable conflict for them at the present time.

This whole complex developed as a function of being relied upon exploitatively as the "family hoist" while simultaneously being blamed for everything that went wrong in the family.

This occurred as a function of being sufficiently superior in some way to their parents that they were subconsciously placed in the *in loco* Deity position by their family. They were literally unconsciously experienced as a "little God" who was betraying the family when they "allowed" negative things to happen.

RIGHT EAR ITCHING

"Leave me alone!" They are being bothered by inputs from the environment concerning their needs, wants and relationship-interest.

LEFT EAR ITCHING

"Vulnerability-alarm." They are being alarmed by their inner thoughts and feelings concerning the possibility of forming relationships.

ITCHING EYES

"Ostrich response." They are engaged in awareness-avoidance and denial-domination, as they become threatened by the prospect of seeing clearly their life history, current situation and intended destiny on their way to enlightenment. There is a lot of fear, grief and guilt coming up as an impending breakout from self-limitations looms on the horizon. They were never supposed to get this far, and there is a feeling of family-betrayal, self-endangerment, and oceanic grief as they progress along.

****

"Outta my sight!" There is a deep sense of irritation by what they see, and they want to rub it out of sight. They find what they are encountering utterly intolerable, and they react to their indignation by trying not to see the full implications and ramifications of what is happening. They are the product of a demoralizingly dysfunctional family where looking the other way was the only way to survive the tumult and torture of their experiences.

RIGHT EYE ITCHING

"I don' wanna know." They have a big fear of seeing too much about the world around them.

LEFT EYE ITCHING

"Let's pretend." They are avoiding knowing their personal characteristics and their situation.

~~~~~~

"ITCH FITS" (Breakouts of itching all over the body, reflecting uneliminated toxins in the body, often caused by kidney problems)

"Ejectee-rejectee-dejectee feelings." They have the feeling that they are somehow "unfit for human consumption" and that they are at some level an unacceptable pariah. There is a good deal of underlying self-rejection and/or blame-throwing by their family.

ITCHING LYMPH BUBBLES

"Fear bubbles." They are generating agitated anticipation and dread of the future. They are being inundated with implication-anxiety. It arose from an unpredictable, uncontrollable, non-intervenable dysfunctional family who lived a "magical misery tour" lifestyle.

ITCHING SCALP

"Direction-debating." They are intensely concerned about the correctness of their intentions and interpretations. They are deeply conflicted about their wants, needs and desires, and about how to go about meeting their many unmet needs.

They are deeply dissatisfied with their situation, and they are also full of self-doubts, self-accusations and self-distrust, along with a lot of remorse and regret over their past activities. They were severely wrong-made and confidence-undermined by their rejecting and accusatory family.

RECTAL ITCHING

"Moral cretin." They are suffering from guilt and remorse over the past and a refusal to forgive themselves. They came up in a highly uncompromising and accusative household.

REFERRED ITCHING

"Displaced dissatisfaction." They are experiencing agitation about their situation, but in a manner which re-locates the problem. They are frustrated with the way their life is going, but they are afraid to face the real issues and processes involved. They come from a reality-avoidant dysfunctional family.

"STING-ITCHES" (Sudden and extremely compelling)

"Emotional starvation." There is an intensely felt basic deprivation and a strong feeling of unmet fundamental needs. They have a pronounced sense of utter isolation and alienation, as though they have no business being here, and as though they will never have any form of support or love in their life. These "sting-itchies" are suppressed deep pangs of pain about all this. It is the result of consistent severe rejection, starting in the womb.

I.T.P. (Interstitial Thrombocytopenic Purpura) [Failure of bone marrow to make blood platelets, resulting in ease of bleeding to death.]

"Burden feelings." They have intensely rejecting feelings about themselves arising from a profound buried guilt over a felt impeding of someone else's life, an existential guilt about being a dreary responsibility. They have difficulties in how well they are taking care of their own needs and getting nurtured. There is also a diminishment of life energy and little vitality-replenishment.

They have a rigid, somber and disaster-deflecting orientation that got started in a severely dysfunctional and ferociously close-mindedly denigrating family in which nothing ever worked. They were held accountable for everyone's misery. There was "no room at the inn" for them -- for their having any needs or any form of hope or joy.
****

"Bitter stagnation." They are suffering from deep-seated negative thoughts and feelings of unwillingness to go on with life. Their emotional body is deeply troubled, and there is a real lack of joy and no generation of new ideas. There is an absence of love in their heart. They come from a severely cynical, self-serving authoritarian and hostile family.

<u>**JAUNDICE**</u> (Bile in the blood, leading to yellowish taint to the skin)

"Cynically disgusted." They are strongly given to sneering pessimism and nihilism. They manifest a notable lack of love, compassion and tolerance. They are deeply disappointed, discouraged and disgusted.

They are handicapped by an unbalanced reason that is dominated by negative internal and external prejudices. They are condescendingly contemptuous, and they have an intense resentment over lack of recognition of who they are and what they contribute. It derives from an intensely injustice-nurturing and nihilistic dysfunctional family.

JOINT PROBLEMS

"Rigidly fixated." They are manifesting rigidity and resistance to change in the direction of their life. They are unbending, locked in their position, and unable to move, out of a fear of what lies ahead and out of a refusal to surrender to the processes of life.

They have a basic distrust of themselves and/or of the Universe, and they decidedly do not like the way things are headed. As a result, there is no ease of movement in their functioning or in their moving through the changes in their life.

Their force-flows of life are not fluid or flexible, and there is a lack of presence and gracefulness in their functioning. However, the changes in direction of their life are in response to multi-life issues that they haven't been able to handle, and that now must be handled. Their reaction to this situation is based on having come up in a rigidly patriarchal and conservative family.

~~~~~~

INFLAMMATION OF THE JOINTS

"Super-glue injustice-nurturing." They are feeling rejected for what they are, in the sense of being totally unappreciated. They are full of repressed resentment and anger, and they have a strongly suppressed desire to hit someone. They continuously ruminate and recriminate over their "indignities," and they cling to every item. They come from a severely injustice-nurturing dysfunctional family.
****

"Rigid will." They are unbending in their expression and self-manifestation. They are feeling very victimized and put upon, and they have a chronic bitterness and resentment, leading to a lack of love. They have very strong opinions that they will not, and probably cannot, change. They are the product of an authoritarian and severely patriarchal family.
****

"Boss of the Universe." They have no trust of the "Home Office" (All That Is), and they feel that "It is botching the job." They never let go of anything, in an effort to make life just the way they want it. They grew up in a highly untrustworthy and incomprehensibly dysfunctional family.
****

"Ambulatory paranoid." They are forever sending out arrows of hatred, jealousy, general discord, and other negative their whole system to a halt. They are pushing another person around, or they are being pushed around by another person, and they are into an arrested "fight or flight" reaction.

Underneath all this is a feeling of utter powerlessness and a severe self-and other-rejection arising from their being treated as the "intimate enemy" by their family. They are the product of an intensely hostile home.

193

DEGENERATIVE JOINT DISORDER (DJD) [Arthritis-like]

"Straight-jacketed." They have a pronounced tendency to immobilization, self-criticism, lack of self-worth, fear, anger and a feeling of being tied down, restricted and confined. They are self-suppressing and self-thwarting. They are not allowing themselves to develop their full potential, due to self-distrust, leading to severe constraints. They desperately want to be free to move around and to make something of themselves.

They feel unloved, with a resulting resentful bitterness and a critical judgmentalness towards others. They are suffering from a lot of suppressed resentment, which tends to result in passive-aggressive behavior. They are chronically anxious and depressed, and they are afraid of being angry because it is "wrong, bad and evil." They are the product of perfectionistic parenting in which in effect they could never measure up.
****

"Unfit for human consumption." They are feeling rejected for what they are, in the sense of being totally unappreciated. They are feeling very victimized and put upon, and they experience a lack of love. They feel somehow that they will never receive the acceptance, validation and affection they need. They are the product of a systematically rejecting family system.
****

"Fight or flight." They are immersed in a strong reaction to their situation, and they are chronically anxious. They feel that things have gotten out of hand, and that they can't regain control. They feel that they can't do anything to change their circumstances, and they are utterly frustrated with the way their life is going. They have no trust of the "Home Office" (All That Is), and they feel that "It is botching the job."

Underneath all this is a feeling of utter powerlessness and a severe self- and other-rejection arising from their being treated as the "intimate enemy" by their family.
****

"Will of iron." They have a rigid will and very strong opinions that they will not and probably cannot change. They are unbending in their expression and self-manifestation. They never let go of anything, as they try to be the "boss of the Universe" in an effort to make life just the way they want it. They grew up in a highly inflexible patriarchal and perhaps authoritarian family, and they "identified with the aggressor."
****

"Super-glue injustice-nurturing." They are feeling rejected for what they are, in the sense of being totally unappreciated. They are full of repressed resentment and anger, and they have a strongly suppressed desire to hit someone. They continuously ruminate and recriminate over their "indignities," and they cling to every item. They come from a severely injustice-nurturing dysfunctional family.
****

"Repressed rage." They are full of suppressed resentment and anger and they have a strongly squashed desire to hit someone. They continuously ruminate and recriminate over their "indignities," and they cling to every item. They have a chronic bitterness and resentment, and they are forever sending out arrows of hatred, jealousy, general discord and other negative vibrations.

Their mind is wound up so tight in their hostile preoccupations that it grinds their whole system to a halt, and they are constantly suppressing their desire to strike out and hit people. They are pushing another person around or they are being pushed around by another person. They are the product of an intensely hostile home.
****

"Rigidly fixated." They are manifesting rigidity and resistance to change in the direction of their life. They are unbending, locked in their position, and unable to move, out of a fear of what lies ahead and a refusal to surrender to the processes of life. They have a basic distrust of themselves and/or of the Universe, and they decidedly do not like the way things are headed.

As a result, there is no ease of movement in their functioning or in their moving through the changes in their life. Their force-flows of life are not fluid or flexible, and there is a lack of presence and gracefulness in their functioning.

However, the changes in direction of their life are in response to multi-life issues that they haven't been able to handle, and that now must be handled. Their reaction to this situation is based on having come up in a rigidly patriarchal and conservative family.

****

"Right and righteous." They are very blaming and critical of people, and they are convinced that others won't help them. They are quite fixed, rigid, intolerant and resistive in their functioning. They are quite angry that people won't "carry their load," so that they have to take on what they consider an unjust load.

They are full of projected self-disgust, finding in others what they most dislike in themselves. There are long-standing maladjustments and stony incrustations based on internal conflicts -- often between a desire to do something and a fear of failure. They have great resistance and emotional struggle, with habitual anxiety and fear, "negative faith," and expectations that of the worst case scenario.

They operate with a strong will, inflexible intentions, intense opinions, and an abiding inability to change with changing circumstances. They have a bad case of the "hardening of the attitudes," and they are highly rigid, opinionated and "hung up in principles." They are forcefully opinion-pushing, and they put out a steady stream of skeptical criticism. They are quite hostile, and they are always angry and tense. Calcium growths indicate the presence of hatred and a severely inflexible mind.

It all came from a "vast wasteland" and "dour destiny" type of family culture in which they never knew when something would go wrong, just that it would, sure as the sun rises. It all fell to them to do the necessaries because no one else could be trusted to do so or to do it *right*. No one was ever there for them, and since everything that went down was their fault, they also felt they didn't deserve anyone to be there for them, bottom line.

****

"Ambulatory paranoid." They are forever sending out arrows of hatred, jealousy, general discord, and other negative vibrations. Their mind is wound up so tight in their hostile preoccupations that it grinds their whole system to a halt.

Underneath all this is a feeling of utter powerlessness and a severe self- and other-rejection arising from their being treated as the "intimate enemy" by their family. They are the product of an intensely hostile home.

"STIFF" JOINTS

"No way, Jose!" They are refusing to move forward, to make a new direction in their life. They are rigidly resistant to change and evolution, preferring to stick with the "good old ways" well beyond its usefulness, if not to the point of severe self-detriment. They come from a family in which there was "one and only one right way" to do everything, and in which any deviation brought severe consequences.

[See **BURSITIS**]

JOINT REPLACEMENT.
"New cup! New cup!" They have in effect completed all the learning and experience-expansion of their heretofore life pattern. It is time to move on with all that under their belt and available for their "stage two rocket" phase of their life.
~~~~~~

HIP REPLACEMENT
"Enough, already!" They have had it with regard to the whole process of potency-suppression that their surrounding environments have always imposed upon them. They are now ready to embark on a world-influencing path.

RIGHT HIP REPLACEMENT
"I'll cause World War III!" They were systematically trained to believe that they are untrustworthy and potentially dangerous in the environmental impact. No more!

LEFT HIP REPLACEMENT
"Not AGAIN!?" They are deeply self-distrusting about their choice of intimates, based on their track record. However, the past was! It's OVER!
~~~~~~

KNEE REPLACEMENT
"I don't DARE!" They were so programmed into their family's values, beliefs, life-way and expectations of an intention for them that they have been highly resistive to manifesting themselves and their destiny.

RIGHT KNEE REPLACEMENT
"Success-avoidance." They were shooting themselves in the foot in reaction to the requirement that they move beyond their family's patterns. Forget it!

LEFT KNEE REPLACEMENT'
"Damn me!" They were systematically refusing to manifest their destiny in accordance with their soul's intents and with the Divine Design Not any longer!
~~~~~~

SHOULDER REPLACEMENT
"Everything always falls on *my* shoulders!" They have the feeling that the burdens they carry are not their own. They resent the "heaviness" of life, and they feel that they are carrying the weight of the world on their shoulders.

RIGHT SHOULDER REPLACEMENT
"Behind the scenes Atlas." They are constantly taking the over-responsible, under-appreciated and hyper accountable role. End of *that* story!

LEFT SHOULDER REPLACEMENT

"Alone and alien." They feel that they have to handle all their needs, with no help from non-existent friends. They have had enough of *that* old story!

"JUNGLE ROT" (Severe fungus infection)

"Swamp growth." They are refusing to release the past, and they are letting the past rule today. They are stuck in stagnating beliefs and stationary strategies. The feeling is that "The war is NOT over," that nothing has substantially changed since they developed their ways of being and doing things in a dysfunctional family.

That, in turn, is a self-fulfilling prophecy effect generated by the assumption that nothing has changed, so that there is continuous re-validation of the assumptions and strategies of the past. They are the product of a retrogressive, past-fixated and rigid patriarchal family who won't let go of what was.

KAPOSY'S SARCOMA (Large red spots all over the body usually arising from sexual promiscuity)

"Unfit for human consumption." They have intense concerns about how they think other people are seeing them, how they fit in to the norms of society, and how they see themselves and their deeper insecurities.

They are embarrassed, ashamed and guilty. There are feelings of inferiority, low self-esteem, ostracism and obstruction. They are concerned about how good an example they are to others. They are troubled by their unexpressed unlovely thoughts about other people that have arisen out of a severely unpleasant life history. They were subjected to severely critical, wrong-making, judgmental and blame-throwing parenting.
****

"Proving themselves." They have real world mastery problems, and they end up trying to demonstrate their proficiency in areas where they aren't really capable. They are deeply bothered by how much they aren't being allowed to use their expertise.

They have been so misunderstood and ill-treated that they feel that they have to withdraw into their core to protect their individuality and integrity. This all got started in their intensely rejecting and exploitative family.
****

"Letting things get under their skin." There is a lot of anxiety and fear from old, buried "gukky" stuff, including from past lives. They have a feeling of being threatened in some way, which is a warning to watch their attitude. They grew up in an infuriatingly and intensely threateningly untrustworthy dysfunctional family.
****

"Sexual guilt." There is a felt need for punishment arising out of their severe sexual and generalized shame. Their gut-level belief that sexuality is sinful or dirty, due to a sexually suppressive and shame-inducing, yet simultaneously "tantalizing tarantula" seductive-destructive sex-ploitive dysfunctional family.

KIDNEY PROBLEMS (Inability to cleanse the blood of waste products)

"Negative thinking." This problem is designed to convey the message that they need to turn off their forever looking at what's wrong about things. There has to be a willingness to repress, suppress or refuse to express negative inner experiences and qualities.

It is a law of manifestation that if you wish to learn that which is within, make it manifest externally or overtly. Now they have done that, they need to master their negativity as a major lesson of this life.
****

"Blew it!" They are having the experience of a failure, a loss, a set-back, a disappointment or a reversal. Their experience is that it is their own entire fault, due to their being a general "fuck-up." They are over-reacting to this disappointment situation. Their family was blame-throwing, accountability-attributing, wrong-making and exploitative.
****

"Shadow-boxing." They are afraid of that which was rejected by their environment, and that was required to be "shoved into the shadow" as a child. So anything that activates their unexpressed aspects frightens them.

They are therefore emotionally confused, and they systematically repress their emotions. This most often shows up in difficulty accepting and getting along with other people, especially intimate partners, who express these repressed qualities they find in themselves. It is an "I just hate that about you!" (as they point their finger at themselves) reaction.
****

"Intense vulnerability-anxiety." They are suffering from a chronic primal fear, with a pronounced tendency to run their life around "saving for a rainy day." They are experiencing considerable anxiety, worries and fears over money. There is no sense of well-being, and they are intensely abandonment-anxious. They have no trust of partnership, commitment or connection, and they feel alone on their own.

They are the product of an intensely anxiety-inducing and rejecting dysfunctional family in which much went wrong over which they had no control and for which there was no solution.
****

"Self-acceptance issues." They have much self-doubt and they are ashamed of themselves. They are feeling like a kid who can't do it right, and who is "not good enough." They have a strong feeling of failure and a profound sense of loss and grief.

There is much self-disappointment, self-disapproval and self-rejection. They are intensely reluctant to release their negative emotions. They have deep feelings of inadequacy, insufficiency, incompetence, worthlessness, and guilt.

They are experiencing intense demoralization, unhappiness and confusion. They have become completely amotivational, and they are manifesting no effort or ability to take care of themselves -- they are showing no self-respect.

There has been a sudden shock or the triggering of a great deal of grief. They were systematically told that they don't have what it takes to make it by a family who were invalidating, denigrating and accusatory.
****

"Selfish judgmentalness." They are intensely prone to criticalness, along with a propensity to jealous possessiveness, envy and greed as a defensive strategy. They could care less about ecological issues, they are severely uncaring and selfish. They have lost their cleverness and capacity for energetic work to an over-riding fearfulness. They are in effect paranoid in their orientation and functioning. They grew up in an authoritarian patriarchal household.
****

"Right and righteous." They come from a moralistic, perfectionistic and demanding family. They therefore are in effect trying to control everything to make things correct according to their criteria. They ended up being rather severely judgmental and resentful towards people for not living up to their standards. They are full of unjustified criticalness and wrong-making.

RIGHT KIDNEY PROBLEMS

"Cope-ability-anxiety." They have feelings of utter incompetence at coping in the world.

LEFT KIDNEY PROBLEMS

"Self-rejection." There are profound shame, guilt, and worthlessness feelings.

~~~~~~

INFLAMMATION OF THE KIDNEYS

"There I go again!" They are having an over-reaction to disappointment and failure experiences. They are flooded with implication-anxiety based on past patterns, in a self-distrust reaction. They have the experience that the universe is unjust, and that they have become the product of that fact. They are convinced that they are trapped forever in the adaptations they made to their original dysfunctional family.

KIDNEY STONES

"Angry despair." They are feeling misunderstood, with an intense feeling of frustrated despondency. There is a large store of unshed tears, fears, and sadness arising from old issues that should have been released but have been instead held onto. They are also storing resentments and holding grudges in such a manner as to result in crystallizations of their rage in the form of stones.

The whole thing is an overlay on top of their underlying feeling of incapacity to cope with the demands of life arising from intensely accusatory and blame-throwing parenting in a highly suppressive household.

KLINEFELTER SYNDROME (XXY genetic structure that generates language-related learning disabilities, with speech delay, extreme shyness, and small genitalia in some cases.)

"Best of both." They have components of both genders in their genetic make-up, and it gives them the capacity for manifesting the qualities and capacities of each of them. However, it does tend to result in some undermining of the operation of the left hemisphere, which requires some compensatory training and intervention, preferably early in childhood, after a chromosomal check.

It is the result of destiny design intentions to be able to manifest the capabilities of both genders in their role, experiences and contributions in this lifetime. Depending on how it has played out in their life, it can either Cosmic consequences for past life abuses in the male role that result in their being able to do neither role well, or dharmic for the purposes of extraordinarily integrated contributions.

LACTIC ACIDOSIS (Burning sugar rather than oxygen, resulting in dissolving of the lungs by the resulting acids)

"Self-suppressing." They are full of family taboos, social restrictions, moral inhibitions, and unexpressed passions, strong desires and emotions. They don't have any sense of freedom or the right or ability to communicate their feelings. They have now reached the point where they just can't take it any more. This whole thing was generated by a self-immersed and dysfunctional family who were severely exploitative, shame-inducing and rescue-eliciting.

****

"Don't deserve." Their family experience was one in which they were made to feel bad, wrong and evil. They therefore feel unworthy of living fully, and they are alone, sad and non-belonging, with no sense of acceptance. They are once again in a smothering and stifling environment like the one they grew up in.

****

"Wrong commitments." They get into consuming passionate involvements that lead nowhere, and to get into repeated devastating unrequited love situations. They have a sensitive mind and a very strong sense of justice, righteousness and generosity that frequently leads them into blind alleys and exploitive situations and relationships.

They come from an injustice-sensitive and righteously indignant family system that taught them to tilt windmills and to set themselves up in relationships which replicate the no-win situations they had at home.

****

"Outta here!" They have a real difficulty in taking in prana, chi, qi, love or life energy as a function of the prideful brutalizing misuse of energy in past lives. They have an inability to renew to the breath of life and a lack of enthusiasm and zeal for living.

They are suffering from depression and chronic grief, because they are deeply afraid of taking in love and life energy. They are joy-avoidant and happiness-squashing, out of a profound fear of the Universe. They lack cosmic, community and conjugal contact. Their family was withholding, rejecting and ejecting.

LACTOSE INTOLERANCE (Suppressed generation of the enzyme necessary to break down the lactose in milk)

"Rejection of the Maternal." They find anything and everything having to do with the Feminine and especially the Maternal rather intensely aversive, and they are consequently consistently avoidant and/or denigrating of it. It arises from maternal parenting that was absent, irrelevant, aversive, exploitative, abusive and/or untrustworthy.

****

"Maternal rejection." They were systematically subjected to pervasive maternal messaging that they were "bad, wrong and evil." They are therefore convinced at a deep level that they are "unfit for human consumption," and they are rather intensely self-rejecting.

LADA (Latent Autoimmune Diabetes in Adults)

"Don't deserve it!" They are systematically engaged in resistance to the sweet part of life, resulting in a continuous ambivalent reaction to good things happening for them. They have to constantly grapple with self-rejection and guilt feelings.

It comes from messaging from the most rejecting parent that they are a continuous problem, when in fact, they have always been the solution to problems in their nature and functioning. They were a threat and a guilt-induction to that parent.
****

"Allergic reaction to themselves." They feel somehow responsible for all the ills of the world, that they are the cause. They are having a "get rid of the problem" reaction. They have ended up with little or no ability to receive or to request or to require a return in kind.

It is a result of having "carried the world on their shoulders" all their life, starting with their dysfunctional family. They were told in effect that they were the source of all the family's problems, while they were actually the only one who was deflecting some of the disasters.

LARGE INTESTINE PROBLEMS (Assimilates nutrients from the food intake)
"Survival-anxiety." They have intense concerns over whether they can really handle life. There is a felt powerlessness arising from "skid row" programming and learned helplessness in the face of a severely dysfunctional family.
****

"Virgo-izing it." They are trying to cover all the details, to organize and coordinate everything, to analyze the situation, and to meet all the needs in the right way. They are given to nit-picking perfectionism, detail-domination, and an inability to see the forest for the trees. It is a pattern that got started in a patriarchal and perfectionistic family.
****

"Papa/Mama knows best!" They are prone to over-criticality and a compulsion to help others that is carried out unwisely. They have a desire to be needed in order to inflate a damaged ego or to manipulate people.

They are pushing ideas or things on people in an unwanted rescue-tripping pattern that is the product of their feeling responsible for straightening things out in their severely dysfunctional family.
****

"Exploitation-rage." They feel used and abused, rushed and over-controlled, and like they are in servitude. They feel injured and degraded by some external malignant force. They have the feeling that what they give is not used, appreciated or utilized its intended purposes.

They feel they are being humiliated, and they want to dispose of it *now*! They want to eliminate the responsible agent. They are bursting with unexpressed rage, and they are super self-suppressing. They come from an exploitative, manipulative and supremely selfishly abusive dysfunctional family.
****

"Ostrich trip." They are a basically sensitive, bright, timid, dependent, Pollyanna-ishly denying, and passive person who are reluctant to take life on. They are in perfectionistic denial of the realities that they are maintaining a "conspiracy of silence" about, and which they studiously avoid looking at.

They have the feeling that if they every really looked at their situation, they would come to a deadly end. Their family was intensely intimidated, dependent, denial-dominated and rug-sweeping, out of an underlying terror of the Universe.
****

"Abandonment-paranoid." They are possessive and emotionally unbalanced, with no sense of being loved, wanted or needed. They come from an enmeshed, ambivalent and acceptance-rejection game-playing family.
****

"Serve-aholic." They are a self-denying, over-responsible, and self-denigrating in a severely self-defeating manner. It is a "Cinderella/Cinderfella" pattern in which they were used and abused for self-immersed purposes in an abusive and "jailing" family.
****

"Intuition-avoidance." They are avoiding their inner knowing, their truth-perceptions, and their reality-reading capacities. They are putting out an over-rational and/or fearfully reality-avoidant pattern. They grew up in a severely dysfunctional and denial-dominated family in which accuracy of understanding lead to great pain and potential disaster.
****

"Abyss trip." They are having problems with intense greed and acquisitiveness to the point of its being an addictive process. They have a gaping maw quality about them, and they can never have enough. They are the product of a severely survival-oriented family.
****

"Yin-paranoia." There are deep-seated fears of the unconscious and of the feminine. They are extremely controlling of their emotions, and they maintain a compulsive rationality and a "hands on control" approach to life. They come from an intensely patriarchal family.

~~~~~~

CROHN'S DISEASE (Chronic inflammation of the large intestine at the ileum)
"I'm not good enough." They are self-disapproving and insecure in an "alone on my own" psychology. Their attitude is that they can't trust anyone to do anything for them, and that they may not be enough to do the job either. They feel that they somehow don't deserve support, and that they are likely to be inadequate to the cause.

It is the result of early emotional neglect, followed by capability-undermining and shame-inducing parenting.
****

"Can't discern." They can't tell which end is up, due to the distortions of their discrimination capability. They just don't know how to tell wheat from chaff, relevant from irrelevant, safe from dangerous, useful from useless, etc. It was generated by their confusion-inducing dysfunctional family.
****

"Royally pissed off." They have the feeling that they have been systematically deprived and derailed all their life. Their experience is that they get the dirty end of the stick and the dregs/leftovers everywhere they go. It is an up with which they will no longer put -- they can't assimilate it any more, period, end of report! It got started in an exploitative dysfunctional family.

DIVERTICULITIS (Inflammation of the tiny pouches in the large intestine)
"Undeserving." They have guilty feelings of unlovability, and they engage in self-punishing self-deprivation for presumed transgressions. They are apt to go off into severe self-recrimination in reaction to rejection.

They are not being able to assimilate or absorb what they are experiencing or who they are. It comes from over-exacting parents who placed their "love-line" on the block with perfectionistic expectations.

INFLAMMATION OF THE LARGE INTESTINE
"Self-rejecting affection-desperation." They have a guilty feeling of unlovability and a great need to be loved that is prevented fulfillment by self-punishing self-deprivation for presumed transgressions that the outside world is unaware of.

Their constantly thwarted efforts to achieve affection that never get results end up in intense self-denigration and severe pessimism. They are apt to go off into a frenzy of self-recrimination in reaction to rejection of love from a dear one. There is a considerable feeling of undue burdens, emotional strain and loneliness.

They are over-conscientious and hyper-sensitively over-conscious, with a false feeling of accountability and moral culpability. They tend to be a self-defeating loser, out of an emotionally immature attitude of self-destruction. They are very insecure, and they have a very difficult time letting go of that, which is over and done with. It came from over-exacting parents who imposed an experience of intense oppression, over-responsibility and defeat.

****

"Ambulatory paranoid." They have a generalized suspiciousness orientation that is derived from persecutory parenting. They believe that virtually everything is dangerous and double-dealing. They feel that they have the right to eliminate the causes of their presumed persecution.

They display extreme distrust, security-freak, and stability-seeking behavior. They are actively suspicious of the environment, and they are intensely control imposing. They have great rageful resentment, feeling like they have received something poisonous. They want to get rid of it, dispose of it, and to destroy its source.

They are the product of a rather severely paranoid patriarchal and authoritarian family who treated them as the "intimate enemy."

REGIONAL ENTERITIS

"Ambulatory paranoid." They have an organized suspiciousness orientation derived from persecutory parenting. They believe that virtually everything is dangerous and double-dealing. They feel that they have the right to eliminate the causes of their presumed persecution.

They display extreme distrust, security-freak, and stability-seeking behavior. They are actively suspicious of the environment, and they are intensely control-imposing. And they have great rageful resentment, feeling like they have received something poisonous. They want to get rid of it, to dispose of it and its source.

They come from an overtly paranoid and hostile family who hid none of their embittered, extremely suspicious and ragefully vengeful attitudes. They treated the individual as the "intimate enemy" as well.

LARYNGITIS

"Radio silence." There is a fear of speaking up, and they are afraid to ask for what they want because they are sure it would be withheld or used against them. There is also a fear of expressing themselves and of not being able to answer questions, criticisms and/or attacks. They are also afraid to express their opinions or to make recommendations. So they repress or suppress their feelings, reactions and interpretations. They weren't allowed to have wants, needs or desires, they weren't allowed to speak up or impact, and they weren't heard or respected.

****

"They don't listen to me!" There is a great deal of anger and resentment, particularly towards the authorities, authority figures and/or authority itself. They are "so mad they can't speak up for themselves" -- rageful that they can't be or express themselves in the world. There is a suppressed order-giver underneath all this -- an "I know better what needs to happen here!" feeling.

This whole experience is an old, familiar theme song for them, as it represents what happened in their dysfunctional family, where things went awry all the time, the "powers-that-be" were a "ship of fools," and they were not able to say anything about it.
****

"Hoof-in-mouth disease." They are experiencing shame and guilt over something they have already said. They are trying to stop themselves from any further ecological disaster episodes. They are afraid of someone hearing what they have to say or what would happen if they said any more. They come from a severely denial-dominated dysfunctional family where any form of "cover-blowing" blew up the whole family.

LARYNX PROBLEMS

"Seen but not heard." Their experience is that it is decidedly not allowed for them to speak their piece or to communicate their truth. In effect, it operates like a tight band around their larynx, which represents a "hob-nailed boot" from the environment.

They feel immensely frustrated, invalidated, ignored, deprived, humiliated and ejected/rejected. They also have a profound conflict about whether and how to express themselves about their needs, awareness's, wisdom, recommendations, interventions, predictions, comprehensions, evaluations etc. The message was very clear that they were to keep their mouth shut.

LARYNGIAL "SPASMS"

"Don't you DARE!" Their experience is that it is decidedly not allowed for them to speak their piece or to communicate their truth. In effect, it operates like a "hob-nailed boot" on their larynx, which represents the reaction from their early environment.

They feel immensely frustrated, invalidated, ignored, deprived, humiliated and ejected/rejected. They have a profound conflict about whether and how to express themselves about their needs, awareness's, wisdom, recommendations, interventions, predictions, comprehensions, evaluations etc.

They are choking to death on their own guilt and shame. They feel that they should be thoroughly punished or even destroyed for their "sins," particularly around their need/desire to communicate the truth.

It comes from a severely accusatory, blame-throwing, moralistic, reality-avoidant and punitive family. The message was very clear that they were to keep their mouth shut -- or else.

"LAZY EYE(S)" (Poor ciliary muscle control, resulting in their eye(s) moving around on their own accord)

"I don' wanna see that!" They are internally conflicted, and they are afraid to see what's out there. It is s if it is so horrifying in the world that they would rather "feel their way along by Braille" than to encounter the full truth of the situation -- in a kind of "Medusa-paranoia" reaction, in which they are afraid of what would happen if they saw themselves and the world in a "mirror."

It got started in horrifically dysfunctional family in which a child seeing the whole scene or seeing all of themselves would indeed be overwhelmed and devastated. So they co-opted the denial-dominated and superficiality-fixated strategy of their family, and they ended up with a "wandering eyes" pattern, in order to avoid seeing too much and to avoid being seen seeing.

By doing so, they took on a "protective coloration" camouflage, while simultaneously calibrating how much of the truth of the situation they could actually handle at a time. However, it has cost them dearly, because they do have great difficulty seeing what's going on, and that has led to many problems in their life.

In effect, they have a rather nasty habit of getting in their own way, in a success-deflecting manner. This, in turn, tends to greatly reinforce their fear of the world and/or of themselves. This is usually, though not always, a soul decision in order to expand their soul's experience, to make a contribution from it all, and/or to pay karmic consequences.

"LAZY" RIGHT EYE
"I can't handle that!" They have a pronounced propensity to not want to know what's going on in the world around them.

"LAZY" LEFT EYE
"I don't dare look in the mirror!" They systematically suppress awareness of aspects of themselves that their family would "kill" them for manifesting.

LEAD POISONING (Forebrain, left hemisphere and midbrain damage)
"Amotivational lethargy." They are not at all certain they want to be here, having to carry the responsibilities of living. Their feeling is something like, "Here's *another* fine mess I've gotten myself into!"

They feel overwhelmed, exhausted and depleted, with little energy available even for maintenance tasks. They want to be taken care of and be free to process things unencumbered. It is the result of severely disempowering and demoralizing competence- and confidence-undermining possessive and denial-dominated dysfunctional parenting.

LEGIONNAIRES DISEASE (Sudden virus-caused failure of the immune system)
"Hardening of the attitudes." They are manifesting a certain mental harshness and hard-nosed closed-mindedness. They have a will of iron, and they are intensely inflexible, out of a "generalized dread." They have taken on their life with self-willed determination and a "true grit" response.

They feel that there is no support or assistance, and that they have to take it all on by themselves. They are very rigid and moralistic, with a steel-reinforced value system, along with a fixed way of looking at the world and of doing things.

This all started in a family in which they were treated as the "intimate enemy." What has happened now is that they have reached the end of their rope with this lifestyle, and they are depleted and exhausted to the point where they don't have the wherewithal to.

LEISHMANIASIS (Debilitating disorder that can result in severe facial disfiguration)
"Here's *another* fine mess I've gotten you into!" They are intensely shameful and self-blaming. They also fear attack and accusation from others, and they feel very vulnerable to devastation by other people. They have a rotten self-image, and they feel they are somehow deserving of their "ejectee/rejectee/dejectee" situation due to their "wrong-being." It is a pattern that was created by a severely rejecting, exploitative and blame-throwing family.

LEPROSY (Bacterial disease leading to slow swelling, disfiguration, disintegration, and loss of sensation)

"I'm not good enough." They have a very strong belief in being "evil," "immoral," and "unclean." They feel that they deserve "just punishment" for their "wrong-being." They have a "rotten" self-image that is massively self-rejecting. They believe that God hates them. They are immobilized by their limitations, both genuine and imagined, and they can't handle life at all.

They are the product of a devastatingly destructive and denigrating dysfunctional family who was abusive, sex-ploitative and shame-inducing. There never was any love in their life.

LEUKEMIA (Excessive white cells leading to self-attack and self-destruction)

"I *am* my limitations!" This is the foundational assumption, and they feel it is totally unsafe to be who they are. They are giving up on life with a massive "What's the use?" feeling and an accompanying severe depression and despair. They feel that their present situation and future prospects are totally unacceptable and intolerable. They feel utterly hapless, helpless and hopeless. Their family was super-subtly viciously violent and accusingly attacking.
****

"Alienated isolation." At base, they are distrusting, dismissive, alienated and confused by love for and from others, and they want to isolate themselves and not feel anything.

It seems to result in intense frustration with themselves, and in a bottling up of their emotions, with especial repression of their disturbed or conflicted attitudes towards love. Underneath, they are also deeply resentful and disgusted by people, with a lot of vengeful thoughts. The disease is often precipitated by the loss of an intimate such as a parent. It apparently comes about as a result the loss's connection with their lack of the expression of the love within them. They are the product of a distantiating, untrusting, and alienated family.
****

"Moral monster." They took all their family's dysfunctional blame-throwing on themselves as God's just judgment because it was so subconscious and subterranean. The result is that they are now brutally killing their inspiration and self-manifestation as a "moral imperative." They are unable to express their feelings about things, their reactions to things, and their position on things. They are the product of an accusatory/attributional rejecting family.

(See **CANCER**)

"LISPING"

"Rejection-expecting." Their social interface is laced with anticipations of negative reactions to what they have to say. It is the result of significant intolerance for who they are and to their informational inputs from their family. They were, in effect, a pariah in their own dysfunctional family, who couldn't deal with the truths they put out.

LIVER PROBLEMS

"Cosmic double play." Their Higher Self manifestation has been thrown off balance by some sort of severe setback or by a catastrophic loss or event. They therefore lack good sense, sanity, equilibrium and "normalcy" at the moment. They also are having difficulties with discrimination, faith and capacity for spiritual knowing. They are having an existential crisis around philosophical, religious and Cosmic issues. It is part of the process of readying them for the manifestation of their intended destiny.

****

"Deflated balloon." They are having trouble standing up to what has to be faced, and to rebuilding and replenishing their life force. They try to hide from themselves, they won't tell themselves the truth, they run away from their issues, they duck out from under their problems, they won't face reality, and they are systematically not noticing what is going on in their life.

They lack the psychological strength to engage in strategic planning and practical execution, and to pull off the transformation in their life and attitudes that is necessary at this time. They feel hapless, helpless and hopeless, and they are convinced that they can't handle life. They have a severe suppressed underlying despondency, along with an overwhelming despair.

They come from a severely demoralizingly dysfunctional family who effectively undermined and prevented the development of their self-sufficiency and life-support provision capabilities.

****

"Unfit for human consumption." They feel like a "bad" person who has no right to live or to have life-sustenance. Their experience is that there is something wrong with this picture -- and that is that they are still in it. They are plagued by continuous self-condemnation, self-attack, and intense regret over things they have experienced or done.

They are the product of a significantly dysfunctional family who gave them the constant message they have no right to support or sustenance, and that they have to continuously contribute to justify their very existence.

****

"Generalized resentment." They are angry and confused about what their life is all about. They have intense resentment and rage about lack of recognition, about unjustified criticisms, and about having to support themselves to such a degree. They are exasperated, judgmental, frustrated, and they are full of primitive emotions like fear, depression, anger, worry, anxiety, hate, self-disgust, hurt, need for power, greed, jealous possessiveness, and critical attitudes.

They are full of feelings of being unjustly treated, and they harbor desires for revenge. They are chronically complaining and finding justifications for petty fault-finding, as a means of deceiving themselves. They are systematically self-misleading and self-deluding to justify their attack behaviors. They are the product of a severely dysfunctional, rageful and blame-throwing family.

INFLAMMATION OF THE LIVER

"Fulminating fury." They are a boiling cauldron of seething resentment of the past, and they manifest an intense resistance to change. They are full of fear, anger and hatred arising out of experienced powerlessness, self-doubts and guilt, all of which are projected out as accusations of corruption and exploitation. They feel totally overloaded with demands and unable to deal with them. It arose in a highly dysfunctional and enraging family who demanded far too much and who instilled deep-seated self-doubt and cope-ability-anxiety.

"LONG QT" SYNDROME (Sudden severe cardiac arrhythmia, possibly genetic)

"One strike and I'm out!" They feel that "the buck stops here," and that they are solely responsible, accountable and capable of handling everything. They are the "lone stranger riding off into the sunset" who walks alone.

It is a pattern that got started intrauterine, when there was at least severe ambivalence about their coming. It continued as the family reacted to them as a resource to rely upon, instead of as a child needing nurturance, support, protection, guidance and training.

LOSS OF ABSTRACT THINKING FUNCTION

"I don' wanna know!" They are into compulsively concrete control-mania, and they are heavily denial-dominated and feeling-avoidant. They don't *want* to know what the meanings of things are. It comes from a severely dysfunctional and stressful family in which they had to develop moment-by-moment survival strategies, and in which awareness was both intensely punished and deeply alarming.

So they concentrated on what was in front of them and ignored the rest. While they were able to utilize the abstract function, they did not like to do so, due to their early history, and that attitude has now resulted in its loss.

LOSS OF BODY AND HEAD HAIR

"Return to infancy." It represents the repudiation of all passion, potency and personhood, along with a retreat into innocence and reactivity. It is a manifestation of an intense abandonment-annihilation-anxiety and rejection-paranoia, along with severe competence-and cope ability-anxiety. It tends to be precipitated by the immanence of a strong destiny-development process possibility.

It comes from being heavily programmed not to be too threatening or self-developing in an intensely conditionally accepting family who were highly possessive and/or alarmed by their potency and potentials.

LOSS OF COORDINATION

"Oh no you don't!" They have crossed the "forbidden line" into self-commitment and destiny manifestation, and a long-ago implanted injunction to the effect of, "If you ever violate this taboo, a hex on you!" from their family has gone off. They were to never abandon the family by bonding with relevant others, developing their capacities, or moving into manifestation of their purpose.

LOSS OF EYEBROWS AND/OR EYELASHES

"Close to the chest." They feel (consciously or unconsciously) that it is not safe to express their feelings directly or in a public manner, given the present circumstances. It should be noted that these circumstances are tapping into an old, familiar feeling and strategy. They found out that letting their family knows where they were coming from was tantamount to disaster, particularly in important matters where strong feelings are involved.

LOSS OF MENTAL FUNCTIONS

"Hell no, I won't go along!" They are engaged in a refusal to deal with the world as it is, out of an enraged helplessness and hopelessness. They feel overwhelmed by the requirements of life and unable to cope any more. There is a great deal of bitterness and disgust with the Universe and with the "Home Office" (All That Is). They are having an "I'm taking my marbles and going home!" reaction.

This is a pattern that started early in life, when they had to face an uncaring and even hostilely demanding environment, which had a demoralizing effect on them. Their response to this generated a setting up of a "self-fulfilling prophecy effect" in which they repeatedly found themselves in repetitions of the formative environment. They kept up as long as they could, and now they have decided that enough is enough.

****

"Phasing out." They are doing a stage-by-stage exit from this plane. They are spending a lot of time in the other realm, processing what has gone on and "going to school" out there. They periodically "check in" here, and they then suddenly become lucid for a while. Then they "head on out" again. It seems to be related to a control trip in which they don't trust anyone or anything unless they are at the throttle. That, in turn, comes from growing up in an incompetent, dysfunctional and untrustworthy family or in a family which treated them as the "intimate enemy."

(See **ALZHEIMER'S DISEASE; SENILITY**)

LOSS OF THE SENSE OF TOUCH

"Shut down." They have disengaged from contact with the world around them because it has become too painful to tolerate. It is due to their having had their boundaries violently invaded on the emotional (and perhaps the physical) level throughout their childhood. This left them "shell-shocked," and they were unable to take the "slings and arrows of outrageous fortune" any longer.

"LOU GHERIG'S DISEASE" (Degeneration of the spinal cord and the muscles)

"I don't dare!" They are experiencing severe annihilation-anxiety around the issue of seeking, manifesting and especially acknowledging success. They have the utter conviction that they are the "turd of the Universe," and that they don't have any worth whatsoever. They deny their success, and they are totally unwilling to accept their self-worth.

They are in effect completely immobilized by betrayal avoidance, in that the family, the mother in particular, conveyed to them very clearly that any form of self-manifestation, success in the world and commitment elsewhere would destroy their family.

It got started at a time when there was, in their experience, no difference between their mother and the Universe, so that in effect, they would be committing "Deicide" if they seek success or if they recognize their worth -- they would be destroying God and all Its creation. So to avoid that "ultimate calamity," they are sacrificing themselves on the altar of "filial piety."

"LOW MILK SYNDROME" (Malnutrition-caused strokes, blood clots and other oxygen deprivation-caused brain damage in the infant, due to low breast milk.)

"Who invited YOU!?" She is extremely unclear on the concept of being a mother -- of this child or at all. She feels totally unprepared for the responsibility and the requirements. She may feel in over her head, or she may be highly unwilling to be a mother. In any case, it reflects the rather strong "unwelcome wagon" reaction to her own birth that she experienced at the hands of her mother.

****

210

"I want out." They have a rather strong lack of interest in and rejection of life. They have a subconscious death wish based on a guilty conscience that got started in the womb, even before the lack of mother's milk. Their experience is that they have no right to be here taking up resources and space, because "God said so." It is the result of the intense maternal ambivalence or rejection of having a child or of having this child.

LOW PLATELETS (Difficulty clotting blood)

"Over-responsibility." They have a sense that they are here to make the world all better, and that they should care-take everything and everyone. It comes from having grown up in a situation of many unmet needs for everyone, and they rose to the challenge to the point where they have some difficulty limiting demands made on them or in taking care of their own needs.

LOW SPERM COUNT

"Not this time around." They don't need to go through the parenting experience, and they are therefore are unconsciously choosing not to sustain the procreation process.
****

"Are you kidding?!" They have had a long-standing pattern of monastic celibacy in past lives, and they intend to continue the tradition.
****

"Karma." They have a past life history of severe abuse and even murder of children. They are being required to work off that karma before they will be allowed to parent again.
****

"Inadequate to the cause." They are having severe self-questioning and self-denigration problems. They are highly prone to blame themselves for any let-downs, set-backs or failure that they encounter. They come from a denigrating, wrong-making and undermining family.
****

"In over their head." They are experiencing great fear and resistance to the process of life. There is a considerable amount of tension, anxiety, emotional conflict and traumatic shock involved in their life history. They are heavily into competence-anxiety, self-distrust and self-inhibition. It arises from a "blame-throwing" dysfunctional family.
****

"Male shame." They feel guilty for being a member of the male race, and they unconsciously do not want to pass on their "sinfulness." They are the product of a severely "tripod-raging" mother -- she had the irresistible urge to kick or even more seriously attack anything with three legs.
****

"Cold-hearted." It is a case of egotism, selfishness and dishonest feelings being expressed in an ignorant manner. In effect, they don't *want* to be a parent for all the wrong reasons (or maybe for the right reasons, given who they are). They are hard, harsh, cold, judgmental, negative assumptive, angry and blaming. They are manifesting a primitive manner of functioning learned in a similar family.

LOW WHITE BLOOD CELL COUNT

"Forget *me!*" There has been a loss of self-commitment, due to a sense of worthlessness being activated by current circumstances that replay in updated form the experiences of childhood. It is an old, familiar theme or a "return of the repressed." In either case, it is the result of being given the message by the way they were raised that they aren't worth a hill of beans.

"LUMBAGO" (Backache at the rear of the groin region)

"All by myself." There is a feeling of injustice and of being over-burdened and under-supported. Indeed, there is a strong sense of insufficient support, along with a considerable resentment over that. There is a fear of financial failure and money, they feel at risk on the survival level, and there are concerns about the need for protection. This can be either current or chronic.

They were more or less left to their own devices from early on, and their family was not able to provide them basic emotional support. There is a significant need for nurturance being displayed with this type of problem.

****

"Cope-ability-anxiety." They are full of self-doubt, competence-anxiety and worth concerns, and they lack the will or strength to overcome the obstacles they face. They are success-avoidant out of fear of abandonment-annihilation built in during their early childhood. They are the product of a rejecting, competence-undermining and blame-throwing dysfunctional family.

****

"Over-burdened." They feel overloaded with excessive demands, because this was the pattern in their childhood. They find this painful, heavy and they want to run away, as well as suppressing a desire to attack. They therefore are into over-control for fear of release of aggression and the misuse and abuse of power.

****

"Enmeshed." They are guilt ridden about sexuality, due to sex-ploitative parenting and to demands that they never commit to themselves or anyone or anything outside the family. They are over-responsible, self-condemning, depressed and despairing, due to feeling trapped in the "tie that grinds" from an engulfing family.

RIGHT SIDE "LUMBAGO"

"No support." There are conflicts over the nature and/or availability of environmental support systems and supplies. The feeling is that there is not what is needed out there for them in one form or another, and they have little or no trust of the environment to provide what they need. It arose in a dysfunctional family who were not able to provide their basic life support systems and resources much of the time.

MIDDLE AREA "LUMBAGO"

"Calamity-concern." There is a considerable amount of annihilation-anxiety and survival-alarm. Their feeling is that they are here on borrowed time, and that there is the real possibility of being "found out." There is also some "run amok-anxiety" -- the fear that they may "lose it" over their situation of non-support and deprivation. It derives from strong experiences of unacceptability or unwelcomeness from very early on.

LEFT SIDE "LUMBAGO"

"Island unto themselves." They have an inability to accept or to utilize intimate emotional support and basic need-meeting. They are excessively self-sufficient in a "sealed unit" pattern. They have a significant trust of the Universe problem, due to early deprivation and untrustworthiness of their maternal and intimate environment.

LUNG PROBLEMS

"Barking up the wrong tree." They tend to get into consuming passionate commitments that lead nowhere, and to get into repeated devastating unrequited love situations. They have a sensitive mind and a very strong sense of justice, righteousness and generosity that frequently leads them into blind alleys and exploitative situations and relationships.

They come from a dysfunctional family in which they held a parental role that led to their repeatedly trying to rescue them from their self-defeating patterns.
****

"Deprivation City." They have a real difficulty in taking in prana, chi, ki, élan vitale, and love or life energy, as a function of their prideful brutalizing misuse of energy in past lives. They have an inability to renew to the breath of life, along with a lack of enthusiasm and zeal for living. They have a real inability to take in life, and they don't feel worthy of living life fully.

They are suffering from depression and chronic grief, because they are deeply afraid of taking in life energy. They are joy-avoidant and happiness-squashing, out of a fear of the Universe. They lack cosmic, community and conjugal contact. They feel unworthy of living fully, and they are alone, sad and non-belonging, with no sense of acceptance or approval. And they are once again in a smothering and stifling environment, with a resulting sense that life is dull and monotonous. They are the product of a withholding and non-accepting family.
****

"Self-suppression." They are full of family taboos, social restrictions, moral inhibitions, unexpressed passions, strong desires and emotions. They don't have any sense of freedom or the right or ability to communicate their feelings. This was generated by a self-immersed and dysfunctional family who were exploitative, shame-inducing and enmeshed.

RIGHT LUNG PROBLEMS

"Exploitation-paranoia." They are struggling with guilt over real and/or imagined abuses of energy and resources.

LEFT LUNG PROBLEMS

"Don't need!" They have shame over having needs for energy and resources.

(See EMPHYSEMA; PLEURISY; PNEUMONIA; TUBERCULOSIS)

LUPUS

"Deep emotional guilt and shame." They have a deep self-hatred and desire for punishment that is so overwhelming that death seems preferable to dealing with forgiving or loving themselves. They are into self-suppressing power-avoidance and expression-squashing. They are intensely self-rejecting and self-disapproving in a resentful self-disgust reaction.

They seek to appear positive and cheerful, but inside they are deeply depressed. They are full of angry punishment-deservingness feelings and self-destructive motivations and manifestations.

They are capitulating and giving up to an extreme underlying abandonment-depression. They literally feel that it's better to die than to stand up for themselves, and they are in essence giving up on life.

It is the result of being massively rejected, accused and wrong-made by a punitive dysfunctional family with a highly self-immersed, self-serving, and blame-throwing mother, who gave them strong "If it weren't for you. . ." messages, usually while simultaneously depending on them in a "role-reversal" or "associate parent" pattern.

LYME DISEASE (Tick-transmitted failure of the immune system)

"Sealed unit." They are an "urban hermit" -- an achieve-aholic, and a self-denying performance-maniac. They feel that they have to take care of everything because no one else will or they'll do it all wrong. They are so caught up in taking care of business and running the show that they have real trouble with intimacy, vulnerability and emotional commitment. Underneath all this, they are support-starved, frustrated and resentful.

It all got started in a "never good enough" parenting situation, in which they were put on a very conditional love basis -- they had to "perform for their breakfast." However, they never seemed to come up to snuff, so there is a subconscious, subtle and subterranean self-disgust and lack of self-confidence. What happened is they became hooked to the "tie that grinds" in an engulfed symbiosis with their parents, who, in turn, functionally relied on them to rescue them.

Now they are in the seemingly untenable position of having to give up the "quest for the Golden Orb" or the "God Housekeeping Seal of Approval" and the parent-rescue and single-handed "Atlas" trip, or they will not make it.

LYMPHOMA (Cancer of the lymph system)

"Unable to forgive and forget." They are sitting on deep-seated resentment and resignation. They have always had to be "running on empty" with insufficient equipment. They have a growing feeling of "What's the use?" along with an abiding anger about their whole situation.

They have always had to suffer silently and to stuff their sorrow. They feel that they have always come up a day late and a dollar short as a function of some inherent vileness or evilness. They therefore have not felt the right to request or require, much less to complain or explain about their situation. Yet at the same time, they are enslaved to negativity in their thinking and expectations.

They have little ability to defend themselves against attack from themselves or from outside agents or forces. They have a poorly developed ability to self-nurture and to fend for themselves. It is the result of a severely shame-inducing dysfunctional family who conveyed that they can expect nothing but the very worst.

LYMPH SYSTEM PROBLEMS

"Running on empty." They are receiving a warning that the mind needs to be re-centered on the essentials of life, namely the need for love and joy in their life. They are handicapped by an inability to release past memories and other wastes such as harmful habits and traits, or to defend themselves against negative thoughts.

They are blocking and/or denying their emotions, thereby leaving themselves unprotected and vulnerable, with no immunity to external and internal poisons and attacking agents. They feel no sense of acceptance and love from their environment. They feel that they are inadequate to the cause, with the result that they have no felt need or motivation in a lazy, being-tired-of-it-all reaction to someone or some situation or some set of circumstances.

Their emotional body is in disrepair, and they have real difficulties in how well they are taking care of their own needs, getting nurtured, and handling their negative feelings about themselves. They are the product of a shame-inducing dysfunctional family who conveyed very clearly to them they have no right to love and joy, and that "There's no joy in Bloodville."

~~~~~~

LYMPHATIC VESSEL PROBLEMS

"Deep resentment." They feel that their life is lacking in peace, love and they are quite bitter and angry about that. They come from an unloving, non-supportive and exploitative family.

MACULA PROBLEMS (See **EYE PROBLEMS**)

MALARIA (Intense fever caused by parasites)

"Out to get me." They are significantly out of synch with the Universe, with nature, with life, and with themselves. They feel totally unsafe, and they have very little trust of the Universe. They feel it is a "me vs. everything else" type of situation. It is the result of being the "sane one" in an untouchable dysfunctional family who were quite invasive with them.

MALE ERECTILE DISORDER

"Can't get it up." They are manifesting the effects of the "tie that grinds," arising from possessive parenting from their mother and/or from a history of aversive experiences in the sexual arena.

"MALE MENOPAUSE" (Post-retirement depression)

"Fifth wheel." They feel that they no longer have any function, purpose or direction. They also feel identityless, useless and worthless without their community contribution capability. They feel like an unlovable obsolete piece of equipment. It is re-activating profound feelings of unacceptability and worthlessness arising from a rejecting and/or perfectionistic performance-demanding patriarchal household.

MALNUTRITION

"I want out!" They are showing a lack of interest in and a rejection of life. They have a subconscious death wish that is based on a guilty conscience. They are inclined to spiteful self-destruction in an "I'll show them! I'll make them sorry!" pattern. They are the product of a severely dysfunctional, blame-throwing and shame-inducing family.

(See **ANOREXIA**)

"MARASMUS" (Protein and carbohydrate deprivation reaction and/or a severe maternal deprivation result -- "failure to thrive")

"Maternal deprivation." It is a severe devastation reaction in an infant whose mother is doing unto others what was done unto her, only in more extreme form. She has no inner or experience-based resources with which to carry out the process of nurturing.

****

"Ultimate atonement." They are unconsciously convinced they don't deserve to take up resources or to have their needs met, and they have now come to the conclusion that it is time to conclude the story. It is the result of intense intrauterine rejection and/or early deprivation.

"MARSH FEVER" (See **MALARIA**)

MASTADENITIS; MASTITIS (See **INFLAMMATION OF THE MAMMARY GLAND(S)**)

MASTOIDITIS (Inflammation of the bone behind the ear -- usually in children)

"Hear no evil." They have strong desire not to hear the hostility, conflict and aggression that going on around them. Their fear is infecting their understanding, and their anger and frustration with the situation has become acute. They feel out of the loop and left out of the care circle of their family. It is, of course, the product of a dysfunctional family in which their needs were often overlooked or belittled or they became the grounds for blame and accusation.

RIGHT MASTOID

"Where is it going?" They have fear and anger over the implications for future developments of the hostility in their environment.

LEFT MASTOID

"More and worse." There is fear and anger over the treatment they have received, and over its implications for their future.

MELANOMA (Skin cancer)

"Thwarted." They have a very strong feeling of frustrated plans and felt blockages by other people and/or circumstances. They feel threatened in some way, and they are letting things "get under their skin." They have strong longings that they haven't been able to realize, and there is deep hurt and long-standing resentment. They are the product of a frustratingly dysfunctional family who constantly prevented them from achieving their goals.

****

"What's the use?" There is a profound grief that is eating away at them. They are carrying deep-seated hatreds of the world around them and of the people in it. They feel that they are in a hostile environment that involves attempts to penetrate their defenses.

Underpinning all this is an unwillingness to forgive and forget the past. They feel that they are in a rotten situation, and that they always have been. They hate it, and see no way out. However, they are afraid to express their rage about it, or to find an outlet for their creative energy. Their family was demoralizingly dysfunctional and invasive, and they nurtured grudges and resentments.

****

"Suppressed resentment." They are a conservative controller and a feeling-avoiding denier who is experiencing deep disappointment while never being able to let love in. They are suffering from loss and hopelessness, morbid fears, abandonment-depression, and deprivation-resentment. They have unresolved hate, revenge desires, envy, jealousy and anger that are expressed subtly, subconsciously and subterraneanly. The whole thing is the result of severely critical parenting and of systematic victimization in childhood.

MENIERE'S DISEASE (Affecting the organs of balance, leading to violent dizziness, severe nausea and intense vomiting.)

"Confusion City." They are suffering from severe disorientation and feelings of being thrown off base. They have a strong sense of being at risk in a confusing and potentially dangerous world. They don't have a clear sense of direction or of the nature of what is happening around them.

They are sick and tired of all this, and they aren't willing to put up with demands for more responsibility and accountability. They are the product of a "magical misery tour" chaotic dysfunctional family in which they were expected to be the "sane one," but where sanity was not attainable.

(See **ABASIA**)

MENINGITIS (Inflammation of the lining of the brain and the spinal cord)

"Pariah/outcast complex." They are convinced that they are unacceptable to human society. They feel attacked for their beingness, their personality. They are enraged at life and inflamed in their thinking, and they are full of blame and frustrated fury. They were regarded and treated as the "Hunchback of Notre Dame" by their family, who, however, at the same time systematically trained them to be a scapegoat.

(See **BRAIN PROBLEMS**)

MENOPAUSE PROBLEMS

"Yesterday's newspaper." They have a fear of no longer being wanted or of having no usefulness. There is a sense of an ending of their purpose for being here as a woman, and they are therefore experiencing a sense of loss of direction and fulfillment. They are deeply afraid that they are no longer lovable and desirable, and that they will be rejected.

They are experiencing significant self-rejection and fear of aging. They have a strong sense of not being "good enough," and they feel "out of the loop." They are therefore resisting the flow of life and the natural change process, especially if it indicates a lessening of acceptability and the possibility of abandonment and isolation.

It comes from having been placed heavily on conditional love as a child, so that they became convinced that they had no inherently lovable qualities, and that they had to continuously "earn" their acceptance.

MENSTRUAL PROBLEMS

"She-jection." They are engaged in rejection of their femininity, along with power-avoidance and self-disapproval. They have guilt and fear about sexuality, and they have the belief that the genitals are sinful and/or dirty. They feel no self-respect or enjoyment as a woman. It is an outcome of a patriarchal and possible severely dysfunctional family.

~~~~~~

(See **PAINFUL MENSTRUATION**)

"MISSED PERIODS"

"I don' wanna!" They have an intense ambivalence about the generative/creative function. They really want to have a child and/or to manifest their creativity, but they are afraid of the responsibilities and ramifications involved. It is the product of a "Peter Panella-inducing, "eternal girl"-desiring, "Keep her around the old homestead" parenting pattern.

MULTIPLE MENSTRUATIONS

"She-jection." There is intense ambivalence about her femininity or her feminineness. She is angry or ashamed about being a woman in part, and that is acting up now. It comes from having been made wrong for being a woman -- "We (I) wanted a boy!" -- "Isn't that just like a woman?" -- "Goddammit, why can't you think like a man?!" -- "Women are the cause of all the world's troubles." -- "It's a man's world," etc.

****

"No way, Jose!" They are engaged in fertility/creativity-avoidance. They are afraid of or resistant to the generative function and its responsibilities and ramifications. Something in her current life is activating this issue at the present time. It arises from being made to be afraid of her intuition, creativity, and/or generativity by her family. Or they over-indulged and under-required her to prevent her from being able to "grow away."

****

"Peter Panella." She is refusing to grow up and become a woman, wanting to remain a little girl who is "taken care of all of" all her life. This imprinting is now surfacing in her life. It is the result of either over-indulgent/ under-requiring parenting or of being given the message that to grow up and grow away is total family-betrayal.

MERCURY POISONING (Nervous system problems, bone damage)

"Red alert." They are having real problems with mental and/or emotional experiences of weakness and vulnerability. Life's vicissitudes and difficulties have undermined their sense of sanity. There is a disruption of the flow of communication, in the form of input-deflecting and/or expression-suppressing, with the result that information-transmission, action-initiation and behavior-facilitation have been effectively derailed.

They are freaked out and distrusting of the universe, and they feel that they have to have "hands on control" of everything. They are the product of an untrustworthy dysfunctional and enmeshed family.

****

"Careening cannon." Their current situation is giving them the overwhelming sense that everything is thoroughly bollixed up, and they feel that they are devastating the environment and that they are endangering themselves seriously at the same time. They have ended up feeling that they "caused World War II" and that they might in fact "cause World War III." They feel that they are back in their severely dysfunctional family, in which they were the only "sane one" upon whom everything and everyone depended.

"METH MOUTH" (Greyish brown, twisting, rotting, falling out teeth caused by meth-amphetamine abuse. Due to dry mouth lack of saliva to combat bacteria, along with super-thirst leading to soda pop abuse.)

"Fulminating fury." They have a bad case of suppressed rage, hard anger, and potential violence. There is a paranoid orientation, and they are prone to have a hateful attitude. They try and "clear their tubes" with the substance. They are also grossly unable to make effective decisions in life, which leads to constant catastrophic situations that refuel their fury.

They were reared with much emotional invasion and abuse, along with profound emotional neglect, lack of nurturance and frequently physical violence.

****

"Love is a poison apple." They have a deep disappointment and disgust over lack of support and not being able to tell it like it is. They have decided that there is no such thing as real nourishment. They are not ready to accept what the universe is providing them.

They are therefore sealed off from taking in any proffered support or any new ideas. Everything fails to "pass the taste test" as far as they are concerned -- they want to stay in their comfort zone. They have become contemptuously closed-minded, set in their opinions.

It is the outcome of a highly negative experience with their untrustworthy, denial-dominated, dysfunctional family and their subsequent stand-ins.

MIGRAINE HEADACHE

"Love-starvation." Longing for mother's love or that of someone close. Their love inputs came out of the mother's priorities and concerns in a patriarchal household, not unconditionally or in response to their needs. They therefore have an abiding fear of rejection and abandonment, in response to which they developed a perfectionistic compensation attempt -- trying to "earn" their right to love.
****

"Driven." They feel they have to "hump" to make it in life, and that they have to "make something of themselves," to accomplish something. They therefore drive themselves, and they strive to get things done. It is a life-and-death imperative feeling that they have to achieve the goal, to accomplish the outcome.

However, when they complete the project, it sets the stage for the realization that this achievement isn't going to bring the desperately longed for unconditional maternal love either, and it sets the stage for another "Golden Orb"-pursuing project. That, in turn, sets off the headache. They are the product of a withholding and performance-demanding mother.
****

"Overload." They feel overwhelmed with information and unable to integrate it. They are having an intense but repressed rage reaction to the situation. It is as if they are being demanded to do the impossible with nothing, and they are extremely angry about it. They can't handle the ordinary requirements and stresses of life. They are prone to denial and awareness-avoidance, due to their dysfunctional family history.
****

"Frustrated." They feel that something has to be achieved or done, that something is being demanded of them. There is a good deal of fear and/or resistance to being able to fulfill that demand. A goal has to be reached, and the thought of it creates pain. They have an introverted feeling of incompetence arising from perfectionistic performance-demanding parenting.
****

"Compulsive conscience." They are pious, staunch and conscientiously uncompromising. They are also rigid, intolerant and duty-dominated. They have an exacting, achieving, "laying everything out in grids, charts and lists" approach. They are "chore-oriented" to the max. It arose from a patriarchal perfectionistic family.
****

"Derailed destiny." They have a pronounced feeling of having been prevented or blocked from achieving what they set out to accomplish, whether in a particular project or with their life. There are unfulfilled plans that are causing them great pain. It is an old, familiar feeling arising from their dysfunctional family background.
****

"Fuck off!" They have an intense dislike of being "driven" by external demands and they are resisting the flow of life. As a result, they are suffering from nervous strain generated by the requirements and responsibilities of life. They want to do things their way, at their pace, according to their standards, and under their control.

It is a "rebellious child" pattern generated by an authoritarian household in which the mother undermined the system, and who subtly or not-so-subtly encouraged them to rebel as their way of "earning" her love.

****

"Worthless turd." They are suffering from sublimated emotions and sexual fears arising from "smother-loving" sex-ploitation by their mother. They are guilt-grabbing, accident-prone, and self-destructive, out of an unconscious feeling that they have caused and deserved the invasive violation. They are hypersensitive to criticism and non-expressive of negative evaluations, lest they be rejected. Events that activate helpless/ hapless/hopeless feelings are often the precipitants of the migraine attack.

****

"Road block." There is a big impediment to the flow of their life that has to be changed. It is an impediment that is a childhood-acquired pattern that was an adaptation to a dysfunctional family - - like getting sick, success-deflecting, self-invalidating, intimacy-incompetence feelings, and such. It was a very broad decision about themselves that limits them severely that has to be re-decided now, in no uncertain terms.

****

"Air head." They are frightened of the requirements, events and experiences associated with the more earthy aspects of life, such as sexuality, aggression, and feelings, and so they seek to "hide in their head." It is the result of growing up in a highly repressive and rationalistic household.

(See **HEADACHES**)

"MISCARRIAGE" (Spontaneous abortion)

"Not now -- Later." There is a profound sense of mistiming, of really serious consequences of the child's coming at this point. The parents of the child are not at peace with each other and/or the circumstances are not right. There is a strong fear of the future in the mother. There is also a deep apprehension of the upcoming responsibilities generated by a severely dysfunctional family in which they had to carry a lot of the load.

In most cases, the visiting soul only wanted this early period experience. In some cases, they themselves decide that the circumstances aren't right, and they opt to come back later. In a few cases, they decide that the circumstances aren't ever going to be appropriate for them, and they move on.

(See **INFERTILITY; STERILITY**)

MISSING PULSE; NO PULSE DETECTABLE (AT TIMES)

"Inner sanctum." They are pulled into their inner core in strategic retreat from everything. Their feeling is that "Just because you're paranoid doesn't mean they're NOT out to get you!" They feel very much at risk in the world, and they are not allowing anything to "get at" them or to "get to" them.

This can be situational and/or chronic, but in either case, their childhood home was highly invasive and untrustworthy, such that they had to develop the process of "shining on" to a world class art, as they pretended to be vulnerable and involved while actually being in deep retreat from the virulence and violence (physical and/or emotional) of their severely dysfunctional family.

MITOCHONDRIAL MYOPATHY (Progressive muscle disorder that deprives the body of energy)

"Why bother?" They are resistant to new experiences, and they are refusing to move in life. Unsettling memories are surfacing, and they must confront issues that have been long put off. They are having great difficulty coordinating the execution of things and integrating ideas of what is wanted to be accomplished with the pragmatic results they are getting. They have trouble dealing with the feelings and issues associated with success, and they have little sense of competence and confidence. They have a sense of being inadequate, incompetent and ultimately uninterested.

They have lost their sense of purpose, and they have gone into an amotivational syndrome. There is a growing weariness with life, an inner tiredness because of having to cope or keep going. It comes from having grown up in a chronically severely dysfunctional family. They have reached the point where their experience is, "Enough, already!"

MITTLESCHMERTZ (Literally: "middle pain" -- pain at ovulation)

"Peter Panella." It represents an unwillingness to grow up and be an adult female, arising from possessive, over-protective and/or under-requiring parenting. They wanted to "keep her around the old homestead" as their "private preserve," and so they generated compulsive immaturity.
****

"I've had it!" They have a resentment of femininity, of maternity and/or of the patriarchy. They feel restricted or required of, and they resist it. It is a function of "tripod-rage" (the irresistible urge to kick anything with three legs) passed on from their mother or from direct experience of exploitation, sex-ploitation or oppression from their father and/or society at large.

MONILIASIS (Fungus infection of the mucous membranes mouth, throat and vagina) (Candidiasis)

"Stick it up your. . ." They have a deep distrust of and disgust with the resources the world has to offer. They have a "love is a poison apple" and "The war is NOT over!" attitude, and they are "hunkering down in the bunker," hanging on to old tried and true strategies of self-containment and self-sustenance. It arises from untrustworthy parenting in a severely dysfunctional family.

"MONITOR FATIGUE" (Computer screen viewing disorder)

"One track mind." They become so immersed in what they are viewing they get lost in it, resulting in eye strain and muscle fatigue. It is a characteristic of how they live their life -- a kind of "lost in the moment" pattern. It is the result of having to "psyche out the situation" on an on-going basis in their unpredictable and uninterpretable dysfunctional family.

MONKEY POX (Fever, headache, cough, painful rash traveling all over the body)

"Moral cretin." There is intense rage about restrictions, along with rage at themselves for bringing these restrictions on themselves. They are highly resentful about rules, regulations and environmental suppression and oppression. They are also convinced that at some level, they deserve the restrictions, and they even take some measure of pleasure out of the "just desserts punishment."

They are full of generalized malaise and contempt, but they are the worst on themselves. They have a great deal of self-disgust and self-hatred for being what they are, and deep inside, they feel they must suffer as "atonement" for their "violations of the moral order." It all stems from a highly oppressive, shame-inducing, blame-throwing and accusatory family.

MONONUCLEOSIS; MONO (Glandular fever)

"Enough, already!" They are an angry achieve-aholic who is sick and tired of pressures from higher ups and/or from significant others to accomplish beyond their desires or abilities. It can also be a romance or relationship that is hard to handle, due to excessive demands. It is the result of growing up in a dependent family who placed them in a parental role from early on.
****

"Burned out." They are facing a crisis without solution, and this, in conjunction with an "up to the eyebrows" situation has led to a generalized malaise, ennui, torpor, lack of concern and no longer caring for themselves.

It is an old, familiar feeling, being as they are the product of an implacably dysfunctional family in which they were the "sane one" and the "disaster-deflector." It is time for a change of premises, lifestyle and commitments.
****

"Don't deserve." They feel somehow lacking in what it takes to make it, that they are in some way unworthy. They were subjected to deprivation, neglect, accusation and/or rejection from early on, and they ended up believing that it's all they can expect.
****

"Surrounded by takers!" They are angry at not receiving the love and appreciation they deserve. They are forever putting out huge amounts of contribution, commitment and concern, all of which is met with more demands and no acknowledgement. They come from an exploitative, self-immersed and non-appreciative family, and they are pulling in "stand-ins for the cast."

MOTION SICKNESS

"Rudderlessness feelings." They have a fear of not being in control, the thought being that they and perhaps everyone else, will be annihilated if they aren't personally handling the situation. It is a pattern that developed in a disorganized dysfunctional family in which they had to take charge of things or all hell would break loose.

MOUNTAIN SICKNESS (Due to low air pressure)

"Invisible deprivation." Their experience is that they are somehow not getting the life-sustaining support they need, yet there is no visible cause for it. Everything looks fine. This is a recreation of their early history, in which they never got what they needed, yet the observables were all in the right place and/order. It is the result of a subtle and subconscious selfishness and subterranean sabotaging dysfunctional family system.

MRSA (Methicillin-Resistant Staphylococcus Aurous – a severe viral infection)
"Resentful resignation." They are having the experience that life is being quite difficult, and they are feeling very little, if any positives in their life. To them, it feels like everything is one long series of responsibilities, traumas and drudgeries. It is the result of a "grimly getting through the night" dysfunctional family.
****

"Well, what do you expect?" They are bitterly of the opinion that "There is no joy in Bloodville!" They are in effect utterly unable to experience the beauty, good and joy of the Universe. They are quite resistive to and angry about the process of dealing with life. They have the feeling that they get every disease and disorder that comes down the pike.

They are the product of a severely ambivalent and self-defeatingly dysfunctional family system. It had the effect of convincing them that love is a four letter word and that joy is a joke. Their experience is that they can and should have no love for themselves, since they are "just getting what they deserve."

MULTIPAL CHEMICAL SENSITIVITY (Fatigue, allergies, asthma, etc., due to chemical, radiation and extra low frequency exposure)
"Alone on my own." They have an overwhelming fear of God, coupled with a profound separation-paranoia. They have the experience that they are struggling along in a cold, hostile and attacking world. They have no sense of connection to the Cosmos, and they feel that they are all they have. There was intrauterine, perinatal, and post-partum ambivalence, and they feel that when they are under stress or vulnerable, the world is decidedly not a safe place to be.
****

"Endangered." They are over-reacting to felt threats to their well-being, to something that is regarded as being hostile to their welfare. There is a deep level of fear about having to participate fully in life or about potential annihilation. There is also an intense distrust of letting something inside their boundaries. They are the product of an untrustworthy and invasive dysfunctional family.
****

"Immobilized." They are dominated by anxiety, suppressed emotions and unresolved aggravation or irritants from childhood. They are engaged in on-the-edge functioning, due to severe emotional difficulties, and due to denying of their own power and self-worth.

They feel stifled and yet at the same time feel that it is unsafe to take charge of their own life. They are full of ideas to get ahead, but they are afraid of pushing on against opposition, should they fail. They are intensely inhibited against free expression, and they are full of unresolved guilt and suppressed grief. Their family was highly enmeshed, dysfunctional and suppressive.
****

"Authority-freak." They are very dependent and afraid to break away, yet they want to control and dominate. They often are possessed by their family, by institutions and by spouse figures. They are a potential leader and independent thinker who is chafing at the bit under what feels like oppressive authority-domination.

They feel held back by fools, unrecognized for their true value and talents, and not given the high place they deserve, so they force themselves to perform to prove themselves to the "boss." It all got started in a self-immersed and possessive family who wanted to "keep them around the old homestead" by undermining their coping capability.
****

"Jealous possessiveness." They are intensely sensitive, fearful and longing for mother love or for love from someone close, and they have a rather pronounced clingingness and abandonment-anxiety. As a result, they are fatalistic, hostility-repressing, compulsive, hypersensitive and lonely, with a very low self-esteem. They have a dampened zest for life, due to their stifling, engulfing and yet abandonment-threatening mothering.
****

"Rejecting first." They have a lot of disappointment, bitterness, unforgivingness and over-worked resentment. They are out of step and in disharmony with their environment. They feel threatened and they fear loss, so they are trying to seize control of the situation.

There is an inability to resolve their resentment, with a resulting rejecting of the breath of life and an emotional suffocation. They have a strong ambivalence towards their mother and against mother-stand-ins.

They are being plagued by unmet dependency needs induced by a "smother-loving" yet rejecting mother who systematically undermined their capacity for independence, identity and destiny-manifestation. There is also a deep fear of letting go of childhood and an intense inner crying.
****

"Wind has gone out of their sails." They have lost their sense of purposes and direction, along with their desire for life. They have developed a deep fear of life, of taking responsibility, of coping with any further demands. The illness can become a safe place to be, a retreat from confrontation and action. They are the product of a destiny-undermining possessive mother who generated a sense of overwhelm and futility in them.

MULTIPLE MYELOMA (Cancer of the plasma cells in bone marrow)

"What's the use?" There is a deep secret or heavy grief eating away at the self. They are harboring deep hurt and long-standing resentment, and they are carrying deep-seated hatreds of the world around them and of the people in it.

They feel that they are in a rotten situation and that they always have been. They hate it and see no way out of it. They have had to bear great troubles and sorrows, which they have had to silently suffer and stuff. They also feel their hopes and plans were always systematically thwarted by other people and/or by circumstances. They are suffering from loss and hopelessness, morbid fears, abandonment-depression and deprivation-resentment.

There is much unresolved hate, revenge desires, jealousy, envy and anger that is either suppressed or expressed indirectly in passive-aggressive and subconscious subterranean subtle sabotage. They are the product of severely critical parenting, and of systematic victimization in childhood.

MULTIPLE SCLEROSIS (Loss of nerve endings, resulting in weakness and incoordination, often leading to immobilization ultimately)

"Hardening of the attitudes." They are being forced to look at things they've never looked at before, including past life stuff. They have to live life for the moment, and to be crystal clear about what they can have and what they can't have.

They have a will of iron, and they are intensely inflexible, all of which arises out of a generalized dread. They have taken on their situation with self-willed determination, in a "true grit" response to the situation, leading to "pit bull" stubbornness and to a "going down fighting" approach. They have taken on a real mental hard-nosed and hard-headed approach._They have typically been highly oppressive and coercively demanding in their pattern in past lives. It is also the result of growing up in a rigidly patriarchal household from this life.
****

"Exploitation-rage." They feel like they have been forced to undertake hard physical work or its equivalent in energy output against their will. They feel there is no support or assistance, and that they have to sustain everyone all by themselves.

They hate it, and they desperately want help and support. They feel that they have exhausted themselves, and they really resent it. They feel alone and alienated, and they are full of despair-rage.

They are in effect wreaking revenge upon those who never loved them. Their family were exploitative and demanding, with little or no concern for their needs or welfare.
****

"Gotta take care of it myself!" They are into severe martyr-tripping, guilt-inducing, and massive control-tripping. They have a real "thing" about reforming and re-forming things.

They are very rigid and moralistic, with a steel-reinforced value system and a fixed way of looking at the world and of doing things. They are fearful that if they don't take a personal hand in things, it will all go to hell in a bread basket.

They have a great deal of bottom line despair in response to their original severely dysfunctional and judgmental family, in which they played the "hero(ine)--rescuer." They were the "family hoist," and inflexible disaster-deflection became their specialty.
****

"Self-straight-jacketing." They are fearful of being free, and they are terrified of their true feelings. They are repressing their emotions, and they are therefore trapping themselves into immobilization and muscular atrophy. They are as a result unable to cope or to flow with change or to work in a co-creative and cooperative relationship with the world. They have then subsequently "selective electromagnetically" attracted and been attracted to overwhelming situations and relationships just like the original family's scene.

They therefore have a strong co-dependent "rescue trip" pattern which is now leading to a final dénouement with regard to learning the lessons involved. They are the product of an oppressive-suppressive-repressive family who would not allow them to be themselves.

MUMPS (Inflammation of the large salivary glands)
"Run amok-anxiety." They are afraid to be themselves for fear of destroying the people and systems around them if they do so. They are immobilized and uncertain as to what to do. In children, this represents a fear that they will wipe out their family if they start being themselves. In an adult, it is a re-run of the same situation they faced as a child in a dysfunctional family.

MUSCULAR DYSTROPHY (Progressive wasting away of the muscles)
"Peter Pan(ella)." They are experiencing a deterioration of their emotional strength, and they are in a crisis of discouragement, self-doubt and competence-anxiety. They are overwhelmed by life, and they feel unable to carry it on any further. They feel insufficient to the cause and that "It's not worth growing up."

It is in response to a "keep them around the old homestead" programming by the parents, in which the injunction was to never become more developed than their parents were. They have now reached a crossroads in what is an issue that they have put off for lifetimes, which is learning to be willing to be the best they can be.
****

"Run amok-anxiety." They are experiencing subconscious fear that they will "lose it" and hit or hurt someone. They have a great deal of resentment-rage for their success-avoidant life history and situation.

They come from a ragefully passive-aggressive family who programmed them to be self-defeating and self-harming. They therefore now feel at some level that they have to suffer to atone for their "evilness," a fact which they find infuriating.

MUSHROOM POISONING

"The old Lucy and the football trick." They have a propensity to "fall for appearances," and to try once again to get the "God Housekeeping Seal of Approval" from "God(zilla)." They were systematically denied any sense of personal worth, while being continuously promised that if they just came up to snuff, things would all change.

It was a "poison apple" experience, but with such high stakes (acceptability, viability and removal of rejection by the "Home Office" [All That Is]) that they keep "trying for the brass ring" in the face of repeated betrayals and let-downs. It's a form of foolish risk-taking.

MYALGIC ENCEPHALOMYELITIS; "M.E." (Exhaustion and irritability that can lead to gland problems, meningitis and immune system breakdown)

"Pooped out." They are pushing beyond their limits, and they have a dread-driven fear of not being good enough, leading to an exhaustion reaction. They were draining all of their inner support, and a stress virus took hold.

They are "running on empty," due to overwhelm and deprivation-exhaustion. They have lost their sense of purposes and direction, of the desire for life, and the wind has gone out of their sails. They have developed a deep fear of life, of taking responsibility, and of coping with any further demands. The illness can become a safe place to be, a retreat from confrontation and action. They are the product of perfectionistic parenting.
****

"Crushed talent." It is an instance of unfulfilled giftedness-suppression, resulting in severe despair-rage, along with emotional commotional episodes of almost psychotic-seeming proportions, and utter exhaustion comparable to Epstein-Barr or Chronic Fatigue Syndrome. They also find themselves being "used" by their gifts, in the form of uncontrollable outbursts and breakouts of their talents in a non-functional and often highly detrimental manner.

They also go into experiences and expressions of intense mental and emotional distress and distortion that are extremely alarming and alienating. They feel possessed by these explosions, and they become quite "run amok-anxious" about it. In addition, they often are possessed by their family, by institutions and/or by spouse figures.

They are the product of extremely possessive and oppressive parenting that got started intra-uterine. They were forbidden and prevented from doing their own thing or from developing their own capabilities, identity and destiny. They were instead forced into playing out their parent(s) (usually the father's) unexpressed destiny.
****

"Allergic to themselves and the world." There is a programmed self-rejection that has resulted in a "belly up" of the immune system, which is in effect working against them.

They were placed in the "family hoist" position of over-responsibility, and they were targeted with the attributed accountability for everything that went wrong in the family -- as if it was a motivated let down betrayal or a personal failure on their part.

This came about as a function of their being a gifted child living in a dysfunctional family who expected them to be able to handle all the family's problems. They played the "hero(ine)" role in the family, and they turned into a work-aholic/achieve-aholic contribution-freak.

They became very accomplished and independent, with perfectionistic standards around worth-earning arising from unpleasable parenting -- they could never, ever measure up. They ended up validation-starved as a result.

****

"Cinderella/Cinderfella." They have a huge control trip that doesn't work that arises because they have no sense of their personal worth or value. They operated in a chronic flight-fight system arousal in childhood, in a context of continual rejection, blame-throwing, and impossible demands. There is a severe "family betrayal" delusion and a guilt-grabbing propensity, due to their being told in effect that they caused World War II. They actually tried to "go for the gold ring" of healing their family because of their gifts.

In the meantime, the family was severely exploitative and betraying, as they overwhelmingly expected of and over-utilized them. No one taught them self-care or self-soothing in their first year of life. They were expected to care for the parents instead. They therefore have no sense of entitlement.

There was little nurturance, compassion or protection in infancy, which resulted in very heavy self-numbing and frantic-fanatic efforting to "make up for what they have caused." They were, in effect, abandoned at an early age by expectations of perfection and miracles. They are now collapsing, out of a sense of non-deservingness and from having run out of inner resources to pull off the "rabbit in the hat" trick any more.

****

"Hapless/helpless/hopeless victimization." There is an inability to self-nurture, to self-appreciate and to self-soothe. As a result of this, they can sometimes end up being care-coercing of the environment, in a very belated attempt to get the fundamental nurturing they never received.

The family was highly authoritarian, non-supportive and repressive-suppressive from the beginning. Often there was also physical and sexual abuse, along with the intense emotional abuse and deprivation. They were subjected to highly conditional, demanding and self-immersed parenting, and "there was no joy in Bloodville." The whole pattern could be summarized in the phrase, *"It's not allowed!"*

MYASTHENIA GRAVIS (Uncontrollably drooping eyelids)

"Resignation-apathy." They have the experience that anything they would do to change things in their life and in the world would only lead to no effect or to worse conditions. They are engaged in systematic self-defeatingness that reflects an underlying sense of worthlessness and undeservingness of love. It's a "Here's *another* fine mess I've gotten myself into!" severe grief and self-distrust pattern going down.

They therefore are fearful and avoidant of change, evolution and transformation. They also have a pronounced propensity to seek to hide their underlying depression with a projection of cheerfulness.

They have a strong tendency to want to just give up and forget the whole thing. They are the product of rejecting and wrong-making parenting in an implacably dysfunctional family in which they were indeed unable to make a difference.

RIGHT EYELID DROOPING

"World-weary." They are convinced that there is nothing that can be done to improve things in their environment. They have a pronounced tendency to get into trouble with the workings of the world as a result.

LEFT EYELID DROOPING

"Bite the bullet." They have become in effect resigned to things being and going pretty much the way that they have so far for them. They have intense problems with self-manifestation processes, inasmuch as it has always been their experience that they are not able to make a difference on their own behalf.

MYOMA (Benign uterine fibroid tumors in menopause)

"Not yet, not yet!" They are afraid of the loss of fertility, as if it were the end of their sexual attractiveness, purpose and life. They fear neglect and rejection, and they are prone to emulate pregnancy as a result. It is an abandonment-anxiety reaction arising from highly conditional loving as a child.

NARCOLEPSY (Uncontrollable urge to go to sleep)

"I want out!" They can't cope, due to extreme fear. They feel cast adrift and abandoned by the "Home Office" (All That Is). They are so freaked out that they want to get away from it all. They don't want to be here at all -- they want to be anywhere else but here.

They encountered an out-of-control dysfunctional family to which they had to adapt, and with whom they had to somehow survive. It has been that way ever since, due to the imprinting effect that leads us to attract to ourselves and be attracted to that with which we grew up.

They are now reaching the point of total demoralization, and they can't take it any more; they can't cope any longer. They are sick and tired of all their responsibilities, and they desperately want them to go away. They need to free themselves from their enslavement to people, systems and situations that resemble or remind them of their family.

NAUSEA

"What a revolting development THIS is!" They are having a fear and disgust reaction to what is happening to them. They are totally rejecting an idea or experience -- they don't want to have anything to do with it. They want to throw it right back out again.

They feel that something wrong or immoral is happening. They are inundated with disgust with the situation and themselves, and they are full of fear of the consequences of what's going down. They feel that something dreadful has happened, and they feel responsible for it. They wish it hadn't happened, and they are truly sorry it has occurred. They deeply wish they hadn't "done it." They want things to return to the way they were before this happened.

They are full of upset, pain and sadness, they don't want the situation anywhere near them. They desperately want to undo the past, and they are afraid of the effects of this on their future. They are full of dissatisfaction, disgust and regret over the way things are. They are saying to themselves over and over, "I should have . . ." They feel personally accountable for everything that happens, particularly the negative outcomes.

Their family held them accountable and responsible for all that took place, and all eyes turned in their direction when anything went wrong -- which was frequently. They were made very aware they had no right to commit to anyone or anything else but the continued maintenance of the family. They therefore have great guilt about sexuality, success, and intimacy, as if these were "evil deeds."

~~~~~~

"MORNING SICKNESS" (In pregnancy)

"Implication-anxiety." They are having second thoughts about the magnitude of the undertaking they are involved with. It activates a sense of queasiness and overwhelm. It is re-activating their childhood experience of having had to in effect parent their family and/or their never having had real nurturing.

"NEAR DEATH EXPERIENCE" ("N.D.E.")

"Time for a change." They have reached a point where they can no longer keep up their pattern of life any more. It is such an overwhelmingly important matter that they literally had to leave body to make a new choice and/or new commitment regarding their destiny. The more profound and dramatic/traumatic the experience and the more extensive the aftermath, the bigger the need for change and/or the more significant the destiny decision.

They are also notably "sensitive" to all manner of experiences and inputs, including intuitive, psychic and "other-worldly," though this may not have been noticed by them prior to the experience.

This type of situation usually arises in persons who have had a severely traumatic and physically or sexually abusive childhood.
****

"Spiritually guiding." They are now an intelligent and life-understanding, wisdom-manifestor. They are now here to assist us in integrating the spiritual with the practical. They were effectively being driven to get in touch with the Cosmic by their dysfunctional family as a child, and they either went to the sidelines to track the flow of human events, or they recoiled into an intensely materialistic orientation. Either way, their destiny now is to share the "good news" about the true nature of the Universe.

NECK PROBLEMS

"No escape." They are being confronted with issues they haven't been able to handle for many lifetimes. They must now finally be handled, and they have to deal with the pressure of this. It got started in their family, who generated circumstances and programming that has resulted in their having to confront the issue now -- or pay dire consequences.
****

"Total control trip." They have clamped down on the system around them, and they are adamantly controlling everything. They have lost almost all poise, fluidity and contact with their feelings. They no longer can integrate and translate feelings and impulses into concepts, thoughts, words, or into strategies and tactics. They can't refine and amplify or dispense and disperse effectively -- they are trying to analyze things into position.

They need and want to release and express their experiences, feelings and interpretations, but they are totally terrified of doing so. They are under a lot of stress as a result, and they are non-accepting and judgmental about it all and of other people. It's all a gigantic pain in the neck for them. It all got started in a highly mentalistic, perfectionistic and control-tripping family.
****

"I don' wanna know!" They don't even want to be here, and they are living in quiet desperation. Unfortunately, they are reacting by being stubbornly, rigidly inflexible and refusing to see other sides of a question. They can't see what's not in front of their nose or what's behind things or what's in the background. They are the product of a denial-dominated dysfunctional family who constantly tried to shove everything under the rug.
****

"Hell-bent-for-leather." They fear death, disaster, dishonor, disgrace, misery, illness, misfortune and failure if they "let loose and let fly with one." Their reaction is to go on a head-lowered pursuit of achievement in ways they regard as representing strength of character.

They are intensely method-oriented, form-fixated and locked into their perspective. They are very set in their ways, and they operate out of a morally convinced reactionary intolerance. They honestly believe it is a matter of pivotal moral magnitude that things be done in the *right* (their) way.

They are now being confronted with a situation or someone whose ideas are at odds with their set ways of doing things. This whole pattern got set up in a highly rigid and patriarchally perfectionistic household.

RIGHT NECK

"Emotional expression problems." They are having hassles around handling emotional manifestation.

LEFT NECK

"Feeling-suppressing." They are engaged in avoidance of tuning in to emotional needs and issues.

~~~~~~

UPPER NECK

"Emotional experience problems." There are issues around handling their emotional experiences.

MIDDLE NECK

"Emotional expression conflicts." They have conflicts about emotional expression.

LOWER NECK

"Emotional channeling issues." They have concerns around the control and channeling into required action and events of their emotional responses.

~~~~~~

FRONT NECK

"Emotional self-rejection." They have guilt and shame around their emotional issues and needs.

BACK NECK

"Caught with their emotional pants down." There is a fear of being in the incorrect psychological position.

~~~~~~

BROKEN NECK

"Loss of control." They have been rather intensely orchestrating and determining their experiences, life and environment, and now they suddenly find themselves "out of the driver's seat."

They were, in effect, preventing the flow of life and learning, and they now have to acquire the ability to being in more sync with things. They grew up in a household in which having the determination of events and processes was critical in their dysfunctional family.

(See **SPINE PROBLEMS** for more information about the particular vertebrae)

"TWISTED" NECK; "WRY NECK" (Due to injury or infection)

"Refusal to face things." They are being confronted with issues which they haven't been able to handle for many lifetimes. They must now finally be handled. Unfortunately, however, they are reacting by being stubbornly and rigidly inflexible, and by refusing to see other sides of a question. They can't see what's not in front of their nose or what's behind things or back there in the background. They have clamped down on the system, and they are adamantly controlling everything.

They have lost almost all poise, fluidity and contact with their feelings. They no longer can integrate and translate feeling and impulses into thoughts, words, concepts, strategies and tactics. They can't refine and amplify or dispense and disperse effectively, and they are under a lot of stress as a result. It's all a gigantic pain in the neck for them.

They fear death, disaster, dishonor, disgrace, misery, illness, misfortune and failure if they "let loose and let fly with one," and they are head-lowered on a hell-bent-for-leather pursuit of achievement in ways that they regard as representing strength of character.

They are intensely method-oriented, form-fixation and locked into their perspective. They are very set in their ways, and they operate out of a morally-convinced reactionary intolerance. They are now being confronted with a situation or with someone whose ideas are at odds with their set ways of doing things.

This whole pattern got set up in a highly rigid and patriarchally perfectionistic household. They honestly believe that it is a matter of pivotal moral magnitude that things be done in the RIGHT (Their) way. They are being told that they need to seek help in alleviating this pattern.

****

"Twisted sister (brother)." They are being caught up in distorted interpretations and intentions, as a function of their fear of what would happen if they faced and acted. They are desperately seeking for some way to re-frame the truth in such a way as to avoid what they deeply fear will be disastrous consequences if they "straighten up and fly right." They come from a denial-dominated and convolutedly collusive dysfunctional family.

"WHIPLASH"

"Catastrophic expectations." They are quite concerned about what would happen if they dealt with a big issue that is coming up for them. They are refusing to go with the flow and to face the issue, leading to non-relevance of functioning in the area in question. They are trying to deny and/or control it away.

The truth is, it is an issue that *must* be handled at this time, as it is effectively preventing the manifestation of their destiny -- and the Universe is not going to allow that to continue. The issue involves early traumatic treatment they are loathe to confront, for fear of the consequences.

They were effectively functioning as the "family hoist" pivotal person, and their impact was huge when they spoke up on anything. In addition, they were subjected to severe trauma by a totally trusted significant other, followed by the overtly or subconsciously given very clear message that they, the perpetrator, and the whole family would be utterly annihilated if they "blew the cover" on the situation.

NECROSIS (Death of part of the body, due to lack of blood supply)

"Moral cretin." They are full of mental morbidity and poisonous thoughts, often arising from guilt or shame over illicit intentions or actions. It comes from growing up in a "there's no joy in Bloodville" type of disintegritous and dysfunctional family who both generated gross situations and then blame-threw and guilt/shame-induced intensely. It was a continuously poisonous environment.

NECROTIZING FASCIITIS (See "FLESH-EATING VIRUS")

NEMATODES (Parasites affecting the nervous system causing constipation, moodiness, etc.)

"Catastrophic expectations." The present situation is activating old abandonment-anxiety and other calamitous anticipations. It is an implication-overwhelm and a severe loss-paranoia reaction. It reflects very early intense insecurity reactions due to uncertainty about maternal commitment and availability.

NERVE PROBLEMS

"Disrupt-power." They are experiencing a disruption of the flow of communication, in the form of input-deflecting and/or expression-suppressing. They are avoiding, preventing and distorting influence, education and evolution. As a result, the flow of information-transmission, action-initiation and behavior-facilitation has been derailed.

They are grimly holding out and holding on to past strategies, resources, people and interpretations. They are freaked out and distrusting of the Universe, and they have to have "red alert" hands on control of everything. However, the result is a thorough bollixing of their situations.

They feel that they are back in their dysfunctional family, and they are the only ones with any sanity in the situation. The result is an escalating situation that emulates the family, as a function of their own interventions.

~~~~~~

NERVE PAINS (Sharp, stabbing pains accompanying movements)

"Oh no you don't!" They are getting "saber-rattle warnings" about "not stepping over that line" of self-commitment and self-manifestation. It is the resultant of an intense "keep 'em around the old homestead" programming.

NEURALGIA (Nerve aches)

"Cut off." They have no self-forgiveness and no self-trust, with the result that they feel they deserve punishment out of continuously guilty feelings. They are in anguish over their communication difficulties with other people, and about their situation. There is very poor communication within them, a blockage or distortion that is causing them great pain. They received very little love as a child, and what there was, was very conditional and interspersed heavily with guilt-induction and shaming.

NEURITIS (Inflammation of the nerves)

"Agitated irritation." They feel that they are continuously subjected to tension-inducing and frustrating stimulation. They feel powerless and undermined because of this. They come from an infuriatingly dysfunctional family who constantly generated situations, events and processes that were highly disruptive and derailing.

"NERVOUS BREAKDOWN;" "NERVOUS PROSTRATION"

"Blown away." They are manifesting an inability to carry on, to cope, and to function. There has been a severe traumatic emotional shock has left them feeling powerless. They are now upset about being upset, and they are feeling continuously attacked. They do not like what they know, and they do not want to act on certain known information.

It is an old, familiar feeling, in that it reproduces the experience they had in their implacably dysfunctional, denial-dominated and traumatic family.

****

"Reality-avoidance." They are misusing their mental gifts with negative thinking habits again, as they did in the prior lives that have laid the foundation for this resolution situation. Their mind is laboring under a delusion, and it is losing its self-reflective consciousness. They are intensely fearful of the future, and they are unable to work with their real feelings and their true comprehensions of things. Their family was severely distorted and nihilistically negative in its thinking.

****

"Stress-out." They are intensely self-centered, and they are jamming the channels of communication and refusing to let input in. They are confused, anxious, hysterical, fearful, strife-torn, resentfully disappointed, overworked and withdrawing from life's activities.

They are overwhelmed with the communication frustrations, and they have exhausted their "nerve force." There is a great deal of tension, strain, struggle, and imposition which has led to total self-immersion.

All of this is all-too-reminiscent of their severely self-defeating and detrimental family of origin, where they learned these strategies that are now getting them into very hot water.
****

"Severely self-centered." They are intensely focused on what's in it for them. They are continuously milking the environment for their gain, with no concern or regard for their ecological impact. They are the product of a convenience-concerned dysfunctional family, and they are the next generation.

(See the book *Problematic Patterns* by the author for information on the particular mental illnesses and other psychological disorders)

NEUROPATHY (Numbness in the extremities, especially the fingers and toes)
"Shadow-shoving." They are systematically suppressing all experiences and expressions of aspects of themselves that they are convinced are so unacceptable as to require total elimination of manifestation. These aspects have caused them so much pain and hurt that they don't want to feel them. The "unacceptable" aspects were reacted to with great punishment, ostracism and rejection when they manifested these qualities and capabilities as a child, so they are now dedicated to never contacting them.
****

They are "going dead" mentally and emotionally -- totally retreating into their core and shutting down feeling, out of fears that they are in a "dog-eat-dog world" in which people are out to do them in. They are vulnerability-avoidant, and they are operating with feelings that the environment is truly dangerous. They have a deep and abiding distrust of intimacy out of an "intimate enemy" experience in their exploitative and untrustworthy family.
****

"Cut off." They are withholding love and consideration, and they are love-deflecting and love-distrusting. To them, love is a poison apple that they want absolutely nothing to do with. It is a resultant of wrong-making and self-immersed parenting.

"NIGHT BLINDNESS;" "NIGHT MYOPIA"
"Automatic pilot." They are prone to run their life on the basis of the most frequently required responses and reactions. It is a kind of "comfort zone efficiency/laziness" that they get into. They are the product of a narrow-optioning family who rather strongly insisted on their adhering to the "tried and true," the "convenient," and the "acceptable."
****

"Overwhelm-anxiety." They are intimidated by their own emotional feelings, reactions and intentions, in a kind of "shadow-paranoia." They are afraid that if they get in touch with these motivations, they will precipitate World War III within themselves, around them, and in their lives.

It comes from an extremely strong "Don't see what we are feeling!" injunction in their severely dysfunctional family. They first encountered it when they gave an "Emperor's new clothes" reaction in response to the feelings activated by what was happening around them early in childhood.

They quickly learned that to get in touch with and express their feelings and reactions is to set off a "dynamite shed" outcome (where you find yourself in a pitch black environment full of rough-hewn square boxes, skinny ropes and a funny smell, so you light a match for enlightenment).

So they have learned to stuff it and sit on their feelings, reactions and intentions, with the result that they are now afraid of what would happen if they ever got in touch with them.

NILE VIRUS; WEST NILE VIRUS (Fever, dizziness, lightheadedness, gastro-intestinal problems, muscle ache, headache and confusion for the 80% mild cases. Disorientation, convulsions, vision loss, neurological damage, coma and perhaps death for the 20% serious cases.)

"Cope-ability concerns." They are experiencing an impaired ability to cope, leading to feelings of being overwhelmed, with a loss of their center. They are have to make high stakes decisions, and they are self-distrusting and competence-anxious.

They are also hung up in the past, resisting life, refusing to move or change, and in denial, with result that they are unable to assimilate what is happening to and around them.

There is a good deal of resentment-rage about all this, and they are staving off despairing depression as a function of the lack of joy in their life. They are rather intensely enmeshed in an achievement-seeking, workaholic or survivalist lifestyle and/or orientation. They have the feeling that the buck stops with them, and one strike and they're out.

They are finding that their usual ways of coping are not working for them, and they are faced with having to develop something new. They are the product of an ambitious or survivalist family who taught them that they are on their own in an indifferent or even hostile/dangerous world, and that they have to look out for "Numero Uno," because no one else will.

~~~~~~

SEVERE CASE; DEATH FROM NILE VIRUS

"God is Al Capone!" They are enraged at the Universe for the "dirty end of the stick" they have gotten since the beginning. They have always felt like a misfit, that they somehow don't belong here.

As a result, their needs have not been met, and they in turn have been unable to fit in, with the result that they have gotten a lot of "You don't belong here!" messages from the environment. They feel totally betrayed by the "Home Office" (All That Is). It all got started in their dysfunctional and exploitative yet wrong-making family.

"NODULES" (Small lumps, bumps or swellings)

"Frustrated ambitions." They are experiencing considerable resentment and frustration over non-manifestation in their career. There is considerable hurt ego over this, and they are manifesting the effects of a severe narcissistic wound. They were functionally emotionally ignored in later infancy, and they ended up with a major worth concern pattern.
****

"Yellow-orange alert." They feel that they are here "on borrowed time," so to speak. They therefore have the experience that they have to constantly "prove themselves," to demonstrate that they have a right to exist and that they have significance and importance. They feel that they are always in danger of being shown to be a hoax, a phony, or an "undesirable."

This is a situation that greatly frustrates and infuriates them. They were treated as if there was something wrong with the picture, and that what was wrong was that they were still in it.

NOSEBLEEDS

"Blown away." They are suffering from some severe emotional shock on the unconscious level, something they thought, saw on TV, heard about, dreamed, experienced, etc. New information has jolted them and altered their perspective. It has resurfaced an underlying chronic issue for them -- which is their worthlessness feelings. They were in effect largely emotionally ignored as a child.
****

"Worth-wound inflation." They have a desperate desire to be noticed, acknowledged, validated and recognized as being significant. They are in effect crying for love and feeling utterly overlooked.

They feel left out of things, and they interpret it to mean they are getting their "rightful treatment." They have deep-seated self-distrust and self-denigration, as they doubt their own perceptions, intuitions, even their sanity, and possibly their very existence.

They are suffering from severe and deep deprivation-grief and rejection-devastation arising from insufficient early emotional support and acceptance.

RIGHT NOSTRIL NOSEBLEED
"Ignored." They are experiencing significant non-recognition and/or invalidation.

LEFT NOSTRIL NOSEBLEED
"Self-denigration." They are having a severe reactivation of their underlying self-distrust and self-denigration.

NUMBNESS
"Shadow-shoving." They are systematically suppressing all experiences and expressions of aspects of themselves that they are convinced are so unacceptable as to require total elimination of manifestation. These aspects have caused them so much pain and hurt that they don't want to feel them.

The so-called "unacceptable" aspects were reacted to with great punishment, ostracism and rejection when they manifested these qualities and capabilities as a child, so they are now dedicated to never contacting them.
****

They are "going dead" mentally and emotionally -- totally retreating into their core and shutting down feeling, out of fears that they are in a "dog-eat-dog world" in which people are out to do them in. They are vulnerability-avoidant, and they are operating with feelings that the environment is truly dangerous. They have a deep and abiding distrust of intimacy out of an "intimate enemy" experience in their exploitative and untrustworthy family.
****

"Cut off." They are withholding love and consideration, and they are love-deflecting and love-distrusting. To them, love is a poison apple that they want absolutely nothing to do with. It is a resultant of wrong-making and self-immersed parenting.

OBESITY; OVERWEIGHT

There are a number of emotional and life history dynamics that can generate this outcome. In addition, they often "mix and match," in effect "doubling up" as motivational systems in the individual.

Here are a few of the most common psychodynamic situations:

"Insecurity." They have fearfulness and a felt need for "protection." They were over-protected and dominated as a child, and now they feel "lost at sea." They have a real need to have something to rely upon and to lean on -- an always available ally. And they found it in food.
****

"What's the point?" They are starved for relevance in their life. They have found from the very beginning that they are surrounded by people, systems, environments, activity requirements and situations that do not relate to where they are coming from. They have therefore been in effect emotionally deprived at a very deep level. They have responded by "self-medication" in the form of food intake as a means of "filling the hole inside."
****

"Anger-absorber." The weight has the effect of assimilating anger from within and from without. It functions as an energy-absorbing shield and buffer for the "slings and arrows of outrageous fortune," and they use it to avoid vulnerability.

Furthermore, it is a feeling-deadening emotional insulation and muffler experiences, so they don't have to feel what happens to them. They can also "sit on," "stuff," and run away from their feelings -- of which they are deeply afraid.

They could do little or nothing to fend off the invasions, intrusions and violations of their intensely dysfunctional family, so they had to develop some means of insulating themselves.
****

"Squashing themselves." They are engaged in a power-paranoia reaction. They are deeply alarmed by their potentials and capabilities, for fear that it will result in their "running amok," "steam-rolling," and/or in being rejected or abandoned.
****

"Too big for their britches." It comes from having been reacted to as an alarmingly potent and powerful being by their family. They were given the very clear message to keep themselves under control at all costs -- or else.
****

"Stuffing it." They are suppressing their feelings, and they are unable to express what they need and desire, and they are avoiding being in touch with themselves. They found out early on that being real led to being hurt badly in their denial-dominated family.
****

"Lowered attractiveness quotient." They deflect sexuality and intimacy, while simultaneously keeping people at a distance. They were the recipient of invasive sex-ploitation and erotic intrusion from their family, and they felt no ability to cope with it, other than to find some way to deflect their interest at the motivational level.
****

"Self-soothing love-substitute." It may be a food-addiction side-effect or a grief-avoiding holding back of an "ocean of tears." It is a means of self-sustaining through "stroke-substitutes" and oral stimulation, due to self-rejecting love-starvation and fear of loss.
****

"Abandoned at an early age." They had to find ways to fend for and sustain themselves. It can function as "emergency storage" for a "very rainy day." They have had to operate as a self-contained "sealed unit" all their life and they grew up in an insecurity-generating dysfunctional and self-immersed and perhaps "survivalist mentality" family.
****

"Emotional-commotional." They tend to be quite reactive in their feelings about things, and to experience things intensely. It is in part temperamental, and in part the result of having grown up in a dysfunctional family in which much of great importance and significance occurred in a non-impactable manner, leaving them with only their emotional reaction to respond with. They then reacted to the emotional upheavals with self-soothing food.
****

"Resentful withholding." They do a systematic refusal to engage in emotional investment. They don't trust anyone as far as they can throw a grand piano, and they have a good deal of anger over their deprivational life history. They have a lot of subterranean resentment, and they are intolerant and unforgiving in their orientation. They are the product of an exploitative family.
****

"Grief-holding." There is resulting semi-edema water retention. They were given the message at the subtle or not so subtle level that they really have no right to exist, and that they therefore can expect no sustenance or nurturance. They were also told that they had no right to "wallow in self-pity."

The food-fixation can be an effort to find so-called "nurturance" that has been denied elsewhere. They were intensely deprived emotionally as a child, and they turned to food as their only means of self-nourishment.
****

"Hunker down in the bunker." It can be a reaction to great emotional shock or loss, as the emptiness within becomes too great to bear. They feel devoid of meaning or purpose, but the attempt to protect themselves from it only makes it worse. They are suffering from excessively fixed mental attitudes and thoughts.

They came from an unstable dysfunctional family, and they are determined to protect themselves from any further such experiences now. They sustain themselves while simultaneously "adding padding."
****

"Big is Bad." It can be a form of power-projection. They come out of a "Don't tread on me!" approach and attitude. It then becomes a means of control, domination and/or protection. They are over-sensitive and self-reassuringly self-protective via increasing their apparent strength and size in a "throwing their weight around" pattern. In addition, it gives them the feeling of being powerful, strong, impactful, self-sufficient -- and invulnerable.

They feel that they need it as a function of their intimidating experiential history, which was full of domineering, oppressive and authoritarian parenting. It can be used as a means of "getting back" or revenge on their family for the treatment they got. The idea is along the lines of, "*I'll* show you what you have done to me! I'll make myself a disgrace!" Their family was rejecting, denigrating, exploitative and abusive.
****

"Spoiled pig." They are a voracious eating machine and a supremely selfish total taker who "vacuums" their way through life. Their only concern is for "more input" of any and all kinds, and they are convinced that they have an absolute right to any and all goodies they want at all times.

They are quite manipulative and malicious about getting it, and they are not in the least bit hesitant to do whatever it takes to keep those goodies coming in. They are also systematically vengeful, passive-aggressive and slyly cruel, out of their intense rage at what they have become and about where their life is going.

They are the product of extremely convenience-concerned, self-immersed over-indulgent and under-requiring parents who in effect cave in and build their life around their "little darling" ego-extension.

****

"Grounding and protection." It can represent a process of keeping the person here and safer when they are channeling Cosmic or "other realm" energies or entities.

~~~~~~

In all cases (with the exception of the "grounding" situation), it reflects insecurity and self-rejection, along with feelings of deprivation, scarcity and loss. It also involves lovelessness and loneliness and a pattern of comfort-seeking.

Their craving for love is expressed in compulsive eating and in accumulating too many possessions. It shows the fear and need for protection that they feel, along with their fear of "growing up" and of taking responsibility for their own life that they family system generated.

There are three types of situation within this general dynamic:

"Love-staved." They are "stroke"-deprived, love-desperate, and likely to be over-giving. There is a distinctly self-punitive and, in severe cases, a self-destructive streak. They are trying to please a family who were invasively intrusive and wrong-making.

****

"Blast from the past." There is much unexpressed longing and holding of unpleasant memories. In some cases, it is a cover for hidden anger and resistance to forgiving. It then often involves systematic self-"blemishing," control-avoidance, and rebelliousness of the "Nobody's gonna tell ME what to do!" type. They come from a domineering household in which one parent colluded with them in their rebellion.

****

"Snail out if its shell." They have difficulty in coping, and there is a child-like need for security. They are cushioning themselves with barricades of material protection. They desire emotional and physical sustenance, with a real fear of lack and of low income.

~~~~~~

The location of the fatty storage is symbolic of the areas of their concerns:

ARMS

"Deprivation-resentment." They have anger at being denied love. Buried in their core, they don't know how to reach out.

LEGS

"Powerlessness-rage." There is anger at their not being able to take charge of their life. They have a lack of initiative and no energy, due to nihilistic lethargy.

THIGHS
"Sex slave." There is stuffed childhood anger over disenfranchisement and sexualization, often at their father. They feel frustrated about their difficulties in moving forward in life.

BELLY
"Developmentally arrested." They are angry at being denied nourishment, and there is an associated passivity and vulnerability.

HIPS
"Sexual suppression." There is anger at both parents for being denied their sexuality and/or over sex-ploitation.

OSTEO-MALACIA (Softening of the bones)
"Enough already!" They are disintegrating under the load of responsibilities they have had to carry all their life. They have the feeling that they just can't support themselves and that their world single-handedly like they have been doing all along.

They are just plain running out of steam from having had to "run on empty" for so long. It just isn't in them any more. It reflects the fact that they had to be the "tower of power" and the "support pillar" for their family as their way of seeking the "God Housekeeping Seal of Approval" from their exploitative, dysfunctional and withholding family.

OSTEO-MYELITIS (Inflammation of the bones)
"Alone on their own." They have a good deal of fear, anger and frustration with the very structure of the Universe, and with the fundamental nature of life. They feel totally unsupported, with no sense of safety. It is a continuation of a feeling they have had all their life, starting in a depriving infancy and childhood in a dysfunctional family where they had to be the "Rock of Gibraltar," the "pillar of strength," the "family hoist."

OSTEO-POROSIS (Porousness of the bones)
"Left to their own devices." They are feeling that there is no support left in life. They feel totally betrayed by the Universe and the "Home Office" (All That Is). They are exhausted and depleted, and they are no longer able or willing to stand up for themselves.

They have a mania for total control of everything around them, and they can't stand the unexpected. They feel there is just no love for them from God. They have a severe "poison apple" reaction to love-inputs, and they therefore won't let love in. It all started in a super-exploitative and dysfunctionally untrustworthy family.

OVARY PROBLEMS
"She-jection." They have a fear of and rejection of their creativity and femininity. They are systematically self-denigrating and ashamed of the feminine role and situation. They would just as soon "take their marbles and go home." They are the product of a misogynistic patriarchal household in which the feminine was denigrated, exploited and abused.
****

"Self-undermining." They have a great desire and need to be respected that is being prevented. Their circumstances are of such a nature as to be exploitative, non-accepting, and denigrating. They come from an enmeshed and undermining dysfunctional household.
****

"Lovelorn." They are in effect love-starved and intensely lonely. They are cut off from any social support, appreciation, affection and acceptance. They were the "odd one out" in their self-immersed and rejecting family.
****

"Erotic conflicts." They are deeply conflicted about and inadequate-feeling in the sexual aspect of their being. They feel that they somehow don't measure up, or on the other hand, that they in no way *want* to measure up to the erotic role. They were sex-ploitated, sexualized and/or sexually abused as a child, or they were sexually denigrated by their family -- father in particular.
****

"Infernal maternal." They are in deep conflict about motherhood, including the way they carry it out, if they are a mother. They feel exploited or inadequate as a mother, and they deeply resent and/or fear the maternal role and aspect of themselves. Their mother was miserable in her maternal functioning, and she passed on her deep issues with motherhood.
****

"Power-avoidant." They are afraid of their personal potency, for fear of what would happen if they released it. They may also be having difficulty giving birth to their identity and destiny. Their early experiences taught them that personal power is both abused and misused, or that disaster follows if they manifest their personal potency.
****

"Tripod-rage." They are afraid of exploitation by the patriarchy, and they deeply resent being a woman in the paranoid patriarchal world of today. It got started with a direct infusion from their mother of the irresistible urge to kick anything with three legs ("tripod-rage"), with behavioral back-up validation by their father and the paranoid patriarchy.
****

"Spousal problems." There may be significant rejection coming from their spouse figure, leading to deep pain and self-questioning regarding their nature as a feminine intimate. It is a repetition of their distorted and disturbed relationship with her father.
****

"Run amok-anxiety." They may be suffering from agitated anxiety about their patriarchy-paranoia and father-fury. They are alarmed at what their "tripod-rage" (irresistible urge to kick anything with three legs) might lead to in the form of their behavior and/or ecological impacts. Their childhood was saturated with infuriating patriarchal processes.

RIGHT OVARY PROBLEMS
"Femininity-rejection." They are engaged in rejection of the feminine, out of "tripod-rage," (irresistible urge to kick anything with three legs) out of patriarchy-distrusting exploitation-paranoia, or out of fear of rejection by patriarchal people.

LEFT OVARY PROBLEMS
"Self-rejection." They are having to deal with self-distrust and/or self-disgust for themselves as a woman, arising either from an underlying acceptance of the patriarchy's rejection of feminine power, or from their underlying "run amok-anxiety" concerning their intense rage at the patriarchy.

OVARIAN CYST (Fluid sac on or near ovary)

"She-jection." They are experiencing a growing conflict regarding their femininity and all of the issues described above. It is the result of systematic rejection on the basis of her gender by her patriarchal family.

(See **GENITAL PROBLEMS -- FEMALE; UTERUS PROBLEMS; VAGINAL PROBLEMS**)

"OVER-ACTIVE" ADRENALS

"Mental run amok." There is an over-production of crushing ideas that results in mental imbalance and feeling overpowered. They have the experience of not being able to select or control the contents of their mind.

It comes from having had to remain continuously open to all inputs as a function of faulty cognitive structure development, arising from a confusion-inducing and intrusive family.

(See **ADRENAL PROBLEMS; GRAVE'S DISEASE**)

OXYCUNESIA (See **PAIN ON MOVEMENT**)

OXYGEN DEPRIVATION -- USUALLY DURING BIRTH

"Who invited YOU!?" They experience no right to be here taking up resources and space, because "God said so." It is the result of intense maternal ambivalence or rejection of having a child or rejecting of having THIS child.

"PACE-MAKER" (Heart-stimulator -- having to have one)

"Sealed unit." They are attempting to compensate for or work their way out of an "urban hermit" heart-shielding self-protection syndrome. They are apt to be one who is all heart, but who found early that l) the world did not want what they had to offer, and 2) that "love is a poison apple" that can't be trusted. So they have lived their life in a self-protective and love-deflecting manner, with a serious inability to let love in.

Now they are trying to change that, or at least to extend the time they have here to deal with that issue. If they do not deal with this issue after the operation, their prognosis is rather poor.

~~~~~~

"PACE-MAKER" PROBLEMS

"Closed heart." They are resisting the necessity to open their heart to the changed world they live in. They are just too distrusting to let go and let God, so to speak. It is, of course, due to a severely untrustworthy early experiential history, with its subsequent "self-fulfilling prophecy" effects.

PAGET'S DISEASE (Thickened bones)

"Cosmic abandonment." They have a profound feeling that nobody cares. The feeling is that there is no longer (or there never was) any foundation to build on. They feel abandoned by the "Home Office" (All That Is), and that there is nothing out there to sustain them. So they became their own "pillar of strength" -- bodily. It is the result of severe deprivation as a child, with a resulting emotional starvation and despairing desperation.

(See **BONE PROBLEMS**)

PAIN

"Karma beliefs." They are engaged in guilt-based self-punishment and atonement-seeking. They have a deep feeling of separation and sinfulness arising from massive guilt-induction from their family for who they were, what they needed, what they did, and what went down in the family.

****

"Trying to slip one past the Cosmos." It is God or Nature's way of warning them that they are off the path, and that something is out of balance. It involves conflict and congestion as they work out an undesirable condition. They now have to clean up their act and the mess they've created. If this is a chronic pattern, it is the result of constant corner-cutting by their family as a lifestyle.

****

"Victim-tripping." They have a belief in bondage and victimization. It has resulted in their being in a relationship that hurts, that is destructive, and that is exploitative. It is a pattern that was generated in a severely dysfunctional and hostile family.

****

"Repressed rage." They are sitting on a lot of resentment-rage that they are afraid to express or act on. Their life is not working, and they are highly frustrated with that, but they dare not do anything about it. They come from an exploitative and suppressive patriarchal family who made it crystal clear that to manifest anger is the kiss of death.

~~~~~~

ACHING PAIN

"Heart-smarts." There has been deprivation, a deep need, or a desire for something that is not being fulfilled. There is an aching imperative for change and fulfillment. They have an intense longing for love and a desperate need for being held, arising from a feeling of undeservingness created by a severely rejecting family. They are being given feedback they need to heal this deep heart-hurt.

BURNING PAIN

"Seething volcano." They are sitting on a great deal of resentment that is causing them considerable discomfort. They come from an exploitative, oppressive, dysfunctional and/or patriarchal family. They are in need of healing this early helplessness hurt and its resulting resentment.

DULL PAIN

"Stoic trip." They are resigned to the "fact" things are never going to get any better and that they just have to "bite the bullet." As a result, they tend to "numb out" and to grudgingly forebear things. They come from an intractably dysfunctional family system. They are being prompted to develop a more initiative action-taking approach.

INTERMITTENT PAIN

"Ya never know." They have the feeling that things are more or less out of control, and that they are unable to determine the flow of events in their life. Their experience is that the Universe keeps sending "curve balls" when they least expect it.

They were the "sane one" in a dysfunctional family upon everyone unconsciously relied. As a result, they felt responsible for everything and the dysfunctionality of the family was most disconcerting to them. They are learning to "share the load" and to find the limits of their responsibilities.

SHARP PAIN

"Getting their attention." They are prone to ignore important emotional processes and issues in their life. They grew up in a denial-dominated dysfunctional family. They are being reminded things don't just go away, that they have to be faced and dealt with.

STABBING PAIN

"Sudden attacks." They have the experience that they are frequently boundary-violated, "bushwhacked" and "broad-sided" in their life. It comes from growing up in an anger-dominated dysfunctional family who were forever attacking each other at one level or another. They are being prompted to develop their ability to trust genuinely trustworthy systems, people and situations.

STINGING PAIN

"Totally attention-arresting." They are intensely aware that something is very wrong with their situation. It operates as a continuous reminder that "they asked for it." They come from an accusatory and rejecting family. They are being prodded to seek the healing necessary to alleviate this heart wound.

THROBBING PAIN

"Never out of mind." They have a propensity to rehearse and rehash past hurts, and to nurse old wounds. They are the product of a never-endingly dysfunctional family who bore grudges and who focused on the negative at all times. They are being given the message that they need to leave their family's pattern behind.

PAIN AT OVULATION

"Tripod-rage." They have a resentment of femininity, of maternity, and/or the patriarchy. They feel restricted or required of, and they resist it. It is a function of the irresistible urge to kick anything with three legs that was passed on from their mother or from direct experience of exploitation, sex-ploitation and/or oppression from their father and/or society at large.
****

"Peter Panella." It represents an unwillingness to grow up and to be an adult female arising from possessive, over-protective and/or under-requiring parenting. They want to be "taken care of" for the rest of their life. Their family was the "keep 'em around the old homestead" type.

PAIN BETWEEN THE SHOULDER BLADES

"Vulnerability-avoidance." They are encountering emotional opening or emotional compression problems. They are unwilling to open their "heart center," due to untrustworthy parenting. Now they are being driven to face this issue by their circumstances because they can no longer afford to maintain this pattern.

PAINFUL BOWEL MOVEMENTS

"Holding in." They are controlling their position in life by trying to create a secure, problem-free and comfortable lifestyle and environment. They are over-concerned with material comfort and physical survival.

They can't give, they hoard, and they are highly possessive. They forcefully hold on to all possible resources, possessions, expressions and extensions of themselves. It is an "armored anus" pattern in which control matters more than anything else. They are intensely feeling-suppressing, and they tend strongly to be asexual.

It all comes from a severely stringent and suppressive dysfunctional family in which they felt that they had to cover all the bases for safety's sake, because no one else had the motivation or the wherewithal to do so. They took over the responsibility for all that happened in the family in a context in which whatever they did was "never good enough." It was a highly patriarchal and penetratingly perfectionistic parenting pattern.

(See **BOWEL PROBLEMS**)

PAINFUL INTERCOURSE

"Erotic avoidance." It was generated by an underlying compulsive immaturity generated by a "Don't grow up!" injunction by their family. Often there was a strong sex-ploitative element in their parent(s) handling of them.

PAINFUL MENSTRUATION

"Femininity-avoidance." They are engaging in a refusal to acknowledge or manifest that they are a woman, arising out of an underlying hatred of themselves and/or of women and of womankind. They thoroughly dislike their body, and they are deeply angry at themselves. There is in effect no self-acceptance or self-love, and they are unable to forgive themselves.

It is a pattern that was generated in a family in which they were systematically devalued, denigrated and disenfranchised, personally and as a female. They felt powerless and a second-class citizen and they hated it. This then turned into hatred of themselves and of womanhood.

PAINFUL URINATION

"Pissed off." They are intensely angry at their life, and they are looking for the one responsible for it. They feel betrayed and victimized, especially by their intimates, particularly those of the other gender. They have the feeling that the parent of the other gender is the cause of all their problems. But underneath all this, they have the uneasy feeling that they are really getting their "just desserts." This whole pattern came about as a result of their being sexualized and sex-ploitated in a seductive-destructive guilt-inducing manner in a severely dysfunctional family.

PAIN IN THE ABDOMEN

"Survival-anxiety." They are laboring under intense concerns over whether they can really handle life. There is much felt powerlessness arising from "skid row" programming and learned helplessness in the face of a severely dysfunctional family.
****

"Nit-picking." They are trying to cover all the details, to organize and coordinate everything, to analyze the situation, and to meet all the needs in the "right" way. They are into perfectionism, detail-domination and an inability to see the forest for the trees. It is a pattern that got started in a patriarchal and perfectionistic family.
****

"Over-critical." They are into a compulsion to help others that are carried out unwisely. They have a great desire to be needed, in order to inflate a damaged ego or to manipulate someone. They are pushing ideas or things on people in an unwanted "rescue-tripping" pattern that is the product of their feeling responsible for "straightening things out" in their dysfunctional family.
****

"Cinderella/Cinderfella." They feel used and abused, rushed and over-controlled, like they are in servitude. They feel what they give is not used, appreciated or utilized for the intended purposes. They are possessive and emotionally unbalanced, with no sense of being loved, wanted or needed. It is a pattern in which they were used and abused for self-immersed purposes in a dysfunctional family.

PAIN IN THE JOINTS

"Judgmental." They feel unloved and "not good enough," with a resulting resentful bitterness and criticality. They are very negatively evaluative of others, and they are convinced that others won't help them.

They are very angry that people won't "carry their load," so that they have to take on what they consider an unjust load. They are full of projected self-disgust, finding in others what they most dislike in themselves.

No one was ever there for them, and since they felt that everything that went down was their fault, they also felt they didn't deserve anyone to be there for them, bottom line. They felt that it all fell to them to do the necessaries because no one else could be trusted to do so or to do it RIGHT.
****

"Lilliput" (tied down with a million little ropes). They feel roped down, restrained and restricted. They are not allowing themselves to develop their full potential, due to severe circumstantial constraints, and they desperately want to be free to move around and to make something of themselves. Yet they feel that if they commit to carrying out their own destiny and goals, it would result in the devastation of others.

They were the "family hoist," the "pivot person" on whom everyone depended in their enmeshed and dysfunctional family. Theirs was a "vast wasteland" and "dour destiny" family culture, in which they never knew when something would go wrong, just that it would, sure as the sun rises.
****

"Negative faith." There are long-standing maladjustments and stony encrustations based on internal conflicts -- often between a desire to do something and a fear of failure. They have great resistance and emotional struggle, with a considerable amount of habitual anxiety and fear, along with expectations that of the worst case scenario. They are the product of a perfectionistic and demanding patriarchal family who had a strongly negative and wrong-making focus.
****

"What's good for General Bullmoose is good for EVERYBODY!!!" They are operating with a strong will, rigid intentions, intense opinions, and an abiding inability to change with changing circumstances. They are forcefully opinion-pushing, and they put out a steady stream of skeptical criticism. Calcium growths indicate the presence of hatred and a severely inflexible mind. They come from a patriarchal and perhaps authoritarian family culture in which "might was right."

(Also, see **JOINT PROBLEMS; RHEUMATOID ARTHRITIS; TENDON PROBLEMS**)

PAIN IN THE MUSCLES

"No way, Jose!" They are resistant to new experiences and they are refusing to move in life. Unsettling memories are surfacing, and they must confront issues that have been long put off.

They grew up in a damaging dysfunctional family who were intensely denial-dominated, resulting in a systematic reality-avoidance pattern.
****

"Self-inhibition." They have great difficulty coordinating the execution of things, integrating ideas of what is wanted to be accomplished with the pragmatic results they are getting, and dealing with the feelings and issues associated with success.

They have little sense of competence and confidence, and they are having significant problems in mobility, flexibility and activity. They have to be extremely inhibited and careful in all they do, or they become immobilized and unable to take action.

It arises from an intensely self-distrust-inducing "keep 'em around the old homestead" family, who programmed them to be super-successful (for the family only), and to otherwise fail. They have "come up a cropper" in reaction to the re-emergence or continued confrontation with this dilemma, and it has effectively immobilized them.
****

"Sinfulness." There is guilt-based self-punishment and atonement-seeking, and/or a belief in bondage, victimization and victim-tripping. In any case, they have a deep feeling of separation and non-deservingness arising from massive guilt-induction their family for who they were, what they needed, what they did, and what went down in the family.

PAIN IN THE RIBS

"Skid Row Syd." They operate with deprivation-expectations and separation- and abandonment-anxiety. They fear that they are going to ultimately end up alone in cold water flat or on the streets.

It arises from a self-immersed and possessive parenting pattern in which they were subjected to lack of consideration of their needs, threats of abandonment, demands that they conform totally to the parent(s) expectations, and systematic subconscious, subterranean and subtle programming to never succeed in the world or in relationships. There was also the injunction that went, "If we can't have you, then you are going to end up alone, alienated and totally deprived."

RIGHT SIDE RIB PAINS

"Self-distrust." They are experiencing fears or manifestations of self-sabotage and "Skid Row-seeking."

LEFT SIDE RIB PAINS

"Self-disgust." There is significant self-rejection, and they have the feeling that they somehow deserve to end up "on Skid Row."

~~~~~~

PAIN IN THE MUSCLES BETWEEN THE RIBS

"Skid Row programming." They feel that somehow they can expect to end up alone in a cold water flat or on "Skid Row." It arises from self-immersed and possessive parenting, which resulted in the injunction never to be able to connect or commit to anyone or anything but the family, along with the message that they deserve no better than "Skid Row" if they break the injunction.

PAIN ON MOVEMENT

"Don't move!" They experience the "balance of the Cosmos" rides on their every move, and that they have to be extremely careful with what they do. They are the product of an extremely blame-throwing and responsibility- and accountability-avoidant family who gave them a very strong "Don't move until I tell you to!" injunction. Now they feel the "weight of the world" and the "brunt of the pain" of the human race.

PAIN TOLERANCE -- HIGH

"The Machine." They are intensely determined to not be done in or to be overcome by any form of vulnerability or weakness. It is a "matter of life and death" to them. This pattern arose out of their feeling utterly alone on their own and/or feeling that they were the "buck stops here" person in their family, due to their being regarded as an inconvenience and/or as the "family hoist" that holds up the whole system like the car repair garage rack.
****

"What, *me* worry?" They are severely denial-dominated and reality-avoidant as a result of having grown up in a family in which that was massively demanded and enforced.

PAIN TOLERANCE -- LOW

They are into "I *knew* it! -- I'm going to die!" emotional commotion reactions. 90% of the experience of pain is psychological, in that it is the activation of the mid-brain or emotional center that creates most of the sensation. The physical basis of pain is primarily in the skin, not in deeper organs, and several inner organs are insensitive to pain.

Pain is our warning system that something harmful is happening. But after the initial shot over the bow, the vast bulk of the pain experience is in the *interpretations* of what it means.

Consequently, hyper-sensitivity to pain represents a generalized dread freak-out about life with associated emotional reactions when something untoward happens. It is an over-reaction to actual damage and danger, and a catastrophizing anticipation of much more serious outcomes.

It is a function of a pronounced propensity to go to and stay at the "worst case scenario." They live in the "cellar of existence" -- survival issues. They are chronically fearful and easily alarmed because they have little trust of the universe.

They therefore over-react to the "danger signal" of pain with massive amounts of anxiety and implication reactions about what it all means and where it is all going. This turns the pain experience into an intolerable torture.

It is the result of a severely dysfunctional family in which the worst often DID happen, producing a conditioned calamity-expectation process. It is a pattern that got started in early infancy, when there was very little protection, sustenance or support.
****

"Enough already!" The experience is of "salt in the wound." They feel like life is adding insult to injury, and that their experiential history has been replete with devastation, deprivation and denigration. They find the current process entirely too much, as a result.

They have undergone much emotional suffering and pragmatic stress in their life, and they find being demanded to endure physical pain as well is the "straw that broke the camel's back"
-- and they simply can't do it.

They are the product of a rather massively guilt-inducing, atonement-demanding, accusatory and dysfunctional family, and they are likely to have been the "linchpin" for the whole system also. They were systematically wounded on the emotional capability level in their severely dysfunctional family. This produced a severely over-responsible and self-blaming, punishment-seeking and success-avoidant lifestyle.
****

"Woe is me!" They have a very strong experience of being the "butt of the Universe," in the sense of its playing "Kick you" with them. They tend to be quite self-immersed and egocentric, with a pronounced pattern of complaining and "groan-moaning." It started in their severely dysfunctional family, where about the only way they could get any attention was to play up their "injuries and tragedies."

PALLEGRA (Niacin deficiency -- skin eruptions, gastrointestinal disturbances. It can lead to nervous disorders and dementia) – (Also Spelled Pellagra)

"It's all my fault!" They have a pronounced tendency to feel negatively evaluated and even attacked for their deficiencies and for the resulting untoward environmental events, as they experience it. There is a considerable lack of harmony and peace in their life.

They tend to be plagued by shame, embarrassment and guilt, along with inferiority, low self-esteem, ostracism and obstruction. They take on too much accountability and responsibility, and they try to do too much too well, as they try to "make up for" their perceived lacks and their "badness." They feel like an "alarming Martian."

They have great trouble being able to say "no" to demands and expectations from their environment, with the result they end up a perfectionistic workaholic who tries too hard. It is a pattern that started in a wrong-making, over-expecting and denial-dominated dysfunctional family.

PALPITATIONS (See ARRYTHMIA)

PALSY (Involuntary tremor with paralysis)

"One and only one way." They are getting stuck, due to paralyzing thoughts. They are fixated on a particular mind set, mental approach, and paradigmatic model. They want to "make things all right," out of having to be the one responsible for everything that happens.

However, they are extremely rigid in how they think that should be. They are trapped in implication-terror at the thought of things being different from what they imagine or of trying a new approach to things. They come from a similar family system.
****

"Cosmic paranoia." They are full of guilt and rejection of life, they are not able to forgive others or themselves. They have an intensely anxious relationship with the Universe that is full of fear, uncertainty and insecurity. They have a "God will KILL me if I do anything different!" feeling. They have ended up feeling stagnated and immobilized.

It is the result of a very rigid adaptation to a severely dysfunctional and frightening family who themselves manifested a very fearfully narrow viewpoint and lifestyle. They played the role of the "family hoist" who was the pivotal point of everything.

PANCREAS PROBLEMS

"Love-incompetent." They are having difficulties in integrating and expressing love. They don't believe they deserve love, and that "Love is a poison apple." They have a lot of guilt and feelings of lack of value, in a low self-esteem process.

It all developed out of a severe worth-anxiety process that arose from intensely ambivalent acceptance-rejection reactions from their family.
****

"There is no joy in Bloodville." They have an angry sourness and bitterness about life, with a feeling that life has lost its sweetness. They have the experience that their quality of life is out of control, and that "life sucks." There is a frustrated desire to acquire goods and friendships, along with a sense of their goals and plans being disrupted.

As they experience it, there is no joy, fun, caring and sharing in their life, and they have lost touch with the enjoyment of life. They feel they can't create anything worthwhile for themselves.

They are harboring a good deal of anger and resentment about all this, and they are intensely judgmental and rejecting of everything and everyone. Now they have reached the point where they are rejecting everything, because they feel totally rejected by the Universe.

They are the product of a severely dysfunctional and unimpactable family system in which they were the "responsible one" who had to sacrifice their joy to the alter of disaster-deflection.
****

"I-me-mine." They are highly egocentric and egotistical in their functioning. They are engaged in over-indulgence and/or in self-indulgence, emotional excess, negative self-expression, and/or violence. Their underlying attitude is the world owes them a living, a loving and a lavish, and they feel betrayed when it doesn't come through for them.

They come from an intensely self-immersed and selfish family who could care less about ecological impact or contribution. It generated a compulsive worth-proof-needing, in the form of a constant input of positive and sweet experiences, along with a simultaneous continuation of the family culture.

~~~~~~

PANCREATIC CANCER

"Where's the exit?" They have in effect given up on life, and they want out of here NOW. They are intensely embittered, and they feel that they in effect have no quality of life or reason to continue. They feel utterly unable to make anything better in their life, and they don't want to bother trying any more.

They are sitting on a great deal of resentment-rage and disgusted distrust about the world and other people. To them, it is as if they are surrounded by a "ship of fools" in an insane world, and they want out. They see no possibility of anything working out or of any sweetness in living.

It all got started in a severely ambivalent and subtly rejecting dysfunctional family, who made it quite clear to that at the underlying message level that they had no right to expect a good life. They reacted initially with a frenetic/frantic effort to "get the God Housekeeping Seal of Approval." However, now they have "thrown in the towel," and their whole concentration is on the Ultimate Route Out.

(See **CANCER**)

PANCREATITIS (Inflammation of the pancreas)

"Bitter rejection." They are disgusted, frustrated and angry, because continuously rejecting of everything they come in contact with. They come from an equally begrudging and grumbling dissatisfied dysfunctional family.

PANIC ATTACKS; PANIC DISORDER

"Run amok-anxiety." They are experiencing a fear of what they would do if they "let fly with one." It is usually set off by symbolic or actual precipitating circumstances that activate their underlying motivational system and/or memories of their past.

There are a number of possibilities here. It can be:

1) "evil-anxiety," where they feel they are "bad," and that they would do dreadful things, or

2) "betrayal -anxiety," a fear that if they did what they want or said what they see, they would destroy the family, or

3) "sex-ploitation-rage," in which they are afraid of what they would do in reaction to having been subjected to invasive possessive and intrusive sexual attentions from their family.

This whole pattern started in the womb, where there was originally a massive rejection reaction from their mother, in fear of the individual's great capabilities (inherent in their soul).

PARALYSIS

"Don't move!" Their experience is that the "balance of the Cosmos" rides on every move. They don't dare move forward on anything, feeling that they might set off World War III. Now they feel the "weight of the world" and the "brunt of the pain" of the human race.

They are the product of an extremely blame-throwing and responsibility- and accountability-avoidant family, who gave them a very strong "Don't move until I tell you to!" injunction.
****

"They're after me!" They are undergoing immobilizing fear and terror, a feeling of utter helplessness. They feel they are under attack from the Universe, and that nothing is trustworthy. They are in a thorough-going escape mode, and they are doing all they can to avoid an unwanted task or experience and/or to escape a situation or person.

They are experiencing an intense resistance to life, people and things in a super-stubbornness reaction. They are fearful of what the future might bring, and they are highly reluctant to engage with life. They are mentally and/or emotionally confused, they feel overwhelmed and inadequate, and they lack self-control at this point.

It is the result of having come up in an irrational and/or chaotic family, in which there was nothing they could do to change the course of events, to improve the situation, or to provide themselves a better experience.

RIGHT SIDE PARALYSIS

A "Don't do!" injunction is being activated. They were programmed not to be effective in the world.

LEFT SIDE PARALYSIS

Their "Don't be!" injunction is operating. They were told by their family that what they are is not acceptable.

PARALYSIS OF THE DIAPHRAM (Iron lung situation)

"I don't deserve to live." They feel they have no right to exist and take up air and space. They have an overwhelming fear of God, and they are convinced that they will be struck dead if they make any waves or demands.

There is an inability to breathe for themselves, and to a systematic suppression of any form of crying, due to guilt- and shame-inducing parenting. They feel stifled and also that it is unsafe to take charge of their own life. They are intensely inhibited against free expression, and they are full of unresolved guilt and suppressed grief.

They feel "left out in the cold," and that there is no place for them here. It is the result of intrauterine and subsequent severe rejection and of massive "If it weren't for you. . ." and accusatory parenting.

PARAPLEGIC [Paralyzed in two limbs] (See **PARALYSIS**)

PARASITES; PARASITIC WORMS

"At effect, not at cause." They are therefore feeling-dominated, in a letting their feelings run them, rather than their taking responsibility for effective manifestation of their reactions to things. They are also giving their power to others, letting them take over everything in their life.

It's a pattern that started in a "never good enough" parenting situation, in which they frantically tried over and over to get the "God Housekeeping Seal of Approval" -- and forever failed to do so.
****

"I don't have what it takes." They feel that they lack the secret for success and worth that everyone else has, and that they have to keep trying with "stand-ins for the original cast" in re-runs of the original scenario until they get it right, finally.

They are terrified to strike out on their own or to stand on their own rights and on their own ground and two feet, for fear of the ultimate "blow-it." They have no trust of themselves, and they are convinced there is an "answer" that they don't have and others do, so they keep on trying to find the "key."

In the meantime, they turn everything over to "those in the know" or to those they think hold the "Golden Orb" of "Final Validation." As a result, they have to deal with constant emotional commotion and external interference and exploitation in their lives. They are the product of an accusative and blame-throwing family.

PARASTHESIA (See **NUMBNESS**)

PARASYMPATHETIC NERVOUS SYSTEM PROBLEMS

"Red-orange alert." They are continuously in a state of mild agitation, somewhat along the lines of Don Knotts in his constant anxiety mode. They feel somehow at least slightly endangered at all times. It comes from growing up in an unpredictably dysfunctional family in which things would come at them "off the wall," so to speak.
****

"Chronically angry." They are forever feeling thwarted, invaded, and even violated. They are instantly irritable and resentfully reactive most of the time. They are the product of a severely frustrating and unassailably dysfunctional family who continuously subjected them to enraging experiences.

PARATHYROID PROBLEMS

"Catastrophic expectations." They operate with constant anxiety, worry and tenseness. They have the feeling that they are one step away from calamity in an unpredictable and uncontrollable manner, and that they have to be on at least "yellow alert" at all times to see if they can't head disaster off at the pass. They also have a good deal of resentment over their whole situation and life pattern, about which they are too afraid to do anything. It comes from having been in a chaotic dysfunctional family.

PARESIS (Paralysis due to brain disease, usually syphilis)

"God is Al Capone!" They have a profound and abiding distrust of the Universe in which their experience is that the "Home Office" (All That Is) has taken charge of their life in a highly detrimental manner.

They feel an immobilizing fear and terror, along with a feeling of utter helplessness. As a result, they have an abiding distrust of the Universe, and they have "thrown in the towel" on managing their own affairs or those of the world around them. They are mentally and emotionally confused, and they feel overwhelmed and inadequate, with the result they have lost their self-control at this point.

They feel that they are under attack from the Universe, and that nothing is trustworthy. They are having an intense resistance to life, people and things in general, in a "super-stubbornness" reaction.

This all developed as a result of having come up in a chaotic and irrational family in which there was nothing they could do to change the course of events or to provide themselves a better experience. There was never anyone there to meet their needs. Indeed, they had to meet the needs of the situation, including their being sex-ploitated and shamed for their sexuality.

PARKINSON'S DISEASE (Progressive palsy)

"I don't dare let go!" There is an intense fearfulness and an overweening desire to control everything and everyone about every aspect of every issue, situation and under-taking. They have no faith in the Universe and in life, and they feel alone and unsafe in an uncaring world.

They have the complete conviction that all hell will break loose and everything will go to hell in a bread basket, unless they personally hands on determine the purpose, flow and outcome of everything. It comes from being the only "sane one" and the "family hoist" in a severely dysfunctional family.

(See **PALSY**)

"PARROT FEVER" (Lung disease with fever)

"Grit and bear it." They are joy-avoidant, happiness-squashing, and love-deflecting, out of a fear of the Universe. They feel unworthy of living fully, and they are alone, sad and non-belonging, with little sense of acceptance.

They tend to get into consuming passionate commitments that lead nowhere, and to become involved in unrequited love relationships. They are full of family taboos, social restrictions and moral inhibitions, all of which generate a great deal of resentment which they are frightened of expressing. They come from a highly exploitative and shame-inducing dysfunctional family.

PENIS PROBLEMS

"Male shame." They are having the experience of being a "moral cretin" for being male. They are either competence-anxious about their ability to carry off the male role requirements or they are guilt-ridden over the state of the male race and/or their own history of functioning.

In all events, their mother was domineering, full of "tripod-rage," (The irresistible urge to kick anything with three legs) wrong-making/ accusatory, and engulfingly dependent.
****

"Raging rapist." They are power-fiend so hell-bent on dominating and domineering everyone. It is the result of their mother's having totally squashed and squelched them throughout their childhood, so that now they are grimly set on getting "on top of" everyone.

****

"Ferocious fierceness." They are into piercing penetration in their mania for making an impact. They are driven to leave their imprint on everything they encounter. This came from being completely ignored and devalued by their family, so that they couldn't make a difference in anything that happened. They ended up furiously determined to "prove" themselves.

(See **GENITAL PROBLEMS -- MALE**)

PEPTIC ULCER (Lesion in the upper digestive tract caused by stomach acid)

"Suppressing freak-outs." They have a very strong fear of not coming up to snuff, of not being good enough. They are convinced that it is their responsibility to please everyone. They are intensely anxious to please, but they suffer from the conviction that they don't have "the right stuff."

This is an area of intense "rawness," causing severe pain and upset. They are suppressing strong anger, fear, aggression or nervousness. They are not being able to take in and assimilate what is happening to them, the realities they have to deal with. They are therefore extremely bothered about their "failure." It is the result of "never good enough" parenting.

PERICARDIUM PROBLEMS (The lining around heart)

"Island unto themselves." They are emotionally closed, love-deflecting and intensely insensitive. They are convinced that "love is a poison apple" as a result of untrustworthy parenting, and they have closed their heart. They have little trust, faith, or capacity for love and joy.

PERINEUM PROBLEMS (The area between the anus and the genitals)

"Self-revulsion." They have strong shame feelings about their fundamental beingness, in the form of intense rejection of their physical nature, especially around elimination and sexuality. They also feel basically unsafe in the world, because they "don't deserve to be here."

They were made to feel profoundly "bad, wrong and evil" as a child for what and who they were. The result is deep questioning about their right to exist.

PERIPHERAL NERVE FUNCTIONING IMPAIRMENT

"Shadow-shoving." They are systematically suppressing all experiences and expressions of aspects of themselves that they are convinced are so unacceptable as to require total elimination of manifestation. These aspects have caused them so much pain and hurt that they don't want to feel them. The "unacceptable" aspects were reacted to with great punishment, ostracism and rejection when they manifested these qualities and capabilities as a child, so they are now dedicated to never contacting them.

They are "going dead" mentally and emotionally -- totally retreating into their core and shutting down feeling, out of fears that they are in a "dog-eat-dog world" in which people are out to do them in. They are vulnerability-avoidant, and they are operating with feelings that the environment is truly dangerous. They have a deep and abiding distrust of intimacy out of an "intimate enemy" experience in their exploitative and untrustworthy family.

****

"Cut off." They are withholding love and consideration, and they are love-deflecting and love-distrusting. To them, love is a poison apple that they want absolutely nothing to do with. It is a result of wrong-making and self-immersed parenting.

PERITONEUM PROBLEMS (Abdominal wall lining)

"This is an up with which I will no longer put!" They are fed up with the "slings and arrows of outrageous fortune." They have a deep-seated resentment of their lot in life, the hard knocks they have experienced (or are experiencing). They feel they have assimilated far more than their share of negativity, and they are putting up a protective shield of vulnerability- and involvement-avoidance as a result. It reflects an underlying distrust of the Universe generated by a "poison apple" dispensing dysfunctional family.

PERNICIOUS ANEMIA (Gradual reduction of red cells, leading to weakness, nervous system problems and digestive disorders)

"I just can't go on like this any more." They are feeling overwhelmed and exhausted by the requirements of life. Rest, joy and love seem beyond their range or rights, as far as they are concerned.

There is an insufficiency of sustaining inputs of resources and support, and they feel overloaded and drained out, due to an excessive sense of responsibility. There is intense deprivation-grief and little trust in the Universe. They are the product of an exploitative and responsibility-dumping dysfunctional family.

****

"But not for me." They have a super-serious and catastrophic expectations approach to life. They don't feel "good enough" to deserve even the basic sustenance resources. They feel undeserving of joy and love, and that God will destroy them if they have any. They feel that they have to be in continuous self-sacrificing service, yet they don't feel that what they have to offer is worth anything.

They are suffering from a profound sense of helplessness, haplessness and hopelessness, and they are driven by an underlying intense depression and sorrow. They are therefore systematically life-negating and love-refusing, and in effect, they are throwing in the towel. It is the result of severely harsh, exploitative and aggressively attacking mothering.

PERTUSSIS (See WHOOPING COUGH)

"PETITE MAL" (Small seizures)

"Fear-freakout." They have a sense of persecution and pressure from the environment, along with a feeling of great struggle. They are rejecting of life, and they have propensity to violence towards the self.

There is a hidden fear amounting to severe "run amok-anxiety" and agitated anticipation of a potential homicidal rampage from themselves. The little seizures are fear paroxysms and intense resentment-energy releases.

There is an extreme need to escape from the experiences of life, along with a great fear of the expectations of society. There is a pronounced sense of being outclassed and overwhelmed by the world, along with a tremendous resentment of their situation.

It came from having too much expected of them, either for what they were capable of or for a child. If the epilepsy appeared in childhood, it added to the sense of their being incapable and "broken brained," which only fueled the flames of the situation.

PFEIFFER'S DISEASE (See MONONUCLEOSIS)

"PHANTOM LIMB" (Sensed presence of an absent limb)

"Deep regrets." They have an intense sense of unfinished business, and they are full of "If only. . ." feelings. Their experience is that they *should* be able to complete their intentions and purposes, and that somehow it got derailed.

Underlying all this is a deep-seated sense of guilt and moral responsibility for making sure everything is right in the world. It is the result of performance-contingent love from their parents, often to the accompaniment of perfectionistic expectations.

~~~~~~

"PHANTOM LIMB" PAIN

"You asked for it, asshole!" Their experience is they deserve their negative circumstances, and that they have to atone for their "evilness" and "accountability" for "all they have done/been." The result is a severe self-punishment reaction in the form of the "phantom pain." They are the product of moralistic, perfectionistic, wrong-making parenting.

PHLEBITIS (Potentially lethal floating blood clot in the blood vessels)

"Trapped." They have an intense anger and frustration with their lives, and they feel caught in a manner in which there is no escape. They feel that their situation can't be alleviated, and that their problems are insoluble, given the nature of the world.

They are blaming others for the limitations and lack of joy in their life that they are experiencing. Their experience is that they are surrounded by a "ship of fools" and by irrelevant resources that simply don't meet the needs of the situation. It comes from having had to take over the helm of a rudderless, highly incompetent and dysfunctional family from a very early age.

PHRENOPLEGIAL (See PARALYSIS OF THE DIAPHRAM)

PICK'S DISEASE (Degenerative brain disease affecting the frontal and temporal lobes)

"Comprehension-collapse." They have lost the ability to accept, organize, store, integrate and interpret information, with the result they can no longer make decisions or function on their own volition. They are having a profound emotional and disorganized reaction to this. It is the result of confusion-inducing and very restrictive parenting.

"PINCHED NERVE"

"Oh no you don't!" They are getting "saber-rattle warnings" about not "stepping over that line" of self-commitment and self-manifestation. It is the result of intense "keep them around the old homestead" programming.

PINEAL GLAND PROBLEMS (Small "master gland" above the roof of the mouth)

"God must be Al Capone!" They have severe issues around sacred-secular interaction. It results in non-communicativeness and distrust. They have little faith in the Universe, and they feel their only real defense is to keep everyone guessing as to who they are, what they are experiencing, what their situation is, and what they are up to. They systematically refuse to be educated and enlightened.

They were subjected to highly invasive and untrustworthy parenting, starting in the womb or early infancy. It resulted in an experience of the "Home Office" (All That Is) as being inimical to their best interests, because of the "in loco Deity" effect of early childhood, where they experienced the parents as the "local reps" of the "Source."

"PIN WORMS" (Rectal parasites)

"Repressed rebellion." They are rather control-oriented and self-suppressing, and they are afraid to "dump their stuff" on the world. Yet they are also resentful of what feels like intrusively invasive restrictions and interventions from their environment. However, bottom line, they feel self-disgusted and self-rejecting as being somehow "unclean." It came about from a restrictive, shame-inducing and boundary-violating family.

PITUITARY GLAND PROBLEMS (The "conductor gland" -- as in an orchestra)

"It's all *their* fault!" They are prone to be arrogantly egoistic and intensely insulted by and unhappy with their lot in life. They are severely disappointed and narcissistically wounded. They have the habit of somaticizing and of claming ill health as the basis of much of their dysfunctionality.

They feel they don't have any control of themselves or of their situation. They feel very unbalanced and out of control. They don't feel they are the master of their own ship and fate, and they have the belief that they are forever experiencing bad luck and misfortune. They are highly negatively focused, and they have real problems with seeing the things that are right and good.

At the base of it is a severe self-distrust and worth-anxiety generated by ignoring, insensitive, exploitative and/or oppressive parenting.

PLACENTA PROBLEMS

"What are *you* doing here!?" There is a rather intense at least ambivalence about being pregnant, or about being pregnant with this particular child. It can come from any number of causes, including situationals, the soul nature of the child, or personality problems in the mother.

If it is the mother's personal characteristics issues, it arises from having been given the same message at about the same time and probably subsequently as a theme in her childhood.
****

"Air supply problem." The fetus feels cut off from the Universe -- rejected by God. They assume they are getting their "Cosmic just desserts," and this conclusion carries into their life as the foundational assumption out of which they operate. It is a destiny design feature for purposes of karma-burning, experience-expanding and/or special training.

PLANTAR WARTS (Painful warts on the bottoms of the feet)
"Cope-ability-agitation." They have deep competence-anxiety and lack of confidence in themselves, and in the very basis of their understanding and functioning. They feel that somehow their foundational equipment or beingness is insufficient to the cause of living.

There is a spreading frustration about where the future seems to be going, and they have little trust or faith in the Universe. There is also a good deal of resentment and anger about all of this. It is the product of "keep 'em around the old homestead" independence- and effectance-undermining parenting.

PLATELETS, LOW (Difficulty clotting blood)
"Over-responsibility." They have a sense that they are here to make the world all better, and that they should care-take everything and everyone. It comes from having grown up in a situation of many unmet needs for everyone, and they rose to the challenge to the point where they have some difficulty limiting demands made on them or in taking care of their own needs.

PLEURISY (Inflammation of the lung lining)
"Exploitation-rage." There is a deep resentment of the inequality of energy exchange and of the unrequitedness of their relationship with the environment, but especially in their intimate relationships. They are prone to rescuing and codependent situations out of an underlying sense of non-deservingness of love and support.

They are now tending to put up an antagonistic and hostile wall around themselves to avoid further such experiences. It is the result of an exploitative and shame-inducing dysfunctional family.

(See **LUNG PROBLEMS**)

PHILTRUM PROBLEMS (The indented area below the nose in the center of the upper lip)
"Run down." They are manifesting low life energy, and their sexual manifestation is diminished, due to being emotionally, physically and/or sexually abused. This issue is now surfacing and calling for rectification.

"P.M.S." (Pre-Menstrual Syndrome); "P.M.T." (Pre-Menstrual Tension)
"Self-suppression." They are feeling powerless and that it is "unfeminine" to be powerful in a patriarchal world. They therefore systematically suppress their anger and personal potency. They hate to feel angry or upset at anyone, and they are prone to give power to outside influences, resulting in their allowing confusion to reign.

They reject the feminine process, while feeling that owning their potency will result in utter rejection and invalidation. They can only vicariously experience validation, significance and worth by assisting others to get it, at their own expense. They feel somehow inferior, dysfunctional and meaningless because of the monthly process of creativity- and generativity-manifestation. There is a lack of self-appreciation and self-love.

What results out of all this is a tendency to become destabilized by physiological changes. They also feel that their physiological condition provides an excuse for rage- and despair-release. They were subjected to intense patriarchal conditioning by both their family and the culture at large. They need to take charge of their own life, and take joy in their potency and worth.

PNEUMOCOCCUS (Airborne lethal lung disease)

"No right to exist." They feel unworthy of living fully, and they are alone, sad, and non-belonging, with no sense of acceptance. They are suffocating from a chronic self-disgust reaction, and they are full of angry punishment-deservingness feelings with self-destructive motivations and manifestations. They are capitulating and giving up, in an extreme underlying abandonment depression around feeling rejected by God and ejected from the Cosmos.

It is the result of being massively neglected, rejected, accused and wrong-made by a severely dysfunctional family, along with a highly self-immersed, self-serving, and blame-throwing mother who gave them strong "If it weren't for you" messages, while simultaneously putting "You can do no right" demands for them to "make it all better" for her.

PNEUMONIA (Inflammation of the lungs)

"Suppressed grief." They are desperate and tired of life, due to generalized disturbances in their processes and situation. They are having a "salt poured in emotional wounds" experience that is not being allowed to heal.

They are suffering under the influence of their lifelong repressed sorrow. They are also fearful and anxious to the point of being overcome with desperation and futility feelings. They are struggling with confusion-inducing emotional conflict, and there is a failure to maintain immunity to negative ideas.

They are the product of a self-defeatingness generating dysfunctional family who instilled a sense of their being hapless, helpless and hopeless.

****

"My way or the highway!" They have a very strong ego that is getting in their way. They tend to believe that theirs is the "only way to fly," and that they are surrounded by people who not only don't understand that, but who also place restrictions on them and who "punish" them for their ways of doing things and their beingness.

They can't let people in or themselves out. They also have the experience that they have to handle the whole of life single-handed, with no help from any friends. While this has made for a modicum of success as a survival strategy, it has cut them off from joy and love, and that is now taking its toll. It came about from effective emotional abandonment at a very early age, to which they reacted with becoming a "self-made person" with a "portable Plexiglas phone-booth" around them.

****

"Tie that grinds." They are feeling totally stifled by an over-close and/or dominating relationship. They are being overwhelmed and restricted, they are very angry about it. However, they don't feel they can do or say anything about it, for fear of catastrophic consequences. It is the result of an authoritarian and oppressive and possessive family.

POLIO; POLIOMYELITIS (Paralysis of the body -- usually the limbs, but it can go to the iron lung level)

"Life-and-death scarcity." They have a very strong feeling of being "done in" by some one, because there are not enough life sustenance resources to go around. They feel they have to stop someone from getting any resources, because it means that they won't get theirs. They are paralyzed with jealousy and feelings of life-and-death restrictions of freedom.

It comes from a family that engendered strong feelings of scarcity of life support systems, and which engaged in competition to the death among the family members.

POLYCYSTIC OVARIAN SYNDROME (PCOS) (Irregular periods, male pattern baldness, depression, infertility, facial hair, acne, weight gain)

"Gender role issues." She is at odds with her situation, function and identity as a female in a patriarchal world. She feels victimized, and she has a significant amount of "tripod-rage" (the irresistible urge to kick anything with three legs). She also feels considerably self-dissatisfied, particularly in the realm of potency, personal power and position. She feels somehow insufficient as a person by being female.

In addition, she tends to have an overdeveloped sense of being personally responsible/accountable for the welfare of those around her by "delivering the goods" and "covering all the bases." She feels that she has to run the whole show with inadequate personal resources and prerogatives. She feels somehow cut off and alone in the world and, in effect, abandoned by God. She was placed in a parental role in her family, where she was depended on to be both the father and the mother of the family.

POLYPS (Cylindrical growths)

"Chained to the wall." They are trapped in "ghosts of Christmases past" emotionally, in the sense that things have not and will not change for them. They are lost in the emotional pain of their childhood, and as a result, they tend to re-create it in their current life. They are rigidly refusing to release the past, and they are experiencing the impact of stagnating beliefs and stationary strategies.

The net effect is a massively convincing experience that "life sucks," "God is Al Capone," and you might as well "hunker down in the bunker," because it's useless to expect any better out of things. The feeling is that the war is definitely NOT over, and that nothing has substantially changed since they developed their ways of being and doing things in their severely neglectful, rejecting and dysfunctional family.

Unfortunately, that sets up a self-fulfilling prophecy effect that continuously revalidates their assumptions and coping strategies of the past. They are drowning in their own sorrow as a result. It is the result of a massively invasive and pervasively accusatory and exploitative family who operated out of extremely pessimistic and nihilistic beliefs and resulting events.
****

"Hunkering down in the bunker." They fear life, and they refuse to take it in emotionally. They feel unsafe in the world, and that they don't dare live fully and freely. Their experience is that "love is a poison apple" that can't be trusted, and that they deserve no better than that, because of who and what they are, bottom line. They are the product of an untrustworthy and rejecting dysfunctional family who were systematically undermining of their capacity to cope.

POROUSNESS OF THE BONES (See OSTEO-POROSIS)

"POST-NASAL DRIP" (Sinus infection)

"Dripping faucet." There is an "inner crying," along with a feeling of being a powerless child victim of a cruel and uncaring world. They are manifesting accountability-avoidant self-pity and a fixation on the conviction they are the down-trodden object of discrimination, deprivation and persecution. It got started with an invasively suppressive, scapegoating, exploitative, emotionally depriving, and ejecting-rejecting family, and it has become a way of life, in a self-fulfilling prophecy manner.

RIGHT "POST-NASAL DRIP"
"Hobnail boot." They have feelings of victimization and powerlessness.

LEFT "POST-NASAL DRIP"
"Vast wasteland." There is long-standing grief and resignation around emotional deprivation.

POST-PARTUM DEPRESSION (After giving birth)
"Running on empty." They are having an exhaustion and abandonment-despair reaction, which is a re-play of their own post-birth experience. They were left to their own devices at that time, and often there was significant maternal deprivation in their childhood.

PREMATURE MENOPAUSE
"Enough, already!" They are going into "early retirement." They are exhausted and/or fed up, and they want to "kick back," and to not have to handle "command generation" responsibilities.

This can be an "eternal girl" pattern in which they don't want to be grown up and/or a situation where they have had it with sexuality, generativity and/or contributory responsibilities.

If it is an "eternal girl" pattern, it arose from a possessive/enmeshing relationship with their mother. If it is a "fed up" response to responsibility, it may reflect an "over-loaded" pattern started by a severely demanding family.
****

"Right to MY life!" They want no more kids or no possibility of any kids in their life. They are becoming totally focused on manifesting THEIR identity and destiny from now on. They may or may not have been caught up in the "eternal maternal" pattern, but they definitely do not intend it to be the pattern of their life now.

If they *were* caught up in the "eternal maternal trip," it was imposed extremely early in their life as a "God says so!" requirement from their family.
****

"Buzz off, buster!" They are thoroughly enraged with the paranoid patriarchy, with the "tripods" of the world, and/or with sexuality and its patterns. They are therefore shutting down sexually (which of course is not at all involved in menopause normally). They have "had it up to the eyebrows," and it is "an up with which they will no longer put." This can either come from a lifetime of victimization and sex-ploitation and/or from an underlying massive rage reaction to sexuality from early sex-ploitation and abuse.
****

"Checking out." They are "winding down" and getting ready to leave. They are tired, disgusted or self-rejecting. If they are tired of it all, it may arise from having had to "shoulder the world" all their life, and they are like a "worn-out horse."

If it is a generalized revulsion reaction, it may reflect a severely cynical and/or an abusive upbringing. If it is a self-elimination process, it would be the result of intensely denigrating and/or accusatory parenting.
****

"I've got WORK to do!" They are in effect ending their period of physical generativity to make room for other forms of generativity (contributing to tomorrow). They feel completed with the physical form of generativity and/or they are not to do the child-rearing thing because their destiny calls for other contributions now.
****

"Femininity-rejection." They feel the sexual/childbearing aspects of themselves are not acceptable manifestations. They were subjected to intensely patriarchal treatment as a child and later in their life, and they are reacting with rageful refusal to play the game any more and/or with revulsion towards the feminine.

"PRICKLY HEAT" (Fever-induced blisters -- usually in infancy)

"Alone in the world." They feel unprotected and unsupported, and they are quite resentful of that. There is a considerable amount of internal conflict about need-seeking and self-expression. They feel that they have to dig in their heels to prevent untoward outcomes of self-release.

It arises from a significantly dysfunctional family who is in effect riding rough-shod over them when they let themselves and their needs be known. This is reflective of an intensely ambivalent or even out-and-out rejecting attitude on the part of the mother about being pregnant, or about being the mother of this particular individual.

PROGERIA (Grossly premature aging -- they die with all the characteristic appearances and limitations of an extremely advanced age person by the age of 6 to 10.)

"Bring back the good old days!" They are incapable of adjusting to being here on the material plane, and they are engaging in a severe rejection of reality and the world. It is an extremely accelerated destiny manifestation, as they only came to take care of some brief unfinished business of the soul. Hence they very much do not feel a part of this world, and that there must be some kind of Cosmic mistake at the basis of their being here at all. At some deep level, they can hardly wait to get out of here.

PROGESTERONE PROBLEMS (Hormone that prepares the uterus for the reception and development of the fertilized ovum)

"Inadequate to the cause." They feel competence-anxious, ill-equipped, unprepared and/or undeserving of generativity and fertility. They are afraid that they have no right or capability to carry out child-bearing and -rearing. They also tend to feel insufficient to the requirements of meaningful service and contribution. Their family denigrated and undermined their self-worth, confidence and competence.

****

"Generativity issues." They are in conflict about or in opposition to building tomorrow's world -- including bearing and rearing children. They tend to be focused or even fixated on personal gain and self-serving, perhaps at the expense of contribution or service to the world. They are the product of a similar family culture.

PROLAPSE (Displacement or protrusion of an organ, such as the vagina, the prostate, the bladder, or the heart)

"Done in." They are engaged in a collapsing, giving up or loss of control, due to there no longer being sufficient energy to maintain their "elasticity." There is a mental prostration, devastation and deactivation. There is an inner hopelessness, depression and sense of no longer having control of their life. It is a reactivation of an old, familiar feeling, arising from having grown up in a hapless and helpless position in their severely dysfunctional family.

PROLAPSED HEART VALVE (Protruding into the heart chamber, leading to back-logged blood, pain, skipped beats and shortness of breath)

"Undeserving." They are struggling with feelings of unlovability, or with the sense that love is never going to come to them. Their experience is that they are somehow "flawed" and that they therefore cannot expect to receive the acceptance and love they so desperately need and desire. It arises from perfectionistic and paternalistic parenting in which nothing they ever did was "good enough."

PROSTATE PROBLEMS

"Male shame." They are plagued with emotional tenseness and sexual impotence, due to emotional conflicts about sexuality. They are self-contained and lonely, with a lot of deprivation-grief and depression.

There is a significant amount of fatigue, along with a breaking down and/or a certain giving up. They feel they just don't cut it as a male, or that to be a male is a shameful thing. It is the result of severe "tripod-rage" on their mother's part (the irresistible urge to kick anything with three legs). Now it is coming to roost in the symbolic center of masculine sexuality.

****

"Can't get it up." There are mental fears that are weakening their masculinity, along with a belief in the deteriorations of aging. There are felt pressures to perform sexually.

They have guilt and concern over past carelessness and exploitativeness. They "bought the whole nine yards" of the masculine projection and manifestation in the patriarchal culture, and they are now feeling the cost. The net effect is one of isolation, self-rejection and power-shame.

It came as a result of being thrust into the masculine role by their mother, who wanted them to be the man in their life or at least a man she could be proud of. They also modeled themselves after their patriarchal father.

~~~~~~

PROLAPSED PROSTATE (Protruding into the bladder)

"Yesterday's newspaper." Due to changes in their life situation such as divorce, aging or illness, there are intense feelings of frustration, impotence and uselessness. They experience themselves as being ineffectual, confused and unable to be a full man.

They are afraid that their purpose in being here is already over. They are having great difficulty expressing or releasing these negative and corrosive emotions. They grew up in a family who equated sexual performance and "macho" masculinity with worth and meaningfulness as a male.

PROSTATE CANCER

"Powerlessness-fury." They are full of repressed resentment at the way that they have been restricted and disempowered in their life. They are prone to turn their personal potency over to others, systems and situations. They are the product of a castrating and "in-yoke"-ing enmeshed and possessive mother.

PROSTRATION (Exhaustion and collapse)

"Burned out." They are overwhelmed and unable to continue on any longer. They have depleted all their resources, and there just isn't any more steam left. They are something of a workaholic or "serve-aholic," who operates in a "Me last!" manner. It is a pattern that started when they were made the "family hoist" in their demanding, enmeshed, dysfunctional family.

PSORIASIS (Scaly red patches on the skin)

"Unscratchable itch." They feel a constant gnawing at them, a boring from within, a continual nagging, irritation or annoyance. They want to achieve something, but they just can't get closure on it. They end up feeling that they just have to settle for putting up with the incompleteness (of themselves) in a resignation-apathy. They come from a family in which they were continuously blocked from developing their personal power and goals.
****

"Feeling-denying." They are emotionally insecure in a feeling-avoidant and accountability/ responsibility-deflecting manner. They try to think and deny their way through life, hoping that their underlying hurt and vulnerability will not surface.

However, they are now experiencing just that, and they are quite disturbed and agitated about that. They are the product of a denial-dominated, feeling-suppressing and reality-avoidant dysfunctional family.
****

"Self-numbing." They are deadening their senses or their sense of self, out of a fear of being hurt further. They refuse to accept responsibility for their own feelings, but the reality is that they can never let themselves alone about their frustrated ambitions.

They gnaw at themselves all the time, as they always strive after the next-to-unattainable "brass ring" of approval and validation from their unpleasant "parent in the head." They are self-depriving and joy-avoidant in a self-disapproving and worthless-feeling manner. It's a self-perfectionism arising from "Never good enough!" parenting.

PSYCHOMOTOR EPISODES ("Non-present"/"automatic pilot" episodes. It is a form of seizure)

"Fear-freak-out." They have a sense of persecution and pressure from the environment, along with a feeling of great struggle. It is a rejecting of life and violence towards the self.

There is a hidden fear amounting to severe "run amok-anxiety" -- an agitated anticipation of a potential homicidal rampage from themselves. The episodes are fear reactions and resentment-energy releases. There is an extreme need to escape from the experiences of life, along with a great fear of the expectations of society.

They have tremendous competence-anxiety and profound cope-ability-anxiety. There is a pronounced sense of being out-classed and overwhelmed by the world, along with a tremendous resentment of their situation.

It came from having too much expected of them, either for what they were capable of or for a child. If the epilepsy appeared in childhood, it added to the sense of their being incapable and "broken brained," which only "fueled the flames" of the situation.

PTERIGEUM (Growth on the cornea of the eye) (See CORNEA PROBLEMS)

"PUFFINESS" (Body-wide water retention)

"Holding on." They are not letting go of something or someone, and they are resistant to changes. They are hanging on to the past for fear that if they let go, something awful will happen. They are repressing, denying or clutching to inner feelings and urges.

They feel emotionally trapped in the direction they are going in, and they feel unable to emotionally assert themselves to bring any release. They feel like they are carrying a heavy load on their shoulders, an overload of responsibility. They want to share the load, but they are afraid to ask for fear of alienating and losing what support they do have.

It's a "Cinderella/Cinderfella" pattern, in which they were held accountable and responsible for the needs and situations of everyone and everything in their family, while the only support they got came from their "unsung hero(ine)" role in a serve-aholic situation.
****

"Suppressed sorrow." Water retention is in effect stored grief from their whole situation and life history. It comes from a fear that any change will result in the loss of even more in their life. They'd rather keep things as they are than take a chance that they will end up with nothing, which is what they fully expect is their "just desserts" for all the "failures" of their "care-taking," as represented by the negative events in their family's history.
****

"Clutching clinging." They have a great fear of losing something vital to their survival and acceptability as a human being. They are intensely abandonment-paranoid and approval-enslaved, and they are into severe self-suppressing and pleasing-appeasing patterns as a rejection-deflection strategy. They are also prone to highly possessive and jealous patterns in their relationships.

It is the result of being placed on very conditional acceptance from very early on. They had to earn their "love-line," which of course "meant" that "God said" that they don't deserve love, -- they "earn" it by "selling out" and hating themselves for it.

QUADRAPLEGIC [Paralyzed in four limbs] (See **PARALYSIS**)

"QUINCY" (Inflammation of tonsils)

"Atonement-freak." They have a strong belief that they can't speak up for themselves or ask for their needs. They believe that they don't have the right, and that they don't deserve to have their needs met or to seek any form of gratification. It is the result of an oppressive and shame-inducing family.

"RABBIT FEVER" (Fever, ache, inflamed lymph glands)

"Life sucks!" They are being consumed with resentment over threatened abandonment. They have very negative feelings about themselves. They feel they have no right to joy and love, and that "there's no joy in Bloodville." Their current situation is re-instating the experiences they had in their shame-inducing and rejecting dysfunctional family.

"RABIES"

"Immobilized by rage." They are full of suppressed rage and festering thoughts activated by their seething volcano-based desire to control everything, along with a systematic refusal to express their feelings.

They don't trust the process of life, and they are full of resentment regarding what they regard as the absolute untrustworthiness of the world. They are convinced that if they ever asked for what they wanted, it would be deliberately withheld from them. They feel constantly betrayed, and they are thoroughly enraged about it. Not only that, they feel that the information would be used against them.

For the same reasons, they in effect can't express their feelings, reactions and interpretations. Their experience is it is dangerous to let the world know where they are coming from and what's happening with them. They may even believe that violence is the answer to many of life's situations. They are trying to control their rage before they run amok with it.

It ends up in constant contractions of both the extensors and flexors, concluding in immobilization and spasms. It is the result of coming from a highly distrusting, untrustworthy, extortionistic and coercive control-manifesting family. They are passing on what they learned at home.

RADIATION SICKNESS

"It's not allowed!" Their experience is that any form of success and quality of life is simply prohibited by the Universe. They feel continuously thwarted by circumstances, and they have little or no self-confidence to boot. They feel betrayed and victimized by life, and that they are continuously devalued and disempowered. They come from a rejecting and disempowering dysfunctional family.
****

"Running on empty." They have a "but not for me" attitude about positive things happening in their life. They feel that they have some sort of inherent "moral cretinism" and/or set of limitations that prevent their having anything meaningful or joyful in their life.

There is a considerable lack of harmony and internal conflict. As a result of this, they are deeply resentful and agitated. Furthermore, there is an ever-present fear of even more losses, and they have the profound fundamental conviction that they don't have the right to complain. Their family was severely accusatory and blame-throwing in an accountability-avoidant and abusive family.
****

"Moral cretin." They are full of unexpressed negative emotions, and they have a major distrust of the Universe. Bottom line, they are convinced in their core of being that they deserve no other, that they need punishment and deprivation to "pay for their sins" and for their "evilness."

They received a *persona non grata* treatment in which they were consistently criticized, attacked, accused and denigrated, and in which they received no support or respect. In the meantime, they were the "family hoist" who held up the whole system in a "Cinderella/Cinderfella" syndrome in their severely dysfunctional unreliable and unpredictable family.

They were actually inherently quite superior to the rest of the family, which led to unconscious extreme expectations of rescue and expectations, that no one could meet, which resulted in unconscious embitterment by the rest of the family members, who then took it out on them.

"RAT BITE FEVER" (Rash, fever, muscle pain)

"Just desserts." They have been trying to "cut corners," to "get to home base" the "quick and dirty" way, and to intimidate with their irritation reactions, and it has come time to "pay the piper." They are intensely enraged at this development, and they are very agitated at this turn of events.

It is the result being cleverly capitulated to in a "keep 'em around the old homestead" -- "tie that grinds" dysfunctional family.

RAYNAUD'S DISEASE (Chronically cold extremities)

"Urban hermit." They have a good deal of vulnerability-resentment and reachability-avoidance. They are a contact-disliking people-avoider who is reticent with strangers and a poor circulator who tends to agoraphobia (the fear of going out of their home). They are rejection-paranoid, and they are retreating into their core.

They feel rejected and not understood, and that any reaching out to touch someone would result in rebuff or worse reactions. They feel like an "ugly duckling" who elicits rejection everywhere they go. It all got started when their parents punished and rejected them for being different and formidable, because they were frightened by the individual's potency.
****

"Learned helplessness." They feel cut off from understanding their life circumstances or their direction. Their family was a confusion-inducing, repressive and power-preventing dysfunctional system. The individual felt no recourse, and, at the same time, they deeply resented the treatment they were getting.

They want to hit or strangle someone as a result, and they want to take any sort of hostile physical action against them. However, they don't want others to know how they feel, so they get "cold feet." But ultimately, they took it all to heart, and they sadly settled into a resignation-apathy, as an overlay on their intense desire to strike out.

RIGHT HAND COLDNESS

"Lying low." They are avoiding contact with the world for fear of what it would do to them.

LEFT HAND COLDNESS

"Run amok-anxiety." They have a deep fear of their own hostile impulses and what they would do to the world.
~~~~~~

RIGHT FOOT COLDNESS

"Forget it!" They do not want support from others or from the environment, out of a deep distrust.

LEFT FOOT COLDNESS
"Environment-protecting." They are systematically vulnerability-avoidance and involvement-deflecting to prevent their engaging in mayhem, they fear.

~~~~~~

COLD NOSE
"Power-avoidance." They are afraid of their personal potency and its potential consequences for them and for the ecology.

COLD EARS
"Awareness-avoidance." They are avoiding tuning into what is really going on in their life and in the world around them.

RECTOCELE (Prolapse in the rectal/vaginal wall)
"Anal-retentive." They are caught up in perfectionistic standards and applications, and they are intensely controlling and dominating in their approach. They are rageful about being restricted, inhibited, boundary-violated and wrong-made about their beingness, particularly around sexuality.

They were severely dominated and monitored in their role-reversing and perfectionistically expecting family.

REFERRED PAIN
"Attention-re-directing." They are self-deluding and/or accountability/responsibility-avoiding around the emotional pain activated in the area affected by the issues involved. They have the habit of deflecting, distorting and focusing attention away from the real cause of their emotional pain onto other areas. This pattern got started in a denial-dominated, awareness-deflecting and situation-distorting dysfunctional family.

(To understand the issues involved, note the meanings of difficulties in the area(s) where the pain is referred to, and also look to the meanings of the problems in the area(s) where the pain should normally be expected to be.)

Some examples of the referred pain dynamics:

"Atonement-seeking." They are engaged in guilt-based self-punishment. They have a deep feeling of separation and "sinfulness" arising from massive guilt-induction from their family for who they were, for what they needed, for what they did, and for what went down in the family.
****

"Get back to where you once belonged!" It is Nature's way of warning that they are off the path, leading to conflict and congestion as they work out an undesirable condition. They have tried to "slip one past the Cosmos," and now have to "clean up their act," and they have to "clean up the mess." If this is a chronic pattern, it is the result of constant "corner-cutting" by their family as a lifestyle.
****

"Victim-tripping." They have a belief in bondage and victimization that was generated in a severely dysfunctional and hostile family.

REFLEX SYMPATHETIC DYSTROPHY (Progressive nerve disorder that in its final stages involves such extreme pain in the hands and feet due to involuntary chronic clenching or cramping that suicide is a not uncommon outcome.)

"Karmic payback." They are engaged in severe guilt-based self-punishment and atonement-seeking. They have deep feeling of separation and sinfulness arising from massive feelings of evilness induced by their intensely-negatively oriented family for being who they were, for what they needed, for what they did, and for what went down in the family.

There is often an underlying vague awareness that they are in effect paying intense karma for extreme abusiveness they exhibited in previous lives. Their deep inner experience is that something is grossly cosmically out of balance, and that it is a Universal requirement that they now "balance the moral budget."

****

"Severe competence-anxiety." It is a reflexive flight/freeze reaction set off by trauma, often starting in the young. It is, in effect, a massive fear of self-release at the subconscious level -- the fear being based on an underlying massive self-distrust and sense of inability to manifest what it takes to make it without disastrous outcomes. It gets started intrauterine out of the mother's conscious or unconscious fear of having a deformed child.

****

"Repressed rage." They are sitting on a lot of fulminating fury that they are afraid to express, act on or even know about. Their life is not working, and they are very frustrated with that.

They come from a severely exploitative and suppressive patriarchal family who made it crystal clear that to manifest personal power and anger is the "kiss of death."

HANDS

"Powerlessness feelings." They have the experience of being unable to effectively impact on the world around them or of refusal to do so.

LEGS AND FEET

"Destiny-resistance." They have a fear of or refusal to move into the manifestation of their life purpose.

REFLUX (Regurgitation followed by choking on food that went down the wind pipe)

"I can't keep up." They feel utterly overwhelmed by life and their circumstances, and they feel there is no way to meet the demands being made of them or that there is no way to realize their destiny due to circumstances beyond their control.

It is a re-appearance of an experience that once was the "warp and woof" of their life, but it now has reached the point where they feel that they simply don't have what it takes to make it and/or that there is simply no point in continuing. They are the product of a highly nihilistic and pessimistic parenting pattern.

****

"I should leave." They are experiencing a resurgence of very early self-rejection and existential guilt arising from intensely accusatory, wrong-making and rejecting maternal parenting.

****

"Time to exit, stage left." They have the feeling that they have completed what they can do here, and they feel that they have nothing more to do, so they are leaving. It is a destiny completion reaction.

RELAPSING FEVER (Alternates with non-fever)

"Magical misery tour." They are caught up in recurring resentment and agitated anticipation. There is severe internal conflict and lack of harmony. They have abandonment-paranoias, and self-induced worry and hurry. It represents an experienced return to the uncertainties and frustrations of their unpredictable dysfunctional family.

REPRODUCTIVE ORGAN PROBLEMS

"Unfit for human consumption." They feel that they were an unwanted gender and/or they are rejecting of sexuality. They feel utterly unacceptable and a "moral cretin." There are many inner conflicts and confusions about identity, worth, vulnerability and procreativity. They come from a non-accepting and devaluing/ denigrating family.
****

"Involvement-incompetent." They are afraid to share themselves intimately, and they have great difficulties in communication, in their ability to trust, in their capacity for considerateness and respectfulness, and in being at peace with the other gender and with sexuality. They are having great difficulty in sharing love and in being in committed relationships. They are the product of an untrustworthy and unloving family.
****

"Sexual shame." They are suffering from guilt, worry, embarrassment, shame, fear, insecurity, and resentment over their sexuality. They are repressing and suppressing their sexuality, and they are frustrated in their expression of their creativity. They have little capacity for joy, pleasure and being vulnerable in the heart, and they lack forgiveness to themselves around the whole area of sexuality.

Traumatic sexual experiences, primarily of a parental sex-ploitative and/or gender-rejecting nature created it, and subsequent traumas in this area compounded it. It is the result of the necessity to pay karma, due to an imbalance in their inner soul in this area as a function of sexual abuses in previous lives.

RIGHT REPRODUCTIVE ORGAN PROBLEMS

"Competence concerns." They have many conflicts concerning their manner of manifestation of their sexuality.

LEFT REPRODUCTIVE ORGAN PROBLEMS

"Worth concerns." They have issues around their self-worth, their right to exist, and their right to love, deriving from their being a sexual (and/or sexualized) being.

(See **GENITAL PROBLEMS -- FEMALE; GENITAL PROBLEMS -- MALE; OVARY PROBLEMS; PROTSATE PROBLEMS; TESTICLE PROBLEMS; UTERUS PROBLEMS; VAGINAL PROBLEMS**)

RESPIRATORY PROBLEMS

"I don't deserve to exist." They feel highly unsafe in the world, and they fear taking in life fully. They feel unworthy of living fully, and they are alone, sad and non-belonging, with no sense of acceptance or approval.

They are joy-avoidant and happiness-squashing, out of an underlying fear of the Universe. They are also love-starved and lonely. It is the result of untrustworthy, depriving and/or self-immersed parenting.

~~~~~~

RESPIRATORY FAILURE

"Enough!" They are now having an "Enough is enough!" reaction, and they are "heading on out." They are desperately tired of life, due to life-long suppressed grief. They are fearful and anxious, and they are in effect too devastated to take it any more.

It came about from effective emotional abandonment at a very early age, to which they reacted with becoming a "self-made person" with a "portable Plexiglas phone booth" around them. They can't let people in or themselves out. This has cut them off from joy and love, and it is now taking its toll.

(See **BRONCHITIS; COLDS; EMPHYSEMA; FLU; TUBERCULOSIS; WHOOPING COUGH**)

"RESTLESS LEG SYNDROME" (Jerking movements of the legs during sleep)

"Survivalist dynamics." They have a bottom line belief that they are all they've got, and that "One strike and I'm out!" They simply have to be in control of everything that happens to and around them. It makes them very anxious when they can't have "hands on" control of things.

It comes from being more or less left to their own devices from the beginning in a rather intensely dysfunctional family.

"RETCHING" (Intense regurgitation)

"Repulsion-expulsion." They are engaged in unsuccessful attempts to rid themselves of a situation. They are violently refusing to accept the current developments, because to them it means something dreadful is about to happen. It just means more responsibility, trauma and pain, and they have a fear and disgust reaction to what is happening to them.

They feel that somehow it is their own fault that this situation exists, and they are desperately trying to convince themselves it really isn't happening. However, it isn't working, and their misery compounds on itself.

Their family made them accountable and responsible for everything, and they had to live with the "finger" of accusation every time something went wrong, which was frequently, in their out of control dysfunctional family.

RETROGRADE AMNESIA (Loss of memory of immediately preceding events)

"Hum a few bars and I'll take it -- and get lost." They are swallowed up in the immediate stimulus situation, in a continuous "living in the moment" pattern. They have lost or never acquired the ability to discern patterns, sequences and meaning.

It is a result of having been required to not know what was happening to them and around them in a dysfunctional, sex-ploitative and/or abusive family. They are deathly afraid of the consequences of their knowing what happens, for them and their "inner cosmos" (the "in loco Deity" experience that the family were the "local reps" of the "Home Office" [All That Is]). Their experience is that remembering would violate a "Divine injunction," and it possibly could result in "Deicide," because of the terror the family had of the individual's knowing what was going down.

"RETRO-VIRUS" (H.I.V.- like, it interacts with other diseases and bodily locations)

"Running out of steam." They have deep grief and a sense of underlying despair and demoralization. It's a "What's the use?" attitude in the making or the expression. They are overwhelmed by too much sorrow, and by the "running on empty" effect of a severe inequality of energy exchange with the world whereby they put out much more than they get.

It is a result of having "carried the world on their shoulders" all their life, starting with their dysfunctional family, with little or no ability to receive, request or require a return in kind as the outcome. They were told, in effect, they were the source of all the family's problems while actually being the only one deflecting some of the disasters.

RHEUMATIC FEVER (Bacterial allergic reaction that causes swelling in the skin, joints and heart)

"I blew it!" They are fearful of lose of love, and they have abandonment-annihilation-anxiety. There is deep grief, and a feeling of deserving this as their "just desserts" from the "Home Office" (All That Is). It is the result of parental rejection, emotional deprivation, and/or separation threats during infancy and childhood.

RHEUMATIC HEART (Swelling)

"Cut off." They are having emotional conflict arising from considerable annihilation-anxiety, often resulting in a submissive manner of being that emulates a "martyr" or "victim tripping" approach. They have been traumatized in such a manner as to lead to a shut down of their "heart center." There is a considerable agitation over their inability to love their parents or family.

They are a sensitive soul who has been shocked by severe emotional deprivation, separation-abandonment threats, and/or the loss or death of loved ones. It is the result of lack of love from those who should have been able to love them, or from a lack of love for someone who should be loved, such as their parents.

RHEUMATISM (Inflammation and pain in the muscles and/or joints)

"They done me in!" They are feeling rejected for what they are, in the sense of being totally unappreciated, and there is a lack of love in their life. They are feeling very victimized and put upon, and they often find themselves being pushed around by others. Underneath all this is a feeling of utter powerlessness and a severe self- and other-rejection arising from their being treated as the "intimate enemy" by their family.
****

"Seething bitterness." They are full of repressed resentment and anger and they have a strongly suppressed desire to hit someone. They continuously ruminate and recriminate over their "indignities," and they cling to every item like "super-glue." They have a chronic bitterness and resentment, leading to a desire for revenge. Their mind is wound up so tight in their hostile preoccupations that it grinds their whole system to a halt. They come from a suppressive and injustice-nurturing, grudge-holding family.
****

"Fixedly inflexible." They are unbending in their expression and self-manifestation. They have a rigid will and very strong opinions that they will not and probably cannot change. They are prone to pushing others around, and to imposing their way in an arbitrary and authoritarian manner. They never let go of anything, as they try to be the "boss of the Universe" in an effort to make life just the way they want it. They have no trust of the "Home Office" (All That Is), and they feel that

"It is botching the job." They are forever sending out arrows of hatred, jealousy, general discord and other negative vibrations. They are the product of an intensely hostile home.

RHEUMATOID ARTHRITIS (Connective tissue in the joints attacked by the immune system.)

"Massive self-rejection." They have a deep self-dislike, shame and guilt. They have an inbred sense of worthlessness and self-criticism. They are, in effect, attacking themselves. They are preventing movement and fluidity in what they are doing and in the direction they are going. They are unassertive and inhibited in their behavior, and they are self-sacrificing and unable to express strong emotions. It is the result of continuous condemnation and denigration as a child.
****

"Authority-freak." They are operating out of a deep criticism of the powers that be, along with a feeling of being very put-upon and exploited. They have an abiding distrust of the Universe. It was generated by an oppressive and patriarchal household. This all arises out of their soul's refusal to handle multi-life problems that have come up again.
****

"Hapless, helpless, hopeless." They feel utterly overwhelmed by the world's requirements. There is no sense of an out route or of an ability to make a difference in their situation. It comes from having been the "pivot person" in their severely and intractably dysfunctional family.

(See **ARTHRITIS**)

RICKETS (Softening and bending of the bones, due to lack of Vitamin D)

"Falling apart." They are disintegrating under the load of responsibilities they have had to carry all their life. They just can't support themselves and their world single-handedly like they have been doing all along any more.

They suffered from emotional malnutrition and a lack of love and security in childhood. They arrived at the conclusion that it is all they deserve and can expect from the Universe. As a result, they have consistently been involved in repetitions of the home situation.

RIGHT/LEFT SPLIT IN THEIR BODY

"Polarized functioning." They are notably lacking in integration and balance of their manifestation. They emphasize one side over the other to a degree that is functionally detrimental to their welfare. They come from a highly patriarchal and domineering family in which role specialization is heavily emphasized.

RIGHT SIDE OVER-EMPHASIS

"Yang-banging." They are hyper-masculinized in their manifestation, with an exaggeration of their protective, impact-making, releasing, taking and fighting aspects.

LEFT SIDE OVER-EMPHASIS

"Yin-dominated." They tend to be over-giving, over-nurturing and over-responsible -- at their own expense. They are excessively receptive and reactive, and they tend to suppress their personal potency.

RINGING IN THE EARS (Mild)

"Voices in the head." They are experiencing a low background "noise" of admonitions, evaluations and injunctions from "Christmases past" telling them that what they are doing/being/having isn't right or the right thing for them.

It indicates that they are "breaking script" or "breaking new ground" in their life. They are the product of a rather possessive, demanding or dysfunctionally dependent family who were very tightly monitoring and controlling of their functioning. They are now leaving all of that behind.

RIGHT EAR RINGING

"What will the neighbors think?" They are getting "flash-backs" of concerns from the family about how things might affect their social acceptability.

LEFT EAR RINGING

"You better watch out!" They are re-experiencing numerous warnings about being "the death of themselves" if they're not "careful" (e.g., not conforming to the family's programs).

(See **TINNITUS**)

"RINGWORM" (Contagious fungus-based skin eruptions of a circular shape)

"Cope-ability-anxiety." They are allowing others to "get under their skin." They have a sense of powerlessness to deflect disaster and to handle the world. They have no sense that things will get any better for them. They are self-denigrating, and they don't feel good enough or clean enough. It is the result of intense oppression and shame-induction by their family.

RITTER'S DISEASE (Severe skin inflammation in infants)

"Freaked out." They are suffering from intense implication-anxiety and ramification-rage. The experience is of being beset on all sides by inexorable and continuously irritating and threatening forces. They have a notable lack of peace and harmony in their lives, and they feel very uneasy and frightened by the world. To make matters worse, they have strong longings that can't be realized at present.

They take it all personally, of course, as if they were the cause of it all. They are already ashamed of themselves, and they feel somehow "monstrous." They have been so misunderstood and ill-treated from the beginning that they have had to withdraw into their core.

It arises from their being a "sensitive" in a denial-dominated dysfunctional family. They feel like an "alarming Martian." It is a result of a hostile atmosphere in their environment, starting in the womb.

ROCKY MOUNTAIN SPOTTED FEVER (Red eruptions, fever, pains in the bones and muscles)

"Rejection-resentment." They feel besieged and restricted on all sides. They feel unsafe, betrayed, rejected and attacked. They have concluded they can't be themselves because that is "wrong, bad and evil." But at the same time, they are burning up with intense anger and stored resentments about how they are treated.

They are also intensely abandonment-anxious and self-disgusted for eliciting this reaction. It is the result of a self-immersed, convenience-concerned, wrong-making and suppressive family.

ROSACEA (Red and rough blotches on the cheeks, nose and lower face -- much more common in males)
"Stressed out." They are feeling the effects of overload and chronic deprivation in their life, due to excessive responsibilities and demands and/or to self-imposed stresses resulting from their over-responsible "serve-aholic" lifestyle. They were placed in a position of extremely excessive responsibility in their dependent and dysfunctional family.
****
"Coals from the fire." It is reflective of a process of insisting on taking coals from the fire of their disorder. They are engaged in a systematically dissipative or self-destructive lifestyle (such as alcoholism). It is a pattern that got started early on in a significantly dysfunctional family, in which they were forced to participate and/or serve as the "sane one" for the family -- to the point where they were programmed to slowly self-destruct.

ROTATOR CUFF TENDONITIS (A tearing and swelling of the muscles and tendons that hold the upper area in the shoulder joint)
"Over-responsibility strains." They are taking on too much in the way of taking care of the world. They feel victimized and overwhelmed, and there is an experience of non-support. It has resulted in their going over the edge of what can be handled and tolerated. They were the "family hoist" in a rather severely dysfunctional family.

RUBELLA (German measles)
"They don't like me." They feel excluded and picked on by their intimate circle. They feel misunderstood and unappreciated. It is a reaction to being regarded as something of an irritant or problem by their family.

RUMINATION DISORDER OF INFANCY (Repeated regurgitation and re-swallowing their food)
"Nobody there." There is intense maternal emotional unavailability (though she may be physically ministering to the child). It is a super-self-sustaining activity and a refusal to rely on anyone for anything.

RUPTURE (Tearing apart of muscle wall, leading to a hernia -- a protruding organ)
"Overwhelm-anxiety." They feel that they are completely in over their head, and that they don't have what it takes to handle the requirements of their present situation. The result is an over-responsible, self-blaming, competence-anxious "serve-aholic" who is constantly feeling they can't deliver the goods. They are the product of an exploitative and competence-undermining family who simultaneously depended on them and blamed them for all that went wrong.
Meanwhile at the same time they were programming them to be a failure in the world so they could "keep them around the old homestead." They are now being told that they need to stop, look and re-choose on how much they take on, how they evaluate their capabilities, and how they scare themselves.
****
"Run amok-anxiety." They are a powder keg of rage about to go off, with a frantic effort to control their anger. They do so by pretending it isn't there, in an ostrich-like manner, which only

generates events and outcomes that feed the volcano inside. They feel that life is "so pressing," and they try to ignore it all, resulting in self-violence and self-injury.

They are super self-suppressing and maniacally controlling of the environment. They try to pin everything down -- especially themselves -- in a "Lilliputian-like million little ropes" pattern. They end up rupturing all their relationships, as they struggle under the strain of enormous burdens, as they experience it.

Much of what they do is incorrect manifestation of creative expression in trying to hands on pin everything down. They have a considerable amount of self-distrust arising from an extremely punitive and controlling upbringing. In effect, they are doing unto others what was done unto them.

RUPTURED DISC (Torn-apart plate-like structure between the spinal vertebrae)

"Cop-out artist." They engage in chronic problem-avoidance, as they try to "put it behind them." It is an "ostrich approach" they learned in their denial-dominated and accountability responsibility-ducking dysfunctional family.

(See **SPINAL DISC PROBLEMS** for what it means to have the particular disc(s) involved rupture.)

REYE'S SYNDROME (Severe endangerment or death of a child or infant, due to giving them aspirin before age five. The dynamics refer to those of the child, unless otherwise indicated.)

"This is as far as I go." It is a soul decision based upon prior intentions, or upon an assessment of the situation in terms of its relevance for the soul's needs.

****

"Self-hatred." Their parents are picking up and unconsciously acting on the individual's intense self-rejection. It is the result of hateful parenting that the parents may or may not be aware of.

****

"I don't deserve to exist." It reflects felt deservingness of non-support and lack of love, to the point of feeling that they shouldn't continue to live. It arises from parenting that made them feel worthless.

****

"Driven to distraction." The parent(s) are under so much stress and tension from current or on-going circumstances that they are not able to track at the level that is required. It is a continuation of the process that went down in their own dysfunctional family.

****

"Shit happens." It was one of the "random generator" events that make up a small percentage of what happens whose purpose is to continuously challenge through a means not of our making or the Divine design. It should be noted here that "shinola happens" too.

SACROILIAC PROBLEMS (Juncture of the hip bone and the lower spine)

"At effect." They are feeling very much that they are not "at cause" in their life. They have a pronounced fear of seductive-destructiveness and the abuse of power from those around them. They are severely conflicted and suppressed with regard to sexuality. They also feel they or others will misuse power, particularly that of sexuality. They feel poorly integrated with the world around them, as if they are in the wrong place, and they feel at risk.

They don't know which way to turn, and they end up not turning anywhere, in a kind of multi-directional thwartedness reaction. They are the product of "seduce-slap" and self-immersed domineering from their mother.

RIGHT SACROILIAC

"In over their head." There is uncertainty as to how to proceed and how to handle the world on its terms. They feel like a child in an adult role, like in the movie "Big."

LEFT SACROILIAC

"Self-shame." They have self-distrust and confusion as to how to deal with their feelings, desires and intentions. They feel guilty for their personal potency, and they are ashamed of their sexuality.

SALMONELLA (Bacterial disorder causing dehydration, diarrhea, nausea, headache, and other symptoms to a severe and potentially lethal degree.)

"Feeling overwhelmed." They are under a lot of stress, and they are feeling quite tense about it. Their fear and anxiety are alarming them to the point of threatening to upset their whole apple cart. They are having strong experiences of internal pressures rising to the point of getting out of control. There is an intense need for them to be able to get on top of their situation so they can problem-solve and issue-resolve.

****

"Here it comes!" They are faced with a heavy and meaningful task, they wish it were over and done with. Something important is pending, and they don't want to go through with it. They have a fair amount of competence-anxiety and built-in programming against success and intimacy.

They were supposed to stick around the old homestead and take care of their parents. Any move towards independence, self-empowerment, and significant involvement/contribution/ commitment activates annihilation-anxiety and betrayal-guilt. The current situation is just such a requirement and issue for them.

****

"What a revolting development THIS is!" They are having a fear and disgust reaction to what is happening to them. They are totally rejecting an idea or experience -- they don't want to have anything to do with it. They want to throw it right back out again. They feel that something wrong or immoral is happening.

They are inundated with disgust with the situation and themselves, and they are full of fear of the consequences of what's going down. They feel that something dreadful has happened, and they feel responsible for it. They wish it hadn't happened, and they are truly sorry it has occurred. They deeply wish they hadn't "done it." They want things to return to the way they were before this happened. They are full of upset, pain and sadness; they don't want the situation anywhere near them.

They desperately want to undo the past, and they are afraid of the effects of this on their future. They are full of dissatisfaction, disgust and regret over the way things are. They are saying to themselves over and over, "I should have. . ." They feel personally accountable for everything that happens, particularly the negative outcomes.

Their family held them accountable and responsible for all that took place, and all eyes turned in their direction when anything went wrong -- which was frequently. They were made very aware they had no right to commit to anyone or anything else but the continued maintenance of the family. They therefore have great guilt about sexuality, success, and intimacy, as if these were "evil deeds."

****

"Left high and dry." They experience life as one long threat. They feel that something disastrous is imminent, and that they are like a fish out of water, in that they feel they don't have what it takes to handle it.

It has been this way all their life, starting in their unpredictably destructive family in which there was much subterranean, subconscious and subtle subterfuge and sabotage going down. No one saw or knew what was happening, just that they couldn't tell when the next piece of traumatic excrement was going to come off the fan. At any moment, something awful could happen, and they have to be on constant at least "yellow alert."

****

"Over-run." They are feeling defenseless and like they have to allow others to take control and run the situation. It is a "learned helplessness" that leads them to feel that they don't have the right to protection, support or nurturance. They simply expect to "eat shit" as a part of living.

It is a pattern that arose in a family where they had few, if any rights, and in which much anger and negativity took place, over which no one seemed to have any control.

SARCOIDOSIS (See IMMUNE SYSTEM PROBLEMS)

S.A.R.S. (Sudden Acute Respiratory Syndrome)

"Urban Hermit." There is an insufficient involvement and interaction with the world, in a kind of "among us but not of us" pattern. Underneath is a buried rage and resentment about being so alone, alien and alienated.

It comes from growing up in a family in which they could do no right, as the unrecognized and unacknowledged "family hoist" upon whom everyone depended and whom no one supported, sustained or validated.

****

"Self-suppression." They are full of family taboos, social restrictions, moral inhibitions, unexpressed passions, strong desires and unexpressed intense emotions. They don't have any sense of freedom or the right or ability to communicate their feelings. This was generated by a self-immersed and dysfunctional family who were exploitative, shame-inducting and enmeshed.

****

"Barking up the wrong tree." They tend to get into consuming passionate commitments that lead nowhere, and to get into repeated disturbing unrequited love situations. They have a sensitive mind and a very strong sense of justice, righteousness and generosity that frequently leads them into blind alleys and exploitative situations and relationships.

They are feeling that they are always in "tie that grinds" relationships in which they feel totally stifled by over-close and/or dominating partners. They are being overwhelmed and restricted, and they are very angry about it. However, they don't feel that they can do or say anything about it, for fear of catastrophic consequences.

They come from an authoritarian, oppressive and possessive dysfunctional family in which they held a reversed parental role that led to their repeatedly trying to rescue their family from their self-defeating patterns.

****

"Suppressed grief." They are desperate and tired of life, due to generalized disturbances in their processes and situation. They are having a "salt poured in emotional wounds" experience that they are not being allowed to heal. They are suffering under the influence of their lifelong suppressed sorrow.

They are fearful and anxious to the point of being overcome with desperation and futility feelings. They are struggling with confusion-inducing emotional conflict, and there is a failure to maintain immunity to negative ideas.

They are the product of a self-defeatingness generating dysfunctional family who instilled a sense of being hapless, helpless and hopeless.

****

"Deprivation City." They have a real difficulty in taking in prana, chi, ki, élan vitale, love or life energy, as a function of their prideful brutalizing misuse of energy in past lives. They have an inability to renew to the breath of life, along with a lack of enthusiasm and zeal for living. They have a real inability to take in life, and they don't feel worthy of living life fully. They are suffering from depression and chronic grief, because they are deeply afraid of taking in life energy.

They lack cosmic, community and conjugal contact. They are alone, sad and non-belonging, with no sense of acceptance or approval. They feel constantly in smothering and stifling environments, with a resulting sense that life is dull and monotonous. They are the product of a severely withholding and rejecting family.

****

"My way or the highway!" They have a very strong ego that is getting in their way. They tend to believe that theirs is the "only way to fly," and that they are surrounded by people who not only don't understand that, but who also place restrictions on them and who "unfairly punish" them for their ways of beingness and of doing things.

They feel that they have to handle the whole of life single-handed, with no help from any so-called friends. While this has made for a modicum of success as a survival strategy, it has cut them off from joy and love, and they can't let people in or themselves out to merge, and that is now taking its toll. It all got started in a severely self-immersed and functionally neglectful dysfunctional family who paid little attention to their needs.

****

"Bitter resentfulness." They are wasting away due to selfishness, intense possessiveness, cruel thoughts and vengefulness. They feel that they have done their level best in a valiant effort, but that circumstances just wouldn't have it so.

They have had unhappy love affairs, resulting in disappointment, disgust unforgiveness and clutchingness. They feel unappreciated, and they play out a "Camille" scenario, in which their feeling is, "They'll be sorry when I'm gone!" They are given to resentfully imagined guilt and remorse reactions from their people.

In addition, there is also a large spiteful revenge streak playing a major part in this process. They are selfishly clinging and controlling, they are slyly passive-aggressive, and they are full of "Feel sorry for me!" strategies. In the meantime, they are seeking and "easeful death."

It is the result of their having a "special" role as a child in their severely passive-aggressive dysfunctional family, and they have never gotten over or wanted to relinquish it.

****

"No right to exist." They feel unworthy of living, and they are suffocating from a chronic self-disgust reaction. They are full of angry punishment-deservingness feelings, with accompanying self-destructive motivations and manifestations. They are capitulating and giving up, in an extreme underlying abandonment depression around feeling rejected by God and of being ejected from the Cosmos.

It is the result of being massively neglected, rejected, accused and made wrong by a severely judgmental dysfunctional family. There was a highly self-immersed, self-serving and blame-throwing mother who gave them strong "If it weren't for you!" messages. She simultaneously put "you can do no right!" accusations out continuously, along with expecting them to "make it all better" -- an utter impossibility.

They are now having an "Enough is enough!" reaction, and they are "heading on out." They are desperately tired of life, due to life-long severe suppressed grief and emotional deprivation. They are fearful and anxious, and they are, in effect, too devastated to take it any more. It came from effective emotional abandonment at an early age, to which they reacted by becoming a "self-made person" with a "portable Plexiglas phone booth" around them. So they are leaving now.

SCABIES (See **SKIN MITES** in **SKIN PROBLEMS**)

SCARLET FEVER (Chills, high fever, sore throat and skin rash)
"Cinderella/Cinderfella." They have a resentful fearfulness about feeling attacked and rejected. They feel they are unappreciated and wrongly accused. They were regarded as the source and cause of everything that happened in the family at the subconscious level, resulting in their being constantly blamed for everything that went wrong.

SCIATICA (Nerve pains in the hips and thighs, due to prolapsed disc or to a "pinched nerve" in the lower spine)
"I don' wanna know!" The direction they are going is causing deep inner pain, which they don't want to feel, so they seek to ignore it. They are avoiding knowing what is really going on and what they are really experiencing. They come from a denial-dominated self-defeat programming dysfunctional family.
****

"Naive." They are being gullible and insufficiently critical in their judgment calls. They are over-accepting and suggestible, and they have a fear of money and of the future. They are being kept "forever young" and incapable of self-sufficiency and identity/destiny-manifestation by the parents in a "keep 'em around the old homestead" possessive abusiveness pattern.
****

"Tie that grinds." They have sexual conflicts and a parent-fixation, due to a sex-ploitative and accountability-attributing treatment from their family.
****

"Creativity-anxiety." They have a great deal of concern, anxiety and dread regarding the release and expression of their creative capabilities. They are of two minds -- one conservative and conforming, and the other creative and individualistic. They are the product of an achievement-oriented family who both admired and disapproved of their creative nature.
****

"Mother, *please*, I'd rather do it *myself!*" They are intensely self-determining, and they are an "island unto one's self" who is super-self-sufficient. They are greatly concerned and agitated about money, security and safety issues.

Underneath all their ferocious independence is an "innocent infant" longing for care and commitment. As a result, they do a "first roar of disapproval" pattern whereby they intensely reject suggestions, and then come around later. This got started in early infancy in reaction to "Child, *please*, I'd rather you did it *yourself!*" parenting.

****

"Hypocritical." They operate in a two-faced manner, putting out what seems to be desired while harboring very different orientations, experiences, interpretations and evaluations inside. They learned it in their highly status-conscious and selfishly ambitious family.

SCLEROSIS (Inflammation and hardening of connective tissue)

"Self-rage." They are attacking themselves at a very deep and essential level, out of an intense anger. They have a long-repressed fury or rage that is coming to the surface, along with a case of "hardening of the attitudes" and beliefs. They are only seeing parts of themselves, not the entire picture, and they are fragmenting as a result. They are full of self-dislike, guilt, shame and inner unhappiness.

It arises out of a profound self-hatred promulgated in their envious, dysfunctional, authoritarian and possessive household.

SCURVY (Bleeding, swelling and weakness due to vitamin C deficiency)

"Singled out for shit." They are feeling singularly mistreated, and they feel that they are unable to do anything about it. They tend to be "victim-tripping" and full of undirected resentment as they get stuck in re-running scenarios of the past and in dreading the future.

Their experience is that they are overwhelmed and exhausted by the requirements of life. It feels like it is too much for them to handle, and they have the conviction they can't expect to have rest, joy and love in their lives. Instead, their lot seems to be one of having to "sit there and take it." It is the result of growing up in a slyly sadistic dysfunctional family.

SEBACEOUS CYST (Infected oil gland)

"Blockage-anger." They are harboring a great deal of anger and inhibited aggression over their circumstances. They feel completely blocked in their situation by the world around them. They have many frustrated desires and resentments over restrictions, in a feeling of victimization. They are in effect running the same old painful movie in their head, and they are nursing old hurts and current examples, all of which creates a false growth. Underlying the pattern is a guilt-based self-rejection generated in a blame-throwing, shame-inducing and victimizing family.

SEIZURES

"Overload." They are being bombarded with "do the impossible with nothing while everything that matters rides on it" demands. They feel pressured and persecuted by the environment, which is an old, familiar story to them. They are full of fear, despair and rage about their condition, and their present circumstances took it over the top.

They were expected to carry the weight of the world (their severely dysfunctional family), while at the same time being told that they can do nothing right and that they are the cause of everyone's problems.
****

"Throwing in the towel." They are running away from themselves, their family, life, everything. They feel totally overwhelmed and outclassed by the demands of life. They have little sense of capability and cope-ability, and there is no feeling of support from the Universe.

It arises from having too much expected of them as a child, a situation made only made worse by the appearance of the seizures and the experience of having a "broken brain." The seizures also often additionally function as guilt-relief from past life events.

(See **EPILEPSY**)

SENILITY

"Slowly disengaging." They are gradually leaving this plane, and they spend long periods of time "out there" processing what has happened in this life, "going to Cosmic school," and deciding what to do as their next step. They have difficulty staying in the here and now, as they want to be "out there."

However, they do "check in" here every once in a while, resulting in brief periods of lucidity. They always were a little detached and uninvolved, due to their partially withdrawing from their dysfunctional and/or possessive family early on.
****

"Return to Childhood." They are seeking to the so-called "safety" of childhood, and they long for the security of the "good old days." They are, in effect, demanding care and attention with no energy or contribution returned. It is a form of escapism, control and/or revenge. It is the ultimate outcome of a severely confidence-undermining childhood.

(See **ALZHEIMER'S; DEMENTIA**)

SENSORY-MOTOR INTEGRATION SYNDROME (In infancy or childhood, usually)

"Booming, buzzing confusion." They are overwhelmed by environmental inputs, either due to sensory overload, or to the incompatibility or contradictoriness's of the inputs they have gotten from the onset of their life.

The result is a "critical period" disruption of the integrative function, and they can't handle the integration demands of the environment. It is the result of a rather massively over-stimulating intrauterine and early infancy experience, arising from primarily maternal severe emotional conflict and/or stress overload.

SEPSIS (Runaway infection due to the body's over-reaction to the poisons bacteria generate. It's often fatal.)

"Fury flare-up." There is a great deal of anger arising out of a chronic resentment-rage over their situation that has now "gone over the top." There is an intense inner conflict and generalized hostility has taken on extreme physical form.

They are being massively stressed by current circumstances, and this has resulted in their becoming furious and suspicious about everything that is happening to them. And now it has gotten to the point where it is out of control -- with very dangerous results. It got started in a severely dysfunctional family in which nothing worked right, and in which nothing could effectively be done about it -- with often disastrous results that just had to be lived with.

~~~~~~

DEATH BY SEPSIS

"Outta here!" At some deep level, they arrived at the conclusion that: a) they couldn't take it any more, and b) they could do nothing about it anyway. So they left.

****

"Shit happens." Sometimes things just show up. It's the result of the "random generator," which sets off events that are neither the result of the Divine Intent nor of the play-outs of our will. The purpose is to continuously challenge us with growth-generating events. It should be noted in this regard that "shinola happens" too.

SEPTIC SHOCK (Shut-down of vital organs by severe infection runaway)

"Going down the tubes." Their fulminating fury has gotten to the point where they can no longer put up with their life the way it has been going. They are in a situation where they have to radically change their way of life -- or leave the planet.

SHIGELLOSIS ("The trots," fever, vomiting, cramps)

"NO! Not now! Not ever!" They are being confronted with a requirement that is totally terrifying them. They will go to almost any extremes not to face this experience, but the Universe is now forcing them to take it on.

It can be anything from cosmic issues such as trust of the Universe to commitment-avoidance, to dealing with their underlying profound depression or self-rejection or whatever. It got started in this life with severe emotional neglect and/or rejection as an infant and beyond by their intensely abusive and awareness-avoidant mother.

"SHINGLES" (Painful viral infection and blisters along the nerves)

"Generalized dread." They are in effect "waiting for the other shoe to drop." They are experiencing much anxiety that things will go badly for them, and they labor under much fear and tension as they anticipate disaster.

They have a great need and desire for nurturance, protection and affection. But their agitated anxiety results in their being hyper-sensitive in the "finding the cat is stomping loudly" fashion. There is also a great deal of anger, frustration, along with a fair amount of hostility expression.

It comes from having been buffeted-about helplessly by the self-destructive lifestyle of their dysfunctional family.

"SHOCK REACTION"

"I'm outta here!" They are into complete overwhelm and overload -- a "too much to handle" reaction. Their system just can't take any more traumas. They simply can't cope with any more negativity in their lives.

While the particular precipitating event is a systems overload, there is still a component to their reaction which reflects an underlying experience of this trauma's being the "straw that broke the camel's back." It is the result of their having been routinely traumatized in their severely dysfunctional family, and subsequently as well.

SHORTNESS OF BREATH

"Catastrophic expectations." They have a pronounced fear of the environment. There is an agitated anticipation of a condition that could cause the loss of life's joys, and they are experiencing tension and mental stress.

So they have taken to "taking first," and to fending off vulnerability whenever possible. They tend to be unable to communicate, and to be angrily selfish and/or misusing of love. However, this results in constant anxiety that someone or something will take it all away from them, in a return of their childhood experience.

It all started with trauma in the womb or shortly thereafter, with the result that they feel that the world is not a safe place when they are vulnerable or under stress. They don't trust the Universe, because it feels like it has never been there for them, and like they have always had to fend off an invasive and exploitative world.

SICKLE CELL ANEMIA (Clogging of the arteries, coupled with severe joint pains)

"Cope-ability-anxiety." They have a firm belief that they are "not good enough" that is so strong that it destroys their capacity for joy of life. They are full of inferiority feelings, and they are utterly self-rejecting. There is and was no love in their life, and those around them were thoroughly convincing they were a "moral cretin" and absolutely worthless.

"S.I.D.S." (Sudden Infant Death Syndrome)

"Job done." This was all the soul wanted, and it selected the situation knowing in advance what would result. It wanted this particular womb and the experiences that would be forthcoming for the soul's own purposes.
****

"Can't handle it." Checking it out and finding that it was too much to handle for them, they wanted out. They'll design more carefully next time, based on this learning experience.
****

"Forget this!" There just wasn't enough relevant support for their particular needs, so they simply stopped breathing.
****

"Shit happens." Sometimes things just show up. It's the result of the "random generator," which sets off events that are neither the result of the Divine Intent nor of the play-outs of our will. The purpose is to continuously challenge us with growth-generating events. It should be noted in this regard that "shinola happens" too.

SINUS PROBLEMS

"Romancing the stone." They feel they have lost someone they loved a great deal, or that they have never had the love they needed from someone they loved deeply. They feel that they somehow caused the abandonment or loss, and they are compulsively "looking for love in all the wrong faces," and they are trying in all the wrong ways to win love via perfectionistic performance. It backfires, though, with the result there is much "inner crying."

They are trying to "put a better ending on the old story" with "stand-ins for the original cast." They are trying to "squeeze blood from a turnip," they are profoundly hurt by and they deeply resent the way it is going. This whole thing got started in an attempt to prevent the loss of parental love, particularly of paternal validation. It never worked.
****

"How dare they!" They are experiencing strong irritation with someone close, in a hyper-sensitive "persecution complex" manner. They are having many irritated feelings, leading to a considerable restriction of their actions.

This whole thing is a warning they are attracting revenge, retaliatory and other negative thoughts in their direction. The reason is that they are being over-discriminating and judgmental in an excessively disciplined and annoying manner. They are the product of an invasive and angry dysfunctional family.

****

"Never at peace." There is chronic agitation and an unsettled condition that is seemingly impossible to heal. They are desperately trying to arrive at some sort of freedom from tension. It seems that everywhere they go, they run into more trouble.

The entire complex got started and was maintained by an intense "never good enough" parenting process. This whole pattern may represent karmic issues that have to be dealt with in this life.

RIGHT SINUS PROBLEM
"Betrayed." They are feeling that the world is letting them down in its manifestation.

LEFT SINUS PROBLEM
"I asked for it." They are engaged in self-rejection based on the assumption that they deserve the disappointments and deprivations they are experiencing.

~~~~~~

SINUS CONGESTION
"Inner crying." They are having a reaction to an experienced rejection from someone they love, or they are undergoing an exacerbation of or a return of their long-standing feeling they have never had the love they needed from someone they loved very deeply. They feel that they somehow caused the abandonment, rejection or loss.

They are trying to put a new ending on the old story with "stand-ins for the original cast." However, it doesn't work, of course, and they end up being dominating, possessive, irritated and controlling. In effect, they are attempting to "squeeze blood from a turnip," and they deeply resent the results. The whole thing started and maintained by an intense "never good enough" parenting pattern.

SINUS HEADACHES (Lollipaloser pain in the sinus cavities)
"Wailing in pain." They are suffering from suppressed grief, abandonment-anxiety, and frustration with their intimates about insufficient support and love -- an issue dating back to childhood.

SINUSITIS (Inflammation leading to blockage, greenish discharge, and pain in the sinuses)
"Intimate irritation." They are having a lot of problems with their closest intimate, and it is making them very despairingly angry. They keep trying to run the show, to make the other person dance to their tune, and it doesn't work. They are very resentful and grief-stricken at the same time. It is a pattern that got started in their oppressive and enmeshed family.

SKELETON PROBLEMS

"Paradigm shift." The basic structure of their life is crumbling around and within them. They suddenly feel like a jellyfish that has no inner structure to rely upon. The foundational beliefs and values upon which they built their life no longer work for them. It is an existential crisis which requires a re-thinking of their entire structure.

They adapted to a family environment that either was tied to dying values or was severely dysfunctional. The result is that now they have to start all over again, and they have to free themselves from dependence on their old values, beliefs and commitments.

SKIN PROBLEMS

"I hope I pass the audition." They have intense concerns about how they think others see them, how they fit into the norms of society, and how they see themselves, along with their deeper insecurities. They are embarrassed, ashamed and guilty, and there are feelings of inferiority, low self-esteem, obstruction and ostracism. They are concerned about how good an example they are to others.

All of this is the result of their being a "sensitive" in a severely denial-dominated dysfunctional family who used and abused them. They were used for their sensitivity, out of the need for contact, for their tenderness, and for their desire to elevate.

The family in effect abused them for being intensely threatening, for being disturbingly different, and for being difficult to comprehend, if at all. So they had to play the role of the "alarming Martian."

****

"Cope-ability-anxiety." They are having real world-mastery problems, and they try to prove themselves in areas where they aren't capable. At the same time, they are bothered by how much they aren't allowed to use their expertise. To make matters more intense, they have strong longings which can't be realized at the present. This often results from a hostile atmosphere in the environment that involves attempts to penetrate their defenses.

They have a notable lack of peace and harmony in their lives, and they are continuously uneasy, unsettled and threatened by the world. At base, they want to elevate other people's consciousness, and to integrate spiritual and sacred information and energies into the world.

They are very sensitive and good at getting the feel of things, and they want to share this. However, they have been so misunderstood and ill-treated that they have had to withdraw into their core to protect their individuality and integrity. They grew up in a family who did not understand them, and who became invasively abusive.

****

"Intensely irritated." They are bored, annoyed, frustrated and impatient. They are troubled by their unexpressed unlovely thoughts about others that have arisen out of all this. There is a lot of anxiety and fear from old, buried "gukky stuff," including from past lives. They have a feeling of being threatened in some way, which is a warning to watch their attitude, because they are letting things "get under their skin."

Underpinning much of their situation is an unwillingness to forgive and forget the past, and they are prone to intensely critical attitudes. They have always felt like some sort of "stranger in a strange land," and they have never "fit in." For some, blemishes become an excuse for withdrawing altogether.

At the base of all this is a hidden habit of fear and "raw nerves," along with a deep-seated emotional conflict between the desire for affection and the fear of being hurt if it is sought. They learned early on that "love is a poison apple" in their severely dysfunctional and ambivalent family.

"HORNY" GROWTHS ON THE SKIN

"Body armor." Their experience is that "love is a poison apple," and they therefore have to maintain an "armed garrison" composed of love-deflectors and vulnerability-avoidance. It is the result of untrustworthy relationships in their dysfunctional family.

INFLAMMATION OF THE SKIN

"Urban hermit." This is a case of a fiery suppressed sexuality and eroticized spiritual longings in an intimacy-avoiding destiny-deflector. They have developed a "pariah complex" in which they feel totally unwelcome wherever they go, arising out of their guilt and shame about their erotic nature. There is a good deal of resentment about that. They are product of an invasively intrusive and over-possessive "tantalizing tarantula" sex-ploitative mother in a patriarchal household.

****

"Irrelevant perfectionism." They are harboring deep narcissistic resentment and hostility towards women, especially their intimates. They are prone to spiritual addiction and impractical idealism, with a systematic refusal to be grounded. They operate out of unrealistic "perfect tree house"-seeking and an inability to manifest. It is the result of over-indulgent and interference-running possessive maternal parenting.

SKIN MITES

"Getting to me." They are allowing others to get under their skin so that their thinking is infected. They are self-belittling and lacking in confidence, and they are very vulnerable to accusation and attribution.

They are also very dependent and structure-seeking, out of feeling they don't have the ability or identity to think for themselves, to run their own life, or to take care of themselves. It comes out of a highly denigrating and competence-undermining family.

SLEEP APNEA (Interruptions of breathing while sleeping)

"Maternal deprivation." They are intensely sensitive, fearful and longing for mother love or love from someone close. They have a lot of disappointment, bitterness, unforgivingness and resentment about being over-worked.

However, at the same time, they dare not express or even acknowledge these feelings out of fear of total rejection and abandonment. They tend rather strongly to be fatalistic, hostility-repressing, compulsively over-giving, hypersensitive and lonely. They are also full of family taboos, social restrictions and moral inhibitions, all of which were learned in an intensely repressive family which forced a "model child" adjustment on them.

There is a great deal of deep-seated guilt, shame and grief arising out of this, and they are joy-avoidant, happiness-squashing and love-deflecting, all in the misguided hope they will thereby finally "earn" the "God Housekeeping Seal of Approval." In effect, they are so self-suppressing that they are suffocating themselves.

SLEEP-DEPRIVATION SYNDROME (Irritability, confusion, fight-flight reaction)

"Red-orange alert." They are on intense vigilance and "hair-trigger" reactivity. They don't dare to relax because they don't trust the process of life. They have a disturbed mental condition, due to a subconscious shock, and/or due to a chronic state of "red-orange alert." They labor under a great deal of guilt and fear over imagined failures and their consequences. There has now also been an "emergency preparation" activated by current circumstances. It arises from their having been the "sane one" in a severely dysfunctional family.

"SLEEPING SICKNESS" (Bacterially-precipitated, compulsive sleep state, often lethal)

"Lem'me outta here!" They are feeling drained and over-demanded, like they have been cast adrift and abandoned by the "Home Office." (All That Is). They can't cope, due to extreme fear, and they are so "freaked out" that they want to totally get away from it all.

They encountered an out-of-control dysfunctional family to which they had to adapt, and in which they somehow had to survive. It has been that way ever since, due to the imprinting effect that leads us to attract to ourselves and to be attracted to that with which we grew up.

Now they have reached the point of total demoralization, and they can't take it any more, and they don't want to be here at all.

SLOWED HEART RATE

"Alone on their own." They have taken care of business with no help from their non-existent friends since infancy. The result is a chronic low-key depression reflected in their slowed down heart rate. They were expected to meet their own needs in a "Child, PLEASE, I'd rather you do it yourself!" parenting pattern.

SMALL INTESTINE PROBLEMS (First wave assimilation of nutrients)

"Assimilation problems." They are having absorption difficulties and problems in separating the wheat from the chaff. They are having difficulties with analysis and with processing things. They are being hampered by distorted discrimination and disturbing distrust generated by a dysfunctional family's "magical mystery tour" pattern, and by their being subjected to systematic invalidation then and ever since.
****

"Self-worth issues." They are experiencing excessive guilt, self-doubt and self-image problems. They feel unappreciated and also unsure of their capability and value. They need appreciation, love, and understanding of the kind they never got as a child in their accusatorially invalidating family.

(See **ILEITIS**)

INFLAMMATION OF THE SMALL INTESTINE

"Roiling turmoil." They are intensely resentful at their lot in life. They are finding that they are experiencing a lot of inassimilable and uninterruptible inputs. They come from a "poison apple" pseudo-loving and systematically misleading, emotionally abusive family.

SMALL POX (Fever, pain, vomiting, boils that leave permanent indentation scars)

"Moral cretin." There is intense rage about restrictions, along with rage at themselves for bringing these restrictions on themselves. They are highly resentful about rules and regulations, along with environmental suppression and oppression.

They are also convinced that at some level, they deserve the restrictions, and they even take some measure of pleasure out of the "just desserts punishment." They are full of generalized malaise and contempt, but they are the worst on themselves.

They have a great deal of self-disgust and self-hatred for being what they are, and deep inside, they feel they must suffer as "atonement" for their "violations of the moral order." It all stems from a highly oppressive, shame-inducing, blame-throwing and accusatory family.

SOFTENING OF THE BONES

"Enough already!" They are disintegrating under the load of responsibilities they have had to carry all their life. They have the feeling that they just can't support themselves and that their world single-handedly like they have been doing all along.

They are just plain running out of steam from having had to "run on empty" for so long. It just isn't in them any more. It reflects the fact that they had to be the "tower of power" and the "support pillar" for their family as their way of seeking the "God Housekeeping Seal of Approval" from their exploitative, dysfunctional and withholding family.

"SOLAR FEVER" (Infectious fever)

"Burning up." They are full of intense anger and stored resentments. They are full of agitated worry and hurry, in fear of anticipated outcomes. There is a severe lack of harmony and a lot of internal conflict. They have a fear of or a reaction to loss of friendships -- abandonment feelings. It represents an experienced return to the uncertainties and frustrations of their dysfunctional family.

SOLAR PLEXUS PROBLEMS (Upper abdomen)

"Cope-ability-anxiety." They are suffering from powerlessness feelings, and they feel overwhelmed by life. They have a strong fear of their gut reactions, their intuitive hits, and their "inner voice." They don't trust their capacity to make discriminations, evaluations and judgments.

They have lost touch with much of their personal potency and life energy. Their feelings are easily hurt, and they are hyper-sensitive to rejection. They are quite abandonment-anxious and betrayal-paranoid.

It comes from having been thoroughly undermined in their confidence and self-trust by a wrong-making, denigrating, untrustworthy, rejecting, abandonment-threatening, and rather severely dysfunctional family.

****

"Papa/Mama knows best!" They are imperatively intrusive in an authoritarian manner. They are full of critical judgmentalness and insensitive boorishness, in a massively egocentric "What's good for General Bullmoose is good for *everybody*!" pattern. This comes from their being positioned in or capitulated into a situation of coercive control within their patriarchal dysfunctional family.

"SPASTIC COLON" (Sudden uncontrollable diarrhea attacks)

"Blow-out." They are frantically sorting and shuffling ideas. They are encountering a situation that requires that they process out the implications and ramifications of what is going down. They fear that they will not be able to have what it takes to handle the needs of the new developments. Their feeling is that "I'm all I've got," and that if they fail, all hell will break loose.

There was never any form of trustworthy support when they were growing up, and they learned to take care of themselves in a "self-made person" manner "disaster-deflecting" psychology.
****

"Papa/Mama knows best!" They tend to push things on other people in a bossy "unilateral good deeds" fashion. They can't seem to "leave well enough alone." They have an abiding fear of the Universe, and they feel that in effect they have to have "hands on" control of everything at all times. They are simply terrified of letting go.

There was never anyone at the helm of the ship in their dysfunctional family, and so they grabbed the wheel and never let go. Now they don't dare let go. Their current circumstances are precipitating a "loss of control" panic reaction.

"SPASTIC" DUODENUM (Convulsive closings of the start of the small intestine)

"I don't need you!" They have severe dependency-independency conflicts resulting in their bending over backwards in ferocious independence, and in their "taking their marbles and going home" refusals to receive and/or to request support.

They have a marked maternal dependency and mother-fixation underlying this pattern -- an extreme need for nurturance and affection arising from a history of maternal deprivation.

SPHINCTER PROBLEMS

"Control issues." They are intensely desirous of control, and yet they are deeply disturbed by the responsibilities and lifestyle that their compulsive control-seeking generates. They are therefore highly ambivalent about control, resulting in a disruption of the "steady state" muscles.

It is a pattern that started when they were the "linchpin" person for their family in childhood, the one whose sanity, solidity and strength deflected disaster continuously.

SPINAL CORD PROBLEMS

"Insufficient to the cause." They feel unequipped and/or permanently damaged at the very core of their being and functioning system. They feel unable to rise to the requirements of life, and they are thoroughly demoralized. They are strongly inclined to "throw in the towel" in a resentful resignation trip. They were systematically undermined in their confidence and competence by an accusatory and passive-aggressively dysfunctional family.

MENINGEAL SUBLUXATION (Spinal cord dislocation)

"Overload." They are feeling taxed beyond their capacities to meet the demands of their life situation. They are under a considerable amount of emotional, mental and/or chemical stress. This is a familiar pattern to them, and it got started in their dysfunctional family, where they felt or were assigned the responsibility to "make it better" or to "make up for it."

MENINGITIS (Inflammation of the lining of the brain and the spinal cord)

"Pariah/outcast complex." They are convinced that they are unacceptable to human society, and that other people are incensed that they are here. They feel attacked for their beingness, their personality.

They are enraged at life and inflamed in their thinking, and they are full of blame and frustrated fury. They were regarded and treated as the "Hunchback of Notre Dame" by their family, who, however, at the same time systematically trained them to be a scapegoat.

SPINAL INJURY

"Don't move!" Their experience is that the "balance of the Cosmos" rides on their every move. They don't dare move forward on anything.

They are the product of an extremely blame-throwing and responsibility- and accountability-avoidant family who gave them a very strong "Don't move until I tell you to!" injunction.

Now they are feeling the "weight of the world" and the "brunt of the pain of the human race."

****

"Under siege." They are undergoing an immobilizing fear and terror, a feeling of utter helplessness and hopelessness. They feel they are under attack from the Universe, and that nothing is trustworthy. They are mentally and/or emotionally confused, they feel overwhelmed.

They are in a thorough-going escape mode, and they are doing all they can to avoid an unwanted task or experience and/or to escape a situation or person. They are experiencing an intense resistance to life, people and things in a super-stubbornness reaction, and inadequate, and they lack self-control at this point.

It is the result of having come up in an irrational and/or chaotic family in which there was nothing they could do to change the course of events, to improve the situation, or to provide themselves a better experience.

SPINAL DISC PROBLEMS

"I can't handle it!" They are feeling outclassed and over-run by the demands of life, and they are seeking to put off, slide around, or ignore the requirements that are giving them the feeling they don't have what it takes to make it. It comes from having grown up in a household that either asked far too much or far too little of them.

Each spinal disc has a different additional meaning associated with problems around that disc. They are listed below:

~~~~~~

SKULL/FIRST CERVICAL DISC (Head/neck)

"Cut off at the pass." They have the intense feeling that they have been cast adrift with no compass in uncharted seas that are potentially very dangerous. They have to watch their flank with others as well, and they are forever on the alert for how people are reacting to them. It comes from their having been enculturated by a severely dysfunctional family's values, orientation and lifestyle that left them no guidelines with which to work.

FIRST CERVICAL/SECOND CERVICAL DISC (Neck)

"Lying low." They are running from life and awareness, in a fearful relationship to the Universe. They are afraid of social ostracism and the truth, out of the expectation they would be in effect "royally reamed" if they spoke up or spoke out.

As a result, they live a self-suppressing and denial-dominated lifestyle, with an underlying deep resentment of having to do so. It arose from a suppressive, repressive and perfectionistic parenting experience.

SECOND CERVICAL/THIRD CERVICAL DISC (Neck)

"I could cause World War III!" They have real boundary problems, in that they take on responsibility for everything that happens around them. They therefore tend strongly to "disaster-deflect" as their primary approach to things, emphasizing awareness-avoidance, guilt-grabbing, intervention-deflection, or indiscriminate intervention.

They were looked to as the primal cause for everything by their family, whether it took the form of blowing the cover on the family denial or of setting off a chain reaction of events in the family. Their family was highly blaming in their treatment of them.

THIRD CERVICAL/FOURTH CERVICAL DISC (Neck)

"I caused World War II!" They feel personally responsible for everything that goes wrong in their vicinity. As a result, they try to sit on themselves and to "atone" for what happened. They allow themselves no leeway or input of joy or resources, for fear of the wrath of God in a non-comprehensible world. They were subjected to intense blame and shame-induction as a child.

FOURTH CERVICAL/FIFTH CERVICAL DISC (Neck)

"Alone on their own." They have lost contact with the higher realms of things, and they are therefore afraid of setting off calamities in an unpredictable manner. They have taken to a self-suppressive and compulsively concretely controlling approach to everything as a result.

They come from a family who blamed them when things went wrong, and who made them wrong if they acted on their intuition.

FIFTH CERVICAL/SIXTH CERVICAL DISC (Neck)

"Hands-on control." They are intensely avoidant of all things intangible and non-rational. They have a strictly three-dimensional model of the world, and they are therefore ferociously determined not to let things get out of hand, because "One strike and we're out!" They feel that they are the only one who can deflect ultimate disasters.

They come from a severely dysfunctional and anti-spiritual/ethereal background, and they were systematically punished if they dealt with anything beyond the five senses realm. At the same time, they were the "sane one," and they felt and were held accountable/ responsible for all that went wrong.

SIXTH CERVICAL/SEVENTH CERVICAL DISC (Neck)

"Desert island." Their experience of life is that it is a "vast wasteland" of heartlessness and grimness. For them, life is about survival and the minimization of pain, so they are inflexibly conceptual and harm-avoidant, with a resulting sense of deprivation and resentment. They come from a dysfunctional and severely dreary family.

SEVENTH CERVICAL/FIRST THROACIC DISC (Upper back)

"Overwhelmed." They feel bereft of support from the Cosmos in an impossible-to-handle world. They feel that they neither deserve nor can have the resources necessary to make their life work. They are the product of a demoralizingly dysfunctional and wrong-making family.

FIRST THORACIC/SECOND THORACIC DISC (Upper back)

"Mother, PLEASE, I'd rather do it myself!" They feel that the world is untrustworthy, and that vulnerability and involvement are unsafe. They also feel that things are out of hand, and that they can do little to make things any better.

So they have retreated into an "island unto themselves" lifestyle. It comes from growing up in an overwhelmingly dysfunctional and effectively neglectful family.

SECOND THORACIC/THIRD THORACIC DISC (Upper back)

"Armed fortress." They feel they live in an indifferent and hurtful world in which no one cares, and in which nothing is trustworthy. They therefore are pulled into their inner core in a constantly on guard, trouble-expecting and wrong-making manner. They are the product of a severely dysfunctional and blame-throwing family.

THIRD THORACIC/FOURTH THORACIC DISC (Upper back)

"Angry agitation." They are intensely emotionally bothered all the time, and they are highly blame-throwing and judgmental about it all. Their experience is that they are surrounded by a "ship of fools" who are causing all sorts of unpredictable mayhem, and they are intensely rageful about it. They come from a severely wrong-making and blame-throwing family.

FOURTH THORACIC/FIFTH THORACIC DISC (Middle back)

"Bitter suppression." They feel that life is dangerously untrustworthy, and that they therefore have to avoid all forms of spontaneity, joy and feelings. The result is a blame-throwing self-squashing that result in much unexpressed rage. They are the product of a severely dysfunctional and wrong-making family.

FIFTH THORACIC/SIXTH THORACIC DISC (Middle back)

"Magical misery tour." They are extremely afraid of feelings and of the future. Their experience is that things just go from bad to worse, and that it is dangerous out there and in here.

So they do an "ostrich" approach to things that results in their having to be fearfully alert for the unpredictable awfuls that are sure to come at all times. Their family was highly reality-avoidant and dysfunctional.

SIXTH THORACIC/SEVENTH THORACIC DISC (Middle back)

"Balled up in pain." They have no trust of the Universe, and they feel that "love is a poison apple." The result is a completely self-contained "sealed unit" who cuts themselves off from contact with the world, with the result they have a great deal of pain that they just have to live with. Their family was thoroughly untrustworthy, self-involved and dysfunctional.

SEVENTH THORACIC/EIGHTH THORACIC DISC (Middle back)

"Vast wasteland." Their experience is that no one can be trusted enough to be vulnerable, and that there is nothing out there for them because they don't deserve any better anyway. Their family was intensely self-serving and shame-inducing.

EIGHTH THORACIC/NINTH THORACIC DISC (Middle back)

"But not for me. . ." They feel completely cut off from all positivity, and that they are utterly powerless to do anything about it. Their experience is that the world is populated with "moral cretins" who victimize them. They feel absolutely bereft of anything of any value, with a good deal of suppressed rage about that. It is the result of an abusive and blame-throwing family.

NINTH THORACIC/TENTH THORACIC DISC (Middle back)

"Suffering succotash!" They are convinced that they can do nothing to make anything work or to prevent their suffering, so they are into a blame-throwing and victim-tripping mode of operation.

They are the product of a severely dysfunctional, disempowering family who systematically imposed and induced suffering as they engaged in continuous accountability-avoidance, attributing and blame-throwing.

TENTH THORACIC/ELEVENTH THORACIC DISC (Middle back)

"Pissed-off passivity." They have the foundational assumption they don't deserve anything positive in their life, and that they are powerless to do anything to make anything happen anyway. So they are resentfully resigned to a negative experience of life. They are the product of a blame-throwing dysfunctional family.

ELEVENTH THORACIC/TWELTH THORACIC DISC (Middle back)

"Worthless turd." They are convinced that they are "unfit for human consumption," and that "love is a poison apple." So they systematically prevent and avoid loving relationships, while they "wait for rigor mortis." They are the product of a severely rejecting and pessimistic family.

TWELTH THORACIC/FIRST LUMBAR DISC (Middle back)

"Outcast on a desert island." They feel that they deserve ostracism and deprivation, and while they feel profound pain over their situation, they don't trust or believe in themselves or others enough to allow anything else to happen. They come from a deeply love-distrust-inducing family.

FIRST LUMBAR/SECOND LUMBAR DISC (Lower back)

"Bitter pill." They feel they have no choice but to "sit there and take it," with regard to having to accept the painful and alienated lifestyle they are living. It is the product of significant early deprivation, and of a "dead end" family system.

SECOND LUMBAR/THIRD LUMBAR DISC (Lower back)

"Screwed, Jewed and tattooed." They feel they have been in effect "raped by God," and that they can trust nothing and no one as a result. They also feel that it is their "just desserts," and that they can therefore do nothing about it. Their family felt utterly powerless and unable to do anything about anything.

THIRD LUMBAR/FOURTH LUMBAR DISC (Lower back)

"Up a creek without a paddle." They feel completely devastated in their ability to have success in any sphere of life, and at base, they feel they deserve no better. They were emotionally and/or physically sexually abused and systematically confidence- and competence-undermined by a severely possessive dysfunctional family.

FOURTH LUMBAR/FIFTH LUMBAR DISC (Lower back)

"Perpetual loser." They feel as though they don't have the right to positivity of any kind, and they don't have what it takes to make it. This makes for a dreary, weary lifestyle that they deeply resent. It is the result of a possessive and punitive family.

FIFTH LUMBAR/SACRUM DISC (Lower back)

"Violation-rage." They feel seduced and attacked by the Universe, and that it is their "evilness" and "worthlessness" that is the cause of it all. They are therefore furiously but helplessly rageful about their whole situation. They are the product of seductive-destructive parenting.

SACRUM/COCCYX DISC (Pelvis/tail bone)

"Pain-blame." They have a great deal of sexual guilt and survival-anxiety in what feels like a "lose-lose life" that they feel that they somehow deserve. They were seductive-destructively and shame-inducingly parented by their sex-ploitative and worth-devastating family.

~~~~~~

SLIPPED DISC (Ill-moved platelet between the vertebrae)

"Cope-ability-anxiety." They feel a great deal of pressure, and that they are completely unsupported by life. They are lost in indecision, in the face of feeling overwhelmed and alone in the world. They feel they are being asked to be more than they are, or to do more than they can handle -- that they have to live up to something beyond their capabilities.

They are full of cope-ability-anxiety and self-disgust for being the way they are. The result is that they are rather intensely indecisive and "waffling" in their functioning. They are the product of a highly unsupportive and wrong-making family.

SPINAL MENINGITIS (Inflammation of the brain and/or spinal cord lining) [See **MENINGITIS**]

SPINE PROBLEMS

"Insufficiency feelings." They feel basically outclassed and overwhelmed by life's requirements. They feel inferior, and they are shyly socially avoidant as a result. They lack confidence, and this operates in a self-fulfilling prophecy manner.

They were placed in positions of responsibility and requirement that were beyond their level of development. And their family reacted with rage, blame, accusations and denigration/ undermining of their capacity to cope.

****

"Take it and shove it!" They are refusing to flow with the support that life provides them, as well as rejecting the spiritual connection. They are convinced that the resources the Universe provides them are irrelevant, "poison apples," potential betrayals, or nothing but requirements, responsibilities and restrictions.

It results in a rigid inflexibility, pridefulness, and inability to support the life process. It is the outcome of a primitive, rejecting, exploitative and untrustworthy dysfunctional family.

Each vertebrate has more specific psychological meanings associated with problems around that vertebrate. These are listed below:

FIRST CERVICAL (Top of the Neck) VERTEBRA -- (The "Atlas")

"Not good enough." They are not able to experience God's support and the Divine Intellect input. They are coming from fear, confusion and endless inner chatter. They are in effect running from life, in a "What will the neighbors think?" ostracism-paranoia and fear of failure arising from a strong feeling of not being worthy and sufficient to the cause.

It arose from an "associate parent" or "role-reversed" experience in which they were expected to perform to perfection in order to receive any love and validation at all.

SECOND CERVICAL (Neck) VERTEBRA -- (The "Axis")

"I don' wanna know!" There is an inhibition of the ability to develop their breadth of understanding and comprehension -- a rejection of wisdom. They are doing a denial-dominated refusal to know or understand.

It feels very dangerous to them to take a stand and make a decision, and they are out of balance with life. They are intensely resentful and full of blame, and they want nothing to do with the spiritual realm.

It is the result of an intensely denial-dominated dysfunctional family who exploded and "blew apart at the seams" if the individual noted or expressed any patterns, or if they shared any understanding (which requires accountability, responsibility and integrity -- none of which the family could manifest).

THIRD CERVICAL VERTEBRA (Neck)

"Serve-aholic frenzy." They have a damaged capacity to perceive spiritual Truth as a means of self-guidance. Instead, they accept blame for others, they bite off more than they can chew, and they grind themselves down in a "codependent runaway." They are guilt-dominated, atonement-seeking, over-responsible, self-denigrating, fearful of making the wrong decision, and feeling in over their head.

It arose out of their being systematically shame-induced, accused and blamed, on the one hand, and out of their being exploited, depended upon and scape-goated, on the other, in their dysfunctional family.

FOURTH CERVICAL VERTEBRA (Neck)

"Bitter joylessness." They have difficulty seeing or knowing the inner essence or truth of things, as a function of losing contact with their Higher Self. They feel lost in a "magical misery tour," and they feel guilty for everything that goes wrong, as if they were somehow responsible and accountable for it.

They are therefore systematically suppressing themselves, and they are stuffing their feelings. They are unable to allow themselves anything and as a result, there are a lot of bottled up feelings, stuffed tears, and repressed rages. The net effect is a resigned resentment over their squelched condition.

They are the product of a highly repressive and blame-throwing family in which they were held accountable for all negative events, as if they had the power to control things magically.

It is the result of their being at a higher state of development than the family in one way or another, so they turned to the individual for care-taking, and then they turned to them in blame when the sub-consciously expected perfection of experience was not forthcoming.

FIFTH CERVICAL VERTEBRA (Neck)

"Self-distrust." They have lost the capacity for "grokking" (perceiving the full nature and import of things in one glance), for getting the whole concept at once, for intuition, and for full comprehension.

As a result, they fear making mistakes, and their communication tends to be partial. They then developed a fear of ridicule and self-expression, and they can't believe they have any good to them. They are constantly trying to anticipate and control everything with the result they are continuously over-burdened.

They are the product of a primitive, pragmatic and/or concrete-minded family who were distrusting and disgusted with non-sensory inputs or sources. They were subjected to derision or degradation when they shared their "hits" and their hunches from their inherent highly developed intuitive capability.

SIXTH CERVICAL VERTEBRA (Neck)

"Walking cerebrum." They are taking a hyper-rational approach to things, with no spiritual essence or connection involved. They try to handle everything with reason, rationality and logical problem-solving. They are afraid of feelings and unpredictability, spontaneity and flow.

They therefore feel heavily burdened and overloaded, as they try to "fix" others. They are highly inflexible, rigid and resistive to influence or change. They feel that they must have "hands on" control of everything, and that everything must be done their rational, logical way.

It comes from their having been in a dysfunctional family that was either emotional-commotional or chaotic, so that they decided never to have to deal with that sort of mess again, or it was a hot-bed of "walking cerebrums."

In either case, they decided to never let things get out of control, and to always make sure that everything makes perfectly logical sense.

SEVENTH CERVICAL VERTEBRA (Neck)

"Cosmic abandonment." They have lost the ability to be in touch with the "Home Office" and the associated capacity for abundance, bounty and beauty. They experience nothing to appreciate and be grateful for, and they therefore feel abandoned or rejected by God.

They feel they have no right to be themselves or reach out for resources because they can't trust others or the Universe, and because they somehow have done something, become something, or is something that doesn't deserve God's love and abundance.

They are therefore very angry about their situation of deprivation, an anger greatly compounded by their confusion as to exactly why they are in this predicament. In essence, they feel resentfully helpless. They are the product of a dysfunctional and blame-throwing family in which nothing ever worked or made much sense.

FIRST THORACIC VERTEBRA (Upper Back)

"Going down." They are unable to keep their faith and hope alive, and they therefore are giving up in despair and resignation. They have a real fear of life, and they feel it is too much to cope with. They can't handle it, and they are closing off from life.

This came about as a result of their being made to feel responsible for the care and maintenance of a severely dysfunctional family. When it became apparent that they were in over their head, they became demoralized and immobilized.

SECOND THORACIC VERTEBRA (Upper Back)

"Closed-off heart." They have had to shut down their "heart center," due to fear, pain and hurt. They are unwilling to feel or be vulnerable, much less to connect and merge. They are deeply distrusting of the Universe and of other people, and to them, "love is a poison apple."

They have no self-love and no inner peace. It is the outcome of a highly untrustworthy and attacking dysfunctional family.

THIRD THORACIC VERTEBRA (Upper Back)

"Grit and bear it." They are suffering from inner chaos and deep, old hurts. They are unable to communicate about these or anything else, out of a lack of forgiveness of self and others. They are very blame-frame oriented, and their basic feeling is "You asked for it, asshole!"

They are convinced that they have to "just sit there and take it." And that, in turn, generates a great deal of inner turmoil that is a combination of outrage, despair, fear, guilt, shame and confusion.

They come from a severely blaming and judgmental family, and the repeated message was, "You made your bed. Now lie in it!"

FOURTH THORACIC VERETEBRA (Middle Back)

"Bitter and blaming." They don't have the ability to have fun, to laugh, to feel joy and elation, to have light in their lives, and to have a sense of humor. They are instead unforgiving, condemning, and needing to make others wrong.

There experience is, "There is no joy in Bloodville" and "Someone is to blame, here and it sure as hell isn't ME!" Needless to say, they are just doing unto others what was done unto them.

FIFTH THORACIC VERTEBRA (Middle Back)

"Feeling-avoidant." They are totally terrified of their emotions and those of others, out of a fear that all hell will break loose if they ever come in contact with feelings. They systematically refuse to process their emotions, and they do all they can to not come in contact with them in others.

They are therefore full of dammed-up feelings and a resulting rage. It is the result of an extremely feeling-suppressing and reality-avoiding dysfunctional family.

SIXTH THORACIC VERTEBRA (Middle Back)

"Chronic agitation." They are in a constant state of worry and fear of the future. They have no trust in the process of life, and they have the feeling it is their own fault, that they don't deserve to have things go right for them.

So they are forever vigilant and on guard, which only serves as a continual "reminder" that they "don't deserve to love themselves." They therefore don't want to have

302

any awareness of or commerce with the negative emotions, and so they "stuff" them. All of this generates a real anger at life.

They come from a reality-avoiding dysfunctional family who systematically shoved their "unacceptable" feelings into the shadow, and who slid the unpleasant realities of life under the rug. The result was an experienced chaos and "magical misery tour," in which they never knew when the next piece of excrement would come off the wall, just that it would.

SEVENTH THROACIC VERTEBRA (Middle Back)

"Love is a poison apple." They have never been able to develop the capacity for *agape*, -- the ability to have selfless affection, to just love and want the loved one to be happy, with no requirements and no desires. They are convinced that love is simply not to be trusted.

They therefore refuse to enjoy, and instead they store pain continuously. They have put up a "psychic deflector shield," and they are shriveling up into a large ball of pain. Their family was extremely self-serving and slyly manipulative in a very untrustworthy and untouchable manner. So they just shut down and shut up.

EIGHTH THORACIC VERTEBRA (Middle Back)

"Non-deservingness feelings." They are convinced that they are a "failure" and a "fraud," and that they have not "earned the right" to the good things in life. They won't let love, joy and abundance in, and they are systematically success-avoidant.

They feel that "God will *kill* me!" if they have success or quality of life. They feel inherently undeserving of anything positive because of something they did, became, or are, and they therefore expect (and bottom line want) nothing but failure.

They hope that by determinedly deflecting any positives in their life, they will avoid being "spiritually annihilated" for having what they "have no right to have," and they will simultaneously thereby earn "atonement points" to compensate to "balance out" their "karmic indebtedness." They come from a heavily blame-throwing and shame- and guilt-inducing dysfunctional family.

NINTH THORACIC VERTEBRA (Middle Back)

"Blame-throwing." They feel powerless in a victimizing Universe, and they feel let down by life. They feel that it is other people's fault, and they are forever looking for whom to blame. Their experience is that they have no capability or culpability in regard to creating their own life, and they are a first class "victim-tripper."

They are the product of a "sado-masochistic minuet" family system. That is, it was a "pseudo-sadist" and a "masked sadist" situation, where nothing was as it seemed. The result was that they found they were able to fill the "victim" role, and they are stuck in it now.

TENTH THORACIC VERTEBRA (Middle Back)

"Woe is me!" They refuse to take charge of their life or their environment. They would rather be a victim and take the position, "It's your fault!" Their basic feeling is that they don't deserve anything positive, so they are "pulling coals out of the fire" by blame-throwing.

It is a function of their being in an accountability- and responsibility-avoidant dysfunctional family in which everyone points the finger of blame at someone else for the "shitty messes" they were wallowing in.

ELEVENTH THORACIC VERTEBRA (Middle Back)

"Intimacy-avoidant." They have a very low self-image and a high self-rejection. They are convinced that they can never make it in a relationship, and they are commitment-avoidant and fearful of relationships as a result. They were systematically told they were unlovable and "unfit for human consumption" by their highly rejecting family.

TWELFTH THORACIC VERTEBRA (Middle Back)

"Hiding in the cave." They are convinced that "love is a poison apple" and that joy is indigestible. They are profoundly insecure and fearful of love, and they are unable to assimilate any form of nourishment.

They are in effect, disowning their right to live, and they have "hunkered down in the bunker" to "wait out the siege" until "their number comes up." It all comes down to believing they deserve and can expect no better out of life. That, in turn, came from a family who lived in a similar manner.

FIRST LUMBAR VERTEBRA (Lower Back)

"Alone and lonely." They have the feeling that there is no support or love in the Universe for them, in a strong sense of insecurity and lack of resources. They are crying for love, and yet at the same time they have the desperate need to be isolated and bereft.

Their experience is they can't count on anyone or anything, and that they "deserve" this being "cast on a desert island" for something they did, became or are. Their relationship to their situation is one of ambivalent "atonement." It is the result of poor early bonding and significant early deprivation.

SECOND LUMBAR VERTEBRA (Lower Back)

"In it for life." They are stuck in childhood pain, and they see no way out. They have a distorted sense of loyalty and betrayal-paranoia about ever living their own life or about having a quality of life that goes beyond that of their parents.

They are the product of powerless-feeling parents who felt trapped in a "dead-end" lifestyle, and who passed on this sense of being unable to break free of their imprinting and circumstances. Their family also sub-consciously conveyed that they needed them to stay and take care of them, and certainly not to have better than they -- the ultimate bitter pill.

THIRD LUMBAR VERTEBRA (Lower Back)

"Trapped in the past." They were the victim of emotional and/or physical sexual abuse, and they are full of guilt and self-hatred as a result. They feel totally unsafe in the world, and that they can trust no one, because it felt like God raped them. They have profound sexual shame and self-revulsion.

Their abuse occurred so early that they took it to be their "just desserts." It also had the effect of generating a deep distrust of the Universe, due to the confusion of the "Home Office" with the parents at that early an age, so that they fully expect the Universe to screw them again.

FOURTH LUMBAR VERTEBRA (Lower Back)

"You belong to us!" They feel powerless and unable to make it in intimacy, sexuality, financial security and career. They feel that they haven't got what it takes to be a mature and empowered individual. They also feel that they have no right to expect success or love in life. They fear failure and the stakes of taking responsibility in the realm of career.

It all comes out of a strong "keep 'em around the old homestead" competence- and confidence-undermining possessive parenting. The message was, "You know better than to ever think that you could make it out there!"

FIFTH LUMBAR VERTEBRA (Lower Back)

"Profound sense of non-deservingness." They have a severe problem wanting, asking for, and accepting any form of joy and pleasure. They are very insecure about their worth and worthiness, and they have a lot of difficulty in communicating because of it. This all leads to a great deal of frustration and resentment-rage about their dreary and joyless, isolated and alienated, and uncertain/insecure experience of life.

They were systematically confidence- and competence-undermined while simultaneously being shame-induced and worth-anxiety-activated by their self-serving and subterraneanly sabotaging dysfunctional family.

SACRUM PROBLEMS (Spinal Cord/Pelvis Connection)

"Sexual shame." They are suffering from sexual guilt and shame induced by a sex-ploitative "tantalizing tarantula" -- "seductive-destructive" -- "seduce-slap" parenting pattern. They feel utterly powerless to do anything about their situation, and at the same time, they are enraged about how they were treated. They have a way of hanging on to old, stubborn anger.

They were made to feel "evil" for having sexual feelings, and at the same time, they were systematically stimulated by the parents and made wrong for responding and for not responding, so they were in a "lose-lose" situation.

COCCYX PROBLEMS ("Tail Bone")

"Putting their tail between their legs." They are being out of balance with themselves, and they are holding on to self-blame for old pain. They are manifesting compulsive conservatism and hyper-caution run by survival-anxiety.

There is an insufficient amount of self-love and a sense of not deserving to have safety and security. There is also considerable sexual shame. They are engaged in self-protective capitulation and sexual guilt.

They are survival-oriented and security-seeking, and they feel that they don't have the right to assert on behalf of themselves because they "don't deserve it." All of this arose in an oppressive family in which there was a large amount of blame and shame-induction, particularly around sexual issues, while it was at the same time intensely sex-ploitative. There was also a considerable amount of generalized survival-insecurity.

~~~~~~

ANKYLOSING SPONDYLITIS (Debilitating disease caused by stiffening of the spine)

"Nobody cares." They are manifesting a profound feeling that they are totally alone on their own. The experience is there never was any foundation to build on. They feel abandoned by the "Home Office" (All That Is), and they feel that there is nothing out there to sustain them.

So they have become their own "pillar of strength." They refuse to accept the support that life provides them. They feel that available resources are irrelevant, "poison apples," potential betrayals, or nothing but requirements, responsibilities and restrictions. It results in a total self-containment lifestyle and a stiff-backed rigid inflexibility.

They are the product of a primitive, rejecting, exploitative and untrustworthy dysfunctional family, with a resulting but unacknowledged emotional starvation and despairing desperation.

EXOSTOSIS (Nerve irritation caused by over-growth of bone on the spine)
"Nobody cares." They have a profound feeling that they are totally alone on their own. The experience is that there never was any foundation to build on. They feel abandoned by the "Home Office" (All That Is) and that there is nothing out there to sustain them.

So they become their own "pillar of strength." They refuse to accept the support that life provides them. They feel that the available resources are irrelevant, "poison apples," potential betrayals, or nothing but requirements, responsibilities and restrictions. It results in a rigid inflexibility.

They are the product of a primitive, rejecting, exploitative untrustworthy dysfunctional family, with a resulting emotional starvation and despairing desperation.

SPINAL FUSION (Spinal vertebrae grow together, causing stiffening of the spine. Or it has been done surgically as a desperate measure.)
"Nobody cares." They are manifesting a profound feeling that they are totally alone on their own. The experience is that there never was any foundation to build on. They feel abandoned by the "Home Office" (All That Is), and they feel that there is nothing out there to sustain them.

So they have become their own "pillar of strength." They refuse to accept the support that life provides them. They feel that available resources are irrelevant, "poison apples," potential betrayals, or nothing but requirements, responsibilities and restrictions. It results in a total self-containment lifestyle and a stiff-backed rigid inflexibility.

They are the product of a primitive, rejecting, exploitative and untrustworthy dysfunctional family, with a resulting but unacknowledged emotional starvation and despairing desperation.

STENOSIS (Narrowing of the spinal column, due to calcium deposits)
"Hardening of the attitudes." They are rigidly adhering to standards and patterns that are unrealistic, out-dated and self-defeating. They are refusing to flow with the support that life provides them, and they are rejecting their spiritual connection.

They are convinced the resources the Universe provides them are irrelevant, "poison apples," potential betrayals, or nothing but requirements, responsibilities and restrictions. They feel they have to rely solely on themselves to provide themselves a sense of security in a highly insecurity-generating world.

They feel that they are in over their head, and that they have to handle it by strictly adhering to the "tried and true." It results in a rigid inflexibility and inability to support the life process.

It is the result of a primitive, rejecting, exploitative and untrustworthy dysfunctional family, of a highly regimented and perfectionistic family, and/or of having to serve as the "sane one," the "Rock of Gibraltar" in a severely dysfunctional and conservative family.

VERTEBRAL SUBLUXATION (Displaced vertebrate)

"Jerked around." They feel being excessively demanded of, restricted or controlled by their environment, in the form of feeling non-supported, exploited and/or abused. They are having difficulty meeting the requirements made of them, due to the lack of the necessary resolve and reserves or to a sense of being unfairly imposed upon.

It is a pattern that started in their under-requiring, competence- and confidence-undermining and/or dysfunctionally demanding family.

SPLEEN PROBLEMS

"Morose rumination." There is a lack of capacity to connect with soul love, resulting in excessive worry and in being obsessed with things. They have a considerable amount of frustration, impatience, over-attachment, possessiveness, anger and antagonism.

All of this plays out in considerable negativism about potential catastrophic outcomes. It also leads to their being critical, skeptical, irritable, and indifferent about others. They are quite unhappy and emotionally unbalanced, and there is a considerable tendency to engage in complaining and "sympathy-sop" behaviors.

They are the product of a grudge-nursing and cynically nihilistic dysfunctional family who take an injustice-nurturing and negativistic approach.

****

"Unfit for human consumption." They feel very unsafe in the world because bottom line, they feel that don't deserve to be safe or nurtured. They have little or no self-love, and they don't experience other's love.

They are abandonment-anxious and alienation-avoidant and they are highly insecure. They feel universally rejected, and they are very agitated and depressed. They have ended up feeling this is their lot in life, and that they somehow had to handle it, which has resulted in a pattern of constant predictions of and preparation for disaster, with the consequent anger, fear and despair.

This whole pattern started in an unpredictable and unstable dysfunctional family in which there were constant difficulties.

SPRUE (Inability to absorb nutrients)

"Cosmic ejectee." There is a simultaneous profound self-rejection and distrust of the Universe. Their experience is they are so unacceptable that anything the environment has to offer is going to be "poison apples," because that's all they can expect.

It is the result either of some sort of karmic issue, of extreme rejection and accusation by their family, or both.

STAPH INFECTION; STAPHYLOCOCCUS (Picked up in hospitals, clinics, etc.)

"Parental violation -- repeated." They are manifesting their underlying unconscious expectations of being betrayed and invaded that arose from a childhood experience of being repeatedly violated by their dysfunctional and self-serving family.

Their experience is that they are still feeling the effects destructive and self-sabotage-inducing "implants" from their invasive family. They also find that the environment has a way of reproducing their home environment -- complete with all the destructive invasions and violations.

"STEALTH VIRUS" (A parasite that comes in below the threshold of the immune system like a stealth bomber flying under the radar. It leads to exhaustion and irritability that can end up in glandular problems, meningitis, and immune system breakdown.)

"Pooped out." They are pushing beyond their limits, and they have a dread-driven fear of not being good enough, leading to an exhaustion reaction. They were draining all of their inner support, and a stress virus took hold.

They are "running on empty," due to overwhelm and deprivation-exhaustion. They have lost their sense of purposes and direction, of the desire for life, and the wind has gone out of their sails. They have developed a deep fear of life, of taking responsibility, and of coping with any further demands. The illness can become a safe place to be, a retreat from confrontation and action. They are the product of perfectionistic parenting.

****

"Crushed talent." They are undergoing unfulfilled giftedness-suppression, resulting in severe despair-rage, along with emotional commotional episodes of almost psychotic-seeming proportions, and utter exhaustion comparable to Epstein-Barr. They also find themselves being "used" by their gifts, in the form of uncontrollable outbursts and breakouts of their talents in a non-functional and often highly detrimental manner.

They also go into experiences and expressions of intense mental and emotional distress and distortion that are extremely alarming and alienating. They feel possessed by these explosions, and they become quite "run amok-anxious" about it. In addition, they often are possessed by their family, by institutions and/or by spouse figures.

They are the product of extremely possessive and oppressive parenting that got started intra-uterine. They were forbidden and prevented from doing their own thing or from developing their own capabilities, identity and destiny. They were instead forced into playing out their parent(s) (usually the father's) unexpressed destiny.

****

"I stink!" There is a programmed self-rejection that has resulted in a "belly up" of the immune system. It in effect works against them, as if they were allergic to themselves and the world. They were placed in the "family hoist" position of over-responsibility, and they were targeted with the attributed accountability for everything that went wrong in the family -- as if it was a motivated let down betrayal or a personal failure on their part.

This came about as a function of their being a gifted child living in a dysfunctional family who expected them to be able to handle all the family's problems. They played the "hero(ine)" role in the family, and they turned into a work-aholic -- achieve-aholic contribution-freak.

They became very accomplished and independent, with perfectionistic standards around worth-earning arising from unpleasable parenting -- they could never, ever measure up. They ended up validation-starved as a result.

****

"Hands on rescue efforts." They have a huge control trip that doesn't work that arises because they have no sense of their personal worth or value. There is a severe "family betrayal" delusion and a guilt-grabbing propensity, due to their being told in effect that they caused World War II.

It is a "Cinderella/Cinderfella" syndrome where, due to their gifts, they actually tried to "go for the gold ring" of healing their family. In the meantime, the family was severely exploitative and betraying, as they over-whelmingly expected of and over-utilized them.

No one taught them self-care or self-soothing in their first year of life. They were expected to care for the parents instead. They therefore have no sense of entitlement.

There was little nurturance, compassion or protection in infancy, which resulted in very heavy self-numbing and frantic-fanatic efforting to "make up for what they have caused." They were, in effect, abandoned at an early age by expectations of perfection and miracles.

They operated in a chronic flight-fight system arousal in childhood, in a context of continual rejection, blame-throwing, and impossible demands. They are now collapsing, out of a sense of non-deservingness and from having run out of inner resources to pull off the "rabbit in the hat" trick any more.

****

"Overwhelmed." They are into a hapless-helpless-hopeless victimization experience. There is an inability to self-nurture, self-appreciate and self-soothe. As a result of all this, they can sometimes end up being care-coercing of the environment, in a very belated attempt to get the fundamental nurturing they never received.

The family was highly authoritarian, non-supportive and repressive-suppressive from the beginning. Often there was also physical and sexual abuse, along with the intense emotional abuse and deprivation. They were subjected to highly conditional, demanding and self-immersed parenting, and "there was no joy in Bloodville." The whole pattern could be summarized in the phrase, *"It's not allowed!"*

STENOSIS (See SPINE PROBLEMS)

STERILITY

"In over their head." They are experiencing great fear and resistance to the process of life. There is a considerable amount of tension, anxiety, emotional conflict and traumatic shock involved in their life history. They are heavily into competence-anxiety, self-distrust and self-inhibition. It arises from a "blame-throwing" dysfunctional family.

****

"Cold-hearted." It is a case of egotism, selfishness and dishonest feelings being expressed in an ignorant manner. In effect, they don't *want* to be a parent for all the wrong reasons (or maybe for the right reasons, given who they are). They are hard, harsh, cold, judgmental, negative assumptive, angry and blaming. They are manifesting a primitive manner of functioning learned in a similar family.

****

"Not this time around." They don't need to go through the parenting experience, and they are therefore are unconsciously choosing not to sustain the procreation process.

****

"Not time yet!" The child's soul intends to come in, but the circumstances are not appropriate at the moment, for whatever reason.

****

"Are you kidding?!" They have had a long-standing pattern of monastic celibacy in past lives, and they intend to continue the tradition.

****

"Karma." They have a past life history of severe abuse and even murder of children. They are being required to work off that karma before they will be allowed to parent again.

****

"More than one way to skin a cat." The parents are destined to express their generativity in other ways that would prevent, derail or distort proper parenting.

STERNUM PROBLEMS

"Vulnerability-avoidance." They are closing off their "heart center" to avoid any further hurt. They feel a strong need to protect themselves, and they have put up an "invisible Plexiglas shield" around their heart area.

They were systematically subjected to betrayal, and they have also consistently chosen to become involved in exploitative and emotionally abusive relationships. As a result, they have built up a plate of armor around their heart. It started in a dysfunctional and hurtful family of such a nature that they concluded this is their "deserved lot in life."

STIGMATA (Spontaneous fluid or blood flow from hands, feet, the side, etc.)

"The real McCoy." For reasons known only to the soul and the "Home Office" (All That Is), they are serving as an emissary and messenger. This situation is ascertainable by the nature of their functioning, which is impeccable and divinely inspired, within the limits of human imperfection.
****

"Trauma drama." They have such passionate, literalistic and dramatic dedication to an identity as a "persecuted saint" that they are able to psycho-physiologically generate symbolic similarities. They are the product of a denial-dominated and pathologically sex-ploitative family.
****

"True believer." They have a profound devotion to the spiritual life as all that matters, resulting in an altered state of being that includes the identification with the utter dedication to their higher purpose to such a degree that "sympathetic symptoms" have appeared.

It came about as a function of their withdrawal from their severely and intractably dysfunctional family into the "other realms."

(See **CONVERSION DISORDER**)

STOMACH PROBLEMS (Assimilation preparation)

"Oh my God!" They are facing an indigestible or nauseating reality in their life. They are full of dread and fear of the future, and they are highly insecure. They are worried, negativistic and decision-anxious, and they fear new notions.

They feel over-burdened with responsibilities already, and they are highly reluctant to take on new ideas and inputs for fear they will result in further increases in restrictions, requirements and responsibilities.

They have an inability to assimilate experiences -- they can't "stomach" them. They have real trouble digesting ideas, and there is a real incapacity to expand their consciousness and to integrate new information. They are unable to comprehend, and they become confused and demoralized.

They were systematically undermined in their coping capability, competence, and confidence by a highly possessive family who depended on them extensively from early on.
****

"Eating themselves away." They have intense power issues and anger that generate resentment, dislike and bitterness that blocks the digesting and assimilating of experiences, as well as disrupting the ability to accept that which the experiences teach.

They are consumed with anger, and they are highly condemning of other people's success. They are rejecting, over-discriminating, dichotomizing and restricting their consciousness. There is much conflict between their head and heart, between their thought and their feeling functions. They are heavily into denial, repression, rationalism and overly mental evaluation. They are displaying inflexible attitudes and systematic assimilation-avoidance.

They have a pronounced male/female split, and they are intensely rejecting of the energy and qualities of the other gender within themselves (the *"anima"* or the *"animus"*). They are self-motivated to the extreme, and they are counter-dependent in a reaction formation to unresolved dependency needs and emotional conflicts.

They are full of hate and disharmony that profoundly affects their digestion of both their physical and mental food. They were brought up in a very closed system family who took a rejecting, condescending and elitist attitude towards others, and who treated them as the "intimate enemy."

****

"Sustenance-rejecting." They have an underlying self-rejection that leads them to deflect nurturance, support and relevant acceptance. They have a difficult time holding nourishment and manifesting a comfortable home, financial security, and a happy personal life, due to severe guilt and shame feelings.

They are unwilling to accept sustenance due to worth issues, and they feel they shouldn't be included in things. They are super-sensitive, highly apprehensive, and they therefore are easily dominated. There is a huge backlog of profoundly hurt feelings.

They are intensely suppressing their self-commitment in a "shadow-shoving" phobic reaction that generates a repressed subconscious super-selfishness. There is also a deep-seated sense of discouragement, disappointment, dread, despair and depression. They are very weary and tired, and they are rather immobilized and amotivational, out of feeling they don't deserve anything positive. It is the result of a severely shame-inducing dysfunctional family.

GASTRITIS (Irritation of the stomach lining)

"Over-burdened." They feel over-demanded of, exploited and prevented from doing what they want to do with their life. They are afraid to refuse the demands for fear of rejection or abandonment, so they grudgingly carry out their imposed responsibilities. However, they dearly wish they could express their true feelings and selfhood.

It comes from having had their "love-line" contingent upon their performing "up to snuff," and upon their meeting their family's needs first.

****

"Hanging fire." They are laboring under the threat of some sort of pending disaster. They have been operating with intense uncertainty about this and other things for a very long time. There is a feeling of doom about the whole thing.

They come from a severely dysfunctional family in which "things went bump in the night" with often calamitous results continuously.

GASTRO-ENTERITIS (Inflammation of the stomach and intestinal lining)

"Self-devastation fears." They have undergone a prolonged uncertainty about how things are going to come out, along with a pronounced feeling of doom and disaster in the making. They have an inability to say "No" to demands, and they end up selling themselves out. It is due to a fear of rejection and abandonment, with an associated grief, despair and guilt and self-disapproval about the loss of their self-values. Their family was at best highly ambivalent towards them, and they underwent a great deal of acceptance/rejection-anxiety producing experiences.

****

"Doing the impossible with nothing." They are a perfectionistic work-aholic who is trapped in inescapable overwhelming responsibilities. They feel that they just have to absorb whatever they encounter or are required to do, and it is seriously upsetting and irritating them. They deeply wish that they could reject what is not good for them.

They are the product of perfectionistic, judgmental, wrong-making and extremely demanding parents.

STOMACH CANCER

"Vengeance vendetta." They are dedicated to the proposition that they are going to get even for all that has happened to them. They are spiteful and bitterly resentful, and they are full of malice, judgmental condemnation and hatred. They are relentlessly unforgiving, and they are constantly scheming and manipulating for sweet vengeance. They come from a ruthlessly vicious family.

(See **CANCER**)

STREP THROAT

"They're talking about me!" They are being subjected to negative evaluation, to being misjudged, to being unfairly criticized, and to being self-righteously gossiped about. Or they are sure that this is the case. They are full of accusation-hatred. This is an old, familiar pattern, as it happened all the time in their family.
****

"Grief-rage." The sore throat represents a suppressed scream of deprivation-frustration. They feel utterly cut off from other people and they feel unable to express themselves. They feel a profound sense of deprivation, and they have an intense sense of helplessness to do anything about it. They are holding in angry words in reaction to what is happening to them. There is a deep resentment of their situation. The withheld expressions of their feelings, needs and information, their refusal to communicate with themselves or others the truth that needs to be told, is resulting in an inflammation of the communication organ.

This all started in a family in which there was much suppression, secrecy and subterranean sabotage, and anyone who spoke the truth was severely punished or attacked.
****

"Moral cretins!" They are being severely judgmental, hyper-critical and intensely resentful of others. They are also being self-righteously gossipy about them. There is an underlying guilt about all this that is showing up as a rage-raw throat. This pattern of negative evaluations of others came out of a wrong-making and contemptuous family.

"STROKE" (Decreased blood flow to part of the brain usually, due to a burst blood vessel in the brain)

"Serve-aholic." They tend to become engaged in compulsive and co-dependent compassion, and to become involved in taking on the problems of the world in an "unsung hero(ine)" pattern. They then get burned out and resentfully burned up about the lack of recognition and support in their lives.

Now they have finally reached the point where they are feeling overwhelmed with the requirements of life, and they are giving up. They are in effect trying to put an end to it all. It is the result of being the "family hoist" in a severely dysfunctional, exploitative and self-immersed family.
****

"Intense bitterness." They have a narrowed, constricted and compressed flow of love energy in their life. It is the result of a subconscious death wish that leads to their rejecting life at a deep level. They have a "No one cares" attitude and an intense resistance to people and things.

They are rejecting life, and they would rather die than change. They are in effect viciously violent towards themselves in their attitudes and in their behavior. They are the product of an authoritarian, condemning and intensely judgmental family.

"ST. VITUS' DANCE" (Involuntary muscular actions)

"Support-preventing." There have had a severe sense of deprivation and degradation all their life. It results in a "self-fulfilling prophecy" effect of driving away of those who might support and love them. It started in a severely rejecting family, and they took it all personally, so that underlying all of this is a basic assumption they and everybody else are no damned good.

(See **HUNTINGTON'S CHOREA**)

SWALLOWING DIFFICULTY

"Look before you leap." They have an unwillingness to "swallow" things in a "hook, line and sinker" manner. They are now having difficulty accepting *anything* for fear of being "had" again. They learned in their dysfunctional family not to take things at face value, and to "toe-test" so as to not get taken in by what seems to be going down.

~~~~~~

GETTING FOOD, PILLS, ETC., STUCK IN THEIR THROAT

"Wizard of Ought." They tend to get caught up in their pictures of how things *should* be, with the result that they are focused on desired outcomes, or the next event or undertaking, as they try to do too much at once or too fast, while not paying attention to the process of the moment. They are prone to be not present in themselves and in the realities of now, as they run their life out of their conceptions of how things *ought* to be. It is a pattern that started in a judgmental and achieve-aholic family.

SWALLOWING REPEATEDLY

"Swallow-wallowing." They are lost in fearfulness about being "caught in the act." They feel they are doing something wrong, and that they are going to be discovered and given their "just punishment." They were made to feel "evil" and deserving of punishment for having wants, needs and desires as a child, and it is now an obsessional pattern with them.

SWELLING

"Plugged drains." They are being stuck in their thinking, and they are "all clogged up" with painful ideas and negative feelings. They can't let go of the past, and they are full of remembrance-resentment. They refuse to flow and grow out of being trapped in the past and afraid of the future.

They are emotionally resisting the flow of life, and they are holding back their feelings. They are afraid to express or experience their feelings, for fear they will be inappropriate, that they will lead to disastrous consequences, or that they will be harmed if they do so. Their family was highly feeling-avoidant and emotionally suppressive.

"SWELLING UP"

"Holding on." They are not letting go of something or someone, and they are resistant to changes. They are hanging on to the past for fear that if they let go, something awful will happen. They are repressing, denying or clutching to inner feelings and urges. They feel emotionally trapped in the direction they are going in, and they feel unable to emotionally assert themselves to bring any release. They had to grit and bear it in their rigidly restricting dysfunctional family.
****

"Over-burdened." They feel like they are carrying a heavy load on their shoulders, an overload of responsibility. They want to share the load, but they are afraid to ask for fear of alienating and losing what support they do have.

It's a "Cinderella/Cinderfella" pattern in which they were held accountable and responsible for the needs and situations of everyone and everything in their family, while the only support they got came from that "unsung hero(ine)" role in a "serve-aholic" situation.
****

"Love-starved." They are desperate for love and afraid of the loss of love. Water retention is in effect stored grief from this whole situation and life history. It comes from a fear that any change will result in the loss of even more in their life.

They'd rather keep things as they are than take a chance that they will end up with nothing, which is what they fully expect is their "just desserts" for all the "failures" of their "care-taking," as represented by the negative events in their family's history.
****

"Clutching/clinging." They have a great fear of losing something vital to their survival and acceptability as a human being. They are intensely abandonment-paranoid and approval-enslaved, and they are into severe self-suppressing and pleasing-appeasing patterns as a rejection-deflection strategy. They are also prone to highly possessive and jealous patterns in their relationships.

It is the result of being placed on very conditional acceptance from very early on. They had to earn their "love-line," which of course "meant" that "God said" that they don't deserve love, -- they "earn" it by "selling out" and hating themselves for it.

SYMPATHETIC NERVOUS SYSTEM PROBLEMS

"Grief-stricken." They are more or less immobilized by their long-standing devastation reaction to their early history of deprivation and non-nurturing. They were more or less left to their own devices from the very beginning, and they have an underlying belief that they got their "just desserts."
****

"Despair-dominated." They have the feeling that nothing they do can change the downhill slide that their life seems to be taking. They are the product of an implacably dysfunctional family who systematically undermined their capacity for independent and effective functioning.
****

"Atonement-freak." They are convinced that they are responsible for World War II, and they are on a systematic "karma-payback" effort. They come from a highly accusatory, accountability-attributing and demandingly-dependent dysfunctional family.
****

314

"Red-orange alert." They are continuously in a state of mild agitation, somewhat along the lines of Don Knotts in his constant anxiety mode. They feel somehow at least slightly endangered at all times. It comes from growing up in an unpredictably dysfunctional family in which things would come at them "off the wall," so to speak.

****

"Chronically angry." They are forever feeling thwarted, invaded, and even violated. They are instantly irritable and resentfully reactive most of the time. They are the product of a severely frustrating and unassailably dysfunctional family who continuously subjected them to enraging experiences.

"SYNDROME X" ("Spare tire," high cholesterol, high blood pressure, elevated blood triglycerides)

"Love-starvation." They have a desperate longing to belong, yet they are intensely emotionally insulated. They also experience much social isolation, with a resulting self-sustaining self-nurturance pattern. They are a self-protective "urban hermit" who was continuously blamed, in an "If it weren't for *you* . . ." pattern.

They ended up believing that they don't deserve any better, so they have withdrawn from social involvement on any close or vulnerable level, and they have turned to self-sustaining love-substitutes such as carbohydrates, sugar and pasta.

(See **DIABETES -- TYPE II**)

SYPHILIS

"Moral cretin." They are giving away their power and effectiveness to the evaluations of others. They are self-rejecting and ashamed of themselves for being who they are. As a part of this, they have severe sexual guilt and a need for punishment. They believe that their genitals are "sinful," "dirty" and "evil," due to puritanical and punitive and simultaneously prurient and sexualizing parenting.

~~~~~~

DEMENTIA DUE TO SYPHILIS

"Gradually leaving." They have a strong belief in not being "good enough,"   with much self-intolerance, self-rejection and self-destructive potential. There is also severe sexual guilt imposed by an over-possessive and seductive-received little or no love/ acceptance from the very beginning.

It is in effect a severe maternal deprivation and familial denigration reaction. They therefore are "following orders" and leaving the planet by self-harming degrees.

TABES DORSALIS (Gradual paralysis and disrupted movement, due to syphilis)

"One and only one way." They are getting stuck, due to paralyzing thoughts. They are fixated on a particular mind set, mental approach, and paradigmatic model. They want to "make things all right," out of having to be the one responsible for everything that happens. However, they are extremely rigid in how they think that should be.

They are trapped in implication-terror at the thought of things being different from what they imagine or of trying a new approach to things. They come from a similar family system.

****

315

"Cosmic paranoia." They are full of guilt and rejection of life, they are not able to forgive others or themselves. They have an intensely anxious relationship with the Universe that is full of fear, uncertainty and insecurity. They have a "God will KILL me if I do anything different!" feeling. They have ended up feeling stagnated and immobilized.

It is the result of a very rigid adaptation to a severely dysfunctional and frightening family who themselves manifested a very fearfully narrow viewpoint and lifestyle. They played the role of the "family hoist" who was the pivotal point of everything.

~~~~~~

SYSTEMIC INFECTION (Out-of-control yeast, protozoa, bacterial, viral, parasitic or other infestations)

"Going up in flames." They are totally enraged at their situation in an all-consuming massive irritation, frustration and outrage reaction. It is a festering condition that is resulting in breakdown of their whole system. They feel cosmically abandoned and betrayed, and they are "running on empty" in profound sorrow.

There is a deep grief, despair, demoralization and devastation experience that results in a "What's the use?" response to the overwhelming inequity of energy exchange in their life. They experience being "asked to do the impossible with nothing" in completely intolerable circumstances.

They had to carry the world on their shoulders in a massively dysfunctional family in which they could do nothing to improve the situation, and yet they were still expected to "make it all better."

The result was a draconian "Cinderella/Cinderfella" profoundly abusive exploitation situation. This can sometimes result in a possession (invasive takeover) by a non-material primitive and/or "evil" being.

TABES DORSALIS (See **SYPHYLIS**)

TACHYCARDIA [Sudden bursts of rapid heart beating] (See **ARRYTHMIA**)

"TAIL BONE" PROBLEMS [Coccyx] (See **SPINAL PROBLEMS**)

TAPEWORM (Digestive system parasite that is about 1/4 inch wide and very long)

"Unclean." They are experiencing self-disgust and self-rejection, along with a strong belief in being a victim. In both a reactive enslavement and a self-fulfilling prophecy manner, they have a sense of helplessness and an utter vulnerability to the seeming attitudes of others as being "God's Gospel Truth."

They then become what was said, or they elicit the negative responses to themselves. They were massively shame-induced by their family.
****

"Goodie-getting." They are consumed with materialistic ambitions, abundance-seeking, and comfort concerns. Sophisticated greediness eats away at them. It arose from a highly self-involved family system that was operating out of an underlying survivalist mentality.

TARDIC DYSKINESIA (Uncoordinated involuntary movements precipitated by psychiatric medication)

"So you think you got away, do you?" They were severely programmed by their family to fail in all aspects of effective functioning. Their attempt to restore some semblance of sanity to their beingness has activated an "Oh no you don't!" sub-routine designed to prevent them from ever engaging in self-committed destiny-manifestation.

TEETH PROBLEMS

"No more putting off." They are being forced to deal with their oldest unresolved issues that span many lifetimes. The area involved is that of responsibility, and as a result, they lack vitality and aggressiveness, due to their great conflict about it.

There are two possible scenarios involved here:

1) "Indecisiveness." Problems in this area are being reflective of long-standing inability to come to decisions that is due to an inability to break things down for analysis and choice-making.

They are prone to be undisciplined in their attitudes and expression, and they are manifesting negligence in their life-management. They are systematically power-avoidant, responsibility-deflecting, unambitious, assertiveness-suppressing, and lacking in determination.

The resulting build-up and sudden release of "Reggie the Raging Room-Wrecker" frustrated rage-outs are one of several processes by which they are therefore unsuccessful in money matters and intimacy. They simply have no idea what the principles of truth and right action are.

The pattern is the result of a systematically power-derailing, competence-undermining, and responsibility-deflecting possessive parenting pattern involving interference-running, do-for-ing, under-requiring, or demoralization- and immobilization-inducting.

2) "Immobilization." They are experiencing overwhelm reactions, due to feeling compelled or required to take on responsibilities that are in effect way over their head. They tend to "bite off more than they can chew," in terms of their capacities and motivational structure.

As a result, they are being inundated with requirements and felt accountabilities. They have not developed or they have lost the ability to set priorities and boundaries, and they are caught up in a "parent-rescue" psychology.

It comes from their having long-standing soul guilt around past life patterns of irresponsibility, coupled with being expected to be the "family hoist" and to "make things all better."

When these expectations were far too much for them to handle as a child, they became targeted for much accusation, attribution and guilt/shame-induction, as if they were the cause of all their family's problems, and as if they were cosmically required to "atone for" and to "make up for" all they have "caused."

RIGHT TEETH

"Hunkering down in the bunker." They are having difficulties in coming to terms with the necessity to develop deliberate conscious attitudes and actions in the world. They were likely to have been hampered in comprehending and mastering the processes of cope-ability.

LEFT TEETH

"Over-mental." They tend to have difficulty handling their instinctual, intuitive, spontaneous, unconscious and non-calibrating reactions. They were trained to be oblivious to how to track or manage this part of their functioning.

UPPER TEETH

"Competence-avoidance." They tend to have problems with coming to effective decisions. They also have problems with authority -- their own. They are the product of an oppressive patriarchal family and/or of a confidence- and competence-undermining enmeshed family.

LOWER TEETH

"Outsider." They are rather resistive to responsibility and receiving, both. They feel not part of the world, alien, incompetent and/or alienated. They were simultaneously under-required and denigrated in their enmeshed, blame-throwing dysfunctional family.

Every tooth pertains to a tendency, trait and/or soul lesson. The following is a map of these qualities, presented in the order that they present themselves to us. Dentists number the teeth sequentially, starting with the right upper jaw most back tooth and going to the most back left upper tooth, and then the numbers go from the most far back left bottom tooth to the most far back right bottom tooth. These numbers appear with each tooth.

RIGHT FRONT INCISOR (Top Center) [# 8]

"Anger-agitated." They tend to have problems with resentment, perhaps even to the point of combativeness and violence-proneness. It is a pattern generated by parenting which was insufficiently structuring. Although they were apt to have "gotten away with murder," they tend to have no sense of sustenance or support from the environment.

SECOND TOP RIGHT [# 7]

"Rootless." They have a propensity to be "footloose and fancy-free," and to have difficulty in their ability to commit or settle down. It is the result of having a "special relationship" with the parent(s) that however was never grounded or solidified, and that tended to be rather gamey and manipulative.

THIRD TOP RIGHT (Canine) [# 6]

"Constant correcting." They are prone to be critical of their intimates, in a shift-over of the resentment they feel toward the capacity-undermining parent(s). They feel that "love is a poison apple," and that it is therefore rather untrustworthy.

FOURTH TOP RIGHT [# 5]

"Perennial child." They have a pattern of displaying a propensity to not take things seriously. They are apt to be rather flippant, and they may lack maturity. Underneath, they have something of a self-respect, self-acceptance and sense of self-worth problem. This is a pattern that was generated by non-requiring and over-doting parenting.

FIFTH TOP RIGHT [# 4]

"Perennial adolescent." They have a tendency to be sarcastic, impudent and rebellious towards their intimates. Bottom line, they were undermined in their ability to be self-expressive, creative, and sexually mature. It resulted from parental interference with their independence-, initiative- and identity-formation processes.

SIXTH TOP RIGHT [# 3]

"Erotic over-do." They tend to display some under-control of their sexual and affectional impulses, due to having been sexualized and interference-run in a "special relationship" with their mother.

SEVENTH TOP RIGHT [# 2]

"Urban hermit." They are likely to be an "among us but not of us" type of person. They have been more or less alone on their own all their life, due to a rather self-immersed and convenience-concerned parenting.
****

"Opportunistic." They tend to want to live by their wits and to milk things for what they can get out of them, with insufficient regard for their environmental impact. It is a result of convenience-concerned parenting that let them "get away with things" as long as it didn't interfere with the parent(s) "comfort zone."

319

EIGHTH TOP RIGHT [# 1]

"Tendency to larceny." They have a propensity to want to operate in a manner in which they seek to sneak one by on people. It's the result of being shaped to unilaterally seek to get their way a lot when they were growing up.

****

"Visiting anthropologist." They are something of a cultural outsider who does not subscribe to the interpretations and values of the mainstream. They have had to fend for themselves from the very beginning, as they were in effect shoved to the sidelines of their family. They have been at the sidelines of society ever since, believing it is their just desserts and the only way they can live.

LEFT FRONT INCISOR (Top Center) [# 9]

"Space case." They tend to lack a sense of groundedness for practical operation. They are likely to have not had to figure things out for themselves, and they therefore don't know themselves, the world, or the Cosmos.

SECOND TOP LEFT [# 10]

"Rudderless." They are rather nervousness and anxious, because they are a bit uncertain as to how to navigate through the world. They feel they have little sense of foundation, and there is a resulting rather unsettled feeling regarding their guidance system. They feel they got little support or guidance for developing their values and comprehension of things.

THIRD TOP LEFT (Canine) [# 11]

"Irritability." They tend to have some anger issues, and they may even display some violent propensities toward their intimates, because of a transfer of their resentment of their parent for tending to derail their destiny with their "love."

FOURTH TOP LEFT [# 12]

"Erotic self-defeat propensity." They tend to have problems in the control of their sexual impulses, due to sexualizing parenting. This tends to undermine their self-trust, self-acceptance, and their sense of self-worth.

FIFTH TOP LEFT [# 13]

"Love-aholic." They tend to be prone to "sudden romantic attractions." This indicates that they are uncertain of their worth, and that they are rather afraid of manifesting their self-expression, creativity and sexuality.

They are also vulnerable to a sense of personal powerlessness and dependency on others' evaluations of them. They were undermined in their sense of their love-ability by "love-gamey" parenting.

SIXTH TOP LEFT [# 14]

"Stranger in a strange land." They feel somehow different and like an outsider, because they were systematically shaped into being a misfit in society by possessive parents.

SEVENTH TOP LEFT [# 15]

"Unfit for human consumption." They have the experience of being somehow unacceptable, as a function of their not fitting into their family system from the very beginning, with the result that the family tended to eject them.

EIGHTH TOP LEFT [# 16]

"Alien." They feel somehow strange, weird and even non-human, due their being of a different soul nature from their family and/or due to rejection and accusations of deviance by their family.

BOTTOM RIGHT CENTRAL [# 25]

"Sustenance-avoidance." They tend to be "allergic" to nourishment and nurturance, including a number of foods. This is a function of the fact that they tended to be rejected at the emotional level by their family.

SECOND BOTTOM RIGHT [# 26]

"Studied incompetence." They are prone to be unable to function effectively in the world, and to be thereby self-defeating. It is a reaction to competence- and confidence-undermining parenting.

THIRD BOTTOM RIGHT [# 27]

"Shooting themselves in the foot." They tend to be somewhat self-sabotaging in their functioning, due to belittling parenting patterns.

FOURTH BOTTOM RIGHT [# 28]

"Self-put downs." They are apt to be rather self-denigrating, as a result of negating and accusatory parenting.

FIFTH BOTTOM RIGHT [# 29]

"Self-undermining." They tend to be success-avoidant, and to experience setbacks, losses and non-optimal of quality of life. It comes from being accused and guilt-induced as a child.

SIXTH BOTTOM RIGHT [# 30]

"Self-defeating." They are apt to be self-undermining in their attitudes and patterns, due to being made to feel somehow unacceptable for being who they are.

SEVENTH BOTTOM RIGHT [# 31]

"Potentially self-endangering." They tend to be somewhat self-destructive in their orientation and inclinations, as a result of rather accusatory and rejecting parenting.

EIGHTH BOTTOM RIGHT [# 32]

"Self-rejection." They have something of a pattern of self-destructive activities, due to being left more or less to their own devices from early childhood.

BOTTOM LEFT CENTRAL [# 24]

"3-D focused." They tend to have a rather over-materialistic orientation and philosophy. It reflects a similar immersion in the world of the senses by their parents.

SECOND BOTTOM LEFT [# 23]

"Is it for real?" They are apt to be rather rejecting of spiritual issues, of religion, and of matters of faith. They were rather poorly received and integrated by their mother in the beginning, and as a result, they have trust of the Universe issues.

THIRD BOTTOM LEFT [# 22]

"Nonsense!" They tend to devalue religion, spiritual issues and matters of faith. They are the product of rather materialistic and selfish parenting that denigrated the sacred realm.

FOURTH BOTTOM LEFT [# 21]

"Cynical inclinations." They tend to have a somewhat nihilistic and pessimistic in their orientation. It arises from a rather self-immersed and self-serving parenting history.

FIFTH BOTTOM LEFT [# 20]

"Depressive." They are apt to have something of a despairing orientation, due to rather unconcerned parenting.

SIXTH BOTTOM LEFT [# 19]

"God is Al Capone!" They are inclined to have the feeling that the world is sort of a "mafia arrangement" -- with them on the "hit list." It comes from a rather intensely self-immersed and self-serving parenting approach where they punished the individual if they got in the family's way.

SEVENTH BOTTOM LEFT [# 18]

"Despairing." They are apt to be a tendency to a "What's the use?" orientation on their part, as a result of having grown up in a non-impactably self-immersed family.

EIGHTH BOTTOM LEFT [# 17]

"Amotivational." They have a propensity to be rather demoralized and uninterested in things. It is a pattern that arises from rather neglectful and uncaring parenting.

~~~~~~

BREAKING OR LOSING FILLINGS

"Immobilized." They are feeling overwhelmed and unable to cope with their current challenges, stresses and difficulties. It arises from intense competence- and confidence-undermining parenting.

****

"Clearing up." Old patterns and issues regarding decision-making, taking stands, understanding what is happening, and the like are leaving, due to healing processes.

(See the particular teeth involved for more information)

"DRY SOCKET" (Tooth infection)

"Desert island." They feel somehow ostracized as a pariah, and that they are somehow "unfit for human consumption." They were severely rejected, neglected and blamed as a child.

FILLING REACTION (Mercury)

"Vulnerable-feeling." They are having real problems with mental and/or emotional experiences of weakness and impactability. Life's vicissitudes and difficulties have undermined their sense of safety.

There is a disruption of the flow of communication in the form of input-deflecting and/or expression-suppressing. They are freaked out and distrusting of the Universe, and they feel that they have to be on "red-orange alert" with "hands on" control of everything.

The current situation is giving them the sense that they are back in their significantly dysfunctional family, in which they were the "sane one" upon whom everything and everyone depended, and where they were in way over their head.

LOSING ENAMEL

"I'm here alone on my own." They feel intensely vulnerable and unprotected around decision-making issues. Their family stayed more or less uninvolved unless the individual did, or they decided, something the family didn't like, and then the family attacked.

(See the information above for more understanding of what is occurring)

LOSING TEETH

"Indecisiveness." They are manifesting learned helplessness and difficulty in making decisions arising from insufficient nurturance, grounding and teaching when they were growing up.

(See the information above on the particular tooth or teeth involved for more understanding of what is occurring)

METAL TEETH PROBLEMS

"Working on it." They are intensively trying to overcome the difficulties indicated by problems with the particular teeth that have been made metal.

(See the information above for more understanding)

PYORRHEA (Inflammation of the teeth sockets)

"Wimp-wilt." They are angry at their inability to make decisions, as they live out a "wishy-washy gutless wonder" lifestyle. They are the product of a systematically confidence- and competence-undermining and potency-punishing "keep 'em around the old homestead" possessive parenting pattern.

"ROOT CANAL" (Boring out the decayed pulp center of the root of a tooth)

"Lost at sea." They can't seem to "bite into" anything any more. Their foundational beliefs and ways of doing things are being destroyed, and as a result, they have lost their grounding and their roots. They feel rudderless and directionless.

It is a result of the emergence of multi-life issues that they haven't been able to handle, and that must be handled now around responsibility-taking, decision-making, and direction-setting.

This all arose out of having had to adapt to a significantly dysfunctional family, with the result they had to adopt erroneous and self-defeating assumptions and strategies.

TEMPORO-MANDIBULAR JOINT ("TMJ") PROBLEMS

"Utterly derailed." They are undergoing total frustration at their inability to make things happen the way they want. They feel it is very important to move things in a direction that will deflect disaster, and they feel completely thwarted in their efforts to make things go the way they

323

need to. It comes from growing up in a significantly dysfunctional family in which they were made to feel responsible for making things work, and they couldn't.

RIGHT JOINT PROBLEMS
"I didn't want *that!*" They are experiencing intense frustration regarding the results of how they go about doing things.

LEFT JOINT PROBLEMS
"Forced suppression." They are intensely frustrated with not being allowed or able to be themselves.

~~~~~~

"TMJ" SYNDROME -- TEETH-GRINDING VERSION (Tempero-Mandible Joint)
"Keep a tight grip!" They have intensely repressed and suppressed rage at their situation which they dare not express. They keep their mouth firmly clamped shut. They don't trust themselves as far as they can throw and grand piano, and they are full of "run amok-anxiety."

They are hugely frustrated with the state of the world, and they desperately want to re-form it, but they have consistently "run into a brick wall" of resistance of refusal from the world. They are "ready to kill" about it.

This reflects a history of their trying to "make things all better" in their dysfunctional family, in the context of perfectionist expectations of them. The result was that no matter what they did, it didn't work, and they are desperately frustrated about their inability to get the "God Housekeeping Seal of Approval," and about their lack of success in making the world work.

RIGHT TEETH-GRINDING "TMJ"
"HOW did I do *that?*" They are experiencing intense frustration regarding the results of how they go about doing things.

LEFT TEETH-GRINDING "TMJ"
"Don't be you!" They are intensely frustrated with not being allowed or able to be themselves.

~~~~~~

"TMJ" SYNDROME -- TRAUMATIC VERSION (Tempero-Mandible Joint)
"You'll pay for this!" They are experiencing a frustrated inability to translate their feelings and intentions into effective action. Their determination has found no place to go, and it has therefore turned into resentment-rage, revulsion, and revenge motivation.

They are utterly disgusted with the way things keep turning out, and they have reached the point where "This is an up with which I will no longer put!" They intend to "set things straight," no matter what it takes.

This whole pattern started in a family in which they were held accountable and responsible for what went down in the family, but in which they were given no functional power to make a difference in how things went down.

RIGHT TRAUMATIC "TMJ"

"God damn it all!" They are experiencing intense frustration regarding the results of how they go about doing things.

LEFT TRAUMATIC "TMJ"

"I want to be *me!*" They are intensely frustrated with not being allowed or able to be themselves.

TENDON PROBLEMS

"Sitting on themselves." There is a deep conflict between what they think they should be doing or going down and what their poisonous "inner voice" is saying that they should do. They are engaged in excessive self-control and fear of letting go.

The fear is of falling in love, of losing touch with reality, of losing consciousness, of being rejected, of being abandoned, of being taken advantage of, of loss of support, of loss of self, of "running amok," and/or of annihilation.

The result is excessive self-control and fear of letting go, along with a refusal to manifest full maturity and stature. They have a certain rigidity and tenacity of their concepts, and they are quite unforgiving of themselves.

They are "freaked out for dear life" by their "dangerous environment" perceptions, and by their equally powerful self-distrust, both of which were generated by a deeply distrusting and distrust-inducing family.

~~~~~~

TENALGIA (Pain in the tendons)

"I don't *DARE!*" They are exercising excessive self-control, and they have a pronounced fear of letting go, due to strong underlying self-distrust and self-non-forgivingness.

They are "freaked out for dear life" by their "dangerous environment" perceptions, and by equally powerful self-distrust, both of which were generated by a deeply distrusting and distrust-inducting family.

TENDONITIS (Inflammation of the tendons)

"Intention irritations." They are intensely inner conflicted about where they are going, and about what they are doing. They are thoroughly frustrated with what is happening in their life, but they are deeply afraid of and guilt-inhibited about changing how they are operating.

They have a strong case of "run amok-anxiety," in the form of a great fear of what would happen if they "let go and let fly" with themselves. So they "sit and seethe." It is a pattern that started in a deeply distrusting and self-distrust-inducing family.

TESTICLE PROBLEMS

"Requirement-deflecting." They are into generativity-resistance and responsibility-avoidance. They don't want to have to deal with the demands of child-rearing or of follow-through on projects and undertakings.

It arises from an under-requiring and over-indulgent parenting pattern, especially by the mother, in a "keep him around the old homestead" subconscious motivation.

****

"Maturity-avoidance." They have a fear of growing up and of their masculinity, which was generated by a "tripod-raging" mother (she had an irresistible urge to kick anything with three legs). She wanted him to remain an "eternal boy," to be there for her as a "safe" male element.
****

"Held by the balls." They are struggling with powerlessness feelings. They feel that they are being taken over, that they are being restricted and restrained. There may also be a fear of losing their masculinity, if it is a woman they feel has "grabbed their balls." It comes from having been reared by a severely domineering family, mother in particular.
****

"Masculinity-anxiety." They have fears, insecurities and doubts about their abilities, and about being a man. There may be conflicts about sexual preference or about sexuality itself. There are likely to be deep concerns about their ability to perform and about their potency. It is the result of systematic undermining and/or denigration by their family when they were growing up.

RIGHT TESTICLE PROBLEM
"Doing it wrong." They have issues around how they want to manifest their creativity or generativity (care-taking today and building tomorrow) -- around how they are going about manifesting it. It comes from a lot of wrong-making about how they went about doing things as a child.

LEFT TESTICLE PROBLEM
"What if . . .?" They are having conflicts about what it is that they want to manifest with their creativity or generativity. It arises from self-distrust activated by negative assumptive parenting.

(See **GENITAL PROBLEMS -- MALE; PROSTATE PROBLEMS**)

TESTOSTERONE PROBLEMS (Male hormone)
"Initiative issues." They are being disrupted in their ability to be effectively assertive, creatively instigating, confronting, aggressive, enduring, strong, etc. They are undergoing difficulties with these impact-making and difference-making motivations and resources. It arises from distorted and dysfunctional parenting patterns with regard to the manifestation of the creative initiative process.

LOW TESTOSTERONE
They are having problems with male shame, amotivational syndrome, effective castration, or other confidence-, competence- and/or one-pointedness-undermining feelings and manifestations. They were subjected to initiative-negating and wrong-making parenting.

HIGH TESTOSTERONE
They are being prone to be aggressive, over-bearing, excessively willful and or insensitive in their functioning. They were, in effect, overly conceded to and "privileged position" parented.

(See **HORMONAL PROBLEMS**)

TETANUS; TETANY (Spasmodic contraction of the muscles)

"Immobilized by rage." They are full of suppressed rage and festering thoughts activated by their seething volcano-based desire to control everything, along with a systematic refusal to express their feelings. They don't trust the process of life, and they are full of resentment regarding what they regard as the absolute untrustworthiness of the world.

They are convinced that if they ever asked for what they wanted, it would be deliberately withheld from them. They feel constantly betrayed, and they are thoroughly enraged about it. Not only that, they feel that the information would be used against them.

For the same reasons, they in effect can't express their feelings, reactions and interpretations. Their experience is it is dangerous to let the world know where they are coming from and what's happening with them.

They even believe that violence is the answer to many of life's situations. They are trying to control their rage before they run amok with it. It ends up in constant contractions of both the extensors and flexors, ending up in immobilization and spasms.

It is the result of coming from a highly distrusting, untrustworthy, extortionistic and coercive control-manifesting family. They are passing on what they learned at home.

THALAMUS PROBLEM (See BRAIN PROBLEMS)

THIGH PROBLEMS

"Cope-ability-anxiety." There is a paralysis of action, an immobilization, a fear of the future at present. They have strong fears concerning their having inadequate capacity, potency and strength. They tend to be success-avoidant, self-restricting, and denying themselves of support.

They feel unlovable, and they are vulnerability-, intimacy- and sexuality-avoidant. They were systematically confidence-undermined, and their sense of worth was consistently denigrated by their possessive family. The net effect is a lot of stored grief over all the deprivation and sex-ploitation, and they have severe issues about lack of support and of strength to support themselves and others.

The family did a "keep 'em around the old homestead" program on the individual which was designed to effectively prevent the individual's capacity to cope, succeed, connect and be involved in intimacy.

RIGHT THIGH

"Damage-control." They have major conflicts regarding how they go about manifesting their strength and providing themselves support. They have considerable difficulty accepting commitments in the world, and in giving support to friends, coworkers and colleagues. They also distrust and don't know how to relate to fellow workers and fellow travelers in the world at large.

They don't know how to handle the world of manifestation, environmental impact, and legacy-leaving very well, because all that was systematically undermined in childhood.

LEFT THIGH

"Am I up to it?" They are very unsure of their personal potency and strength. They aren't certain they can count on it or whether they have enough of what it takes to make it. They also have great difficulty receiving support, with intimate love and with sexual connection. All of this came about because of an extremely exclusive claim-laying that their parent(s) did on them.

~~~~~~

INNER THIGH
"Sexual shame." They are engaged in sexual guilt and incest-avoidance. They feel both immoral for having an erotic nature and emotionally inhibited in sexuality, due to the sex-ploitive parenting pattern they experienced.

OUTER THIGH
"Potency-shame." They are handicapped by systematic success-avoidance. They feel it would somehow be "parenticide" to develop their environmental impact capabilities or to manifest their destiny, due to the intense possessiveness of the parenting they underwent.

THROAT PROBLEMS
"Grief-rage." It is a case of intense sorrow-resentment over all the pain and deprivation they have experienced. They are full of criticism and judgment about how the world is, and they want no part of it any more.

They have reached the point where they are "gagging" on it, and they can't swallow any more of what life has been giving them. They've had enough, thank you, and screw you all! They are the product of a severely self-immersed dysfunctional family.
****

"Feeling-avoidance." They are deeply suppressing their emotions, and they are intensely avoidant of self-expression. They have an inability to speak up for themselves, out of a feeling that they have no right to "make noise."

There is also a fear that what they would express would set off World War III. They are "sitting on" themselves, and they are stifling their creativity, expressivity and transmission of information.

They are afraid of power, and they have catastrophic expectations of what uses and abuses of anything they would put into words would be subjected to. They are afraid to articulate what they know, feel, want and sense. They grew up in a repressive and oppressive denial-dominated and blame-throwing/accusatory family.
****

"Vast wasteland." Their family was withholding, with no nurturance, and any time they did get something, it was invariably taken away. They have had many loses and much insufficiency. They have had to swallow a lot of hurts without saying anything, and they are very angry about that -- but they dare not let that out. They are over-concerned with possessions as "security blankets." They underwent severely repressive and suppressive enforcement of the "seen and not heard" mode.
****

"Reality-refusal." They are having difficulty with resistance or reluctance to accept their reality, and they don't know how to take it in. They are experiencing a lot of confusion, and they are lacking in discernment.

They therefore tend to utilize their knowledge in insensitive, inappropriate and harmful manner. They come from an intensely denial-dominated and uninterruptible dysfunctional family.
****

"Pulled in." They have some very deep distrust of the Universe issues, and they are like a turtle in its shell, refusing to come out. The feeling is very, very strong that it is just too dangerous and disastrous to open their mouth and speak out their truth.

So they keep their peace, huddle in their shell, and stuff their creativity. Their life history has been replete with oppression and deprivation in a highly authoritarian and abusive household.
****

"No way, Jose!" They are under a great deal of pressure to change their way of being and functioning in their present circumstances. They have decided to "hunker down in the bunker" to ride out the siege, but they are *not* going to change, as far as they are concerned.

They are the product of an entrenched conservative family system who felt extremely strongly that theirs was the *only* way to fly. Or they decided to withdraw from the family fray early on, and to march to their own drummer, come what may.

RIGHT THROAT

"Dare I say it?" Their fear is that if they speak out or express what they know, the environment will abuse or misuse what they have shared.

LEFT THROAT

"I'll cause World War III!" They are either "run amok-anxious" self-distrusting and/or afraid that if they express themselves, it will result in the people in their environment abusing it, misusing it, or "losing it."

THRUSH (Fungus in the mouth)

"What have I DONE?!" They are very angry about having made the *wrong* decisions. It is a "TIGA!" ("There I go *again!)* self-distrust and self-disgust reaction. It comes from a family who focused heavily on what went wrong with everything, and who were intensely harm-avoidant. They hated hassles and trauma, and they made it very clear to the individual that if the individual is going to do or decide anything, they had better get it RIGHT!

THYMUS GLAND PROBLEMS ("Master gland" of the immune system)

"Singled out for shit." There is a consistent lack of fulfillment in their life, and they have many difficulties of living. They have taken a passive responsibility-deflecting approach in desperation, because nothing else seems to work.

They have the experience that they are being persecuted, and they experience life in a "Just because I'm paranoid doesn't mean they're not out to get me!" manner. They feel picked on and besieged from all sides on all issues. They literally feel attacked by life and by the Universe. It's so intense that it is seriously affecting their immunity to environmental irritants and traumas.

Underneath all the survival struggle and feeling assaulted stuff is the Big Question, "Why Me?" and their conclusion in their guts is that they asked for it by being who and what they are inherently. The siege started in the womb, and it has never let up, so they have a "gut conclusion" that they somehow deserve it. So the breakdown of the immune system is a response to both external attack and internal feelings of culpability.

It is the result of being treated like the "intimate enemy" in their family, with a resulting "self-fulfilling prophecy effect" subsequently revalidating that nothing has changed, and that they continue to deserve such treatment. It is, of course, a "delusional conclusion," but it is one that seems to have had all of reality on its side from the "git-go."

THYROID PROBLEMS (Neck gland that secretes life-vital substances)

"But not for me." They have a very strong experience in life in which everything seems to be made and geared for everyone but them. They feel that everyone else has some sort of secret for success that they will never have.

For some reason involving a mysterious set of inherent "moral cretinisms" and limitations on their part, above and beyond the ones they actually know about, they are just never destined to have success, quality of life or love, as they experience it. They feel that they have no right to express who they are, to develop, to put out and apply their creativity, or to succeed. They are the product of a withholding, suppressive and depriving dysfunctional family.
****

"Persona non grata." They get loud and clear that no one wants to hear from them. They are utterly and universally humiliated by being the *only* one who doesn't fit, who doesn't get any support, who has to scrounge up and "spit-and-haywire" together what they need, who no one wants anything to do with, etc., etc., etc. They were the ejectee/rejectee/dejectee of their family who had to do everything for themselves on their own hook.
****

"Humiliation-rage." They have a great deal of humiliation about the fact that no one respects them. Their experience is that their existence and importance is constantly being overlooked. They were the "odd one out" in their accusatory and denigrating family.
****

"Infantile tyrannosaurus." Their experience is that "I never get do what I want to do." "When, is it ever going to be MY turn?!" They are the product of convenience-concerned parenting in which giving in to their whims was the line of least resistance.

They ended up believing that they are being constantly denied their fair share of things, due to the necessity of having to cooperate with the larger picture in life. They decidedly have no concept of that or any intention of participating in the give and take of life.
****

"Unclear on the concept." They have conflicts between what their conscious mind intends and what their unconscious dictates, and the result is a certain lack of discernment that gets them in trouble. They come from a family who confused them constantly on what is right and proper.
****

"Cowering in the cave." They fear that they will lose out all their life and they also fear for their life, in a form of annihilation-anxiety. There is also a great deal of emotional imbalance relating to the past and to their personal feelings.

They have the experience that if they do come out, they will be torn apart by a hostile and wrong-making world. Their family undermined their ability to cope and contribute, and they were subtly and continuously attacking.

"TICS" (Chronic uncontrollable movements, usually in the face)

"Nervous Nelly." They are very fearful and attack-anticipating, and they feel that they are being watched hostilely and judgmentally by others all the time. They have the feeling that they can do no right. So they have curtailed all their "unacceptable" feelings -- especially their sexuality and their anger.

They are super-self-suppressing, and they are very nervous, tense, and "run amok-anxious" -- both about "blowing it" and about "blowing up" at all the wrong-making, oppression and rejection that they have experienced.

They are intensely afraid that they'll "let their internal cat out of the bag," and that'll be the end of everything. They have an intense self-distrust arising from a severely stultifyingly suppressive and simultaneously sex-ploitative and sadistic parenting pattern. They were treated as if they existed only for their family's gratification, edification and glorification, with no room for them or their needs.

TINNITUS [Loud ringing or other sounds in the ear(s)]

"Drowning it out." There are messages from their Higher Self and the Other Side, as well as from their outer environment, but they are a case of a completely closed mind. They don't want to hear any of it, and they are refusing to listen. They are not hearing their "inner voice," and they are being intensely rejecting and stubborn.

They were so mistreated by their environment from the very beginning that they have no trust in the Universe, in the world, or in others. They listen only to their own long-established beliefs.

It all started in a severely oppressive and hostile home in which they were treated as the "intimate enemy." That happened severely and long enough that they completely came to a "My mind's made up -- don't confuse me with facts!" orientation. That has done a never-ending self-fulfilling prophecy effect re-validation of the original conclusions drawn so long ago and far away.

RIGHT EAR TINNITUS
"Shut up!" They are refusing to listen to information from the environment.

LEFT EAR TINNITUS
"Go away!" They are stubbornly ignoring their inner knowing and their "inner voice."

TOE PROBLEMS

"Pie in the sky." They are having real difficulties in getting a grip on their grounding, direction and purpose in life. They have trouble integrating what's on their mind with the process of making things happen.

They tend to get "lost in space" and to be idealistic and impractical, or they are prone to be unconcerned about or inept with the process of mastering the details of manifestation. They can't seem to translate ideas, values and goals into plans, action and production.

They have an underlying fear that they don't have what it takes to make things happen, and they are competence-anxious and cope-ability-concerned. They are the product of a severely competence-undermining family who effectively prevented their developing the wherewithal to make things happen on the practical level.

****

"I don't want to bother!" They don't want to be hassled by all the mundane details of handling things, and of translating their impulses and images into effective productivity and contributory manifestation. The just don't see the point of becoming involved with things at that level.

They were motivationally distorted in such a manner that they now have trouble dealing with the details of working towards the future. It was either "keep 'em around the old homestead" possessiveness and/or a dysfunctional incapacitation process arising from their inability to handle life themselves.

~~~~~~

BIG TOE PROBLEMS

"Lacking in manifestation resources." They are having difficulties in the enablement of the grounding process. They are having problems concerning the capacity to connect with the necessary life-sustenance and intention-manifestation resources.

RIGHT BIG TOE PROBLEMS

"No programs." They are having trouble generating life-support and plan-implementation strategies and tactics. They have the feeling that they just don't have the internal sub-routines to pull off life's requirements.

LEFT BIG TOE PROBLEMS

"Don't want to develop." They have motivational issues about whether to come up with or to develop sources of support, or about what kinds of sources of support to develop.

They have conflicts about whether to come up with the wherewithal for making their dreams, desires, intentions and plans happen, or for which future scenarios to develop the manifestation resources.

~~~~~~

BIG TOE BASE SEGMENT PROBLEMS

"Responsibility-avoidance." They are in conflict about whether they should really undertake full engagement requirements, and they therefore are ambivalent about going after fundamental self-sufficiency and contribution.

RIGHT BIG TOE BASE SEGMENT PROBLEMS

"Can I follow through?" They are deeply concerned about their ability to complete things.

LEFT BIG TOE BASE SEGMENT PROBLEMS

"Why bother?" There feeling is that they just can't "get it up" for taking care of business.

~~~~~~

BIG TOE BASE SEGMENT -- BONE PROBLEMS

"Cope-ability-anxiety." They feel as if they are lacking in the basic capabilities of making it in life.

RIGHT BIG TOE BASE SEGMENT -- BONE PROBLEMS
"I just don't have what it takes." They are convinced that there is something basic missing in their make-up regarding self-sufficiency.

LEFT BIG TOE BASE SEGMENT -- BONE PROBLEMS
"I can't and I can't care about it." They are in effect amotivational regarding taking care of themselves.
~~~~~~

BIG TOE BASE SEGMENT -- JOINT PROBLEMS
"Hunkering down in the bunker." They are in effect rigidly refusing to undertake self-responsibility and contribution. At the same time, they need to do so intensely. They are severely ambivalent, and they are therefore hiding out.

RIGHT BIG TOE BASE SEGMENT -- JOINT PROBLEMS
"Could I?" They aren't sure they have the wherewithal to pull off self-responsibility and contribution.

LEFT BIG TOE BASE SEGMENT -- JOINT PROBLEMS
"Should I?" They have great reservations about their motivation to take on life's responsibilities.
~~~~~~

BIG TOE TIP PROBLEMS
"Can't garner their resources." They are having deep difficulties getting the resources they need to implement self-responsibility and contribution and/or they are tending to "shoot themselves in the foot" when they try, due to all their conflicts in this area.

RIGHT BIG TOE TIP PROBLEMS
"How do I get it together?" They feel that they just can't seem to pull themselves and the necessary resources into a workable system.

LEFT BIG TOE TIP PROBLEMS
"Dear Prudence." They are so conflicted about this whole business of taking care of business that they end up not being willing to get it together to "come out and play."
~~~~~~

BIG TOE TIP -- BONE PROBLEMS
"Competence-anxiety." They feel like they are in over their head, and that they don't have what it takes to make it in the world.

RIGHT BIG TOE -- BONE PROBLEMS

"How can I do it?" Their experience is that they just plain don't have the know-how.

LEFT BIG TOE -- BONE PROBLEMS

"I don' wanna!" They are so traumatized by the prospect of the requirements of life that they are demoralized and anti-motivational.

BIG TOE TIP -- JOINT PROBLEMS

"Self-distrust." They have a profound underlying motivational questioning that is making them intensely resistive to garnering the resources for implementation of their purposes in life.

RIGHT BIG TOE -- JOINT PROBLEMS

"I'll screw it up!" They are so unsure of their motives that they won't even get things together to try.

LEFT BIG TOE TIP -- JOINT PROBLEMS

"I won't follow through!" They are convinced that they are so intensely resistive that it would actually cause more trouble that it's worth to try.

SECOND TOE PROBLEMS

"Strategy questions." They are having hassles in deciding which way to proceed and where to go for gaining grounding, for getting life supports, and for grasping the resources needed for the implementation of their intentions.

RIGHT SECOND TOE PROBLEMS

"Garnering problems." They have issues about how best to go about getting what they need to make things happen.

LEFT SECOND TOE PROBLEMS

"Decision-resistance." They are having difficulties in arriving at decisions concerning what they need to make things happen.

SECOND TOE BASE SEGMENT

"Direction-questioning." There are deep conflicts about which direction to go around getting the resources they need to live their own life.

RIGHT SECOND TOE BASE SEGMENT PROBLEMS
"Too many issues." They have the experience that they don't have what it takes to make sense of things and to take a direction. They feel inundated by all the desiderata of life.

LEFT SECOND TOE BASE SEGMENT PROBLEMS
"Unclear on the concept." They feel like they are lost at sea with regard to how to go about garnering what is needed for self-sufficiency.

~~~~~~

SECOND TOE BASE SEGMENT -- BONE PROBLEMS
"Severe cope-ability anxiety." They have great concerns about their sanity and about their ability to even pull off living as an independent person.

RIGHT SECOND TOE BASE SEGMENT -- BONE PROBLEMS
"What if . . .?" They are full of scenarios of disaster should they try to take life on its own terms.

LEFT SECOND TOE BASE SEGMENT -- BONE PROBLEMS
"Run amok-anxiety." They are in effect terrified of what they might do if they were forced to try to operate independently -- they literally fear that they would "go crazy."

~~~~~~

SECOND TOE BASE SEGMENT -- JOINT PROBLEMS
"No way, Jose!" They are strongly resisting taking on life on its own terms.

RIGHT SECOND TOE BASE SEGMENT -- JOINT PROBLEMS
"You can't make me!" They are grimly determined not to be required of by life, out of an underlying profound competence-anxiety.

LEFT SECOND TOE BASE SEGMENT -- JOINT PROBLEMS
"I *REFUSE!*" They are absolutely committed to being taken care of and to not having to expend or extend themselves into the world.

~~~~~~

SECOND TOE MID-SEGMENT PROBLEMS
"Intervention questions." They are highly uncertain how to go about translating their intentions into proper-direction interventions.

RIGHT SEOND TOE MID-SEGMENT PROBLEMS
"How do I know what to do?" They are unclear on the concept of how to about intervening in things.

LEFT SECOND TOE MID-SEGMENT PROBLEMS
"Muddy waters." They don't have a clear-cut value or priority system upon which to draw for determining directions to go.

~~~~~~

SECOND TOE MID-SEGMENT -- BONE PROBLEMS
"Direction questions." They are intensely concerned that the just don't have the wherewithal to pull off being able to know which way to go in life.

RIGHT SECOND TOE MID-SEGMENT -- BONE PROBLEMS

"How do *I* know?" They feel like they're navigating in a fog.

LEFT SECOND TOE MID-SEGMENT -- BONE PROBLEMS
"How can I know?" They are just sure that they are lacking in basic equipment regarding knowing which way to go.

~~~~~~

SECOND TOE MID-SEGMENT -- JOINT PROBLEMS
"Change-resistance." They are really strongly resisting the changes in direction in their life that are being required.

RIGHT SECOND TOE MID-SECTION -- JOINT PROBLEMS
"I *can't!*" They are convinced that they just don't have the abilities required by the new direction things are going.

LEFT SECOND TOE MID-SECTION -- JOINT PROBLEMS
"I *WON'T!*" They are heavily digging in their heels, in a stubborn refusal to go with the flow.

~~~~~~

SECOND TOE TIP PROBLEMS
"Decision-anxiety." They are intensely competence-anxious about their ability to decide and to implement their decisions regarding fundamental support systems in their life.

RIGHT SECOND TOE TIP PROBLEMS
"I don't know how!" They feel in over their head with regard to having to process information and to arrive at decisions about their basic resources.

LEFT SECOND TOE TIP PROBLEMS
"I don't trust myself!" They are very unsure about their own trustworthiness regarding decisions about their life support systems.

~~~~~~

SECOND TOE TIP -- BONE PROBLEMS
"Overwhelmed." Life's vicissitudes and difficulties have undermined their sense of sanity and ability to know what's real and possible.

RIGHT SECOND TOE TIP -- BONE PROBLEMS
"How do I know what's real?" They don't have any confidence that they can tell reality from wishful thinking.

LEFT SECOND TOE TIP -- BONE PROBMLEMS
"How can I trust *me!*" They are convinced that they are vaguely crazy, and that they would go off half-cocked if they tried to make distinctions and discernments.

~~~~~~

SECOND TOE TIP -- JOINT PROBLEMS
"Scared to death." There is a real rigidity and resistance to change in the direction of their life that arises out of a deep-seated terror of the world.

RIGHT SECOND TOE TIP -- JOINT PROBLEMS
"I'll drive right off a cliff!" They feel severely unaware and unequipped to deal with the requirements of the changes in the direction things are taking.

LEFT SECOND TOE TIP -- JOINT PROBLEMS
"They'll *KILL* me!" They are thoroughly unnerved and paranoid about how the world will react to and deal with any changes on their part.

~~~~~~

MIDDLE TOE PROBLEMS
"Wherewithal difficulties." They are having problems in the realm of getting the resources for the grounded manifestation of their life energy, sexual expression, creativity and personal potency.

RIGHT MIDDLE TOE PROBLEMS
"Inner spark"-handling issues. They are encountering hassles around their ways of dealing with the practicalities of channeling their internal initiative and their impact-making resources

LEFT MIDDLE TOE PROBLEMS
"Self-release issues." There and considerable concerns about whether to express or release their creativity, sexuality, potency and life energy, or concerning in what arenas and with what resources to do so.

~~~~~~

MIDDLE TOE BASE SEGMENT PROBLEMS

"Motivational questions." They are experiencing conflicts of motives regarding whether and how to manifest their life energy, creativity, personal potency and sexuality.

RIGHT MIDDLE TOE BASE SEGMENT PROBLEMS

"I'm not equipped to handle that." They have the experience that they lack certain fundamental resources for the manifestation of their soul and life purpose.

LEFT MIDDLE TOE BASE SEGMENT PROBLEMS

"Who am I?" They have a rather intense identity diffusion and a lack of direction problem that makes it very difficult for them to commit to anything.

~~~~~~

MIDDLE TOE BASE SEGMENT -- BONE PROBLEMS

"Support issues." They feel bereft of support for their manifesting their soul energies, passion and potency.

RIGHT MIDDLE TOE BASE SEGMENT -- BONE PROBLEMS

"Is there anybody out there?" They feel they landed on the wrong planet -- that what and who they are is "unfit for human consumption."

LEFT MIDDLE TOE BASE SEGMENT -- BONE PROBLEMS

"What am I *doing* here!?" Their experience is that they are on a desert island with no relevance, no peers and no purpose.

~~~~~~

MIDDLE TOE BASE SEGMENT -- JOINT PBOBLEMS

"Distrust of the Universe." They have deep underlying doubts-about-the-Universe issues around their being even allowed to, much less supported in manifesting their beingness in the world, and they are therefore resisting movement in that direction.

RIGHT MIDDLE TOE BASE SEGMENT -- JOINT PROBLEMS

"It's not safe out there!" They feel that the world is no place for them to be, and they are avoiding involvement like the plague.

LEFT MIDDLE TOE BASE SEGMENT -- JOINT PROBLEMS

"I don't *belong* here!" They have the experience that there is something inherently at least not acceptable, if not bad, wrong and evil about them that makes them unwilling to trust the universe in any way.

~~~~~~

MIDDLE TOE MID- SEGMENT PROBLEMS

"Unclear on the concept." They are intensely unsure as to what it would take to be able to express their creativity, potency, sexuality and life energy in the world.

RIGHT MIDDLE TOE MID- SEGMENT PROBLEMS
"I don't know how." They are so out of the loop that they feel unable to implement their beingness in the world.

LEFT MIDDLE TOE MID- SEGMENT PROBLEMS
"Lost at sea." They are so befuddled about what it is to be who they are that they have no effective means of navigating themselves through the world.

~~~~~~

MIDDLE TOE MID- SEGMENT -- BONE PROBLEMS

"Vulnerability-anxiety." They are having real problems with mental or emotional experiences of weakness and violability.

RIGHT MIDDLE TOE MID-SEGMENT -- BONE PROBLEMS
"Outclassed and over-run." Their experience is that they don't have what it takes to make it in this dangerous world.

LEFT MIDDLE TOE MID-SEGMENT -- BONE PROBLEMS
"Weirded out." They believe that there is something inherently distorted and dysfunctional about their inner workings that make them greatly at risk.

~~~~~~

MIDDLE TOE MID- SEGMENT -- JOINT PROBLEMS

"Soul-avoidance." They are rigidly resisting moving in the direction of the expression of their soul characteristics.

RIGHT MIDDLE TOE MID-SEGMENT -- JOINT PROBLEMS
"How do I do it?" They don't know how to go about the business of manifesting their soul.

LEFT MIDDLE TOE MID-SEGMENT -- JOINT PROBLEMS
"What is it?" They are not at all sure of who and what they are at the soul level.

~~~~~~

MIDDLE TOE TIP PROBLEMS
"Manifestation-incompetence." They feel unable to implement their potency, creativity, passion and sexuality.

RIGHT MIDDLE TOE TIP PROBLEMS
"Unequipped." They feel lacking in the resources necessary to manifest their beingness.

LEFT MIDDLE TOE TIP PROBLEMS

"Untrustworthy." They feel that their inner soul is in effect unsafe to loose upon the world.

~~~~~~

MIDDLE TOE TIP -- BONE PROBLEMS

"Catastrophic expectations." They are afraid of their making deadly mistakes if they tried to translate their intentions into implementations regarding their true soul motives.

RIGHT MIDDLE TOE TIP -- BONE PROBLEMS

"I don't dare!" They are rather intensely competence-anxious about their ability to implement their intentions without creating disaster.

LEFT MIDDLE TOE TIP -- BONE PROBLEMS

"Self-distrust." They are quite ashamed at what might lurk within that could lurch out in "Mr. Hyde" style if they got in touch with their inner intentions.

~~~~~~

MIDDLE TOE TIP -- JOINT PROBLEMS

"Self-suppression." They are refusing to surrender to their inner soul characteristics and motivations, for fear of not doing it correctly.

RIGHT MIDDLE TOE TIP -- JOINT PROBLEMS

"I'll blow it!" They are afraid that they are too incompetent to manifest their inner soul.

LEFT MIDDLE TOE TIP -- JOINT PROBLEMS

"I can't be trusted." They feel that their inner intentions are of such a nature as to make it undesirable to release them.

~~~~~~

FOURTH TOE PROBLEMS

"Resource-garnering problems." They have issues regarding the generation of the resources and supports for the implementation of meaningful involvements in life, such as relationships, work, responsibilities, authority/ respectability, success and spiritual manifestation.

RIGHT FOURTH TOE PROBLEMS

"Can't come up with the ability to get resources." They are encountering difficulties in working out or coming up with the resources, strategies, tactics and methods of bringing about significant and worthwhile involvements and manifestations.

LEFT FOURTH TOE PROBLEMS
"Amotivational."   They are having conflicts concerning whether to be involved in intimacy, efforting, requirements, authority issues, productivity and with their sacred connection-maturity and contribution issues.
****

"Motivational ambivalence." They are experiencing ambiguities as to WHAT significant involvements to manifest -- values/ethics and motivation issues.

FOURTH TOE BASE PROBLEMS
"Ability-generating difficulties." There are problems in their coming up with the resources and supports for meaningful involvements in life, such as love and work.

RIGHT FOURTH TOE BASE PROBLEMS
"No comprehendo." They feel like an outsider who doesn't have the wherewithal to garner the resources necessary for involvement in life.

LEFT FOURTH TOE BASE PROBLEMS
"Stranger in a strange land." Their experience is that they are somehow inherently different from everyone else in a manner that blocks their getting it together so as to become involved.

FOURTH TOE BASE SEGMENT -- BONE PROBLEMS
"No support." They feel that they are not going to be able to have the support they need from others if they become significantly involved in life.

RIGHT FOURTH TOE BASE SEGMENT -- BONE PROBLEMS
"Forget it!" Their experience is that there is just not enough support available from others for them to become engaged.

LEFT FOURTH TOE BASE SEGMENT -- BONE PROBLEMS
"I don't deserve it." They feel that due to something about their inherent nature, they cannot and should not count on support from others for their becoming involved in life.

FOURTH TOE BASE SEGMENT -- JOINT PROBLEMS
"Involvement-avoidance." They are locked into their position of non-involvement in life, and it is causing problems.

RIGHT FOURTH TOE BASE SEGMENT -- JOINT PROBLEMS
"I can't." They feel like they lack the necessary competences that are involved in becoming engaged in life.

341

LEFT FOURTH TOE BASE SEGMENT -- JOINT PROBLEMS
"No way, Jose!" They are adamantly refusing to take life on, out of an underlying fear of what would happen if they did.

~~~~~~

FOURTH TOE MID-SEGMENT PROBLEMS
"Method-ambivalence." They have profound uncertainty about how to become actively involved in life.

RIGHT FOURTH TOE MID-SEGMENT PROBLEMS
"How do you do it?" They are quite uncertain as to how to go about becoming engaged.

LEFT FOURTH TOE MID-SEGMENT PROBLEMS
"What do I engage?" They don't know who they are enough to become engaged in life.

~~~~~~

FOURTH TOE MID-SEGMENT -- BONE PROBLEMS
"Alone on their own." They feel that they have no standing or support in the world.

RIGHT FOURTH TOE MID-SEGMENT -- BONE PROBLEMS
"Out on a limb." They feel that they don't have the acceptance or the commitment they need from the surrounding social environment.

LEFT FOURTH TOE MID-SEGMENT -- BONE PROBLEMS
"Why bother?" They have the experience that no matter what they do, no one will be there for them, so they disengage.

~~~~~~

FOURTH TOE MID-SEGMENT -- JOINT PROBLEMS
"Involvement-resisting." There is a lack of grace and presence in their functioning, due to their own aloneness experience.

RIGHT FOURTH TOE MID-SEGMENT -- JOINT PROBLEMS
"Socially incompetent." They have a way of alienating others, due to their alienation.

LEFT FOURTH TOE MID-SEGMENT -- JOINT PROBLLEMS
"A pox on *all* your houses!" They feel that there is no point to their becoming involved, due to their experience that they are a "stranger in a strange land."

~~~~~~

FOURTH TOE TIP PROBLEMS

"Wherewithal questions." They have real concerns about their having the ability to be involved, meaningfully invested and vulnerable in life.

RIGHT FOURTH TOE TIP PROBLEMS

"I'm not sure I can do it." They are highly uncertain about how to go about becoming involved and invested.

LEFT FOURTH TOE TIP PROBLEMS

"I may be lacking." They have an underlying fear that there is something fundamental missing in their make-up that makes it impossible for them to become involved in life.

~~~~~~

FOURTH TOE TIP -- BONE PROBLEMS

"Annihilation-anxiety." They feel that to become involved is to be in essence killed, because they would be in over their head, and they would enrage the world.

RIGHT FOURTH TOE TIP -- BONE PROBLEMS

"They'll kill me!" They are convinced that the social environment is so hostile to them that they don't dare become involved.

LEFT FOURTH TOE TIP -- BONE PROBLEMS

"Mr. Hyde." They are afraid that if they get involved, their "inner demon" will come out -- with disastrous results all the way around.

~~~~~~

FOURTH TOE TIP -- JOINT PROBLEMS

"Won't budge." They have a deep fear of what would lie ahead if they became involved meaningfully in life and they therefore refuse to move.

RIGHT FOURTH TOE TIP --JOINT PROBLEMS

"They'll run amok." They have a deep and abiding distrust of other people, so they refuse to become meaningfully engaged.

LEFT FOURTH TOE TIP -- JOINT PROBLEMS

"I'll set off World War III." They have an underlying fear of themselves and of what they might do if they got involved.

~~~~~~

LITTLE TOE PROBLEMS

"Interpersonal incompetence." They are having difficulties in the realm of their development and utilization of their social skills, their interpersonal orientation, and the interactional manifestation resources.

Such actions as social connection, communication, gender identity, persona projection, conducting business, family relationships and personal freedom of expression are involved here.

RIGHT LITTLE TOE PROBLEMS

"Unclear on the concept." There are issues concerning how to go about such things as connecting with people, communicating, image-projecting, etc.

LEFT LITTLE TOE PROBLEMS

"Interpersonal involvement questioning." They have rather intense conflicts about whether, how much, with whom, under what conditions and for what purposes to develop the resources for manifestation of significant interpersonal involvements.

~~~~~~

LITTLE TOE BASE SEGMENT PROBLEMS

"Involvement-avoidance." There are internal issues about whether to become involved with and connected to other people. There is a resulting lack of development of interpersonal resource skills.

RIGHT LITTLE TOE BASE SEGMENT PROBLEMS

"No know-how." They are lacking in some foundational interpersonal interface capabilities.

LEFT LITTLE TOE BASE SEGMENT PROBLEMS

"I don' wanna!" They are quite ambivalent and alienated, and they therefore avoid social involvement.

~~~~~~

LITTLE TOE BASE SEGMENT -- BONE PROBLEMS

"I'm outta here!" They would rather "take their marbles and go home" than to face the challenges interpersonal connection.

RIGHT LITTLE TOE BASE SEGMENT -- BONE PROBLEMS

"Social competence-anxiety." They are afraid that they don't have what it takes to succeed interpersonally.

LEFT LITTLE TOE BASE SEGMENT -- BONE PROBLEMS

"Alienated." They are so disgusted with other people that they would just as soon stay away.

~~~~~~

LITTLE TOE BASE SEGMENT -- JOINT PROBLEMS
"Basic distrust." There is a fundamental suspiciousness of other people that makes them intensely resistant to developing interpersonal capabilities.

RIGHT LITTLE TOE BASE SEGMENT -- JOINT PROBLEMS
"I can't fend them off." Their experience is that they lack the wherewithal to cope with other people's untrustworthiness.

LEFT LITTLE TOE BASE SEGMENT -- JOINT PROBLEMS
"Bah! Humbug!" They want nothing to do with other people, out of their underlying paranoia.

~~~~~~

LITTLE TOE MID-SEGMENT PROBLEMS
"Contact-conflicted." They are in great internal ambivalence conflict about whether and how to connect socially with others.

RIGHT LITTLE TOE MID-SEGMENT PROBLEMS
"What would happen?" They are quite alarmed at the possible scenarios of interpersonal involvement.

LEFT LITTLE TOE MID-SEGMENT PROBLEMS
"I'm not so sure I want to." They are not at all certain that they really care to become interpersonally involved.

~~~~~~

LITTLE TOE MID-SEGMENT -- BONE PROBLEMS
"Out of the question." They feel that they have no standing in the world, and that they therefore are not in a position to develop interpersonal connections.

RIGHT LITTLE TOE MID-SEGMENT -- BONE PROBLEMS
"Bereft." They feel socially bankrupt, and they therefore avoid social contacts.

LEFT LITTLE TOE MID-SEGMENT -- BONE PROBLEMS
"Ejectee-rejectee-dejectee." Their experience is that they just don't fit in anywhere.

~~~~~~

LITTLE TOE MID-SEGMENT -- JOINT PROBLEMS
"Catastrophic expectations." They are unbendingly refusing to develop the wherewithal to connect with others, out of the fear of what would happen if they did.

RIGHT LITTLE TOE MID-SEGMENT -- JOINT PROBLEMS
"Are you kidding?" They have the conviction that interpersonal involvements are inherently dangerous.

LEFT LITTLE TOE MID-SEGMENT -- JOINT PROBLEMS
"Run amok-anxiety." They have no faith that they wouldn't do a bunch of awfuls if they got interpersonally involved.
~~~~~~

LITTLE TOE TIP PROBLEMS
"Social competence-anxiety." They are feeling utterly inept socially and interpersonally, and they have no idea how to go about doing that successfully.

RIGHT LITTLE TOE TIP PROLEMS
"Befuddled." They are so socially out of the loop that they haven't the foggiest notion how to proceed.

LEFT LITTLE TOE TIP PROBLEMS
"No redeeming social significance." They have the feeling that they are in essence "unfit for human consumption."
~~~~~~

LITTLE TOE TIP -- BONE PROBLEMS
"Can't handle it." They feel that they are in effect in over their head when they are dealing with other people.

RIGHT LITTLE TOE TIP -- BONE PROBLEMS
"I wouldn't dare!" They have the experience of being overwhelmed in the social sphere.

LEFT LITTLE TOE TIP -- BONE PROBLEMS
"I shouldn't!" Their feeling is that they are such a "moral cretin" that interpersonal involvement is out of the question.
~~~~~~

LITTLE TOE TIP -- JOINT PROBLEMS
"Won't budge." There is no ease of movement in their interpersonal functioning, and they are refusing to move into interpersonal involvement.

RIGHT LITTLE TOE TIP -- JOINT PROBLEMS
"What's the use?" They feel in over their head interpersonally, and they just won't even try it.

LEFT LITTLE TOE TIP -- JOINT PROBLEMS
"Forget the whole thing!" They are convinced that whatever they are is inherently not cut out for interpersonal involvement.

~~~~~~

"STUBBED TOE"
"Implication-freak-outs." They are experiencing conflicts between their direction of development or movement and their inner desires or intentions. They are having big concerns over the potential ramifications of what is in process.

They grew up in a family in which things all too often went into "escalating disasters." They are therefore reluctant to take on things or to take the initiative.

TOE INTERSPACE PROBLEMS
"Detail-handling competence concerns." They are having problems regarding whether and how to retain, sustain and maintain their resources for pragmatic manifestation on the daily operation and detail consideration level.

They were competence-, confidence- and/or motivation-undermined in this area by their family, so that, in effect, they don't know how to handle their resources. In the worst case scenario, they received "Skid Row" programming.

~~~~~~

BIG TOE/SECOND TOE INTERFACE PROBLEMS
"Grounding resource questions." They are having difficulties in the realm of being practical and connected to Earth, and in the realm of sustenance processes and outcomes, regarding their acquisition and the management of the resources involved.

RIGHT BIG TOE/SECOND TOE INTERSPACE PROBLEMS
"How to get them?" They have issues around how to go about coming up with ways of getting what they need.

LEFT BIG TOE/SECOND TOE INTERSPACE PROBLEMS
"Don't deserve them." They are involved in conflicts about their right to have support, resources and aspiration-activation processes happen for them, and about the necessary decisions involved.

~~~~~~

SECOND TOE/MIDDLE TOE INTERSPACE PROBLEMS
"How do I do it?" They are encountering difficulties concerning how to go about gaining life support, being grounded, and expressing their life energy, creativity, sexuality and relational needs.

RIGHT SECOND TOE/MIDDLE TOE INTERSPACE PROBLEMS
"How to decide?" They have issues regarding how to come to a resolution on the practicalities of the meeting of their life energy, creativity, sexuality and relational needs.

LEFT SECOND TOE/MIDDLE TOE INTERSACE PROBLEMS
"Decision-avoidance." They are having conflicts regarding decisions regarding getting what they need, especially regarding the expression of their life energy, creativity, sexuality and relational needs.
~~~~~~

MIDDLE TOE/FOURTH TOE INTERSPACE PROBLEMS
"Resource-garnering problems." There are difficulties in garnering what they need to manifest their life energy, creativity, sexuality relational needs, work, respect, responsibility, success and spirituality.

RIGHT MIDDLE TOE/FOURTH TOE INTERSPACE PROBLEMS
"Inner spark" expression problems. They have issues in regards to how to handle the expression of their internal soul in significant and worthwhile manifestations.

LEFT MIDDLE TOE/FOURTH TOE INTERSPACE PROBLEMS
"Inner release issues." They have conflicts concerning in what arenas and with what effect to release their "inner spark," in terms of motivational and values concerns.
~~~~~~

FOURTH TOE/LITTLE TOE INTERSPACE PROBLEMS
"Life resource problems." They have difficulties in coming up with the wherewithal to allow their becoming involved in meaningful relationships, social connections and identity-expressions.

RIGHT FOURTH TOE/LITTLE TOE INTERSPACE PROBLEMS
"Means problems." They have run into difficulties regarding the resources and approaches for bringing about significant and worthwhile involvements, relationships and social connections.

LEFT FOURTH TOE/LITTLE TOE INTERSPACE PROBLEMS
"Person without a culture." They are experiencing conflicts involving value and motivational concerns regarding the resources for significant involvements and connections because they feel like a "visiting Martian."

TOE NAIL PROBLEMS
"Confidence problems." They are feeling unprotected and vulnerable in the realm of their ability to be grounded and to handle the details of life, due to competence-undermining by their family.
****

"Lack of support." They are experiencing a sense of non-support for their taking on the realm of handling the details of manifestation, due to motivation-undermining programming.
****

"Assertion problems." There are difficulties with their displaying either the lack of or too much assertiveness and aggressiveness in taking on the tasks of taking care of the details of living, as a function of their having been shaped into ineffectiveness in this area.
****

"Fussiness." They are prone to perfectionistic and pointillistic control of the details of their manifestation process, due to growing up in either a perfectionistic or a chaotic family system.
****

"Selfish insensitivity." They are apt to manifest self-immersion problems in the realm of covering all the bases and he handling of the details of living, as a function of their having been allowed to develop a coercive lifestyle.
****

"Discombobulation." They are caught up in confusion, demoralization and immobilization in the realm of actually making things happen, as a function of having been devastatingly ambiguously parented, so that they have in effect withdrawn from the fray.
****

"Amotivational syndrome." They are having problems bothering with the details of handling things, due to under-requiring and over-indulgent parenting, so that they lack "true grit."
~~~~~~

BIG TOE NAIL PROBLEMS
"Competence concerns." They have issues about their ability to handle the life-sustenance and intention-manifestation processes and requirements of life. These concerns involve either a fear of lack of the wherewithal needed or an over-insistence on their way of doing things
----

RIGHT BIG TOE NAIL PROBLEMS
"Resource-generation problems." They are having difficulties regarding their ability to generate life-sustenance and intention-manifestation resources, due to competence-anxiety or excessive willfulness.

LEFT BIG TOE NAIL PROBLEMS
"Impetus problems." They are encountering conflicts concerning their right or motivation to come up with the life-sustenance and intention-manifestation resources they need, due either to overwhelm-anxiety or to insistence on having thing their way or no way.
~~~~~~

SECOND TOE NAIL PROBLEMS
"Making-it-happen problems." They have issues regarding deciding how to proceed in the matter of their getting grounding and life-sustenance, as well as of in their expression of their will. It is either because of cope-ability-anxiety or of their anticipation of the environment's reaction to their way of doing things.

RIGHT SECOND TOE NAIL PROBLEMS
"Unsureness problems." They are having difficulties in coming up with ways that work for them in getting things done, due to their not knowing how to or due to their being too sure of how they will get things done.

LEFT SECOND TOE NAIL PROBLEMS

"Desire uncertainty." They have conflicts about deciding what they want to happen with regard to life-sustenance and will-expression -- whether they have the right or the wherewithal to do so or whether their way is really the right way.

MIDDLE TOE NAIL PROBLEMS

"Am I going to blow it?" They have concerns about the process of getting what they need to manifest their life energy, creativity, sexuality and relational connections in relation to their sense of competence, or in relation to their "right and righteous" attitude.

RIGHT MIDDLE TOE NAIL PROBLEMS

"Approach problems." They have difficulties in coming up with effective ways of manifesting their "inner spark" and their impact-making process, as a function of their overwhelming feelings or as a function of their insistence pattern.

LEFT MIDDLE TOE NAIL PROLEMS

"Expression-questioning." They have conflicts about their right to express their life energy, creativity, sexuality and relational needs or about the impact of their way of doing so, in the form of insufficiency feelings or of negatingness.

FOURTH TOE NAIL PROBLEMS

"Am I doing it right?" There are concerns around their generating the resources they need for meaningful impacts in relationships, in terms of their sense of a lack of abilities or of their excessive weddedness to their way of doing things.

RIGHT FOURTH TOE NAIL PROBLEMS

"Caught up in their concerns." They are encountering difficulties in working out effective ways of bringing about significant and worthwhile involvements and manifestations, due to their competence-anxiety or to their excessive willfulness.

LEFT FOURTH TOE NAIL PROBLEMS

"Moral cretin." They have value and ethical concerns about their way of handling intimacy, contribution and spirituality around their felt lack of abilities or around their intense intentionality.

LITTLE TOE NAIL PROBLEMS

"Can I do it?" They have concerns about their ability to come up with workable social connection, acceptance and standing resources, as a function of their sense of lack of the capacity, or of their over-intense imposing of their will.

RIGHT LITTLE TOE NAIL PROBLEMS
"Doing it *wrong*!" There are difficulties regarding how to go about dealing with social communication, connection and commitments, due to competence concerns or to over-bearingness.

LEFT LITTLE TOE NAIL PROBLEMS
"Motivational problems." They are experiencing conflicts about whether and in what form to become involved with and connected to others, due to inadequacy feelings or to judgementalness and willfulness.
~~~~~~

"IN-GROWN" TOE NAIL
"Self-squashing." They are struggling with worry and guilt about their right to move forward. They are afraid to take their own direction in life. They are into power-avoidance, identity-squelching, growth-suppressing and turning inward.

It is a result of an engulfing dysfunctional family who conveyed that to "grow away" would be to betray their family.

(See the particular toe nail(s) for more information)

TONGUE PROBLEMS
"I shouldn't." They are dealing with guilt over their enjoyment of the realm of the senses, sexuality, and surface satisfactions like entertainment, activities and consumption, or about their tastes and preferences.

They were made to feel "bad, wrong and evil" for who they are and what they like by their rejecting family.
****

"Watch my mouth!" They have an overdeveloped sense of accountability and responsibility for everything that happens around them, particularly with regard to what they say. They feel that harm has come from their speaking out about things.

It arises from their family's putting them in the "in loco Deity" position, in which they were subconsciously expected to be the Source of everything. It was due to their superior equipment as a soul and as a being. The family then ended up blaming them for all that went wrong.
****

"Karma." They are reaping the bitter returns of their misuse of the power of the spoken word by false speaking, lying, gossiping, setups, etc. in past lives. As a result, they learned this way of functioning again in a family who did the same. They are now learning to do better next time around.
****

"There is no joy in Bloodville." They are cut off from the beauty and joy in life, due to their shut-down to the positives. They are the product of a grimly survivalist, pessimistic, judgmental and punitive family.

RIGHT TONGUE PROBLEMS
"Moral cretin." They are experiencing guilt and/or karma for how they relate to the environment around them, particularly in the realm of the senses and with the spoken word.

351

LEFT TONGUE PROBLEMS

"Wrong, bad and evil." They have shame and self-distrust and/or self-disgust over their sensual desires and/or over what it is that they wish to say.

TIP OF THE TONGUE PROBLEMS

"Sealed lips." They are having difficulties related to speaking out. It arises out of their fear of the consequences of telling it like it is, of experiencing the play-outs of their saying their piece, and/or of problems in articulating what they want to say.

FRONT OF THE TONGUE PROBLEMS

"Speak no evil." They have anxieties about what they want or what they want to say. They fear it will cause harm to them and/or others.

CENTER OF THE TONGUE PROBLEMS

"Bad me!" There are conflicts concerning enjoyment and appreciation of experiences and sensual stimulation, as well as shame around their tastes.

REAR OF THE TONGUE PROBLEMS

"I shouldn't." They have issues around receiving, accepting and/or swallowing what life brings to them.

UNDER THE TONGUE PROBLEMS

"Shadow-shoving." They are engaged in systematic avoidance of their innermost subconscious motivations, feelings and impulses. They strongly shove underground those inner stirrings which were not acceptable to their family or to the "world of agreement."

SIDE OF THE TONGUE PROBLEMS

"What should I do?" They have conflict concerning their role in life, particularly as to what they say and partake in. It comes from an intensely socially anxious "What will the neighbors thing!?" family culture.

RIGHT SIDE OF THE TONGUE PROBLEMS

"What am I supposed to be?" They are greatly concerned about their role in the world at large.

LEFT SIDE OF THE TONGUE PROBLEMS

"Motive-questioning." They are agitatedly unsure of themselves as to the acceptability of their intentions and motivations.

TONSILLITIS

"Expression-anxiety." They live in fear of expressing themselves, especially their emotions and their creativity. So they repress and suppress their anger, fear and other feelings, and they are stifling themselves.

They have a feeling of lost personal potency and of bondage, which results in considerable "inner crying." They have much agitated anxiety and conflict about the intensity of their need to express deep feelings, to release themselves, and to manifest their creative capabilities.

They are the product of an oppressive patriarchal family who took the old position that children are to be seen and not heard.
****

"Whim of iron." They are finding that the reality that they have to swallow to the effect that they can't have what they want is causing an intense irritation, frustration and anger. They are intensely willful and selfish, and they can't stand not getting their own way. They are the product of a highly patriarchal and arrogant family system, and they are a chip off the old block.

(See **QUINCY; SORE THROAT; STREP THROAT**)

TORPOROUSNESS (Sluggishness, lethargy, amotivational)

"Nothing stirs them." They are manifesting a demoralization syndrome, and they are feeling utterly overwhelmed or under-motivated, as a result of having the experience that they don't have what it takes to make it in their current situation or in life in general. Or conversely, they have found that for them, very little is worth doing or pursuing, because it all goes nowhere. So they are very slow to start up on or to progress on anything.

In either case, it is a re-experiencing of their destiny-derailing, competence- and confidence-undermining childhood in a severely dysfunctional family.

TORSO PROBLEMS

"Self-punishment." They are into intense self-rejection and self-attack, as reflected in their having difficulties in the part of the body that contains their internal essence and their "private preserve."

This area is the "core of the self," and it is the seat of the emotions, feelings and impulses -- the "guts" of the persons, their "beingness," and they find that area totally unacceptable. Their self-revulsion is the result of severe shame-induction and denigration by their rejecting family.

RIGHT SIDE OF THE TORSO

"Impact-shame." They are deeply concerned about the effects they are having on the world around them.

CENTER OF THE TORSO

"Self-shame." They have great shame over being who they are, their inner soul.

LEFT SIDE OF THE TORSO

"Motivation-shame." They are experiencing severe guilt over their intentions and desires.

UPPER TORSO

"Shut down." They have in effect closed off their heart, and they are therefore rather unconnected to the world and to other people.

LOWER TORSO

"Paranoia." They live in a good deal of fear most of the time, and they operate out of a deep-seated distrust of the world and of other people.

TORTICOLLIS (See **NECK PROBLEMS**)

TOURETTE SYNDROME (Sudden intense shouts and movement, often involving profanity)

"Shadow burst-outs." They are subject to outbursts of repressed and suppressed intense impulses and intentions. It is the result of subtly oppressive parenting involving much shame-induction, judgementalness and accusation, often on a subliminal or sub-rosa level.

TOXOPLASMOSIS (Virus that causes inflammation in targeted organs that is recurrent and degenerative. It is intensified by a compromised immune system.)

"Running on empty." They are harboring deep grief and a demoralized resigned attitude in the making or in their manifestation. They are plagued by too much sorrow, and by the effect of a significant inequality exchange with the world, whereby they put out much more than they get.

They also live with chronic uncertainty and confusion as the nature of reality that arises from a "magical mystery tour" family experience. It led to a "dance with the second" as the "only way to fly," with the result that they are highly susceptible to momentary variations in the stimulation and situation.

It is the result of having carried the world on their shoulders all their life, starting with their severely dysfunctional family. They were allowed little or no ability to receive or to require return in kind. They were told in no uncertain terms that they were the source of all the family's problems, while they were actually being the one deflecting some of the disasters.

TRACHEA PROBLEMS

"Clutching their throat." They have a lot of anxiety and fear about life, the world and the Cosmos. Their experience is that it is not safe here, that their needs are not going to be met, and that they somehow deserve this.

It feels to them that the world is rather like a tornado, where everything is tossed around violently and randomly. They have little or no trust in the Cosmos. They feel constantly threatened and that the "breath of life" is highly fragile, vulnerable and apt to leave them at any time.

They are the product of a severely dysfunctional, chaotic, abrasive family who were so involved in their "trauma dramas" that the individual was lost in the mayhem, the shuffle and the upheavals. Their needs were simply not taken into account.

TRAUMATIC BRAIN INJURY (TBI) [Caused by having the brain bounce hard against the skull] (Persistent headaches, difficulty remembering, trouble concentrating, learning disability, feeling unusually tired, mood changes, ringing in the ears, confusion, irritability, dis-inhibition, exaggerated startle reactions, learning problems handling crowds, sometimes violent confrontations with people in more severe cases.)

"Brain bruise." Their feeling is, "What happened to my mind/self!?" Coping has become overwhelming to them, and they have lost their sense of center, stability and groundedness. They feel threatened and/or intensely challenged by life's demands and realities all of a sudden, and the world feels unsafe, with a looming possibility of there being no more joy in their life.

They are freaked out, and they are intensely alarmed by the implications and ramifications of their condition. They are having a profound emotional reaction to this. It is composed of feelings of falling apart, self-blame/shame, grief, anxiety, fear, despair and rage.

It is caused by events so intense, severe, and at some level inexplicable and unjustifiable, that the whole thing has been stored in the "older" brain systems related to sheer survival issues. The result is the "automatic pilot" activation of all these very strong reactions, leading to further self-doubt, confusion and fear.

There are also caught up in a "What was *THAT!*" and "What does *THAT* mean!?" pattern, in which they are handicapped by a pronounced propensity to respond with generalized anxiety or fearfulness, with all the associated patterns of functioning in reaction to common stimuli and situations.

Improvement and the recovery process are dependent upon the trauma not being a repetition or representation of an abusive/traumatic childhood history. In the absence of this complication, the usual response is a digging into their internal and external resources to engage in a rather strongly motivated and effective rehabilitation.

If, however, there are detrimental psychodynamic re-activations involved, it will require immediate and ongoing therapy so that the rehabilitation process can proceed without counter-motivations, fear-overwhelm, immobilization by depression and/or rage-aholic patterns.
****

"Who's in charge here!?" They are in deep conflict with their "Higher Self" and/or the "Divine Authority," a conflict in which THEY want to be the one running the show. They feel denied, humiliated and undermined/prevented, and they are full of rage and despair about everything involved in this, from the occurrence and nature of the trauma to all of its play-outs. They have had authority conflict problems all their life, either internally and/or externally/behaviorally. It has now "come to a head."

They are the product of an authoritarian patriarchal family in which they were perennially butting their head against the authority system, or they were programmed to go into conflict with authority as a means of preventing their success in life as a hidden agenda on the part of the family, the mother in particular.
****

"God is Al Capone!" They are feeling betrayed, devastated and over-demanded and reactively furious. Their experience is that they have been abandoned by the "Home Office" (All That Is). As they see it, there is a serious case of crossed purposes between their personal goals and the Divine Intent, and they are extremely anxious/worried and resentful as a result. There is a profound inner conflict within their operational ego and/or between the desires and intentions of the personality and their perception of their unfolding destiny.

They feel completely caught up in some sort of "glitch in the Cosmic computer," such that they are in effect, a totally innocent bystander who got clobbered by whatever negatives are happening as a part of the Divine Design.

Or they have the feeling that the "Home Office" (All That Is) has taken the helm against their will and desires, and that they therefore unable to manage their life. They feel completely at the mercy of the Moral Order, the Judgmental Universe and an Angry God. This reaction to the trauma and its aftermath as a result of a family history in which a lot didn't make sense, and yet it was justified in one form another as being "God's Will" or the equivalent.

They are the product of a significantly dysfunctional family who did not respond to their needs or in which they were forced to take over the meeting of their own needs because no one else would. As a result, they developed an abiding distrust of the Cosmos.
****

"Who's in charge here!?" They are in deep conflict with their "Higher Self" and/or the "Divine Authority," a conflict in which THEY want to be the one running the show. They feel denied, humiliated and undermined/prevented, and they are full of rage and despair about everything involved in this, from the occurrence and nature of the trauma to all of its play-outs. They have had authority conflict problems all their life, either internally and/or externally/behaviorally. It has now "come to a head."

They are the product of an authoritarian patriarchal family in which they were perennially butting their head against the authority system, or they were programmed to go into conflict with authority as a means of preventing their success in life as a hidden agenda on the part of the family, the mother in particular.

****

"No driver of the vehicle." The trauma has knocked out their "executive self" system, and there is something of a "comprehension collapse" that has disrupted their ability to accept, organize, store, integrate and interpret information for purposes of running their life.

They are having a profound emotional and disorganized/disoriented reaction to this. There is simultaneously a release of subconscious, shadow-shoved or suppressed emotional/motivational/cognitive distortion processes which they are trying to "sit on."

They have an over-riding sense of powerlessness, helplessness and hopelessness in the face of overwhelming odds and of on-rushing disaster. They feel immobilized and completely done in by the world, and that they utterly are unable to do anything about it.

They also have a strong belief in their not being good enough, with much self-intolerance, self-rejection, and self-destructive potential. In addition, their experience is that if they encounter something that is beyond their coping capabilities, they are in over their head and any attempts to improve the situation just makes it all the worse, in an "escalating disaster" pattern.

They have the conviction that they are totally unfit for Divine acceptance, and that they are consistently failing in their desperate efforts to use atonement to alleviate their severe chronic shame and their "evilness," as they seek the "God Housekeeping Seal of Approval."

It has in effect completely demoralized them, and that in turn is generating "*waiting for rigor mortis*" resignedly inactive pattern. They seek to keep the damage down as much as possible as their lifestyle.

They have no sense of being able to impact or to protect themselves, and they feel that if they can't kill themselves, at least they can make themselves as small as possible to avoid notice and devastation.

It is the result of having grown up in an extremely pervasively dysfunctional family. There was also a great deal of sexual guilt-inducing by an over-possessively rejecting and wrong-making mother, along with severe maternal deprivation.

They were denigrated and told they could do no right, while at the same time they were being universally turned to with demands, blame and restrictions, in a never-ending barrage. They were in effect subjected to unrelentingly ruthless and utterly unpredictable and uncontrollable subtle rage-based attacking parenting in which there was no response possible.

****

"Woe is me!" They are a "professional victim" who turns everything to their selfish advantage in a master manipulator pattern. They are brilliantly effective at taking advantage of the many things that are involved in dealing with Traumatic Brain Injury. It's the jackpot for life, as far as they are concerned.

They are martyr-tripping, "Jewish mothering," "Why me, God!?"-ing, supremely opportunistic, massively draining of energy, time and resources, audience-demanding, worming, cheating and continuously righteously self-justifying. They are in effect an advancing steamroller in their impact on the environment and the people and systems around them.

Many such individuals have a boiling cauldron of indiscriminate vengeance-vendetta rage in which they subtly slyly and passive-aggressively make life miserable for everyone around them in a "share the misery" pattern.

They are the product of a mutually manipulative and parasitic, severely selfish, and dysfunctional family in which there is an enormous undercurrent of seething fury of the "Somebody's Gonna PAY for this!" and "I gotta right, given what I have to endure!" attitude and tactics. And you open yourself to life in hell if you ever try to give feedback or to correct the situation.
****

"Devil incarnate." This the "sick McMurphy" and the "Milo Minder-Bender" type of situation in which a psychopath takes advantage of every opportunity to precipitate a riot, carry out a vendetta, lash out indiscriminately, and make a personal bonanza at the expense of everyone and everything in sight, including colluding with and selling to the enemy, such as ambulance-chasers, criminals, psychotic relative-triggering, black marketing, supplies and equipment stealing, etc.

They are the product of a totally amoral and exploitative/abusive family system in which it was "everyone for themselves and damn the consequences!" -- with a "What can I get out of this?" value system.

Or they ended up falling between the cracks of a severely dysfunctional and self-immersed family, where they learned the tricks of the trade between the lines, so to speak. In any case, it is utterly untouchable, and all you can do is to confine and restrict them as much as possible.

"TRAVELER'S THROMBOSIS;" "ECONOMY CLASS SYNDROME" "DEEP VEIN THROMBOSIS" OR DVT. (Blood clots in the legs that can even become fatal while on a plane.)

"Pulling the world in over their heads." They have an intensely conservative and restrictive reaction to life. They are resisting change and expansion, closing down on the flow of joy and growth in their life. Change usually meant things got considerably worse when they were a child, and their subsequent experience has done little to change that impression.
****

"Love retard." There is a blocking off of self-love, the ability to express love to others, and the capacity to receive love. They are feeling neglected, abandoned and/or unacceptable, due to the lack or loss of love in their life. They cling to or to hold on to love for fear of its moving away or of our moving away from it. It is the result of an emotionally-depriving early environment.

TREMOR (Constant low-key shaking)

"Cosmic paranoia." They have an intensely anxious relationship with the Universe that is full of fear, uncertainty and insecurity. They have a "God will KILL me if I do anything different!" feeling. They have ended up feeling stagnant and immobilized. They have little faith in the Universe and in life, and they feel alone and unsafe in an uncaring world.

It is the result of a very rigid adaptation to a severely dysfunctional and frightening family who themselves manifested a very fearfully narrow viewpoint and lifestyle. They played the role of the "family hoist" -- the one who was the pivot point of everything.
****

"I don't dare let go!" There is an overwhelming desire to control everything and everyone about every aspect of every issue, situation and undertaking. They have the complete conviction that all hell will break loose and that everything will go down the tubes unless they personally hands-on determine the purpose, process and outcome of everything.

They were the "sane one" in an out-of-control self-defeating, ungrounded and potentially self-destructive family. Without their interventions, things WOULD have gone over the edge into catastrophic disaster.
****

"Annihilation-anxiety." They are deeply afraid of disastrous events about to do them in. They feel very much "at effect," rather than "at cause," and they are in a state of continuous alarm as they feel profoundly at risk all the time. They come from an unpredictably and devastatingly dysfunctional family in which awful things did routinely happen. There may well have been severe violence and abuse as well.

****

"Wreak-freak." They are experiencing intense "run amok-anxiety" about what they might do if they "let fly with one" or if they "let themselves loose on the world." It often has an intense rage underlying it. This rage is the massive indignation-outrage reaction to being subjected to felt completely undeserved violation and deprivation as a child in their severely dysfunctional and destructively self-immersed family.

"TRENCH MOUTH" (Severe stress-precipitated intense gingivitis and infection of the gums) [It got its name from the outcomes of trench warfare in WWI.]

"Overwhelmed." They feel severely out-classed and over-run by life. They have the experience that they lack the resources to handle things, and they also believe that the world is going out of its way to traumatize and persecute them.

They feel intensely vulnerable, unable to cope, and severely deprived in a learned helplessness and intense resentment reaction to the course of their life. They grew up in a dysfunctional and chaotic crisis-courting family who had no time or energy for them.

TRICHINOSIS (Fever, nausea, diarrhea and muscle pains from worms in pork. Often lethal)

"Desert island." There is severe internal conflict and lack of harmony arising from a deep-seated fear of abandonment and of the loss of support systems. They were put on highly conditional acceptance as a child, with the implied threat of abandonment hanging in the air all though childhood.

****

"Can't cope." They feel in over their head, that things have gotten out of hand, that they don't have what it takes to handle their situation. They have a lot of agitated worry and hurry, in fear of anticipated outcomes. They are intensely fearful, and they want to run off.

They want to be rid of the whole thing, and to give their power to others, to let them take over everything. They are afraid of the "ultimate blow it," out of a profound competence-anxiety. They have now reached the point where they just don't have the confidence to carry it off any more.

They were the "family hoist," and at the same time they were the "family scapegoat," and they were made to feel totally responsible for the welfare of the family.

****

"Let me be!" They have an underlying passivity and desire not to be bothered with the requirements and responsibilities of life. They want to be left alone and to be taken care of. They were over-indulged and under-required in their enmeshed family.

****

"Revolting development." They are intensely disgusted with, angered by, and frightened about this turn of events in their life. They feel personally responsible for it. It is the result of having had to take accountability for everything that happened in their family.

TUBERCULOSIS

"Bitter resentfulness." They are wasting away, due to selfishness, intense possessiveness, cruel thoughts, and vengefulness. They are determined to have their own way, as a false consolation for the harsh realities of their life. They feel that they have done their level best in a valiant effort, but that circumstances just wouldn't have it so.

They had unhappy love affairs, resulting in bitterness, disappointment, resentment, unforgivingness and clutchingness. They feel unappreciated, and they play out a "Camille" scenario, in which their feeling is, "They'll be sorry when I'm gone!"

They are given to resentfully-imagined guilt and remorse reactions from their people. In addition, there is also a large spiteful revenge streak playing a major part in this process. They are selfishly clinging and controlling, they are slyly passive-aggressive, and they are full of "Feel sorry for me!" strategies. In the meantime, they are seeking an "easeful death."

It is the result of their having had a "special" role as a child in their severely passive-aggressive dysfunctional family, and they have never gotten over or relinquished it.

TUBEROUS SCLEROSIS (Degenerative connective tissue disorder)

"What am I *doing* here?" They are manifesting a dismayed discombobulation about the world and the way their life is going. It is the result of growing up in a vaguely overwhelmed and enmeshed family or out of being here as a "visitor" from another soul pool for soul experience and destiny-manifestation purposes.
****

"Hapless, helpless, hopeless." They have a great deal of sorrow, deep-seated grief, and despair, and they are chronically crying on the inside. They feel overwhelmed and unable to handle the requirements of life. They have in effect "thrown in the towel" on even trying to make it in life. They come from a massively dysfunctional and demoralizing family.
****

"Allergic reaction to themselves." They feel somehow responsible for all the ills of the world, that they are the cause. They are having a "get rid of the problem" reaction to themselves.

It is a result of having "carried the world on their shoulders" all their life, starting with their dysfunctional family. They ended up with little or no ability to receive or to request or to require a return in kind. They were told in effect that they were the source of all the family's problems, while they were actually the only one who was deflecting some of the disasters.

TULAREMIA (See "RABBIT FEVER")

TUMOR(S)

"Cosmic victimization." They are holding on to thought patterns and attitudes that have been ignored and no dealt with for a long time, and they can now no longer appropriately be held onto or ignored. They feel victimized by the Universe, and they see no way out of it. It feels like it is either justified punishment or the capricious nature of the Universe for them to be forever entrapped in re-runs of the old traumas.

They want to grow, but they feel utterly unable to do so. They feel utterly powerless, and that they just have to accept the way it is. They have a lot of remorse and regrets, and they have the experience that no one cares about them. They are operating out of a hapless, helpless, hopeless orientation. They are the product of an exploitative, abusive and oppressive dysfunctional family.
****

"How Dare they!?" They are nursing old wounds and shocks, and they are building up intense resentment. They have many unresolved rages and hatreds, they refuse to forgive and forget. They have an inflated sense of their importance and worth, and they are prideful and bitterly disgusted with the human race. This nihilistic disdainfulness trip comes from their having grown up in a bitterly dysfunctional and intractable family.

"TWITCHING" (Sudden involuntary gross motor movements)

"Twisted itches." They are suppressing actions and feelings to the point where it leads to stress. They fear letting go or letting people know their feelings, lest all hell break loose or they get strung from the yardarm. They come from a severely dysfunctional family in which "a slip of the lip could sink the ship" -- in actuality.

TYPHOID FEVER (Severe fever, diarrhea)

"Fed up." Things are moving too fast, and they are taking a direction that brings up all kinds of intense anger and stored resentments. They are intensely internally conflicted, and they want to get out of the situation somehow.

They want to get this over with as quickly as possible, and they feel "left in the lurch holding the bag -- again!" They feel overwhelmed by things, and their experience is that no one cares or ever has. It is the result of "keep 'em around the old homestead" parenting in which they were expected to take care of everything.

TYPHUS FEVER (Fever, red eruptions, weakness, nervous disorders)

"Under siege." They feel besieged and restricted on all sides, and they feel unsafe, betrayed, rejected and attacked. They have concluded that they can't be themselves, because that is somehow "bad, wrong and evil."

However, at the same time, they are burning up with intense anger and stored resentments about how they are treated, and they are quite self-disgusted for having elicited this environmental reaction. To top it all off, they are intensely abandonment-anxious as well. This is all the result of a self-immersed, convenience-concerned, wrong-making and suppressive family.

ULCERATED LARYNX (Backed up stomach acid burning the larynx)

"The British are coming!" They are in deep conflict about speaking (or singing) out. They have consistently found that when they do so, they receive large amounts of attack and unjustified criticism. At the same time, they have a profound sense of responsibility to communicate the truth and what they are aware of.

The result is a generalized rage over not being able to express themselves in the world, coupled with anxiety over the fact that if they don't communicate the truth, all hell will break loose, as they experience it. They feel responsible and accountable for what will come out of the present situation, yet at the same time, they feel that their hands are effectively tied. They in turn are "fit to be tied."

It is an old, familiar story that got started in their dysfunctional family, in which they were the only one who saw and knew what was happening, what was coming, and what was needed. They kept trying to convey desperately important realities -- to no avail.

ULCERATED SPOTS ON THE SKIN (Eroded holes, open sores)

"Inferiority complex." They have feelings of low self-esteem, along with a sense of ostracism and obstruction. They are ashamed of themselves, and they are troubled by their unlovely thoughts about others that have arisen out of their life history. They have a lot of anxiety and fear from old, buried "gukky stuff," including from past lives. To make matters worse, they have strong longings which can't be realized at present.

At the base of all this is a conflict between their desire for affection, on the one hand, and their fear of being hurt if it is sought, on the other. Underpinning all this is a tendency to be unwilling to forgive and forget the past. They have a notable lack of peace and harmony in their life, and they feel continuously uneasy and threatened by the world. All of this is an outcome of being a "sensitive" in a severely denial-dominated dysfunctional family who used and abused them.

ULCERATIVE COLITIS (Lining-damaging inflammation of the large intestine)

"Hands-on control." They are rather intensely alarmed about things getting out of hand, and they are prone to obsessive-compulsive patterns. It results in their being indecisive, detail-fixated, decision-anxious.

They are excessively conforming, and they suppress themselves out of fear of ostracism, rejection and retribution. They feel like they are being martyred, and they have a good deal of resentment and anger about that. However, they don't dare express it. They come from a suppressive, rigid, patriarchal family.
****

"Guilty unlovability." They have a great need to be loved that is prevented fulfillment by self-punishing self-deprivation for presumed transgressions that the outside world is unaware of. There is desperation for affection that they never got. This results in self-denigration and pessimism.

They are over-conscientious and hyper-sensitively over-conscientious, with false feelings of accountability and moral culpability. They are a self-defeating "loser" out of an emotionally immature attitude of self-destruction for their "evilness."

There is a considerable feeling of undue burdens, emotional strain, and loneliness. They are apt to go off into a frenzy of self-recrimination in reaction to rejection of love from a dear one. They are very insecure, and they have an intensely difficult time letting go of that which is over and done with. It came from over-exacting parents who imposed an experience of severe oppression, over-responsibility and defeat.
****

"Get out of my life!" They feel injured and degraded by some external malignant force. They want to eliminate the responsible agent. They feel humiliated, and they want to dispose of it NOW! They are bursting with unexpressed rage, and they are super-self-suppressing out of "run amok-anxiety." They are in perfectionistic denial of the realities that they are maintaining a "conspiracy of silence" about, and which they studiously avoid looking at.

They are basically a sensitive, bright, timid, dependent, Pollyannaishly denying, and passive person who is reluctant to take life on. They are indecisive, ingratiating, immature, and impotent. Underneath, they are fulminatingly furious about both their incapacity and their situation.

They are the product of a dysfunctional family in which the mother was dominating and repressive and the father was passive and jealous. There were many miseries and health hassles in the family, and yet it was a "tight little island" from which there was no escape.

ULCERS

"Catastrophic expectations." They have a well-ingrained habit of fearfulness, anxiety and tension. They are forever agitated about the possibility of calamity hitting them. They worry about details, and they are intensely competence-anxious about their ability to cope.

They have a fearsome strong belief that they are "not good enough," and they worry a lot about their "inferiority." They are guilt-grabbing, doubt-dominated, and agitatedly anxious all the time. The pressures of their felt responsibilities are in effect too much for them to handle. Their family was simultaneously perfectionistically expecting and denigrating of their every effort.
****

"Yearning for love." They have severe abandonment and betrayal feelings, along with pronounced dependency and separation-anxiety, some of which is derived from past lives. They are desperate for mothering, but they feel that they have to "earn" it with "achieve-aholic" accomplishments.

They are trying their damnedest to do enough to "deserve" the nurturance they so desperately desire, yet they are at the same time feeling the load of excessive responsibility and a lot of anxiety about failing to pull it all off. They are the product of an agitatedly anxious and catastrophizing family in which they were placed in a position of responsibility that was way over their head.
o so, on the other.

They are frustrated, angry and hostile about their whole situation, and they are undergoing a lot of stress, anxiety, agitation and upset due to too many demands. They have as a result great difficulty assimilating their experiences.

They are deeply frustrated at the way things don't go their way, and they are seeking revenge. As a result, they go into "Reggie the Raging Room-wrecker" rage-aholic reactions, and they are resentful, fault-finding and judgmental. The entire process is "eating away" at them.

The whole pattern started in a withholding and depriving household in which they had to take on too much responsibility too early, and in which they had to "earn their breakfast."

UMBILICAL HERNIA (Bulging inner organ through the belly button)

"Power issues." They feel prevented from accessing their personal potency and/or they are afraid to access their personal power, community clout, and initiative impact-making capabilities. It is the result of being reacted to as being threatening and/or "evil" when they did so as a child.
****

"Cut off from the Universe." They feel somehow rejected by God. They assume that they are getting their "Cosmic just desserts," and this conclusion has carried into their life as the foundational assumption out of which they operate. It started in an at least ambivalent, if not a hostile womb experience. It is essentially a destiny design feature for purposes of karma-burning, experience-expanding, and/or special training.

****

"Powder keg." They are a ball of rage about to go off, and they have a good deal of "run amok-anxiety," with a frantic effort to control their anger. They do so by pretending it isn't there, in an ostrich-like stance, which only generates events and outcomes that feed the volcano inside. It ultimately ends up erupting through their power center and their connection to the Universe.

They have been intensely frustrated in their relations with the world since the beginning, with their suppressive and repressive mother.

UNCONTROLLABLE RESPONSES FROM THE CENTRAL NERVOUS SYSTEM

"Overwhelm!" They are having intense reverberation reactions to a severely threatening and/or traumatic set of circumstances. Their limits of ability have been far exceeded, and their whole operating system is flailing away desperately, in a frantic attempt to regain some semblance of sanity and solubility to their situation.

It arises from having been required to live at the extreme edge in a situation that in effect pushed them to expand their abilities continuously, with profound stakes involved, all through their childhood. The family depended on them as their lifeline, and they responded by rising to the challenge at all costs. Now they have reached the point where "This is an up with which I can no longer put!"

UNCOORDINATED INVOLUNTARY MOVEMENTS

"Oh no you don't!." They have crossed the "forbidden line" into self-commitment and destiny-manifestation, and a long-ago implanted injunction to the effect of, "If you ever violate this taboo, a hex on you!" from their family has gone off. They were never to abandon the family by bonding with relevant others, by developing their capacities, or by moving into manifestation of their purpose.

UNDER-ACTIVE ADRENALS

"Emotional malnutrition." They have a lot of anger at themselves that is resulting in and which comes from severe non-support. They feel that they are "alone on a desert island," with no sustenance from anyone. It has the effect of "pulling the plug" on their motivational system, and they are ending up effectively an amotivational "couch potato." Their family was intensely accusatory and depriving.

"UNDULANT FEVER" (Recurring fever, enlarged spleen, joint pains, sweating)

"Catastrophic expectations." They have very little trust in the Universe, and they are quite unhappy and emotionally unbalanced. There is a certain rigidity and resistance to change, and they are burning up with intense resentment about their situation.

Bottom line, they don't feel safe in the world, and they are very angry about the way things are happening in their life. This has resulted in a constant "prediction and preparation for disaster" pattern.

All of this started in an unpredictable and unstable dysfunctional family in which there were constant difficulties. They feel that this is their lot in life, and that they somehow have to handle it.

UREMIA (Poisoning from urinary substances in the blood)

"Pissed off at the Universe." They have a need to get rid of something in their life, to clear out toxic things, situations, people and environments from their life. However, they have a fundamental lack of love for themselves which prevents them from doing this effectively.

They have a fearful orientation towards the world, and they therefore take a conservative and cautionary approach that results in their hanging on to old ideas, and in their being afraid of letting go. They have an underlying intense abandonment-resentment.

They have the distinct feeling that nothing new is going to make any difference, so they clutch to the "tried and true." The trouble is that it is exactly the "bad old ways" that are now getting them in trouble. This whole pattern got started in a restrictive and depriving dysfunctional family.

URETHRA PROBLEMS; URINARY TRACT PROBLEMS

"Cope-ability anxiety." They are chronically alarmed that they may not have what it takes to make it. They have the feeling that they are somehow inadequate to the cause. They are therefore generally anxious all the time. They are the product of a competence- and confidence- undermining possessive family who wanted to "keep 'em around the old homestead."
****

"Sexual fearfulness." The whole erotic realm "sends them up the skimmer handle." They feel that they can never win and that they always lose and are hurt in this arena. It is the result of being sexualized and sex-ploitated in a seductive-destructive "seduce-slap" type of parenting pattern in which they were enticed and then attacked for being both attractive and responsive by their parent (usually the mother) in their dysfunctional family.
~~~~~~

URINARY TRACT INFECTION(S); URETHRITIS

"Ethical problems." They are having deep conflicts about their ability to manifest their values and priorities. It arises from a non-comprehending, dysfunctional, incompetencing, belittling and/or accusatory family.
****

"Downloading time." There is a need to get rid of something in their life -- they are desperately trying to clear the toxic things, situations and people out of their life. They feel the necessity for the release of pressure. However, their lack of self-love makes this a quite difficult undertaking. They come from a severely dysfunctional family who held them accountable for all their misery.
****

"Hunker down in the bunker." They have a fearful orientation towards the world, along with a cautionary conservative approach which results in their hanging on to old ideas and in their being afraid of letting go. They are lacking in adaptability, and they have a fear of change, because they don't believe that anything new would work on their behalf.

They have a certain difficulty with inner direction arising from the fear that if they have any hopes, they will prove to be false and they "will blow up in their face." They are the product of a demoralizingly dysfunctional family in which any efforts to improve the situation only made things far worse.
****

"Abandonment-anticipation." They have a strong underlying abandonment-anxiety and a resulting tendency to dependent attachment and to vulnerability-avoidance at the same time their experience has to suppress resentment over vulnerability and abandonment-anticipation. They also have the feeling that their need for love is unfulfilled and unfulfillable, with the result that they are prone to depression. They have a fair amount of guilt and grief, arising from a severely suppressive and non-supportive childhood.
****

"Cope-ability-anxious." They have a lack of self-confidence, and they feel insufficient to the cause. They feel tired, and that they are "running on empty." There is poor endurance and a considerable amount of inner agitation and irritation. There is very little basic trust that things are going to go well for them, and they are deeply unhappy.

It is a pattern that got started in a rigidly denial-dominated and bitter dysfunctional family who would systematically see to it that anything they got would be destroyed or removed, out of a generalized envy and alarm reaction to the individual's (to them) incomprehensible capabilities and potentialities. They intended to "keep 'em around the old homestead" as their "private preserve" and their "whipping kid."
****

"Royally pissed off." They are thoroughly enraged at their life, and they don't trust the Universe one iota. They are full of resentment, blame and angry emotions, and they feel betrayed. They are looking for who is responsible for all their troubles, trials and tribulations.

Much of their venom is directed at their intimates, especially those of the other gender. They feel that the parent of the other gender is the cause of all their problems. However, underneath all this is the uneasy feeling that they are really just getting their "just desserts." This whole pattern came about as a result of their being sexualized and sex-ploitated in a seductive-destructive "tantalizing tarantula" -- "seduce-slap" and accusatory manner.

URIC ACID RETENTION (See "GOUT")

URTICARIA (See "HIVES")

UTERUS PROBLEMS

"I don't dare." She feels that it is not safe for her to manifest her creativity or her generativity, and she therefore distrusts and has disgust towards such undertakings. She fears rejection, abandonment and attack, along with envy, jealousy and retaliation.

She has real problems with her mother, as a result of the mother's capitulation or cooperation with what went down in her family. It comes from her experience in a patriarchal and dysfunctional family, in which the feminine and the creative were greatly feared and devalued.

UTERINE CANCER

"Martyr trip." She feels victimized by the Universe and by God (Who is a male, in her experience). She has a great deal of "tripod rage" -- the irresistible urge to kick anything with three legs.

She is plagued with a huge amount of repressed rage, and she is prone to severe passive-aggressiveness and to subtle subterranean subconscious sabotage. They are constantly irritated and enraged by others, particularly males, and especially by her male intimate. They are the product of a repressedly rageful and patriarchy-hating mother, usually with a highly ineffectual and enraging father.

(See **CANCER**)

VAGINAL PROBLEMS

"Self-rejection." She has many worries over not being good enough, along with self-denigration and self-disgust. She doesn't trust her feminine receptivity, and she won't surrender to herself. She also has a fear of sex and sexual desire, along with a fear of procreativity and vulnerability.

It is the result of an intrusively controlling, sex-ploitative and "never enough" withholding and judgmental father.

****

"Tripod-rage." They have an intense urge to kick anything with three legs. It was generated originally by an equally misanthropic mother, but re-validated by an abusive and sex-ploitative father and by the patriarchal culture.

~~~~~~

PAINFUL VAGINAL SPASMS; VAGINISMUS; VAGINITIS

"Womb-rage." They have intense anger at the whole business of being a female. There is a goodly amount of "tripod-rage" (an intense urge to kick anything with three legs) directed at the whole patriarchy, but particularly towards their mate. However, bottom line, it is reflective of a severe self-rejection and self-punishment coming out of sexual guilt. They are the product of a femininity-devaluing patriarchal family.

****

"I don't cut it." They have worries over not being good enough, along with self-denigration and self-disgust. They don't trust their feminine receptivity. They also have a fear of sex and sexual desire, along with a fear of procreativity and vulnerability. It is the result of an intrusively controlling, sex-ploitative and "never good enough" withholding and judgmental father.

"VALLEY FEVER" (Viral flu-like, frequently fatal disorder)

"Persecuted urban hermit." They have profound feelings of being under the influence of malevolent forces and of being weak and helpless. They have a fear of attack from others, and of taking life in fully. There is a strong feeling of lack of support and protection.

They manifest insufficient involvement and interaction, in an "among us but not of us" pattern. They have a lot of conflict, confusion and susceptibility to suggestion, especially from the "world of agreement" or the group mind or statistical "proofs." Underneath is a buried rage and hatred for their being so alone, alien and alienated.

It comes from a family in which they could do no right, where they were unrecognized, and where no one supported, sustained or validated them. It also reflects the sense of utter vulnerability, despair and nihilism that accompany times and processes of great change.

VEIN PROBLEMS

"Grudge-nursing." They are unable to forgive and forget or to cleanse their consciousness or to let go of the garbage from the past. They get caught up in all the little things in life as "symbolic" and "representative" of how it was and how "it always happens that way."

They are prone to be resentment-carrying, to be injustice-nurturing, and to live in the past. They lack understanding, and they have little flexibility of thought. They are full of bitter grudgingness, and they are convinced that what is given out will not be returned.

It is the result of a rigid, conservative, and unchangingly massively dysfunctional, victimizing and mutually exploitative family who continually complained of all the betrayals, denials and injustices they have had to bear as a function of their own malfunctioning.

~~~~~~

INFLAMMATION OF THE VEINS

"I hate my life." They have an intense anger and frustration with their life. They are blaming others for the limitations and lack of joy in their life that they are undergoing at present. Their experience is that they are surrounded by a "ship of fools," and by irrelevant resources that simply don't meet the needs of the situation. It comes from having had to take over the helm of a rudderless, highly incompetent and dysfunctional family from a very early age.

VARICOSE VEINS (Swollen veins due to improper heart valve functioning)

"Love is a poison apple." They are experiencing deep emotional conflict and tension concerning being able to love and nourish themselves, and about letting love in. They are also feeling that they are going in the wrong direction, and that they are not being able to be nourished by their surrounding resources.

They don't feel that they deserve love, and in their experience, what passed for love in their family was most untrustworthy. So they now distrust love in all of its manifestations, and it is causing great problems for them in dealing with life. It started in a severely exploitative and rejecting family in which love was malevolant.

****

"Leave well enough alone!" They are a situation they hate, and they are full of seething resentment about the slow return of invested love. They are also feeling over-worked and over-burdened.

Yet they are convinced that they dare not speak the truth about the situation, for fear of the dire consequences. It is a discouragement and despair life orientation generated by an exploitative, withholding and suppressive dysfunctional family.

****

"Overload." They are living a lifestyle that involves their being responsible for more than they can handle, and they are feeling over-burdened and burned out. They desperately want to put an end to that, and they really want to run away from it all. They are deeply discouraged, and they are highly negative and resistant to their situation.

They were placed in a position of heavy responsibility that was beyond their capacities by their dependent and dysfunctional family.

"WHITE LEG" (Blanching of the leg by clots in the veins)

"Responsibility-resentment." They have a lot of anger over having to stand on their own two feet, and over having to stand up for themselves. They have a strong desire to run away and escape from the responsibilities of life.

They are "pulling the world in over their head," in an intensely change-fighting and responsibility-deflecting manner. They are highly resistive to the requirement to "grow up," and they are on a "sit down strike." The net result is that they are having difficulties in the realm of success, and they are constantly fending off losses and failure.

This whole pattern is the result of "keep 'em around the old homestead" parenting in an over-indulgent, under-requiring, and growth- and change-preventing pattern.

VENEREAL DISEASE

"Mea culpa." They have a felt need for punishment arising out of sexual guilt. They have the gut-level belief that genitals and sinful and dirty, due a sexually suppressive and shame-inducing dysfunctional family, who were at the same time "tantalizing tarantula" -- "seductive-destructive" -- "seduce--slap" sex-ploitative.
****

"Take that!" They are deeply resentful over exploitation, oppression and/or abuse. They are now taking it out on their intimate or someone close, in a "kick the cat" or "passing it on" reaction. They grew up in abusive, blame-throwing, authoritarian and exploitative family.

(See **ACQUIRED IMMUNO-DEFICIENCY SYNDROME (AIDS); GONORRHEA; HERPES; SYPHILIS**)

VERTEBRAL SUBLUXATION (See **SPINE PROBLEMS**)

VERTIGO (Violent dizziness)

"New cup! New cup!" They are finding that the processes and resources they have been relying upon for quite a while now are suddenly unavailable and/or unworkable. They are being required to come up with new approaches to things.
****

"Flying off in all directions at once." They are being inundated with mental confusion and flighty, scattered thinking, due to outside pressures. They are refusing to look at things directly and squarely in the eye. They feel threatened by life's demands and realities. It feels very unsafe to them, and that it is impossible for them to have any joy in their life.

Now they are faced with a high intensity and/or a high stakes decision, commitment, undertaking or experience, and they feel overwhelmed. It is a pattern that got started in a denial-dominated dysfunctional family in which they were required to function in the face of chaos and refusal to deal with reality.

VIRAL INFECTION(S)

"Resentful resignation." They are having the experience that life is being quite difficult, and they are feeling very little, if any positives in their life. To them, it feels like everything is one long series of responsibilities, traumas and drudgeries of late. It is a result of a "grimly getting through the night" dysfunctional family.
****

"Well, what do you expect?" They are bitterly of the opinion that "there is no joy in Bloodville!" They are in effect utterly unable to experience the beauty, good and joy of the Universe. They are quite resistive to and resentful of the process of dealing with life. They have the feeling that they get every disease that comes down the pike.

They are the product of a severely survivalist and self-defeating dysfunctional family system. It had the effect of convincing them that love and joy are a joke and that they can and should have no love for themselves, since they are "just getting what they deserve."

VISION PROBLEMS

"I see too much." They have the feeling that they can't quite handle life the way they want to. They are feeling overwhelmed in the face of the difficulties of life. They are seeing too much for them to handle.

So they are disrupting their vision so they don't have to see what they're going through, even though they have to go through it anyway. It was an adaptation to a significantly dysfunctional family in which it was clearly not O.K. for them to see what was going on, going down, and coming down.

RIGHT EYE VISION PROBLEMS

"Upset by what they see." There are disturbances created by what they see in the world around them.

LEFT EYE VISION PROBLEMS

"I don't like what I see about me." They are having intense conflicts concerning what they see within themselves or concerning what is happening to them.

~~~~~~

ASTIGMATISM (Distorted visual perceptions.)

"I trouble." They are having difficulties with distorted perception do to a confusion-inducing and clarity-preventing family system in childhood. They have an abiding fear of really seeing themselves and what's going on, lest they set off the "dynamite shed" outcome (in which they light a match to see where they are in this strange-smelling pitch dark room full of rough-hewn boxes and skinny little ropes). They are manifesting self-suppression and deep fear of seeing their real worth.

There was much abuse and many fear-inducing experiences during childhood, and they are now trying to create a different reality, one that isn't the same as that playing out in front of their eyes.

RIGHT EYE ASTIGMATISM

"I don't see it." They have a deep fear of seeing what's happening in the world around them.

LEFT EYE ASTIGMATISM

"I don't see me doing it." There is an avoidance of perceiving who they are out of an underlying "monster-anxiety" about themselves.

~~~~~~

"FAR-SIGHTEDNESS"

"Present-avoidance." They have a bad case of hope-addiction of the "grass must be greener over there" and "It's bound to be better then!" variety. They have a real fear of the here and now realities of things and of the present. They focus instead on the future, as they avoid the present.

They are future-fixated, and they forgo much for what they hope will be long range gains. They are extroverted and outgoing, always looking for something or someone better over there.

At base, it's a self-avoidant and self-distracting activity-addict pattern of functioning. In this, they are just passing on what they learned in their denial-dominated dysfunctional family system.

RIGHT EYE FAR-SIGHTEDNESS
"Future-hoping." They are looking for things to be better tomorrow in the world around them.

LEFT EYE FAR-SIGHTEDNESS
"Self-avoidance." They have a real fear of looking at themselves and their inner nature.

VITILIGO (White patches on the skin, sometimes turning the whole body white)
"Stranger in a strange land." They are feeling completely outside of things, like they just don't belong anywhere. They distinctly feel not one of the group, and that they are on the fringes of life.

It came about through the process of their being held accountable and responsible for everything that happened in their dysfunctional family, with the result that they ended up in the "family hoist" and the "family scapegoat" at the same time.

That in turn led to their being apart from the family and everyone else. Being vulnerable, involved and intimate was and is both too painful and too destructive to them, so they have operated like a "Martian anthropologist" -- "urban hermit" on the sidelines of society from the very beginning.

WEEPING SKIN ERUPTIONS (Leaking lymphatic fluid)

"Seeping sorrow." They are plagued by suppressed grief and deprivation-depression. They received very little love and acceptance as an infant and child.
****

"Freak-out." They are being over-run by repressed anxiety and fears derived from a thoroughly frightening family history.

WEST NILE VIRUS (See NILE VIRUS)

"WHITE LEG" (See VEIN PROBLEMS)

WHOOPING COUGH (Intense gasping coughing, with a "whooping" sound in between coughing episodes)

"Expression-suppression." They have intense inhibition around self-expression, along with guilt over what they want to say. There is something they need to speak out about, but they can't bring themselves to do it. They have a strong desire to bark at the world in a "See me! Listen to me, damn it!" manner.

They feel not noticed, appreciated or loved. They are abandonment- and rejection-paranoid. However, at the same time, they are agitated, disturbed and rejecting of ideas that scare them, or that might lead to total rejection.

It comes from a smothering, severely suppressive and intensely rejecting family system in which the message was loud and clearly a "Don't be you!" injunction. They were told in no uncertain terms that they are to be seen and not heard, and that they are in effect "the cause of World War II."
****

"Just ignore me." They feel that they are so unimportant that they have nothing to say, and that they have no right to expect any form of attention or acceptance from other people. They feel that they are in effect "trivial" and "worthless."

In such a situation, illnesses and dramatic symptoms like the coughing and whooping are a "sad settle-for" attention-getting mechanism acquired in a family who would otherwise pretend they didn't exist.
****

"Run amok-anxious." They feel that they are in effect an out-of-control "careening cannon" that would, if they spoke up or were heard, in effect devastate the world. They are therefore terrified of speaking out, and they are profoundly ashamed of themselves for what they would say and do if they could.

It reflects perfectionistic parents who induced a fear of being caught in a mistake. The net effect here is that they become extremely cautiously critical of themselves and all they do, in a worried, confused, mentally conflicted and rejection-anticipating manner.
****

"Self-hatred." They are choking on life in a guilty and self-disgusted manner. They feel that they are in effect a "piece of shit" whom everybody should ignore anyway. They are also sure that what they would say or do would only lead to negative outcomes, they have the feeling that they are "unfit for human consumption," and that they are in effect the precipitator of all the evils in the world. They are the product of a severely rejecting and denigrating dysfunctional family.

"WORMS" (Parasitic)

"Going for the God Housekeeping Seal of Approval." They are giving their power to others, letting them take over everything in their life. It's a pattern that started in a "never good enough" parenting situation, in which they frantically tried over and over to get the "God Housekeeping Seal of Approval" -- and forever failed to do so.

The result is that they now feel that they lack the secret for success and worth that everyone else has, and that they have to keep trying with "stand-ins for the original cast" in re-runs of the original scenario until they "get it right," finally.

****

"Self-distrust." They are terrified to strike out on their own or to stand on their own rights, ground, and two feet, for fear of the ultimate "blow-it." They have no trust of themselves, and they are convinced that there is an "answer" that they don't have and others do, so they keep on trying to find the "key."

In the meantime, they turn everything over to "those in the know" or to those they think hold the "Golden Orb" of "Final Validation." As a result, they have to deal with constant interference and exploitation in their life. It got started in their enmeshed, possessive and competence-undermining "keep 'em around the old homestead" family.

****

"Self-disgust." They are full of self-rejection, along with a strong belief in being a victim and being "unclean." In both a reactive enslavement and a self-fulfilling prophecy manner, they have a sense of helplessness.

They feel an utter vulnerability to the seeming attitudes of others as being "God's Gospel Truth," and they then become what is said, or they elicit the negative responses themselves. They were massively shame-induced by their family.

****

"I want it all!" They are consumed with materialistic ambitions, abundance-seeking, and comfort concerns. Sophisticated greediness is eating away at them. It arose from a highly self-involved family system.

(See **TAPEWORM; TRICHINOSIS**)

YAWS (Skin eruptions, destructive lesions of the skin and in the bones)

"Overwhelmed." Life's vicissitudes and difficulties have undermined the depths of their sense of sanity and survival. They feel inferior, inadequate, and full of shame. They are having real problems with feelings of weakness, vulnerability and worthlessness.

There is also a strong feeling of lack of support from the Universe. They have a great deal of resentment and rage about their whole life pattern. Underlying all of this is a pronounced tendency resist forgiving and forgetting the past, including past lives. They have a notable lack of peace and harmony in their life, and they feel continuously uneasy and threatened by the world.

This all got started when they were the "sane one" in a highly dysfunctional family, with the result that they had to take on too much as a child. They were in over their head then, and they now feel unable to carry on any more.

YEAST INFECTION (In the female sexual organs)

"Me last!" They are a "serve-aholic" co-dependent who is denying of their own needs and who is not supporting themselves. They feel that they don't deserve love, that they have to "earn" it, and they therefore lack self-love.

They feel that they have to "serve themselves up on a platter" to get the "God Housekeeping Seal of Approval" that never comes. They were put on highly conditional and demanding love by their enmeshed and possessive but ambivalent mother.
****

"Self-rejection." They feel that there is something "bad, wrong and evil" about them. They are therefore incapable of accepting or providing support for themselves, and they are unable to own or manifest their personal power. They are the product of a denigrating family who undermined their competence and confidence.
****

"Tripod-rage." There is a considerable amount of the irresistible urge to kick anything with three legs, and of patriarchy-paranoia, which they carefully repress and suppress. They come from a highly exploitative, patriarchal and oppressive/suppressive family.

YEAST OVER-PRODUCTION (Leading to debilitation of the immune system)

"Low self-commitment." They are handicapped by an inability to release past memories and other wastes, such as harmful habits and traits. They are also unable to defend themselves against negative thoughts and internal and external attacks.

They are in effect "running on empty," and they are feeling utterly inadequate to the cause. Their emotional body is in disrepair, and they are having real difficulties in how well they take care of their own needs, getting nurtured, and handling their negative feelings about themselves. They are the product of a shame-producing dysfunctional family who conveyed very clearly to them that they have no right to have love and joy.

YELLOW FEVER (Jaundice, fever, nausea, vomiting)

"I refuse!" They are engaged in a thorough-going rejection of their situation and of life's requirements. They are cynically pessimistic and nihilistic, and there is a lack of love, compassion and tolerance on their part.

They are intensely resentful and ragingly angry at everything, and they are violently ejecting ideas and anything new. They are condescendingly contemptuous and distrustingly discouraged. Their experience is that anything different would just involve more responsibilities and negativity of outcomes. All of this derives from a highly accusatory and blame-throwing dysfunctional and nihilistic family.

YELLOW SKIN (See **JAUNDICE**)

REFERENCES

Arehart-Treichel, J. BIOTYPES. Time Books, New York, 1980.

Blackwell, J. and Blacwell, G. BODY MAGIC. Devon Press, Devon, Alberta, CANADA, 1985.

Booth, R. "The Relationship Between Archetypal Medicine and Past Life Therapy: Interdisciplinary Alternatives to Reductionistic Practice." The International Journal of Transpersonal Studies, 17, l, 1998, 7-16.

Buess, L. M. SYNERGY SESSION. DeVorss & Co., Marina Del Rey, CA, 1980.

Carlson, S. "Body Analysis." Seminar, Portland, OR, 1982.

Clark, M. C. "Spiritual Causes of Physical Pain, Part I." The Michael Connection, Orinda, CA, Fall, 1989.

Clark, M. C. "Spiritual Causes of Physical Pain, Part II." The Michael Connection, Orinda, CA, Winter, 1990.

Cooke, M. B. SYMBOLS. Marcus Books, Agincourt, Ontario, CANADA, 1980.

Cooke, M. B. BODY SIGNS. Marcus Books, Queensville, Ontario, CANADA, 1982.

Dennison, P. and Hargrove, G. "Integrated Movements for Meridian Over/Under Dependency." Unpublished manuscript, San Anselmo, CA, 1984.

Dethlefsen, T. and Dahke, R. THE HEALING POWER OF ILLNESS: The Meaning of Symptoms and How to Interpret Them. Element Press, Rockport, MA, 1991.

Dychtwald, K. BODY/MIND. Jove Publications, New York, 1978.

Ekman, P. TELLING LIES: Clues to Deceit in the Marketplace, Politics and Marriage. Norton, New York, 1985.

Friedman, H. S. (Ed.) PERSONALITY AND DISEASE. Wiley, New York, 1990.

Friedman, H. S. THE SELF-HEALING PERSONALITY: Why Some People Achieve Health and Other Succumb to Illness. Henry Holt, New York, 1991.

Friedman, H. S. (Ed.) HOSTILITY, COPING AND HEALTH. American Psychological Association Press, Washington, D.C., 1992.

Friedman, H. S., Tucker, J. S., Schwartz, J. E., Tomlison-Keasey, C., Martin, L. R., Wingard, D. L. & Criqui, M. H. "Psychosocial and Behavioral Predictors of Longevity: The Aging and Death of the Termites." American Psychologist, 50, 2, 1995, 69-78.

Gach, M. R. and Marco, C. ACU-YOGA. Japan Publications, Tokyo, 1981.

Gibson, W. and Gibson, L. COMPLETE ILLUSTRATED BOOK OF THE PSYCHIC SCIENCES. Doubleday, New York, 1966.

Graham, D. T. "Verbal Attitudes Associated with Physical Disorders." Paper presented at the meetings of the American Psychosomatic Society, Rochester, N.Y., 1962.

Hay, L. HEAL YOUR BODY: METAPHYSICAL CAUSATIONS FOR PHYSICAL ILLNESS. Self-published, Santa Monica, CA, 1984.

Hay, L. HEAL YOUR BODY: THE MENTAL CAUSES FOR PHYSICAL ILLNESSES AND THE METAPHYSICAL WAY TO OVERCOME THEM. Hay House, Santa Monica, CA., 1988.

Hay, L. HEAL YOUR BODY: A TO Z. THE MENTAL CAUSES FOR PHYSICAL ILLNESSES AND THE WAY TO OVERCOME THEM. Hay House, Carlsbad, CA, 1998.

Janov, A. THE ANATOMY OF MENTAL ILLNESS. Berkeley Publishing Corp, New York, 1971.

Kellerman, S. SOMATIC REALITY: Bodily Experience and Emotional Truth. Center Press, Berkeley, CA, 1979.

Kellerman, S. EMOTIONAL ANATOMY. Center Press, Berkeley, CA, 1985.

Kellerman, S. EMBODYING EXPERIENCE: Forming a Personal Life. Center Press, Berkeley, CA, 1987.

Kellerman, S. PATTERNS OF DISTRESS: Emotional Insults and Human Form. Center Press, Berkeley, CA, 1989.

Khalsa, G.S.S. CHUA KA': Zones of Karma. Unpublished manuscript, Los Angeles, CA, 1981.

Kurtz, R. THE BODY REVEALS. Harper & Row, New York, 1976.

Kurtz, R. HAKOMI THERAPY. Hakomi Institute, Boulder, CO, 1988.

Kurtz, R. BODY-CENTERED PSYCHOTHERAPY: The Hakomi Method. Life-Rhythm, Mendicino, CA, 1990.

Kushi, M. ORIENTAL DIAGNOSIS. Sunwheel Publications, London, 1978.

Lewis, H. R. and Lewis, M. E. PSYCHOSOMATICS: How Your Emotions Can Damage Your Health. Viking Press, New York, 1972.

Lincoln, Ph.D. Michael J. (FKA Narayan Khalsa-Singh) "Illnesses and Ailments." Unpublished manuscript, San Francisco, 1985.

Lincoln, Ph.D. Michael J. (FKA Narayan Khalsa-Singh) "Physical Feelings." Unpublished manuscript, San Francisco, 1985.

Lincoln, Ph.D. Michael J. (FKA Narayan Khalsa-Singh) "The Body Speaks." Unpublished manuscript, San Francisco, 1985.

Lincoln, Ph.D. Michael J. (FKA Narayan Khalsa-Singh) WHAT'S IN A FACE? Unpublished manuscript, Boulder, CO, 1995.

Lincoln, Ph.D. Michael J. (FKA Narayan Khalsa-Singh) ADDICTIONS AND CRAVINGS: Their Psychological Meaning. Boulder, CO, 1996; Revised 2006

Lincoln, Ph.D. Michael J. (FKA Narayan Khalsa-Singh) ALLERGIES AND AVERSIONS. Boulder, CO, 1996; Revised 2006

Lowen, A. THE BETRAYAL OF THE BODY. MacMillon Co, New York, 1967.

Lowen, A. THE LANGUAGE OF THE BODY. Collier Books, New York, 1971.

Luscher, M. THE FOUR-COLOR PERSON. Simon & Schuster, New York, 1977.

Luscher, M. PERSONALITY SIGNS. Warner Books, New York, 1981.

Lynn, H. DISEASE, THE CAUSE AND CURE. Coleman Graphics, Long Island, N.Y., 1982.

Morris, D. MANWATCHING. Abrams Press, New York, 1977.

Morris, D. BODY WATCHING. Crown, New York, 1985.

Moyer, B. HEALING AND THE MIND. Doubleday, New York, 1994.

Murray, L. S., Proud, P.M. and Tripp, J. M. TURNING AROUND: A Healing Workshop. Powerline Press, San Jose, CA, 1981.

Ogden, P. "Dimensions of Character." (In) Kurtz, R. HAKOMI THERAPY. Hakomi Institute, Boulder, CO, 1988.

Ornstein, R. and Sobel, D. "The Healing Brain." Psychology Today, New York, 1987.

Pelton, R. W. THE COMPLETE BOOK OF DREAM INTERPRETATION. Arco Press, New York, 1983.

Pennebaker, J. W. OPENING UP: The Healing Power of Confiding in Others. Morrow, New York, 1990.

Reich, W. THE FUNCTION OF THE ORGASM. Orgone Institute Press, New York, 1942.

Reich, W. CHARACTER ANALYSIS. Orgone Institute Press, New York, 1949.

Rolf, I. P. STRUCTURAL INTEGRATION. Guide for Structural Integration, Boulder, CO, 1962.

Rush, M. DECODING THE SECRET LANGUAGE OF THE BODY: The Many Ways Our Bodies Send Us Messages. Simon & Schuster, New York, 1994.

Saltrus, C. and Maisel, E. BODY SCOPES: The Revealing Link Between Body and Personality. Bantam Books, New York, 1986.

Serinus, J. "Permission to Heal." (In) Lee, P., Smith, I. and Adair, M. (Eds.) PSYCHO-IMMUNITY AND THE HEALING PROCESS: Focus on Immune Dysfunction and A.I.D.S. Celestial Arts, San Francisco, 1986.

Shapiro, D. THE BODYMIND WORKBOOK. Element Books, Longmead, Shaftesbury, Dorset, ENGLAND, 1990.

Schenck, Ruthanna HEAL THYSELF: A TEXTBOOK OF DIVINE HEALING. Unity School of Christianity, Kansas City, MO, 1928.

Siegel, B. LOVE, MEDICINE AND MIRACLES. Harper and Row, New York, 1988.

Siegel, D. J. THE DEVELOPING MIND: How Relationships and the Brain Interact to Shape Who We Are. Guilford Press, New York, 1999

Steadman, A. WHO'S THE MATTER WITH ME? ESP Press, Inc., Washington, D.C., 1973.

St. John, G. and Shapiro, D. THE METAPHORIC TECHNIQUE. Element Books, Longmead, Shaftesbury, Dorset, ENGLAND, 1983.

Truman, K. K. FEELINGS BURIED ALIVE NEVER DIE . . . Olympus Distributing, Las Vegas, Nevada, 1996.

Vaughn, B. L. BODY TALK. Argus Publications, Allen, TX, 1982.

Whitmont, E. C. THE ALCHEMY OF HEALING: Psyche and Soma. North Atlantic Books, Berkeley, CA, 1994.

Books Now Available
by Michael J. Lincoln, Ph.D.

In 2006 Dr. Lincoln decided to revise and expand all of his works. We are pleased to present you his latest revised work. See our website www.talkinghearts.net for the latest information on releases.

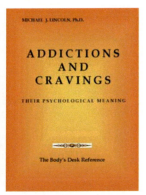

Addiction and Cravings: Their Psychological Meaning (1991, Rev. 2006)

This book is an outstanding overview on the nature of Addictions and Cravings. In addition, a "Dictionary" of the Psychological (and occasionally the sacred) meanings of various addictions and cravings ranging from "Crack" to Mozart. Spiral binding, 369 pages

Retail $69.00

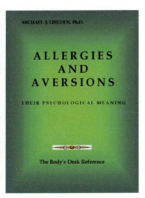

Allergies and Aversions: Their Psychological Meaning (1991, Rev. 2006)

Allergies and Aversions A dictionary of the psychological dynamics and learning history underlying 300 of the most common allergies is presented for the purposes of understanding the meaning of having an intolerance response to these substances. Spiral binding, 123 pages

Retail $34.00

What's in a Face? (1990, Rev. 2007)
The "Dictionary" for Heart Centered Face Reading

An exhaustive dictionary of the psychological (and occasionally the sacred) meanings of facial structure, including head characteristics and hair qualities. It coalesces the ancient Chinese system for doing this is called "Siang Mien" (pronounced SEE-ahng MEE-un), which means "investigating spirit." The contents of this dictionary include the utilizable contents of Siang Mien, plus the best of the West and the author's own experiences over the last 40 years of study of this subject. Spiral binding, 273 pages

Retail $59.00

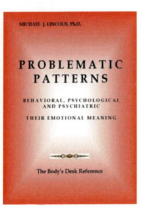

Problematic Patterns (1991, Rev. 2007)
Behavioral, Psychological and Psychiatric Their Emotional Meanings

A brief discussion of the nature of Problematic Patterns of personal and behavioral functioning, followed by a "dictionary" of a considerable number of patterns, including the psychiatric diagnostic system, Michael J. Lincoln's diagnostic system, the enneagram point problems, the deadly sins, numerous traits and many, many more patterns. Using the DSM's as a benchmark you will find items like Drama Triangle-Addict, Compulsive Disorders, Perfectionism and Stress-Seeking Patterns to name a few. Comb binding, 799 pages

Retail $149.00

Visit our website to Order www.talkinghearts.net

Books Now Available
by Michael J. Lincoln Ph.D.
www.talkinghearts.net

Honey, I Blew Up the Kids! (1992, Rev. 2007)
Comprehensive approach to Parenting

An in-depth exploration of the issues, parameters, and experiences of parenting. Also provided is a comprehensive approach to parenting based on realistic, vital awareness and values also explore the dictionary on problematic parenting patterns. Learn how to parent the soul, deal with an old soul child, Indigo/Crystal children as well. Spiral binding, 149 pages

Retail $36.00

WHAT'S HAPPENING TO ME!!?? (1981, Rev. 2007)
A Road Map to the Journey of Change and the Healing Process

This book is about what happens when you reach a place where it is necessary to reconstruct yourself. The idea is to get an overview of what the various events in this process mean. It has the effect of clarifying this process so that it's not so confusing, demoralizing, enraging, and alarming. It also has the effect of accelerating the healing process when you have some sort of understanding of What's Happening to you. Spiral binding, 139 pages

Retail $34.00

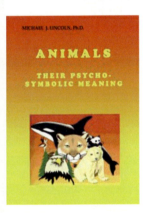

Animals Their Psycho-Symbolic Meaning (1991, Rev. 2007)

A discussion of the nature of animals as symbols in our society and how to interpret them. The ways in which they appear in our lives, the sources of their significance, and the types of indications involved. This leads into a dictionary of the archetypic symbolic and psychological meanings of over 500 animals. Also discussed are the varieties of symbolic meaning in the literature, along with the nature of the purposes of the animal's entering your life at this time.
Spiral binding, 490 pages

Retail $79.00

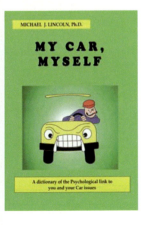

My Car, Myself (1991, Rev. 2008)

A dictionary of the psychological meanings of having your car break down with regard to what the breakdowns indicate about what is happening for you at the time, as a kind of early warning system. It covers most of the major components of the car, ranging from the fuel pump to the floor mats. It also interprets other aspects of your relationship with your car, such as driving habits, traffic tickets, disruptive behaviors and car attitudes It actually works!
Spiral binding, 305 pages

Retail $59.00

Visit our website to Order www.talkinghearts.net